THE RED PRINCE

Timothy Snyder is Professor of History at Yale University. He was a British Marshall Scholar at Oxford and has held fellowships in Paris and Vienna, as well as an Academy Scholarship at Harvard. He has written and edited a number of critically acclaimed books about twentieth-century European history, including *The Reconstruction of Nations: Poland, Ukraine, Lithuania, Belarus, 1569–1999*, which won awards from The American Historical Association, The American Association for Ukrainian Studies and Przeglad Wschodni, and *Sketches from a Secret War: A Polish Artist's Mission to Liberate Soviet Ukraine*, winner of the Pro Historia Polonorum award. He is currently at work on a history of political atrocity in Eastern Europe from 1933 to 1953, and a family history of nationalism. He teaches undergraduate and graduate courses in modern East European political history at Yale University.

TIMOTHY SNYDER

The Red Prince

The Fall of a Dynasty and the
Rise of Modern Europe

VINTAGE BOOKS
London

Published by Vintage 2009

2 4 6 8 10 9 7 5 3 1

Copyright © Timothy Snyder 2008

Timothy Snyder has asserted his right under the Copyright, Designs
and Patents Act 1988 to be identified as the author of this work

First published in Great Britain in 2008 by The Bodley Head

Vintage
Random House, 20 Vauxhall Bridge Road,
London SW1V 2SA

www.vintage-books.co.uk

Addresses for companies within The Random House Group Limited
can be found at: www.randomhouse.co.uk/offices.htm

The Random House Group Limited Reg. No. 954009

A CIP catalogue record for this book
is available from the British Library

ISBN 9781845951207

The Random House Group Limited supports The Forest Stewardship
Council (FSC), the leading international forest certification
organisation. All our titles that are printed on Greenpeace approved
FSC certified paper carry the FSC logo. Our paper procurement policy
can be found at www.rbooks.co.uk/environment

Mixed Sources
Product group from well-managed
forests and other controlled sources
www.fsc.org   Cert no. TT-COC-2139
© 1996 Forest Stewardship Council
FSC

Printed and bound in Great Britain by
CPI Cox & Wyman, Reading RG1 8EX

For I. K., for T. H., for B. E.,
for those that came before,
and those that may come after.

This life, your eternal life!
NIETZSCHE

Contents

Prologue

ONCE UPON A TIME, a lovely young princess named Maria Krystyna lived in a castle, where she read books from the end to the beginning. Then came the Nazis, and after them, the Stalinists. This book is the story of her family, and so it begins with an ending.

An hour before midnight on the eighteenth of August 1948, a Ukrainian colonel lay dead in a Soviet prison in Kiev. He had been a spy in Vienna, working first against Hitler during the Second World War and then against Stalin in the early cold war. He had eluded the Gestapo, but not Soviet counterintelligence. One day the Ukrainian colonel told colleagues that he was going out for lunch, and he was never seen in Vienna again. He was kidnapped by Red Army soldiers, flown to the Soviet Union, and interrogated beyond endurance. He died in the prison hospital and was buried in an unmarked grave.

The Ukrainian colonel had an older brother. He too was a colonel, he too had resisted the Nazis. For his courage, he had spent the war in German prisons and camps. The torturers of the Gestapo had left half of his body paralyzed and one of his eyes useless. Returning home after the Second World War, he tried to claim the family estate. The property was in Poland, and the older brother was Polish. Having been seized by the Nazis in 1939, the estate was confiscated again by the communists in 1945. Knowing that his family had a German background, his Nazi interrogators had wanted him to admit that he was racially German. This he had refused to do. Now he heard the same argument from the new communist regime. He was racially a German, they said, and so had no right to land in the new Poland. What the Nazis had taken, the communists would keep.

Meanwhile, the Polish colonel's children were having problems adapting to the new communist order. In applications to medical school, his daughter had to define the family's social class. The options included working class, peasantry, and intelligentsia—the standard categories of a Marxist bureaucracy. After a long hesitation, the puzzled young lady wrote "Habsburg." This was true. The medical school applicant was the young princess, Maria Krystyna Habsburg. Her father, the Polish colonel, and her uncle, the Ukrainian colonel, were Habsburg princes, descendants of emperors, members of Europe's grandest family.

Born at the end of the nineteenth century, her father Albrecht and her uncle Wilhelm came of age in a world of empires. At the time, their family still ruled the Habsburg monarchy, Europe's proudest and oldest realm. Stretching from the mountains of Ukraine in the north to the warm water of the Adriatic Sea in the south, the Habsburg monarchy embraced a dozen European peoples and recalled six hundred years of uninterrupted power. The Ukrainian colonel and the Polish colonel, Wilhelm and Albrecht, were raised to protect and enlarge the family empire in an age of nationalism. They were to become Polish and Ukrainian princes, loyal to the larger monarchy and subordinate to the Habsburg emperor.

This royal nationalism was their father Stefan's idea. It was he who abandoned the traditional cosmopolitanism of the imperial family to become Polish, hoping to become a regent or prince of Poland. Albrecht, his oldest son, was his loyal heir; Wilhelm, his youngest, was the rebel, the boy who chose another nation. Both sons, though, accepted their father's basic premise. Nationalism was inevitable, he thought, but the destruction of empires was not.

Making a state for every nation would not liberate national minorities. Instead, he foresaw, it would make of Europe an unseemly assemblage of weak states dependent upon stronger ones to survive. Europeans, Stefan believed, would be better served if they could reconcile their national aspirations to a higher loyalty to an empire—to the Habsburg monarchy, in particular. In an imperfect Europe, the Habsburg monarchy was a better theater for national drama than any of the alternatives. Let national politics go on, thought Stefan, within the comfortable confines of a tolerant empire, with a free press and a parliament.

The First World War was thus a tragedy for Stefan's branch of the Habsburg family, as for the dynasty itself. Over the course of the war, the Habsburgs' enemies, the Russians, the British, the French, and the Americans, turned national feeling against the imperial family. At war's end, the Habsburg monarchy was dismembered and disemboweled, and nationalism reigned supreme in Europe. The tragedy of the defeat of 1918 was greatest for Wilhelm, the youngest son, the Ukrainian. Before the First World War, Ukrainian lands had been divided between the Habsburg and Russian empires. Thus arose the national question that Wilhelm had posed for himself. Could Ukraine be unified and joined to the Habsburg monarchy? Could he rule Ukraine for the Habsburgs, just as his father had wished to rule Poland? For a long moment, it seemed that he could.

Wilhelm became the Ukrainian Habsburg, learning the language, commanding Ukrainian troops in the First World War, binding himself closely to his chosen nation. His chance for glory came when the Bolshevik Revolution destroyed the Russian Empire in 1917, opening Ukraine to conquest. Dispatched by the Habsburg emperor to the Ukrainian steppe in 1918, Wilhelm worked to build national consciousness among the peasantry and helped the poor keep the land they had taken from the rich. He became a legend across the country—the Habsburg who spoke Ukrainian, the archduke who loved the common people, the Red Prince.

Wilhelm von Habsburg, the Red Prince, wore the uniform of an Austrian officer, the court regalia of a Habsburg archduke, the simple suit of a Parisian exile, the collar of the Order of the Golden Fleece, and, every so often, a dress. He could handle a saber, a pistol, a rudder, or a golf club; he handled women by necessity and men for pleasure. He spoke the Italian of his archduchess mother, the German of his archduke father, the English of his British royal friends, the Polish of the country his father wished to rule, and the Ukrainian of the land he wished to rule himself. He was no innocent, but then again, innocents cannot found nations. Every national revolution, like every bout of lovemaking, owes something to the one that came before. Every founding father has sown some wild oats. In matters of political loyalty and sexual candor alike, Wilhelm exhibited true shamelessness. It did not occur to him that someone else could define his loyalties or curb his desires. Yet this very insouciance conceals a certain ethical premise. It denies, if only by the whiff of perfume in a Parisian hotel room or a smudge of forger's ink on an Austrian passport, the power of the state to define the individual.

At this most essential level, Wilhelm's attitude to identity was not so different from his brother Albrecht's. Albrecht was a family man, loyal to Poland, the good son of their father. In the age of totalitarianism, both brothers, in perfect ignorance of each other's actions, behaved in much the same way. Both knew that nationality was subject to change, but refused to make changes under threat. Albrecht denied to Nazi interrogators that he was German. Although his family had ruled German lands for centuries, he rejected the Nazi idea of race, that his origin defined his nation. He chose Poland. Wilhelm took great risks to spy against the Soviet Union in the hope that the western powers could protect Ukraine. During his months of interrogation by the Soviet secret police, he chose to speak Ukrainian. Neither brother recovered from their treatment at the hands of totalitarian powers, nor, indeed, has the Europe they represented. Both Nazis and Soviets treated the nation as expressing unchangeable facts about the past rather than human volition in the present. Because they ruled so much of Europe with so much violence, that idea of race remains with us—the undead hand of history as it did not happen.

These Habsburgs had a more lively notion of history. Dynasties can last forever, and rare is the dynasty that believes it deserves anything less. Stalin ruled for a quarter of a century; Hitler for only an eighth. The Habsburgs ruled for hundreds of years. Stefan and his sons, Albrecht and Wilhelm, children of the nineteenth century, had no reason to believe that the twentieth would be their family's last. What was nationalism, after all, to a family of Holy Roman Emperors that had survived the destruction of the Holy Roman Empire, a family of Catholic rulers who had survived the Reformation, a family of dynastic conservatives who had survived the French Revolution and the Napoleonic Wars? In the years before the First World War, the Habsburgs adjusted to modern ideas, but rather as a sailor tacks to an unexpected wind. The journey would continue, on a slightly different course. When Stefan and his sons engaged the nation, it was not with a sense of historical inevitability, with the premonition that nations had to come and to conquer, that empires had to shudder and fall. They thought that freedom for Poland and Ukraine could be reconciled to the expansion of Habsburg rule in Europe. Their own sense of time was one of eternal possibility, of life as composed of moments full of incipient rays of glory, like a drop of dew awaiting the morning sun to release a spectrum of color.

Does it matter that the dewdrop ends up on the black sole of a jackboot? These Habsburgs lost their wars and failed to liberate their nations in their own lifetimes; they, like their chosen nations, were overcome by the Nazis and the Stalinists. Yet the totalitarians who judged and sentenced them have passed, too. The horrors of Nazi and communist rule make it impossible to regard the European history of the twentieth century as a forward march to a greater good. For much the same reason, it is difficult to see the fall of the Habsburgs in 1918 as the beginning of an era of liberation. How, then, to speak of contemporary European history? Perhaps these Habsburgs, with their weary sense of eternity and their hopeful appreciation of the color of the moment, have something to offer. Each moment of the past, after all, is full of what did not happen and what will probably never happen, like a Ukrainian monarchy or a

Habsburg restoration. It also contains what seemed impossible but proved possible, like a unified Ukrainian state or a free Poland in a unifying Europe. And if this is true of these moments of the past, it is true of the present moment as well.

Today, after long exile, Maria Krystyna lives again in the castle of her youth, in Poland. Her father's Polish cause has been won. Even her uncle's exotic dream of an independent Ukraine has been realized. Poland has joined the European Union. Ukrainian democrats, protesting for free elections in their own country, wave the European flag. Her grandfather's idea that patriotism can be reconciled to a higher European loyalty seems oddly prescient.

In the year 2008, Maria Krystyna sits in her grandfather's castle and tells tales from the end to the beginning. The story of her uncle, the Red Prince, is one that she does not know, or will not tell. It ends with a death in Kiev in 1948. It begins earlier, before her birth, with her uncle Wilhelm's rebellion against her grandfather's Polish plan and his choice of Ukraine rather than Poland. Or earlier still, with the long reign of the emperor Franz Josef von Habsburg over a multinational empire that allowed Poles and Ukrainians alike to imagine a future of national liberation. Franz Josef was in power when Stefan was born in 1860, and still in power when Wilhelm was born in 1895. He reigned when Stefan decided to make the family Polish, and reigned still when Wilhelm chose Ukraine. So the story might begin a century ago, in 1908, as Stefan settled his family in a Polish castle, Wilhelm began dreaming of a national kingdom of his own, and Franz Josef celebrated the sixtieth anniversary of his own imperial rule.

GOLD

~

The Emperor's Dream

No EUROPEAN DYNASTY had ruled as long as the Habsburgs, and no Habsburg had ruled as long as Emperor Franz Josef. On the second day of December, 1908, the highest society of his empire gathered in his Court Opera in Vienna to celebrate the sixtieth jubilee of his rule. The nobles and the princes, the officers and the officials, the bishops and the politicians came to celebrate the durability of a man who ruled over them by the grace of God. The meeting place, a house of music, was also a temple of timelessness. Like the other grand edifices constructed in Vienna under Franz Josef, the Court Opera was in the historical style, referring to the Renaissance, yet faced the most beautiful of Europe's modern avenues. It was one of the gems of the Ring, the circular avenue laid down during the reign of Franz Josef to define the inner city. Then, as now, the humble and the grand could mount a tramway and ride around the Ring, endlessly, with a ticket to eternity in hand.

The celebration of the emperor had begun the night before. The Viennese, around the Ring and around the city, lit a single candle in their windows, casting a dim gold glow through the black of the evening. This custom had begun in Vienna sixty years before, when Franz Josef ascended the Habsburg thrones amidst revolution and war, and had spread throughout the empire during his long reign. Not only in Vienna but in Prague, Cracow, Lviv, Trieste, Salzburg, Innsbruck, Ljubljana, Maribor, Brno, Chernivtsi, Budapest, Sarajevo, and countless other cities, towns, and villages throughout central and eastern Europe, loyal Habsburg subjects paid their respects and demonstrated their devotion. After six decades, Franz Josef was the only ruler the vast majority of his millions of subjects—Germans, Poles, Ukrainians, Jews, Czechs, Croatians, Slovenians, Slovaks, Hungarians, Romanians—had ever known. Yet in Vienna the golden glow was not one of nostalgia. In the center of the city, the thousands of flickering candles were outshone by millions of electric light bulbs. All of the grand buildings of the Ring were illuminated by thousands of bulbs. Squares and intersections were decorated with giant electric stars. The emperor's palace itself, the Hofburg, was covered with lights. A million people came out to see the spectacle.

On the morning of the second of December, in the Hofburg, the imperial palace on the Ring, Emperor Franz Josef received the homage of the archdukes and archduchesses: princes and princesses of the blood, heirs like himself to Habsburg emperors of the past. Though most of them had palaces in Vienna, they came from across the empire, from their various refuges from court life, or their various seats of ambition. Archduke Stefan, for example, had two palaces in the imperial south by the Adriatic Sea and two castles in the north in a Galician valley. Stefan and his wife Maria Theresia brought their six children to the Hofburg that morning to pay their respects to the emperor. Their youngest son, Willy, was thirteen, just old enough according to the court ceremonial to take part. Willy, raised by the blue sea, found himself surrounded by the gilded display of his family's power and longevity. It was one of the rare occasions when he saw his father, Stefan, in full ceremonial dress. Around his neck he wore the collar of the Order of the Golden Fleece, the insignia of that most exalted of chivalrous societies. Willy seems to have kept a certain distance from the grandeur. While he did take the opportunity to inspect the imperial treasury, where the thrones and jewels were kept, he remembered the master of ceremony as a golden rooster.

In the evening, at the Court Opera, the emperor and the archdukes met again, this time before an audience. By six o'clock the other guests had arrived and taken their places. At just before seven o'clock, the archdukes and archduchesses, including Stefan, Maria Theresia, and their children, awaited their cue. At the proper moment, the archdukes and archduchesses made their grand appearance in the hall and strode together to their loges. Stefan, Willy, and the family took places in a box on the left side, and remained standing. Only then did Emperor Franz Josef himself appear, a man of seventy-eight years of age and six decades of power, stooped but strong, wearing imposing side whiskers and an impenetrable expression. He acknowledged the applause of the gallery. He stood for a moment. Franz Josef was known for standing: he stood at all engagements, thus keeping them blessedly short. He was also known for withstanding: he had survived the violent deaths of his brother, his wife, and his only son. He outlasted people, he outlasted generations, he seemed able to outlast time itself. Yet now, at precisely seven o'clock, he took a seat, and everyone else could as well, and another performance could begin.

When the curtain rose, the audience's gaze shifted from the emperor of the present to an emperor of the past. *The Emperor's Dream*, a one-act play written to celebrate the jubilee, took as its hero the very first Habsburg emperor, Rudolf. The audience recognized Rudolf as the Habsburg who, in the thirteenth century, had made the Habsburg family the ruling dynasty it had been ever since. He was the first Habsburg elected by his fellow princes to be Holy Roman Emperor, in 1273. Though this title had limited power in a medieval Europe of hundreds of smaller and larger sovereignties, its bearer claimed the legacy of the defunct Roman Empire as well as the leadership of the entire Christian world. It was Rudolf, too, who had seized by war the lands of Austria from the fearsome Czech king Ottokar in 1278. They became the core of a hereditary domain that Rudolf would pass on to his sons, and they to all of the Habsburgs thereafter, down to Franz Josef himself.

On stage, Emperor Rudolf begins to worry aloud about the fate of these Austrian lands. His conquests behind him, his cares are of the future. What will happen to the territories he will bequeath to his sons? Will they be worthy successors? And what of the Habsburgs to follow? Rudolf, a towering, lean, and rather cruel figure in life, was played by a short, plump, and endearing actor. A man of brutal action in reality, on stage he becomes a winsome fellow who needs a nap. He goes to sleep on his throne. A spirit of the Future rises from behind him and tells him of the glories of the House of Habsburg in the centuries to come. As gentle music begins, Rudolf asks Future to be his guide. Future then presents to him five dream pictures, meant to reassure him that what he has won will be cherished and protected.[1]

The first dream picture is of a wedding pact made between two great royal houses. In 1515, the Habsburgs took a gamble with the Jagiellonians, the rulers of Poland and the leading family of eastern Europe. By arranging a double marriage, they put their own crownlands at risk against the possibility of gaining those of the Jagiellonians. Louis the Jagiellonian was king of Poland, Hungary, and Bohemia when he led his armies against the Ottoman Empire at the Battle of Mohács in 1526. His forces defeated, he died as he fled, in a river and under a horse. As a result of the wedding pact, his wife was a Habsburg; after his death, her brother claimed the Bohemian and Hungarian crowns. Bohemia and Hungary became Habsburg crownlands, claimed by all succeeding Habsburg rulers, down to Franz Josef himself. The Hungarian king Matthias Corvinus had written in the fifteenth century, "Let others fight wars! Thou Happy Austria marry. What Mars gives to others, Venus bestows on thee." He was referring to the acquisition of Spain, when a Habsburg had married a girl who was sixth in line to the throne and then watched as the other five obligingly died. His own Hungarian kingdom had followed.

Yet mastery of Hungary was not so simple, as Future explains to Rudolf. War raged between the Habsburgs and the Ottomans. In 1683 the Ottomans marched on Vienna itself with one hundred thousand soldiers. Across the Habsburg domains, church bells rang and fell silent, sending the alarm before their towns fell to the Turks. Vienna was besieged and the Habsburgs entrapped. The Habsburgs got help from their northern neighbor and fellow Catholic realm, Poland. The Polish king sped south with his fearsome cavalry and made camp on a hill just above the city. His knights stormed the Ottoman camps, as a Muslim chronicler recalled, like a flood of black pitch that consumed everything it touched. Vienna was free. In the second dream picture, Future shows Rudolf the meeting of the Habsburg emperor and the Polish king. The Ottomans were vanquished, and the Habsburgs became the undisputed rulers of Hungary and central Europe.

Having won a war, the Habsburgs now had trouble with marriage. As Future explains to Rudolf, they faced crises of succession. The Habsburgs ruled much of Europe and the world as two lines of the same family, one producing the lords of Spain and its far-flung colonial possessions, the other Holy Roman Emperors and masters of central Europe. In 1700 the Spanish line of the family died out, and the central European branch fought, without success, for control of Spain and its empire. This branch, too, had no male heir to take up the succession. The solution to this problem was the Pragmatic Sanction, portrayed in Future's third dream picture. In the picture, the emperor proclaimed, in the presence of the eight-year-old Archduchess Maria Theresia, that she would be his successor. She ascended to the Habsburg thrones in 1740 to become the most famous of all Habsburg rulers. Future assures Rudolf that Maria Theresia ruled with a firm hand.

Empress Maria Theresia took the family principle of nuptial imperialism to its logical extreme, as Future reveals to Rudolf in the fourth dream picture. It displayed Maria Theresia and her family in 1763, applauding the young Mozart at the piano. In the picture were Maria Theresia's sixteen children. The reference to Mozart was a nice way of suggesting that the Habsburgs were civilized rulers and patrons of the arts, but the picture's central message was that Maria Theresia had extended the family's power in Europe with her womb and her wits. She groomed the eldest son to rule and then ruled with him, and she married as many daughters as she could to the monarchs of Europe. The eldest son was Josef, an enlightened absolutist who, like his mother, wished to transform the sprawling territories of the Habsburg monarchy into a well-administered state. The youngest daughter was Maria Antonia, better remembered under her French name, Marie Antoinette, as the villain of the French Revolution.

When Maria Theresia dispatched her daughter to marry the French crown prince, this was a typical example of Habsburg marital diplomacy. France was a traditional enemy of the Habsburgs. Although both France and the Habsburg monarchy were Catholic countries, France had supported the Islamic Ottomans as they marched on Vienna. A French diplomat had even tried to prevent the Polish intervention by distributing bribes. During the religious wars of the sixteenth and seventeenth centuries, France supported Protestant princes against the Habsburgs. The French dynasty, the Bourbons, were the main rival of the Habsburgs for power on the continent of Europe. The French invented modern diplomacy, with its axiom of the superiority of the interests of the state to all other concerns, during their long confrontation with the Habsburgs. Against this ruthlessness, the Habsburgs sent a girl to disrobe. When the fourteen-year-old Maria Antonia was separated from her clothing at the River Rhine in 1773, she was transformed symbolically into the French princess Marie Antoinette, confirming the legitimacy of the old order by taking part in a marriage pact between its two greatest houses.

Sixteen years after Maria Theresia tried to tame the enmity of the Bourbons with the gift of her daughter, that royal house was overthrown in the French Revolution. Marie Antoinette, deposed as queen of France, found herself a simple citizen facing charges of treason and worse. The guillotine touched the necks of people she had known and loved. In prison in 1792, she was asked to kiss the lips of the severed head of a princess who had been, according to rumor, her lesbian lover. In 1793, she was convicted of hindering the revolution and sexually abusing her son. She was guillotined at the Place de Révolution.[2]

As the French Revolution careened into terror and then dictatorship in the 1790s, Napoleon Bonaparte and his grand armies tried to overturn the old order in all of Europe. He brought a new kind of politics, rule by monarchs who claimed to represent peoples rather than a divine hierarchy. Having crowned himself emperor of the French in 1804, Napoleon placed relatives upon the thrones of new kingdoms created from the lands he took from the Habsburgs and other rivals. In 1810, the Habsburgs tried marriage again, offering the daughter of their emperor to Napoleon as his bride. The deal was struck by a clever Habsburg diplomat, Klemens von Metternich. The two were indeed married and were a happy couple. With the Habsburgs neutral, Napoleon marched on Moscow in 1812. The doomed invasion of the Russian Empire was the disaster that turned the tide. In 1813 the Habsburgs joined a victorious coalition against Napoleon, and he was finally defeated.

The French Revolution and the Napoleonic Wars were prelude to the fifth dream image that Future presents to Rudolf: the Congress of Vienna in 1814–1815. In a second-story room, with three windows affording views of the imperial capital, four grates in the ceilings for Metternich's spies, and five doors for the negotiating parties, peace was made in Europe. The guiding principles were the rule of law, that dynasts should rule monarchies; and the balance of power, that no one state should disrupt the rest of the continent. This, the last dream picture that Future shows Rudolf, is a hopeful one. The Habsburgs had emerged from the Napoleonic Wars not only victorious but pivotal, the power with an interest in stability in Europe, and the power whose stability was in the interest of the other European powers. Their allies in the final coalition, the British, Russians, and Prussians, all endorsed this outcome. France, its monarchy restored, returned to its previous position as a European power.

All is right with the world as Future concludes. Rudolf's domain, built of his cunning and violence, is sustained and enlarged by lucky marriage, female power, and tactful diplomacy. As the play nears its end, Rudolf endorses this soft story of his dynasty, saying that he himself is tired of war and is glad to see the making of peace.

The author of the play, a countess aided by a government commission, sidestepped the issue of lost glory by emphasizing the theme of peace. The Habsburgs had done well at the Congress of Vienna, confirming claims to old Polish lands in the north and the Adriatic Sea in the south, but their realm, even thus enlarged, was still nothing more than a central European empire.

As the audience knew, emperors between Rudolf and Franz Josef had pressed far broader claims, and ruled far greater domains. Several emperors had claimed the entire world, or indeed more. Karl von Habsburg, on whose empire in the Old and New Worlds the sun never set, chose as his personal motto "Plus ultra," or "Beyond and beyond." His son Philip coined a medallion inscribed "Orbis non sufficit," or "The world is not enough." Enduringly resonant, too, was Friedrich von Habsburg's famous deciphering of the vowels AEIOU: in the Latin of his fifteenth century, "Austriae est imperare orbi universo"; in the German of centuries to come, "Alle Erdreich ist Österreich untertan"; or in the universal language of our own age, "Austria's empire is our universe."

Another translation of AEIOU was perhaps closest to Franz Josef's heart: "Austria erit in orbe ultima"—"Austria will outlast all others," or "Austria will endure until the end of the world." This motto was the favorite of Franz Josef's own father, and one that had been prominently recalled by his own son, named Rudolf in homage to the first Habsburg emperor. Twenty years earlier, in 1888, Crown Prince Rudolf had passionately criticized his father for abandoning the glory of the imperial past in favor of a mediocre destiny as a second-rate European power. As Rudolf argued, it was hard to reconcile traditional visions of endless ambition with a history that ends in diplomatic compromise. That frustration was one of the reasons why the modern Rudolf, Franz Josef's son and heir, shot himself in the head in 1889.[3]

Perhaps Franz Josef could accept the renunciation of glory. Perhaps, paradoxically, that was the key to his greatness. Even so, Franz Josef must have noticed something else about the play. This was a piece written to celebrate him. Nevertheless, none of the dream pictures concerned the sixty years of his reign. Indeed, the action of *The Emperor's Dream* ends in 1815, fifteen years before his birth. He himself had been edited out, along with all the events and achievements of his long life.

Franz Josef was born along with the age of nationalism, in 1830, the year revolution broke out in Paris against the restored monarchy,

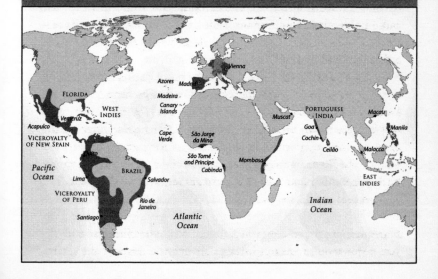

HABSBURG EARTH c. 1580

and the year Polish rebels almost broke the hold of the Russian Empire. The Habsburgs, having enlarged their domains at the Congress of Vienna, found themselves confronting Italian, German, Polish, and south Slav (or Yugoslav) national questions.

These national questions were parting gifts from Napoleon. He had called himself king of Italy. He had dissolved the Holy Roman Empire and dozens of petty German states, thus preparing the way for German unification. He had created a Kingdom of Illyria, a name for the lands of the south Slavs, peoples who would later be known as Serbs, Croats, and Slovenes. He had partially restored Poland, removed from the map by imperial partition in the late eighteenth century, as a Duchy of Warsaw. Having destroyed these Napoleonic entities, the Habsburgs and their allies treated nationalism as a revolutionary idea to be stifled throughout Europe. Metternich, now chancellor, ordered his police to arrest conspirators and his censors to excise suspicious passages from newspapers and books. The Habsburg monarchy of Franz Josef's youth was a police state.[4]

While Franz Josef was educated to rule a conservative empire in the 1830s and 1840s, patriots painted a blurry map of a future Europe where local color bled through the black boundaries of empires. In February 1848, another revolution broke out in Paris. Within the Habsburg domains, nations with proud histories and large noble classes—Germans, Poles, Italians, and Hungarians—seized the occasion to challenge the Habsburgs with protests and uprisings. They cloaked the traditional demands of the nobility for greater local authority in the new rhetoric of national freedom for the people. Chancellor Metternich had to escape from Vienna in a laundry cart.

Franz Josef was brought to the throne at the tender age of eighteen. Against the rebellious noble nations, he turned for help to others, to the Romanians, Croats, Ukrainians, and Czechs. Some nations rebelled against their emperor, others remained loyal to him, but either way all had declared their existence. So even as rebellious nations were defeated on the battlefield, the principle of nationalism was generalized and confirmed. What was more, the new emperor had begun a quiet social revolution. To gain the support of the peasant nations, he had liberated the peasantry from its traditional obligations to landlords. Children and grandchildren of the peasants would become prosperous farmers, or even townsmen. Peoples without historical noble classes would come to see themselves as nations deserving of rights.

In 1848, patriotic ideas found great resonance, but revealed their practical contradictions. The nations capable of fighting against their emperor in the name of national liberation all wished to oppress other nations: the Hungarians the Slovaks, the Poles the Ukrainians, the Italians the Croatians, and so on. In this situation, Franz Josef could navigate among enmities and chart a course back to supreme power. The nation that could raise the most impressive army, the Hungarians, were defeated in the end by officers and soldiers loyal to the monarchy (although Franz Josef, humiliatingly, also had to call in the army of the neighboring Russian Empire for help). National questions could be raised by writers and pressed by rebels, but they could not be answered without monarchs and generals.

The revolutions of 1848, remembered as the springtime of nations, were a lesson for kings and emperors. After 1848 the monarchs understood the risks and opportunities of nationalism, and began a new kind of rivalry among themselves. Nations had failed to choose their rulers, so now rulers would chose their nations. The prize was Germany, thirty-odd states that, when combined, would be the richest and most powerful country in Europe. In the 1850s, Franz Josef tried and failed to unite all of the German states beneath his sceptre by asking for the submission of inferior rulers.

Germany was unified without the Habsburgs. It was Prussia, a nimble young German kingdom, that found the way to unite dynastic rule with German nationalism. Prussia was a large German monarchy, with a capital in Berlin, ruled by the Hohenzollern dynasty. The Hohenzollerns, once subordinate to the Habsburgs, had become their rivals. When the Habsburgs needed votes to remain Holy Roman Emperors, Hohenzollerns got favors. When the Habsburgs needed support during the war for the Spanish succession, they agreed to grant the Hohenzollerns a royal title. The greatest Hohenzollern ruler, Friedrich Wilhelm, established the two pillars of state power, finances and an army. In 1683, as the Habsburgs were melting sacred objects for the gold they needed to defend their capital from the Ottoman siege, Prussia was establishing a taxation system. In 1740, Prussia denied the validity of the Pragmatic Sanction, challenged Maria Theresia's right to rule, and attacked the Habsburg monarchy, eventually seizing most of the rich province of Silesia. The Hohenzollerns were now not only a royal house, but a great power that had defeated the Habsburgs on the battlefield.[5]

In 1866 the Prussia of King Wilhelm I attacked the Habsburg monarchy of Franz Josef. At Sadova, numerically inferior Prussian forces won a decisive victory thanks to superior weaponry and organization. The troops might have pressed on to Vienna, but the Prussian chancellor, Otto von Bismarck, had no wish to destroy the Habsburgs. He wished to keep their monarchy as a barrier to Russia and the Ottoman Empire, while himself uniting the remaining German lands into a national monarchy. Once Bismarck provoked and won a war against France in 1870, he had succeeded. That war brought many of the smaller German states to his side, and the victory made Prussia the greatest military power in Europe. German unification was proclaimed at the Hall of Mirrors in Versailles in January 1871. A great Prussian general had once said that the security of the throne was poetry. The greatest of German poets, Friedrich Schiller, believed that Germany would be a nation when it had a national theater. As it turned out, war abroad was the national theater. The pen is mightier with the sword.

The defeat of 1866 and the exclusion of the Habsburgs from Germany exerted a profound influence on the next generation of the Habsburg family. Archduke Stefan, born in 1860, was a child of Bismarck's age of national unification. In the war of 1866, the Prussian army drove quickly through his home province of Moravia, where the peace was signed. As Stefan was educated in Moravia in the 1870s, the province was neighbor to an enviably powerful Germany. German unification placed the Habsburgs on what seemed to be an eternal defensive. Either they would resist the Germans as a weak foe, or join the Germans as a weak ally. The generation of Franz Josef knew that world power was out of reach, but until 1866 could still dream of

Europe and Germany. Stefan's was the first generation of archdukes to come to maturity in a monarchy that was no longer a European great power and no longer even a candidate to rule Germany.

Even marriage, that traditional tool of Habsburg expansion, now brought only reminders of defeat. In 1866, when Stefan wed a Habsburg archduchess who was also a princess of Tuscany, he was joining his destiny to that of an orphan of another national unification, the Italian. While Stefan's childhood was shaped by the new Germany of Bismarck, his bride Maria Theresia's was determined by the national imperialism of France in Italy. The French emperor Napoleon III had fanned Italian patriotism, allying with the Kingdom of Piedmont-Sardinia in its attempt to win northern Italy from the Habsburgs. In 1859 France and Piedmont defeated Austria at the Battle of Solferino. This began the cascade that Italians call the "resurgence," the unification of Italy from the plenitude of smaller states on the peninsula. The Italians rode German coattails as they made their own state. In 1866, when Prussia defeated the Habsburg armies in Stefan's homeland of Moravia, the Habsburgs also lost Venice. They ceded it to France in exchange for neutrality, only to see the French grant it to Italy.

Italy was becoming a united national monarchy. Flushed with victory, Italian patriots then aimed for the withdrawal of all foreign authority from their country, and that included the French themselves. In 1870, when Prussia attacked France, French troops had to withdraw from Rome to defend their homeland. The Prussian army reached Paris anyway. As Berlin became the capital of a united Germany, Rome became the capital of unified Italy. France and the Habsburgs, historical rivals for the domination of Europe, were both humbled, and the new Germany was unrivalled on the continent. Both of Archduchess Maria Theresia's grandfathers had ruled Italian domains; the formation of a unified Italian kingdom now left two lines of succession that led nowhere. Her marriage to Stefan was thus a retreat from an Italy where Habsburgs would no longer rule.

The dream pictures had to stop in 1815, lest these nightmares of nationalism begin. Franz Josef was born in a police state seeking to maintain what it had, and he ascended to the throne during a revolution. His reign had seen not peace but defeat, not stability but loss, not universal power but corrosive particularism. Every monarch but Franz Josef, it seemed, had mastered nationalism and found a glorious place in modern Europe by making a national monarchy. None of this seemed appropriate subject matter for dream pictures.

In the play, the six decades of Franz Josef's rule had to be revealed by a different kind of art. Near the end of *The Emperor's Dream*, Rudolf pronounces himself satisfied with the dream pictures and asks for the rest of the story. He helpfully presents a new account of glory, one that required no territorial expansion and thus could enshrine Franz Josef as the greatest of the Habsburgs. Facing the emperor and addressing him with both arms outstretched, Rudolf, citing the New Testament, names love as the highest of all virtues and attainments. Future agrees with him, claiming that Rudolf and Franz Josef, like all the Habsburgs, were much loved by all of their peoples.[6]

Then Love herself appears, female in the German language, portrayed onstage by a woman who claims center stage from Future and Rudolf. She has the final word about the emperor and his peoples. Having flown over the mountains and the dales, across the rivers and over the seas, Love has watched, she says, the humble subjects of Franz Josef in their daily lives. She reports, reassuringly, that they all love their emperor. The last words of the play, an expression of thanks to the emperor, belong to Love, speaking for all the peoples of the monarchy. By this point, it was perfectly clear to the audience that the emperor meant was no longer Rudolf, but Franz Josef. When the curtain fell, all eyes and all applause were directed to Franz Josef. Love united past and present through its seemingly harmless theme and brought the history of the Habsburgs to an end on a note that could be celebrated.[7]

Nor was it entirely false. Habsburgs did love their peoples, at least inasmuch as they signified crownlands, power, and wealth. For centuries Habsburgs had used the languages and adapted the customs that best allowed them to rule. Their love was cosmopolitan, indiscriminate, selfish, unreflective, and thus in some sense perfect. They could hardly be said to be of any one ethnicity. As young Willy understood, "ethnically my family was very mixed." Insofar as Habsburgs had something like an inherited nationality, it was their own family. Modern nationalism works in family metaphors, asserting that the people are brothers and sisters, sharing a fatherland or motherland. What need had the Habsburgs for such metaphors, when their family did in fact rule, century upon century, generation after generation; and when their emperor was still perceived, in the twentieth century, as a father or grandfather by millions of his subjects? Their fatherland was where their fathers had trodden, all over Europe, or sailed, all over the world. The nationalism of their subjects could be indulged, endured, and perhaps one day mastered.[8]

The theme of love allowed for a transition from one era of Habsburg history to the next. For centuries, Habsburg love had meant marrying into territory. In the nineteenth century, the love in question was no longer between nubile Habsburg princesses and foreign rulers, but between the many Habsburg peoples and their own ruler, Franz Josef. Love could no longer extend empire, but perhaps it could maintain it. The history of Franz Josef's rule since 1848 was that of the emerging nationalism of his peoples, and the question of his rule was whether nationalism could be reconciled to a higher loyalty, to his person and throne. Precisely because the Habsburg monarchy, with its dozens of peoples, could not became a national state, Franz Josef and his governments sought and found ways to manage national difference as the great national unifications took place. The last fifty years had been a time of national compromise.

Bargaining from a position of weakness after battlefield defeats in the wars with Italy and Prussia, Franz Josef and his ministers made concessions to one nation after another. After the Italian shock of 1859, Emperor Franz Josef promulgated the October Diploma, a kind of constitution, in 1860. It granted some authority to the provincial assemblies of the Habsburg crownlands, thus pacifying the traditional noble ruling classes of the older nations. The Diploma signified that the power of the emperor, though in principle absolute, could be reconciled in practice with regional sources of authority. After the Prussian debacle of 1866, Franz Josef came to terms with the largest and most difficult of the noble nations, the Hungarians. The Hungarian rebellion of 1848 had been by far the most serious. By the terms of the Compromise of 1867, the Hungarian nobility gained control over half the empire.[9]

After 1867, the Habsburg monarchy was known as Austria-Hungary, and the history of its nations divides. Hungary pursued a policy of centralization, designed to keep power and wealth in the hands of the Hungarian gentry. In the other half of the empire, which had no name but which is usually called "Austria," different principles prevailed. It was a strange entity, embracing Hungary from northeast to southwest like a voluptuous woman sitting on a rock. It included crownlands as various as Galicia in the northeast, taken from Poland and inhabited by Poles, Ukrainians, and Jews, and Istria and Dalmatia in the southwest, former possessions of Venice, peopled by Croats, Slovenes, and Italians. In between were the old Habsburg crownlands, provinces dominated by Germans and Czechs. Jews were everywhere but were especially numerous in Galicia and Vienna; and in truth, members of all of the nations could be found almost everywhere. Assimilation and bilingualism were widespread. A large class of imperial officials and military officers regarded themselves as above and beyond nationality, as loyal servants of the dynasty.

The national policies of Franz Josef, unsuitable as they were for dream pictures, did not lack a certain grandeur. He presided over a great and unprecedented experiment: Could a multinational empire survive in a Europe of nations; and, if so, on what principles? The first principle was that of compromise with the historical nations, those with large nobilities who claimed traditional rights to self-government. Soon after the Habsburgs had granted sovereignty within Hungary to the Hungarian nobility, they passed administrative control of Galicia to the Polish nobility. The second principle was the support of peasant societies to balance these very noble nations. In 1848 Franz Josef had removed the remnants of serfdom. In 1867, he proclaimed a constitutional law that made all nations formally equal. Beginning in 1879, Franz Josef's ministers progressively extended an equal vote to all adult males, reaching full suffrage by the

Jonathan Wyss, Topaz Maps

**HABSBURG EUROPE
1908**

elections of 1907. The lower house of parliament came to represent the populations of the monarchy rather than its nobles.

A third principle was perpetual negotiation with the Czechs. Czechs inhabited Bohemia and Moravia, the center of the monarchy, and their lands were the richest and most heavily taxed. Czechs were important for who they were and where they lived, but also for what they represented. Czechs were a Slavic people, and thus symbolized the future of the monarchy. Now that the Habsburgs were cut off from Germany and Italy, they were destined to rule an empire that was predominantly Slavic in population. Almost half the population of the monarchy was Slavic (Czech, Slovak Polish, Ukrainian, Slovenian, Croatian, or Serbian); only about a quarter was German and a quarter

Hungarian. The Habsburgs had to keep the loyalty of their Slavic subjects, which meant satisfying the ambitious Czech national movement. If the individual Slavic nations were not satisfied, they might band together against the Habsburgs, portraying the dynasty as German and oppressive. Slavs might also decide to associate themselves with Slavic states beyond the Habsburg borders, such as the Russian Empire or Serbia. In 1905, in Stefan's home province of Moravia, Germans and Czechs were separated as political groups and provided with separate elections for adults and separate schools for children.[10]

The early twentieth century was the age of national revivals, as poets and historians created national histories meant to draw the masses into a single collective movement. National dramas always involved three acts: a past golden age ended by foreign invasion, a present darkened by foreign tyranny, and a future defined by liberation. As the writers spun the straw of folk nations into the gold of forgotten glory, the Habsburgs, old alchemists themselves, looked on with professional interest. The Habsburgs wished for the oppression act of every national drama to be cast in local terms: that Czechs limit their complaints to local Germans rather than see the Habsburgs as a tyrannical German dynasty, for example; or that Ukrainians regard themselves as humiliated by Polish nobles in Galicia rather than by the Habsburgs who had given Poles the right to rule. If the story were told thus, the Habsburg monarchy could figure as the European stage on which national drama was played, rather than an actor that might be cued to exit.

By making compromises with the noble nations, the Habsburgs hoped to satisfy them before they demanded complete national independence. By supporting the peasant nations, the Habsburgs hoped to enchant the masses at the moment when they entered politics. These peasant societies, they believed, would bring a traditional habit of imperial loyalty to the age of democratic politics. Disputes could be heard and compromises arranged in the crownlands, with Vienna as the arbiter. The Habsburgs would remain at the center, balancing the noble nations against the peasant peoples, gaining the loyalty of each, directing their grievances away from Vienna and towards each other.

Despite these accommodations to the modern politics of nation-alism, Franz Josef was, as he once told Theodore Roosevelt, the last monarch of the old school. An admiring biographer said that he was strong precisely because he knew nothing of the ideas of his age. The emperor would not use a telephone or an elevator. Even when ill at night he refused to see his doctor unless the latter was properly dressed in a formal frock coat. He remained an absolute ruler, claiming power by the grace of God. Constitutional law, manhood suffrage, and parliament itself were to be understood as gifts from the sovereign to his subjects. They could be given, and taken away. The monarch chose to rule according to the constitutional law he granted and in accordance with the laws the parliament passed. Franz Josef chose to endorse the gradual extension of voting rights, believing that this would increase his actual power. His motto was "Viribus unitis," which means "with united strength."

The successes of Franz Josef's reign, though real enough, were too unglamorous for dream pictures. So in the final act Rudolf gestured to Franz Josef, covering the missing century with dra-matic energy, and Love was called in to hold the stage at the end of the play and direct the audience's attention to their monarch. Everyone in the audience knew, of course, that the empire's com-plicated arrangements were a matter of compromise among con-testing forces. Old nations were given regional parliaments, new nations the right to vote in the imperial one. Old nations gave Franz Josef ministers, deputies representing new nations drafted progressive laws. Old nations got a place close to the emperor, new nations schools for the next generation. Each compromise would inevitably resolve one crisis and give rise to others, which in their turn could be addressed within the legal and political frame-work of the monarchy. Such a reality, uncomfortable but accept-able, flattered both the nationalists who had their moments of moderate success and an emperor who had his decades of power. It lasted long and might have lasted longer.[11]

Archduke Stefan applauded from his box, though he had his wor-ries. He understood that love meant national compromise, and was all in favor of both; but he was concerned that the era of national compromise was coming to an end. He knew that the Habsburg stage, on which the various nations could show their colors, make their claims, and resolve their disputes, had a dark back entrance.

National compromise worked reasonably well within the Habsburgs' own domains, but it could not stop national challenges from beyond the monarchy. Nationalism on its northern and western frontiers had driven the Habsburgs from Germany and Italy; other threats loomed in the east and south. The German and Italian unifications were complete, but two others were not: the Polish and the south Slav, or Yugoslav. Stefan, who had an estate in the Balkans, was most worried by the Habsburgs' southern neighbor, Serbia, ruled by a dynasty that hated the Habsburgs and wanted their lands. Between the Habsburg monarchy and Serbia lay the contested provinces of Bosnia and Herzegovina, which the Habsburgs had annexed a few weeks before, in October 1908. Now, in December 1908, the newspapers were full of rumors of war. In the Court Opera that evening was the head of the Habsburg general staff, who wanted to wage preventive war against Serbia.[12]

When the applause for *The Emperor's Dream* stilled, Franz Josef got some bad news. Vienna had bathed him in golden light, the Opera in the praise of his peoples and the ages. His jubilee, however, had not been celebrated so peacefully everywhere in his empire. In Prague, where the same play was being performed at the same time, Czechs were protesting and rioting. Habsburg flags of black and gold, hung ceremoniously for the occasion, were torn down and desecrated. Sometimes they were burned, just as they were in Serbia. Indeed, some of the Czechs had decided to make the Serbian cause their own. Protesting the annexation of Bosnia and Herzegovina, they cried out, "Long live Serbia!"[13]

Franz Josef had little time to consider the matter. Martial law was declared in Prague. In Vienna, in the Court Opera, the curtain rose again, and a second performance began. In a light ballet number, *From the Homeland*, dancers and singers in national dress made their way across the stage, proclaiming the love of each nation for the emperor. By the end, they had assembled themselves in a giant chorus, facing the emperor and proclaiming their collective loyalty. Stefan watched the dancers from his place in a loge. He saw the dozen nations of the monarchy, presented as so many types of folk costume. He was wearing the collar of the Order of the Golden Fleece, the mark of a Habsburg prince, but he knew that costumes could be changed. He himself preferred less predictable transformations. In his own castle, back in Galicia, he liked to announce costume balls on short notice. He himself would always appear, wise jester that he was, in comic disguise.

Stefan understood the emperor's dream: an empire of peoples devoted to their ruler, despite nationalism. He had a dream of his own. Nationalism was inevitable, national unification was inevitable, but it need not weaken the Habsburgs. Germany and Italy had turned nationalism against the Habsburgs, Poland and the south Slavs remained. These were the national questions suppressed by the Congress of Vienna in 1815 and suppressed in the dream pictures, only to be posed in life by bullets and bayonets. Franz Josef had found that compromise was the key to durability; but no Habsburg yet had found the blazing colors of national fervor on the cool palette of the static dream pictures, or reconciled the strong melodies of marches to national liberation with the gentle harmonies of traditional empire.

Poland remained, believed Stefan, the last best hope. Stefan had found a way, he thought, of reconciling national compromise with imperial glory. He would make the national compromise within himself, offering himself to the Polish cause. He would not await the adoration of a subject people, but join that people himself. He would abandon the Habsburg stage for the rough reality of national politics, leave the capital after the jubilee, and return to the crownland of Galicia as a Habsburg archduke, but also as a Polish prince. He had learned the Polish language and studied Polish art and history. He had rebuilt his castle in Polish style, and engaged Polish tutors for his children. His three daughters received visits from scions of the Polish aristocracy. Stefan would let others fight the Balkan wars to come; he preferred to watch his children marry. He would found the royal family of a nation that did not yet know it needed one.

Poland was an imagined kingdom, and Stefan had a good imagination. He also had a lifetime of experience. As a child in Moravia, he had watched the Prussians humiliate the Habsburgs and build their Germany. As a young man he had married a princess in flight from the wreckage of Habsburg power on the Italian peninsula. He took her to a palace on the Adriatic, where they watched the rise of Serbia and the threat of a Yugoslav unification. Poland had to be next. Stefan would be ready, and so would his family.

Willy, the youngest son, also had a good imagination. Of all the children, he had inherited Stefan's sense of fantasy. He was old enough to grasp his father's plans, old enough to imitate, and almost old enough to rebel. The rebellion would begin in Galicia, in a cold castle in the far north of the Habsburg monarchy, where he would choose to love the people that his father ignored, the Ukrainians. Yet the beginnings of Wilhelm's Ukrainian dream, like that of his father's Polish dream, are to be found in the imperial south, by the warm waters of the Adriatic Sea. It was there that the dream pictures began to shimmer and move, like golden sunshine on the waves.

BLUE

Childhood at Sea

IT WAS DECEMBER 1908, and Stefan von Habsburg was in a loge of the Court Opera, wearing his collar of the Order of the Golden Fleece, watching *The Emperor's Dream*. Onstage, Future was beckoning Emperor Rudolf on a journey through the centuries to show him the glories of the Habsburgs to come. She showed him battlefield victories, the rise of great cities, the flowering of trade. At the very end, Future gestured to the Adriatic Sea, where she saw "floating on the blue waves of the sea, passing the dark cypress groves of the harbor, the brilliant fleet of an undefeated navy." Stefan had sailed that blue sea, planted those cypresses, and served that navy. That world of blue was the world where he raised children. It was where his son Wilhelm spent most of the early years of his life.

It was July 1934, and Wilhelm von Habsburg was in a fancy Montmartre club, spending his father's inheritance. Buildings were illuminated by red light, the Moulin Rouge cut its lazy circle through a darkening sky. Wilhelm sat chatting with a journalist friend, a chronicler of celebrity life. At a certain moment, Wilhelm raised his arm to check his watch. As he did so, his cuff fell away to reveal an anchor tattoo. A woman at a nearby table gasped. Believing herself to be in the company of a rough sailor, she summoned the maître d' to complain. Wilhelm and his friend had a good laugh, and Parisian newspaper readers could chuckle at the story the next day.

It was August 1947, and Wilhelm von Habsburg was in the back of an unmarked car, speeding towards a Soviet prison. As the guards removed the watch, they must have noticed the anchor tattoo beneath. In the interrogations that followed, Wilhelm mentioned his father Stefan and his childhood at sea. This meant nothing to his questioners, who were concerned only to prove that he was a Ukrainian nationalist and thus an enemy of Stalin. That he certainly was, but how did he become so? His journey to nationhood began by the sea, in a warm land under Habsburg rule, under the influence of his father. The tattoo records a forgotten quest for naval power that formed both father and son. It was there at the end of his story, and it suggests the beginning.[1]

Stefan and Wilhelm were the last Habsburgs to try to master the seas, but they were not the first. At the height of their glory, in the sixteenth century, the Habsburgs were the leading sea power in the world. By the eighteenth century, the loss of Spain, Portugal, and the Netherlands left them foundering in Europe, with little claim to a world empire. Victory over Napoleon brought a welcome outlet to the sea, the west and the east coasts of the Adriatic Sea. The Habsburgs made Venice their naval base and chief port. Then, during the revolutions of 1848, Italian rebels murdered the commander of the Habsburg arsenal at Venice. The empire would need a better port, its navy a safer base.[2]

At the north end of the Adriatic, the Habsburgs rebuilt the city of Trieste as a modern seaport. By 1859 Trieste was connected to Vienna by rail; after the opening of the Suez Canal in 1869, its ships could sail to Asia and Africa. In these two quick steps, the Habsburgs entered the age of globalization. In these same years, the 1850s and 1860s, the Habsburgs rebuilt the village of Pula, on the eastern shore of the Adriatic, as their naval base. When they began construction, Pula was inhabited by a few hundred people, and many more ghosts. It was there that Medea betrayed her brother to his death at the hands of Jason in the myth of the Golden Fleece. Pula had a forum under the Romans, and it was the residence of the provincial authorities of the Byzantine and then the Holy Roman

Empire. Then there had been a slow half millenium and a reversion to older ways of life. When the rebuilding began, Pula's Roman ruins echoed the bleating of goats. Within two decades, it became, like Trieste, a modern and multinational city with tens of thousands of inhabitants.[3]

The new Adriatic sea empire had to be defended against Italian nationalism. Italians had rebelled against the Habsburgs in 1848 and defeated them in 1859. Italian unification was a process with no natural endpoint. Italian patriots saw no reason why their new national kingdom should not continue to expand around the Adriatic— to Trieste, to Pula, and even further south along the eastern coast. In the Italian imagination, there was no difference between that sea's eastern and western coasts. Even under the Habsburgs, the cities of the eastern Adriatic spoke Italian, a legacy of centuries of rule from Venice. Naval equality with Italy was a pressing matter of security as well as prestige. A naval arms race with Italy was a contest that the Habsburgs could win, and did. The age of national unification forced the Habsburgs to master the seas. In the war of 1866, in which the Habsburgs lost leadership of Germany to Prussia and control of Venice to Italy, they did at least defeat the Italians at sea.[4]

The reform of the Habsburg navy was the work of Archduke Maximilian, the brother of Emperor Franz Josef. It was he who had laid the first stone in the new arsenal at Pula after the revolutions of 1848, he who drew the conclusion from the fiasco of 1859 that the Habsburgs must control the Adriatic, he who had persuaded Franz Josef that a modern battle fleet was possible and necessary. Studying the deployment of ironclads in the American Civil War, Maximilian saw that the day of the wooden battleship had passed. He was the force behind the naval budget of 1862, which guaranteed the Habsburgs a fleet of ironclad ships in the years to come. All the while, Maximilian recalled the naval glory of Habsburgs past. At Trieste, he built his palace, Miramar, to resemble a ship, with round windows like portholes. Even from the inside, it gave an impression of depths, rocking with the soft echoes of footfalls. He decorated its halls with portraits of his Spanish Habsburg forebears,

Jonathan Wyss, Topaz Maps

RUSSIAN EMPIRE

GERMANY

Prague

BOHEMIA

MORAVIA

SILESIA

Žywiec

Cracow

GALICIA

Lviv

Stuttgart

BAVARIA

Danube

Brno

Munich

HABSBURG MONARCHY

Bregenz

Salzburg

Vienna

Danube

AUSTRIA

Budapest

TYROL

STYRIA

Graz

CARINTHIA

HUNGARY

CARNIOLA

Drava

Trieste

Venice

ISTRIA

CROATIA-SLAVONIA

Po

Sava

Pula

Belgrade

ROMANIA

Lošinj

BOSNIA-
HERZEGOVINA

DALMATIA

Sarajevo

SERBIA

Danube

ITALY

TUSCANY

Adriatic Sea

MONTENEGRO

BULGARIA

Sofia

KOSOVA

Rome

OTTOMAN
EMPIRE

Naples

ISKODRA

MONASTIR

Tyrrhenian
Sea

YANYA

Corfu

Ionian
Sea

GREECE

Sicily

Athens

THE HABSBURG ADRIATIC
c. 1908

Malta

rulers of the Atlantic world. He ordered the crew of a wooden ship, the *Novara,* to circumnavigate the globe in a Habsburg còda to the Age of Exploration.[5]

Then the opportunity arose for Maximilian to imitate the exploits of the Spanish Habsburgs by becoming emperor of Mexico. Mexico was by this time an independent but indebted country, and its European creditors, especially France, wished to collect. France presented Maximilian with a proposition from some handpicked Mexican notables that he come to Mexico and rule them as emperor. He hesitated, but his wife wished to be an empress, so he finally agreed. In April 1864, he set out for Mexico on the *Novara,* with French military backing. His empire was resisted by Mexican republicans, whom the French had never subdued. The French departed in February 1867, and the Mexicans captured Maximilian that May. His captors laughed as he invoked the special rights of his family. He had sentenced the republicans' leader to death, and now he was sentenced to death himself.

On the morning of 19 June 1867, seven shots rang out on a sand dune in Querétero. Five of them struck Maximilian's body. After he fell, still breathing, still speaking, quite likely in the Spanish he had learned in order to rule, an officer pointed his saber at Maximilian's heart. A soldier fired the mercy shot, and the Mexican Empire was no more. To the end Maximilian preserved a certain dignity. Before the execution he forgave each of his seven executioners, gave each of them a gold coin, and asked them not to shoot him in the head. The *Novara* returned to Austria, bearing his corpse.[6]

The Mexican debacle left the Habsburg navy without a great leader, and without an archduke to represent its special interests within the ruling family. The next generation seemed to provide a worthy replacement, the young Archduke Stefan. Stefan, born in 1860, hailed from a martial line of the Habsburg family. He was a grandson of Archduke Karl von Habsburg, the victor over Napoleon at Aspern. After the death of his father, Stefan was adopted and educated by his uncle, Archduke Albrecht, the field marshall of the Habsburg army and a decent military strategist. Albrecht raised Stefan and his three siblings to be leaders. One of Stefan's brothers, Friedrich, became field marshall of the army. The other, Eugen, was the grand master of the Teutonic Knights. His sister, Maria Christina, succeeded where Maximilian had failed. She renewed the Habsburg connection to Spain by marrying the Spanish king.[7]

Tall, spirited, and athletic, Stefan was dispatched to the navy to continue Maximilian's other mission, the Habsburg control of the Adriatic Sea. After two years at the imperial naval academy, he was commissioned an officer in 1879. As Stefan rose through the ranks, he remained popular with the younger officers, if less so among their superiors. He was a founding member of the Imperial and Royal Yacht Squadron, an honorary society with no formal relationship to the navy. At the time, most aristocrats found yachting to be fearfully bourgeois, so Stefan's support of the sport expressed a progressive viewpoint. He was thought to be a man of modern convictions.[8]

Stefan was traditional in his romantic life, courting Archduchess Maria Theresia von Habsburg, a Tuscan princess. One of her grandfathers was Leopold II von Habsburg, the last Grand Duke of Tuscany, toppled in 1859. Maria Theresia's other grandfather was Ferdinand II of Bourbon, king of the Two Sicilies, known as "King Bomb" for his brutal suppression of revolt in 1848. When Maria Theresia, born in 1862, was a little girl, Italy was becoming a single kingdom with no need for foreign dynasties. She was fortunate to be wooed by Stefan. If she followed him to Pula, to the Habsburg Adriatic, she could continue to speak her mother tongue, Italian. Their union represented the continued aspiration of the Habsburgs to be a sea power.

Maria Theresia was rather closely related to her suitor. Stefan's grandfather Karl was also her great grandfather. Maria Theresia and Stefan were thus first cousins once removed. This was in the best tradition of Habsburg matchmaking. A marriage between two Habsburgs was a marriage of equals, bound to satisfy the court at Vienna. Emperor Franz Josef soon sent out handwritten wedding announcements to heads of state and a set of fine silver to the couple. The American president, Grover Cleveland, wrote to wish Stefan and Maria Theresia a blessed family life. Their prospects for such a life were excellent. They were married on 28 February 1886 in the imperial palace in Vienna. Stefan had married slightly above his station: his bride was more closely related to the emperor than he, and so closer than he to the court. Maria Theresia had found herself a place at the center of a new Habsburg ambition, mastery of the Adriatic. The couple settled in Pula. They were perfectly placed to found a new line of Habsburgs with appropriately modern ambitions.[9]

The marriage of Stefan and Maria Theresia von Habsburg was a small source of joy for a dynasty in troubled times. The young couple had been brought together by the decline of the Habsburg domains, the bride finding a substitute Italy on the Habsburg Adriatic coast, the husband compensation for the Habsburg army's defeats in the growing and modernized navy. The fleet, with its promise of exploration, could create at least the appearance of a return to international power. Stefan himself spent much of his youth sailing around the Mediterranean and then to Latin America.

Yet for most of the Habsburgs, the monarchy seemed like a mediocre land empire, and they often felt enclosed in a girdle of responsibility. Franz Josef's monarchy, humbled by its ally Germany and locked in compromise with its peoples, could not satisfy most of the Habsburg princes. Such an empire traded glory for durability, abandoning the ancient dream of universal power in favor of a shaky promise of continued security in Europe. For the first time in centuries, Habsburg archdukes had no one to marry to win thrones, and no army that they might lead to great victories. They were contained by seemingly invincible European rivals and kept from the succession by the emperor's seemingly interminable life.

Thus Archduke Maximilian, far more gifted than his brother the emperor, chased a Mexican dream to his death in the New World. Archduke Rudolf, the crown prince and Franz Josef's only son, also suffered from ambition. Like most heirs to thrones, he had a difficult relationship with his father. Franz Josef approved of a tutor who, when Rudolf was a teenager, awakened the youth with pistol shots in the middle of the night and made him exercise in the snow. Rudolf's rebellion was one of ideas rather than actions. He was a believer in the rights of man and of nations. Yet as long as his father ruled, he could say nothing in his own voice about policy. He wrote anonymous newspaper articles criticizing government policy. He was particularly embittered by the Habsburg monarchy's alliance with Germany. He preferred France, which he understood as the homeland of the liberalism and democracy that he himself supported. He was also, quite likely, jealous of Emperor Wilhelm II of Germany. Wilhelm II was almost exactly his own age, and was already in power.

In 1888 Rudolf turned thirty: an age of which to be ashamed, the more so given that his father had come to power at eighteen. He was estranged from his wife and wished to annul his marriage. She had borne him a daughter; he had infected her with venereal disease, and she would never bear him a son. The pope sent his petition for annulment to his father, which must have accentuated Rudolf's sense of childish powerlessness. Rudolf consoled himself with alcohol, morphine, and women, all of which heightened his distress. The venereal diseases were likely driving him mad. Of the many mistresses, the seventeen-year-old, half-Greek baroness Mary Vetsera was not his favorite. His favorite lover, probably the love of his life, was Mizzi Casper. Rudolf had given Mizzi a house in Vienna, where she lived and where a mutual friend ran a high-class bordello. He consoled himself with her in these sad days by going to wine bars and singing popular songs. Yet Mizzi laughed at Rudolf when he spoke of his desire for a double suicide, and reported him to the police in the hope of stopping him. Mary Vetsera, on the other hand, was a *femme fatale* in the truest sense; she actuated Rudolf's fascination with death. On 30 January 1889, Franz Josef was given the awful news that his only son had been found dead at his hunting compound in Mayerling. The doctor who investigated found both Rudolf and Vetsera shot through the head, with the gun near Rudolf's right hand.[10]

The death of the crown prince ended the direct line of the emperor. Franz Josef and his wife, Empress Elisabeth, would have no more sons. She was too old, and the couple was estranged. Franz Josef awoke each morning on a hard cot, bathed himself in cold water, and arranged his day around meetings and paperwork. Elisabeth arranged hers around mirrors and calisthenics to maintain her nineteen-and-a-half-inch waist. "I am a slave," confessed the empress, "to my hair." It grew to her heels and required constant attention. She collected portraits of other beautiful women, asking Habsburg diplomats in Istanbul to procure "photographs of beautiful women from the world of the Turkish harems." She had a certain penchant for kissing girls. She spent her time away from Vienna, often sailing in the south among the Greek islands. In the 1890s, when she appeared in Vienna at all, she hid her aging face behind a veil. On 10 September 1898, while boarding a steamer in Geneva, Elisabeth was killed by an Italian anarchist with a single stroke of a carpenter's awl. She died of internal bleeding without realizing that a thin blade had pierced her heart.[11]

Emperor Franz Josef had lost his brother Maximilian, his son Rudolf, and his wife Elisabeth. These were personal tragedies, to be sure. They were also a challenge to the Habsburg dynasty. Franz Josef ruled long, but one day he must die. Who, then, would succeed him? Aside from Maximilian, the emperor had two more brothers. The younger of them, Archduke Ludwig Viktor, collected art and built palaces, acceptable occupations for an archduke. Yet he also dressed in women's clothing, the better to seduce men. Practiced discreetly, this habit might not have been disqualifying, but Ludwig Viktor, "Lutziwutzi" to his intimates, was not known for discretion. After one too many adventures in the Central Bath House in Vienna, he was dispatched to a castle near Salzburg. He invited army officers to join him there and applied a number of stratagems designed to get them to take off their pants. This left one more brother, Archduke Karl Ludwig, who contrived to kill himself by the very zeal of his Catholic faith. In 1896, he died after drinking the holy but contaminated waters of the River Jordan.

It was nevertheless Karl Ludwig who sired the next crown prince. By the second of his three wives, he had fathered three sons: Franz Ferdinand, Otto Franz, and Ferdinand Karl. Otto Franz, the best known of the three, was prone to dancing naked in cafés, and once poured a bowl of spinach over a bust of the emperor. For another offense, the dishonoring of his own pregnant wife, he was slapped in the face by Franz Josef. It is unclear whether it was Otto Franz or Franz Ferdinand who tested his horse by jumping it over a coffin carried in procession during a funeral. However that may be, Franz Ferdinand, though not as colorful as his brother, was also notoriously unstable. But he was alive, he was the emperor's oldest nephew, so he was crown prince.[12]

Otto Franz was syphilitic, and died a horrible death. His brother, Crown Prince Franz Ferdinand, suffered from tuberculosis, and so traveled south to the Adriatic for the air. There he saw Maria Theresia, who was his first cousin on his mother's side, and sailed with her husband Stefan. He found in their company an entirely different atmosphere fom the one he left behind. Far from the imperial capital of Vienna, in the warm and safe haven of Pula, Stefan and Maria Theresia were renewing the Habsburg family, founding an impressive line of their own. Their children were not long in coming, six of them within nine years.

The first was a daughter, Eleanora, born in 1886. The first son, Karl Albrecht, was born in 1888, a few months before Rudolf's suicide. Karl Albrecht was named for the two Habsburg military heroes: for Albrecht, his father's uncle and guardian, and Karl, his father's grandfather and mother's great-grandfather. These choices of names were traditional, a respectful nod to previous generations. In the case of Albrecht, who was still alive, it was also a very prudent move. Stefan was not at this point among the wealthiest of the archdukes, but he stood to inherit fabulous riches upon his adoptive father Albrecht's death. After Karl Albrecht, Maria Theresia gave birth to two daughters: Renata and Mechtildis. Mechtildis, too, was named in homage to Albrecht. Albrecht's daughter Mechtildis had killed herself by accident, setting her dress on fire while trying to hide a cigarette from her father.

Stefan had designs on a future dynasty, and the naming of the two youngest sons revealed a powerful political imagination. The next son, born in 1893, was christened Leo Karl Maria Cyril-Methodius. Cyril and Methodius, two brothers, were saints, although not of the Catholic but of the rival Orthodox Church. Missionaries to the Slavs a thousand years before, the brothers had created the language that became the traditional one used in the Orthodox liturgy. Although they lived and died before the schism of Christianity of 1054, their achievement came to be associated with Orthodoxy thereafter. Leo was born on their feast day, the fifth of July. Traditionally celebrated by the Orthodox, this feast had just been recognized by the Catholic Church, a tactical move to gain influence among the Orthodox populations of the Balkans. Pope Leo XIII had ordered the change, which seems to explain Leo's first name. His third name, Maria, seems a clear reference to the Virgin Mary, more venerated at that time and place by the Catholics than the Orthodox. Yet according to tradition, Cyril and Methodius's father was named Leo, and their mother, Maria. So the two names Leo and Maria, Catholic references to the reigning pope and the Virgin Mary, were also legibly Orthodox. These four names (Leo, Maria, Cyril, Methodius) could be understood as naming the two Orthodox saints and their parents.[13]

The name cast a bridge across the great schism of Christianity. Since 1054, Christendom in Europe had been divided between east and west. Stefan's son Leo, heir to the most important Catholic family in Europe, was named so that he might one day also appeal to the Orthodox. In the late nineteenth century in the Balkans, religious references were a kind of national politics. Stefan was proposing a Habsburg answer to the "Eastern question," the most pressing diplomatic problem of the day. In southeastern Europe, the Habsburgs' traditional rival, the Ottoman Empire, was in decline. The Eastern question regarded the fate of its Balkan territories, largely inhabited by Orthodox believers. Would they be seized by national monarchies, such as Serbia? Or by the Russian Empire, Orthodox itself and eager to treat Orthodox Serbia as its client? Stefan knew, after the experience of Italy and Germany, that national unifications could threaten the monarchy. The Croatians, who inhabited the southern reaches of the Habsburg monarchy, were Catholic, like the

Habsburgs, but the dialects they spoke were very similar to those being codified as Serbian. A Serbia that unified a "Yugoslav" or south Slavic nation would embrace the Adriatic coast, including Pula and Stefan's own palace there.

Leo was Stefan's answer to the Eastern question: let nationalism continue, let the nationalists unify territory, let a Yugoslavia come into existence and unite Serbs and Croats, Orthodox and Catholics—but let this take place under Habsburg rule and let the reigning Habsburg be my son. Newly unified nations could become Habsburg crownlands, satisfying their local aspirations while taking part in a peaceful and prosperous empire and a superior civilization.

Stefan was not the only Habsburg with such ideas. Prince Rudolf had believed that the Habsburgs should become the dominant power in the Balkans and claim, as he put it in 1886, "supremacy in the European Orient." This dominance was to be achieved by a policy of seeking alliances with the Balkan national monarchies, along with the penetration of their economies and the support of German as the language of culture in the Balkans. His successor as crown prince, Franz Ferdinand, had similar preoccupations. On his yachting trips with Stefan in the Adriatic in the late 1880s and early 1890s, Franz Ferdinand likely spoke of his idea of peacefully absorbing south Slavic domains within the Habsburg monarchy. In this scheme, the dual state Austria-Hungary would become a triple state, an Austria-Hungary-Yugoslavia. The Habsburgs would somehow overcome the Orthodox states of the Balkans, probably during a crisis occasioned by the final collapse of the Ottoman Empire, and incorporate their peoples into new Habsburg crownlands. It seems that Stefan took the step that Rudolf and Franz Ferdinand had not, preparing a Habsburg candidate for the future Balkan zone of influence. Most likely, Leo was intended by his father to be the regent of some kind of Habsburg Balkan kingdom.[14]

Stefan expressed a similar ambition in the name of his youngest son, Wilhelm, born 10 February 1895. Wilhelm was the name of a

Habsburg Family Portrait, 1895. From left to right: Renata, Leo, Wilhelm, Maria Theresia, Eleanora, Albrecht, Stefan, Mechtildis

Habsburg archduke who, in the late fourteenth century, was poised to gain the Polish crown by marriage. He was engaged to Poland's young girl king, Jadwiga—she was king because Poland had no reigning queens. When Wilhelm entered Poland to consummate his marriage with the eleven-year-old girl in 1385, Polish nobles caught him and expelled him from the country. This was no question of delicacy; the nobles wanted to see her wed to someone else. She was married to the Lithuanian grand duke, and together they founded the Jagiellonian line that ruled Poland and much of eastern Europe for the next two centuries. It was a Jagiellonian who lost Bohemia and Hungary to the Habsburgs in 1526. Poland itself remained independent, however, for more than two centuries after that.[15]

Yet the Habsburgs, who knew how to wait, took a good deal of Polish territory in the eighteenth century, collaborating in the partition of old Poland with neighboring empires. In the nineteenth century, the old Polish lands were still divided among the Habsburg monarchy, Germany, and the Russian Empire. As Stefan knew, it was not an especially stable arrangement. His adoptive father Albrecht owned vast tracts in the Habsburg partition of Poland known as Galicia, and Stefan visited him there. He would have known the general history of Polish resistance to imperial rule. Napoleon had rallied Poles against all three of their oppressors. In 1809 the army of the Duchy of Warsaw, a Napoleonic state, had even invaded Habsburg Galicia. In 1830 and again in 1863, Poles had tried to throw off Russian rule. In the 1890s, Poles in Germany resisted campaigns from Berlin to buy their property and weaken their Catholic Church. In the Habsburg domains, conditions for Polish culture were favorable, and opportunities for Polish political life were bountiful. Poles administered the province of Galicia and provided two prime ministers. Some Poles believed that the Habsburgs might one day, in return for their loyalty, support the creation of a unified Polish kingdom within an enlarged Habsburg monarchy.[16]

This was a national wish that Karl Stefan thought his family could fulfill. In 1894 and 1895, as Maria Theresia was pregnant with Wilhelm, Stefan knew that his own destiny was about to be joined to Poland. Albrecht was dying. Upon Albrecht's death, which followed Wilhelm's birth by eight days, Stefan inherited the Galician estate. Stefan knew that he was the archduke best placed to address the Polish question, which, after the Eastern question, was the most pressing national problem in the Europe of the day. His experience in the Balkans had taught him to imagine national unifications. From his southern perspective, Stefan had already developed the notion that future national unifications should take place under the aegis of the Habsburgs. Wilhelm was born to be the answer to the Polish question. The Polish question was: would the three partitions of old Poland ever again unite, and if so, as an independent state or as a crownland of an empire? Stefan's answer was: should Poland unite, let it be under the realm of the Habsburgs, let Poland become a Habsburg crownland, and let the regent of Poland come from my family. All of Stefan's children would learn Polish, but only Wilhelm learned Polish from birth.

Stefan's plan depended upon some future collapse of the Russian Empire, which held more than half of the old Polish lands. It also depended upon the benign attitude of Germany, Poland's other partitioner. Wilhelm's name, as it happened, also referred to Germany. The most famous Wilhelm in 1895 was the German emperor, Wilhelm II. The Habsburgs had signed an alliance with Germany in 1879. In the 1890s, relations between Germany and the Habsburg monarchy grew closer, in some part thanks to the personal diplomacy of Stefan. A few weeks after his son's birth, Stefan commanded the flotilla that sailed to Germany to celebrate the opening of the canal that connects the North and Baltic Seas. Stefan was a better sailor than Wilhelm II, but the Imperial War Harbor at Kiel was imposing. It dwarfed the Habsburg base at Pula, and the German navy was incomparably stronger. Austria could never rival Germany on land, as the war of 1866 had shown, and Stefan now saw that the same was true of the high seas. If the Habsburg monarchy could not oppose Germany, it would have to be an ally. It was a mixed pleasure to tell the German emperor of the birth of a son named Wilhelm. It was meant to be seen as a small gesture of loyalty from one ally to another.[17]

Stefan then retired from the navy. Perhaps the German spectacle had convinced him that naval service was no route to glory. The navy had provided him with only a glimpse of the blue seas that other Habsburgs once had mastered. Most likely, Stefan now saw the vanity of an ambition to rule the seas, especially in light of the growing German and, for that matter, British fleets. He was an anglophile himself, ordering his yachts from Britain and speaking proper English. If the sea offered no satisfying solution, perhaps the nation could. Perhaps an age of national compromise could be transformed into an age of national glory. His retirement was the end of one Habsburg dream—that of a young and virile archduke taming the high seas. But Stefan now had new dreams. He was very wealthy, happily married, and had six healthy children. He was thirty-six, old enough to understand how the world was changing around him, but young enough to believe that he could stay ahead.[18]

Stefan left the navy to try a national policy, one that could serve himself and his family's empire. He had named his sons in ways that symbolically prepared them to rule new kingdoms along the borders of the empire, a Balkan kingdom and a Polish kingdom. If more national unifications were inevitable, let them take place under the guidance of archdukes, within enlarged Habsburg domains. If nationalism must come, let it work for the enlargement of the empire rather than for its disintegration. For such a plan to work, Habsburg archdukes would have to re-create themselves, in advance, as national leaders. With Stefan showing the way, princes could trade their traditional role as commanders of armies for a new dignity as creators of peoples. As a hypothesis about the changing nature of power, this was rather good. Now all he needed was a laboratory.

The Adriatic island of Lošinj, where Stefan built his retirement villa, was to become the Garden of Eden where he could raise his colorful brood of modern monarchs. The island had paths but no proper roads; centuries of building and rebuilding stone fences had cleared the soil while creating a complicated lattice of barriers. Stefan had his villa, called Podjavori, or "Under the Laurels," built far away from the shore, high in a pine forest, on a site picked for its climatological properties. The moisture level was supposedly ideal for a family often visited by tuberculosis. A visitor to Stefan's villa walked west away from the harbor, then up a hill called Cavalry on a rugged path, most likely with a hired man and a donkey for the luggage.

Podjavori was a planned paradise, meant to preserve the health and delight the senses. It was far from civilization, but not too far. Even a careless observer could see that nature had been altered by the hand of man. Stefan brought in two hundred species of plants from around the world, with which his Viennese designers and Italian gardeners transformed the terrains around the villa into a spectacular garden. Some of the most vivid flora were native, such as a spider orchid that bloomed blue inside black. An English governess who arrived in winter found the island to be "a dream of delight." "The air was laden," she wrote, "with the scents of orange and citron-trees, roses and mimosa."[19]

Stefan's Palace on Lošinj, View from Balcony

This governess, a cheerful young lady called Nellie Ryan, was confronted upon arrival with the bright and whimsical world that Stefan had created for his family on the island. She was greeted by his aide-de-camp, who kissed her hand and apologized that his only three words of English were, "I love you." At her very first meeting with Stefan, the archduke insisted that they immediately play tennis. He had at his disposal a tennis court, lined by palm trees, and staffed by four local ball boys who stood at the ready, in folk costume, carrying nets on long poles. "It was a splendid game," she wrote of her first match with the archduke, "but I soon discovered that he was a bad loser."[20]

A few days later Stefan introduced himself into her room. He had designs on her furniture. Explaining that her arrangement was "inartistic," he threw all of her things into a pile in the middle of the room. As he heaved and sweated, the governess expressed concern that his wife would be most surprised to find him in such a state. Maria Theresia appeared, on cue, but only laughed at her husband's typically obsessive behavior. A moment later, a visitor appeared with news of a hunt to take place the following day. Stefan forgot what he was doing. Leaving the mess behind him, he strode into the hall with his new companion, gesticulating wildly.[21]

Stefan no longer seemed to work. He would rise in the morning and put on his painter's uniform: baggy corduroy pants, a shapeless jacket, a straw hat. He would then set out with a canvas under his arm and a servant at his heel. He was not in the least discouraged by his complete lack of artistic talent. Some mornings he would sail out into the Adriatic, returning a few days or a few weeks later with several new paintings. In the evenings, Stefan fussed pointlessly around the house, or played the piano, or threw parties.[22]

His true occupation was the education of his children. He ordered their lives down to the minute, every day, though not entirely unpleasantly. The six of them, known as Leanora, Karl, Renata, Tildis, Leo, and Willy, were schooled at home by teachers drawn from the lower nobility and bourgeoisie. Just as they had been wet-nursed by local women to dilute, as their governess put it, "any too much blue blood," so they were taught by people believed to represent the more vigorous classes. The children rose each day at 6:00, had mass at 7:00, lessons at 8:00, a sandwich and a glass of wine at 10:00 (even the small children always had wine), a walk speaking a foreign language at 11:00, lunch at 12:00 with more wine, then tennis or skating, then tea and cakes at 3:30, lessons at 3:45, and dinner at 7:00.[23]

Willy and his brothers and sisters had to dress for every lunch and every dinner, assisted by their maids and valets. They proceeded into the dining room in proper order of rank for every meal, even if the family was eating by itself with no guests. They had to wear black when in mourning for close relatives, which was rather often. On their father's birthdays, each of the children had to compose a letter to him in a different language. The children spoke Italian, the language of their mother and the Adriatic; German, the language of their father and the empire; as well as French and English, the languages, as Stefan saw matters, of civilization. After 1895 they were also instructed in Polish. Over the course of the day, the children would speak to each other in German, Italian, French, English, and Polish. In one sense, they were native speakers of all five of these languages; in another, they had no native language at all.[24]

On Lošinj, Stefan remained a sailor. He would often sail with artists, sometimes with other guests, such as Franz Ferdinand. He taught his three sons to sail. He ordered yachts to his own specifications, to be constructed in English shipyards. He wrote to the shipbuilders in English, demanding minor modifications, explaining that "this adds to the look of the boat." The delivery of a new yacht was an occasion of great excitement. The family sailed around the Adriatic, to Trieste, Venice, or elsewhere in Italy. Once the family visited Bari, to see the Cathedral of St. Nicholas. There Stefan insisted on buying a black goat that caught his fancy.[25]

In summer 1900, the family made for Petersburg, the capital of the Russian Empire, the Habsburgs' powerful eastern neighbor and rival. The Habsburg monarchy had a long eastern border with Russia, and relations were rather strained. The two empires were rivals in the Balkans: Russia wished for the Orthodox monarchies in the Balkans to be numerous and subordinate to itself, while Austria wished somehow to preserve its own hold on the Adriatic and gain from the decline of the Ottoman Empire. They were also rivals in the Polish question. Russia, which pursued a strict policy of centralization, was suspicious of the freedoms that Poles enjoyed in Galicia. If Galicia was going to become the basis for a Polish unification, its expansion could only come at the expense of Russia.[26]

Stefan's love for the sea kept him in contact with other royals, and kept him thinking about avenues to power. In 1902, Stefan visited Madrid as the Austrian delegate at the coming-of-age ceremony of his nephew, King Alfonso XIII of Bourbon and Habsburg. Alfonso's father had died before his birth, so he had been born king, his mother Maria Christina serving as regent for the first sixteen years of his life. Maria Christina, Stefan's sister, had succeeded in raising her son to his royal destiny. Stefan wanted no worse for himself. His children grew up knowing that their cousin was a king. Alfonso had been born to a throne. Willy was born to create one.[27]

The journeys by sea from Lošinj around Europe provided small lessons in how the children might achieve such transformations. To alter the map of Europe, the children had to learn to modify their own identities and comportment as appropriate. As the family traveled, Stefan instructed Willy and the other children on how and when to shift public identities; nothing was to be more natural than the mask. In 1905, for example, Stefan and the family traveled to Paris "incognito." Stefan took on a false name so that his visit might be considered unofficial. In the elaborate diplomacy of the day, this relieved the French government of its obligations to receive the family as imperial archdukes and archduchesses. It was also something of a comedy: when a Habsburg archduke arrived at a harbor "incognito," the local authorities still had to be informed of exactly what was taking place. This was the task of the Habsburg foreign minister, who was also responsible for monitoring the behavior of the archdukes while they were abroad.[28]

The voyages were part of Willy's political education. He and his family were received by royalty and heads of state wherever they went, for they themselves were royalty. They were addressed as "your imperial and royal highnesses," for they were imperial and royal archdukes and archduchesses and possible future rulers themselves. Kings and queens visited them upon the yachts. The children learned that the world was divided into three kinds of countries: empires and kingdoms ruled by Habsburgs or their relations, empires and kingdoms not ruled by Habsburgs and their relations, and republics such as France. The voyages by yacht must have been a more pleasant kind of schooling than the children's daily routine on Lošinj. Telling signs emerged of untoward contact with hired sailors.[29]

When it was time for the next expedition, in summer 1906, Willy was old enough to be a hand on deck. His father was planning a grand journey to Istanbul. Once again Stefan desired to travel "incognito," informing all and sundry that he would be arriving in a major port with families and servants in tow, while simultaneously maintaining the pretense of discretion. For this journey, his pseudonym was "the Count of Żywiec." It was a telling choice of identity.

Żywiec was the Polish name for the town and region where Stefan had inherited his Galician estate. He used the pseudonym in correspondence with the Habsburg foreign minister, in letters composed entirely in Polish. The foreign minister at the time was indeed a Pole, but like all Habsburg officials, he used German at work. The letter had to be translated so that beleaguered ministry officials could respond. In 1906, as Stefan's children were becoming young men and young women, he demonstratively gave the Polish language precedence over German.[30]

In 1906 Willy turned eleven. He was a happy child of the sea: tan, strawberry blonde, blue-eyed, and by all accounts beautiful. In the Adriatic, he could swim in water so clear as to be transparent to the depths, so saline that it would hold the bones of a thin boy such as himself. Dolphins were plentiful. Fishermen waited quietly for what they called the blue fish, the pilchard. Time was defined by the weather—in Willy's mother tongue, Italian, the words are the same—and especially by the winds, which had their own names: the Tramontane, the Scirocco, the quick-rising Bora from the northeast. Willy was raised a bit incongruously, prepared for northerly Galicia while living by the southern sea, born in Pula and bound for Poland. His father had given Willy his Polish name in 1895, yet did not make Galicia the family's main residence until 1907.

In that year, Stefan proclaimed the family's Polishness and began his own campaign for a Polish throne. The move to Galicia, after a childhood in Istria, must have been a challenge, perhaps even a shock, to the boy, an interruption of the timelessness of childhood. Yet Willy had been raised to expect change; most days of his young life he spoke five languages and wore three suits of clothes. At home and abroad he learned both protocol and flexibility, both of them meant to serve the higher purpose of family ambition. The conviction of an eternal right to rule provided the confidence for flexibility; the confidence in flexibility allowed for the conviction of the eternal right to rule. The Habsburgs saw themselves as inside this virtuous circle, as somehow free of time.[31]

Yet Stefan's embrace of the Polish nation was something more than a typical Habsburg maneuver for power. It involved an abandonment of the calm sense of eternity, of the sea as a source of boundless power, of the island as a site for the perfection of human nature. The family would have to experience time as rough forward motion toward national liberation. Stefan would find in Galicia a Polish nation that he could join, though not one that he could arrange like a garden or steer like a yacht. In his new home, even the family would slip free. Willy would reject his Polish inheritance in favor of a rival nation of his own choosing, Ukraine.

Stefan and Willy leapt ashore in search of national kingdoms. As sailors will, they found the earth moving beneath their feet. Willy went forward, with his father, into an unsteady future of nations, but not without recording the timelessness of his imperial childhood on his own wrists: the down anchor of a boat rocking gently at harbor, the north star of an uncharted journey through darkness. Blue was under his skin, and there it would remain, to be spotted across the shadows of a Parisian restaurant by the attentive eyes of a nervous lady, or noted in the harsh glare of an interrogation chamber by an indifferent servant of Stalin.

GREEN

~~❦~~

Oriental Europe

I N AUTUMN 1906 Archduke Stefan took his family on a sea journey from Lošinj to Istanbul to meet the sultan of the Ottoman
Empire. With Willy happily on deck, he piloted the yacht south,
through the mouth of the Adriatic. Along the way he and the crew
repelled pirate attacks with rifle fire. Willy and his brothers must
have enjoyed the spectacle and the thrill. When the echoes of the
shots quieted, they found themselves in the Mediterranean, sailing
around Greece and through a realm of myth.

Stefan put down anchor on the Greek island of Corfu to visit a
palace built for Empress Elisabeth. She had called it the Achilleion,
after Achilles, the Greek hero of the legend of the Trojan War. The
Trojan War began because the Greek goddesses could not agree
upon which of them was the fairest; it was an appropriate story for
Elisabeth, who spent her life worrying whether she was the loveliest
of queens. Achilles, like Elisabeth, was selfish and petulant. At Troy
he chose to fight or sulk in his tent for the most capricious of reasons. These were the legends that Elisabeth rendered modern by
building a palace on Corfu. She had been one of the many Europeans who persuaded modern Greeks that they were the descendants of the Greeks of antiquity, and that the classics belonged not
just to Europe but also and especially to the Greek nation.[1]

On Corfu, Stefan praised Elisabeth's palace in all its particulars.
For both Habsburgs, the ancient Greeks signified the origins of the

European civilization that, as they saw matters, their family continued. Stefan, for his part, was a knight of the Order of the Golden
Fleece, a chivalric society governed by the Habsburgs and named
for the Greek myth of Jason and the Argonauts. In that ancient tale,
Jason had gathered the greatest heroes of the world and led them on
a naval journey to the east in his ship, the *Argo*, in search of a
miraculous Golden Fleece. Medieval knights of the Order, founded
in 1430, had understood Jason's journey as a model for a Christian
crusade. They vowed to take the Ottoman capital of Istanbul and
reclaim it for Christendom. When Philip II, a Habsburg king of
Spain, raised a navy to defeat the Ottoman Empire on the Mediterranean Sea in the 1570s, he built a magnificent ship called the *Argo*.
The Ottoman Empire, defeated at sea by that strange charge of symbolism, remained a threat to the Habsburgs on land. Its armies besieged Vienna in 1683. Stefan, student of Polish history that he was,
knew that only the Polish cavalry had saved the Habsburgs. The
Polish king's teenaged son, who fought to rescue Vienna that day,
was a member of the Order of the Golden Fleece. Stefan's own sons
would soon join the Order.[2]

Achilles and Jason, the heroes of myth, had both sailed east with
thoughts of conquest. Achilles conquered Troy with a petulant fury,
killing its greatest champion and dragging him naked around the
city walls. Jason seduced Medea, who then betrayed her family to
help him win the fleece. The Habsburg vision of crusading civilization, advancing sometimes by the hero's sword but more often by
Cupid's arrow, was turned against Islam and the east, the seemingly
eternal threat of the Ottoman Empire. The Ottomans had established themselves in the Near East at about the same time that the
Habsburgs had made themselves the central power of Europe. For
half a millennium the two dynasties fought at land and at sea, defin-
ing by their enmity the whole history of southeastern Europe.

Yet now, in the twentieth century, in the age of nationalism, all of
this had changed. Islam, once so fearful because of its might, was
now threatening the Habsburgs by its weakness. The Ottoman Empire was a worrisome neighbor to the Habsburgs not because it
seized territory from Christian empires, but rather because it yielded

lands to new national Christian kingdoms. The first of these, Greece, was distant enough from the Habsburg monarchy to be a charming addition to the European map. One of the artists Elisabeth most admired, the English Romantic poet Lord Byron, had died in the Greek wars of independence. Yet the next independent kingdom, Serbia, was something else entirely. It bordered the Habsburg monarchy, and its populations spoke dialects very similar to those of the inhabitants of the Habsburg south. After 1903, Serbia was ruled by a hostile dynasty plainly interested in territorial expansion at the expense of surrounding empires. Serbia, and nationalism generally, was a threat to the Habsburgs as much as it was to the Ottomans.

Though a sea voyage to the east summoned the spirits of Achilles and Jason, Stefan's journey was of an entirely different sort. He brought the family to the Ottoman Empire on a mission of peace and tourism. Willy, then a boy of eleven, was enthralled by the sights of Istanbul, just as he was supposed to be. Decadence has its charms, especially for the young. Political decline might be overlooked by a young boy overwhelmed by the sultan's court, by the Hagia Sofia, by the Blue Mosque. Like tourists before and since, he found himself lured by rug merchants to inspect their wares. This was a first taste of the Islamic world for Willy and the children, but not the last. In 1907, the family set out for Algiers and Tunisia. North Africa was the place that made the greatest impression on Willy, who remembered it fondly as an adult. He loved Arabs for the rest of his life.[3]

Stefan was something of an orientalist, though his fantasies now reached no further east than Poland. The family found what he was seeking on the island of Malta, which they also visited in 1907. It might seem that Malta and Poland have nothing in common, other than the fact that the Maltese and Polish alphabets both include the letter "ż." As it happens, Malta illustrated the kind of imperial nationalism Stefan wished to employ and indeed embody. Malta, the southernmost island of Europe, was a British possession. For the past two decades, Britain had cultivated the English language and a separate Maltese national identity on the island. This served to insulate the Maltese, whose educated classes spoke Italian, from Italian national unification. Malta showed that national unifications could be contained and that national identity could serve empire. Young Willy did not grasp any of this. He did become an anglophile, however, enjoying the British royal visits to the family on the yacht. He may have also noticed that, besides the English and Italian that he spoke on the island, the Maltese spoke their own language, descended from Arabic.[4]

When the family returned to North Africa in 1909, Willy was thirteen, and Stefan was sailing a yacht with a Polish name. The two of them had seen *The Emperor's Dream* in Vienna, and Stefan had begun to realize his own Polish dream in Galicia. Even as Stefan guided Willy and the family around the eastern Mediterranean, his servants and hirelings were preparing a new family palace, far to the north, in Galicia. The move to Poland was no doubt a source of strife within the family, to which these journeys offered some release. Having heard the call to prayer from towering minarets, young Willy was not much impressed with the pretty wooden Catholic churches of Habsburg Galicia.[5]

These formerly Polish lands were in the Habsburg periphery in the northeast, associated in the popular mind with backwardness and bears—even, absurdly, with polar bears, since eastern Galicia in the Viennese imagination was the Habsburg Siberia. Yet for Willy, who in these years was going back and forth from Istria to Galicia by train, and traveling to the Islamic world by sea, Poland was the least exciting version of the Orient. His father was moving him away from the sea of his boyhood to landlocked borderlands, while at the same time teasing him with the tang of the Islamic east. Before Poland could become fixed as the family's new home, it was already unsettled by the warm winds of the Orient. Willy never quite settled down in Galicia, or indeed anywhere, and the longing for the East never left him.

Willy was learning to wander just as his father was finally settling down, creating for the family a miniature royal Poland inside Habsburg Galicia. Stefan's two castles in Żywiec had their own do-

mains: forty thousand hectares of woods, an area almost four times the size of the Principality of Liechtenstein, or a fifth the size of the American state of Rhode Island. The realm even had its own economy; Stefan inherited a brewery that his uncle had founded in 1856. Stefan invested massively in it, buying the latest equipment, installing electric lighting, purchasing railway cars. These were also used to ship timber from the massive forested estate. He used the

The New Castle, Żywiec

profits from these enterprises to reinforce the majesty of the "new castle," built in the nineteenth century, which he had chosen for the family's Polish residence.[6]

Stefan's builders added whole new wings to the castle, giving each child a suite. Stefan commissioned family portraits, which he hung next to likenesses of Polish kings that he collected during tours of Europe. The castle walls displayed a fine mixture of Habsburg royalty, Polish royalty, and the likenesses of Stefan's family. Buildings in the park recalled the lodges in the nearby mountains. Stefan built a chapel in the Polish Renaissance style for his wife. Maria Theresia, for her part, wrote the pope in her native Italian for permission that mass be said in the private chapel three times daily. The pope granted her requests, although they both knew that there was an admirable Catholic church just beyond the castle grounds. That, though, was beyond the world that these Habsburgs bought, built, and controlled.[7]

Stefan remained impossibly fickle, as Polish artists and architects learned. He once sent an urgent telegram to change the location of a window, an alteration that has not only aesthetic but structural implications, especially when building in stone. He patronized modern designers, in both senses of the word. He was in touch with the

The Old Castle, Żywiec

leading Polish modernist painters of Galicia, for whom the drawing rooms of his castle became a kind of salon. He seemed to like their Polishness more than their modernism. Even as he subsidized the latest styles, he could not keep himself from criticizing them. He said that the art nouveau furniture built for his daughter Eleanora's room looked as if "made from the bones of the nervous dead."[8]

If Stefan was continually irritated by some imperfection, he was also always eager to arrange preposterous kinds of fun. He devoted a room of the castle to a game called Railroad, played with miniature engines powered by steam, involving scenarios that invariably led to collisions. Out of doors, Stefan now took to cars with the same passion he had once reserved for yachts. He test-drove vehicles across Europe, visited factories in Britain and France, and had cars designed according to his own plans. In summer 1910 he organized a "Congress of the Automobiles of Our Friends," which brought the motorized nobility of the Habsburg monarchy, Germany, and Russia to Żywiec to congratulate itself on its modernity. Stefan used his cars for feats of Polish national prowess, as when he managed to attend the performance of a tragic drama by a Romantic poet in Cracow one day and the unveiling of a patriotic statue in Żywiec the next.[9]

Wojciech Kossak 1911

Zywiec, Zamek, Galicya

Family Portrait, 1911, Wilhelm in first row

From the backseat of his father's cars, Willy saw a landscape in green. The castle lay in a valley, in a town surrounded on all sides by the gentle slopes of the Beskidy range of the Carpathian Mountains. Spruce forests covered the mountains from base to peaks, heights that were snowy in winter but passable for much of the year. When weather permitted, the family would hike into the nearby mountains. They would find picnics awaiting them at a summit, servants having heated soups, sausages, and potatoes in the ashes of campfires. During the winter the family skated on a little river, or went sleighing in the castle's park.

So the years passed, marked by daily duties and predictable pleasures. This was a family where girls not only asked for but got ponies for Christmas. When dismantling the enormous Christmas trees, Stefan generally made sure to set them on fire. The family even owned a yew tree. It was never cut down for Christmas. It grew peacefully back on Lošinj, where it still grows, among the gardens that Stefan had made, in that other, warmer, world of pine.[10]

In Stefan's realm of the imagination, childhood never ended, and yet it was ending. The six children emerged from the homes their father had built into the wider world for which their father had tried to prepare them. In Galicia, Willy had to watch as his three sisters received suitors chosen from the Polish aristocracy. This was a tricky business. As the Viennese court saw matters, the Polish princes who came calling were not equal matches for Willy's sisters, who were Habsburg archduchesses. Stefan knew what he stood to lose but also what he stood to gain. If his daughters married Polish aristocrats, they could not produce sons eligible to rule the Habsburg monarchy. On the other hand, such marriages, by helping the family to seem Polish, might create a number of candidates for a future Polish throne: himself, his sons, his sons-in-law, his grandsons.

Habsburgs married to rule, and the marriages came quickly. In September 1908, Stefan and Maria Theresia announced the engagement of their daughter Renata to a Polish prince, Hieronymus Radziwiłł. The Radziwiłłs were one of the grandest families of old Poland, producing princes, bishops, and warriors. They also had a knack for romance. Earlier in the nineteenth century, the German emperor had lost his heart to a Radziwiłł; later in the twentieth, a Radziwiłł would marry the sister of Jacqueline Bouvier. Hieronymus and Renata had to pass through an embarrassing set of court procedures before they could wed. His various titles were not recognized by Vienna. Renata had to renounce all of her titles, as well as the right to be addressed as the "Imperial and Royal Highness." The couple also had to accept a prenuptial agreement and the separation of property.[11]

Stefan helped Polish society understand what was about to happen. On 15 January 1909, the day before Renata's wedding, Polish newspapers in the Habsburg, Russian, and German empires proclaimed that the union connected "the imperial family of the Habsburgs with an excellent Polish family." When Renata and Radziwiłł wed in the chapel at Żywiec castle, they were creating something new: a Polish branch of the Habsburg family. The guests from the Radziwiłł side, clad in fur and tall winter hats with feathers, gave exuberant voice to their joy. They had been recognized as a great family by the greatest of families. Hieronymus gave his new wife a fur coat; another Radziwiłł gave Stefan a sleigh lined with bearskin.

For Stefan and the Habsburgs, it was a moment that called for careful diplomacy. The Habsburg court kept the new clan from succession to the thrones, but wanted to maintain contact with the newly Polish branch of the family. Emperor Franz Josef knew that the issue of Polish unification was alive in all three empires, and that a Polish branch of the family gave him a certain advantage over his fellow emperors in Russia and Germany. His own policy of national concessions dictated a certain cautious endorsement of the Polish national cause. The emperor's representative tactfully pronounced his toast in French rather than in German. Żywiec was very close to the border with Germany, where Poles were forced to hear German in schools and churches. Stefan gave his own speech in both Polish and French.[12]

Mechtildis soon brought a second marital connection to the historical Polish ruling classes. In 1911 she followed the same procedure with her own betrothed, Olgierd Czartoryski. Like Renata, she lost her titles, and the rights of her children to the Habsburg succession. She had to pronounce them to renounce them, using the royal "we" for the last time in her life: "We, Mechtildis, by the grace of God imperial princess and archduchess of Austria, royal princess of Hungary and Bohemia"—and so on. Her groom hailed from another princely Polish family from the east who had preserved wealth and renown after Poland ceased to exist. Olgierd Czartoryski had to follow the same irksome path as Hieronymus Radziwiłł. Because there was no Poland, no Polish court could establish his princely rank—not that the old Poland could have confirmed any such Polish title had it still existed; its political system was based upon the equality of all nobles and recognized no differences in rank among them.[13]

The marriage of a second Habsburg princess with a second Polish prince enlarged the Polish royal family. Stefan's project gained still greater resonance and recognition. When the couple was married on 11 January 1913, the Polish bishop presiding over the ceremony wore historical vestments from the royal castle in Cracow. Emperor Franz Josef sent a representative and a diamond necklace. Queen Maria Christina of Spain, Stefan's sister and the bride's aunt, sent a

Olgierd Czartoryski and Mechtildis
Czartoryska née Habsburg

brooch of diamonds and sapphires. The pope sent a blessing of the union of two great Catholic families, written in his own hand, on parchment inscribed with the Habsburg coat of arms and the Czartoryski motto: "Come what may."[14]

Willy watched the courting; he was lonely, perhaps, but he was not the only outsider. Eleanora, his oldest sister and his favorite, seemed unresponsive to gentlemen callers. In autumn 1912, as a second younger sister prepared for the altar, the whispering started: Eleanora, at twenty-four, risked becoming an old maid. Beautiful Eleanora had a secret. Nine years earlier, at fifteen, she had promised herself to a sailor. During the family's childhood journeys, she had fallen in love with the captain of her father's yacht, the naval officer Alfons Kloss. As Mechtildis was preparing to wed, Eleanora let slip in a letter that she and Kloss were engaged. As she

perhaps intended, word got back to her father. Stefan, as a good
Polish dynast, had good reason to be disappointed by a lost opportunity for a third match with a third Polish aristocratic family. Stefan, as Habsburg rebel, must have been impressed by Eleanora's
audacity. Eleanora wanted be the first Habsburg archduchess in history to marry a commoner with the permission of the emperor.[15]

Stefan wrote to the court to get permission for the wedding. Emperor Franz Josef, no doubt amused that Stefan faced the same types
of problems that he had caused for others, gave his consent to the
marriage, with conditions. The Habsburg court treated Eleanora's
match with Kloss as unequal—but not much more unequal than Renata and Mechtildis's weddings to Polish princes. The feelings of the
Princes Radziwiłł and Czartoryski are unrecorded. Having been
raised to the level of Habsburgs, they now faced years of family re-
unions with a simple naval officer. Yet Eleanora was a beloved daughter of their father-in-law, who was the key to their future fortunes;
and Kloss was a bluff and appealing companion, a hard man not to
like. Perhaps they, like the rest of the Habsburg family, made the best
of it. No less than nationalism, romance was a curse of modernity;
embracing the first was certainly no protection against the second.[16]

Eleanora and Kloss were married in a small family ceremony on
9 January 1913. The wedding was hasty and unceremonious. The
correspondence between Vienna and Żywiec is full of errors of protocol made in haste. Eleanora's statements of renunciation of her
titles and honors arrived in Vienna only after the wedding had taken
place. Eleanora had thought that she and Mechtildis would marry
on the same day, but in the end her ceremony took place two days
earlier. Perhaps this was to grant Eleanor some sort of precedence
over her younger sister; more likely it was to spare her the compar-
isons by guests who would have attended a double wedding. Yet her
fate was hardly a sad one. On her wedding day she was "bubbling
over with love and happiness." Eleanora and Kloss went to live in
the family villa on the Adriatic Sea. Their first child was born nine
months to the day after their wedding.[17]

Young Willy looks ill at ease in the wedding photographs, and it is
not hard to imagine why. His favorite sister Eleanora would be going

Double Wedding Portrait for Renata and Eleanora. Wilhelm third from right.

back to the sunny Istria of their childhood. He was probably resentful of the two proud Poles who had entered the family. They took his other two sisters away to their own estates—and took Willy's place in the Polish schemes of his father. He had been born to be the answer to the Polish question. He had entered the world just as Stefan inherited the Polish estates, the son named for the Habsburg who by rights should have been king of Poland, the only child taught Polish from birth. Now, with the marriages of his sisters, his place in the imaginary Polish succession had taken a tumble. He was suddenly behind not only his father and two older brothers but behind his two new brothers-in-law and their future children. At the ages of fourteen and seventeen, at his sisters' weddings, Willy watched the secure order of childhood dissolve. The interests of the family were not the same as his. A child of destiny had become surplus material. To find his own way, he would have to find his own nation.

The years 1909–1912, as his sisters courted and wed, were a trying time for Willy. While the girls stayed at home in Żywiec to receive suitors and plan weddings, Willy and his brothers went away to board at military schools. In 1909 Willy enrolled at a military school in the town of Hranice in Moravia. Like Sigmund Freud's parents, Stefan was a native of Moravia, a landlocked, mostly Czech-speaking crownland in the middle of the empire. Like yachting and motoring, military school for his sons was another of Stefan's progressive innovations, and he chose a school not far from his own childhood home. Although Habsburg archdukes were expected to command armies or navies, they were not traditionally trained to do so. Stefan's proud martial forebears were usually amateurs, gifted or less so. Stefan, who had studied as an auditor at the naval academy, wished for his own sons to complete a full military education. He sent Willy to a kind of school he had never experienced himself, at least not as a boarder.[18]

Willy was fourteen when he began school at Hranice, and seventeen when he left without passing his exams. This is an awkward time in any boy's life: the moment when a child's inability to control the world yields to a man's inability to control his body. Willy left no written trace of these years. The uncharacteristic silence and the early departure suggest that the period was a troubled one.

The school was most memorably described by the greatest Austrian novelist of the day, Robert Musil, who called it "the devil's asshole." Himself an alumnus, Musil based his elegantly disturbing first novel, *The Confusions of Young Törless,* published in 1906, on his experiences there. In the novel appears a young "Prince H." "When he walked," wrote Musil, "it was with soft, lithe movements, with that contraction of the body that goes together with the habit of walking erect through a suite of empty halls, where anyone else would seem to bump into unseen corners in the empty space." In the story "Prince H." is unhappy, and leaves the school. The main story concerns the unlimited urges of teenage boys to organize homoerotic humiliation, and the unavoidable connections between sexual and intellectual development. Willy, who entered the school three years after the novel was published, was tall, blonde, blue-eyed, and lovely. Was he the graceful prince, or the buggered boy? Perhaps he was both.

Willy was maturing in a central Europe where homosexuality, royalty, and the military were closely associated. In 1907, Willy's

Polish State Archives, Żywiec

Wilhelm as a Schoolboy

namesake, Emperor Wilhelm II of Germany, found himself at the center of a homosexual scandal. In a series of lawsuits that continued until 1909, it transpired that several members of the emperor's most intimate circle, including his closest friend and main civilian advisor, were practicing homosexuals. The friend, Philipp von Eulenberg, always referred to the emperor in correspondence as "the little darling." The Eulenberg Affair was followed by the newspapers of the day with great attention in Germany and throughout Europe. Wilhelm II, a man who liked to choose hats for his wife, never quite escaped the association with homosexuality.[19]

In 1907 a homosexual scandal also broke in Vienna. A popular newspaper founded that April began to publish articles intimating that the Habsburg monarchy's political and financial elite was highly homosexual. There was a suggestion of blackmail in these articles, since "lechery with the same sex" was a criminal offence in the monarchy. Someone identifying himself as a member of this homosexual elite responded. A pseudonymous "Countess Merviola" told newspaper readers that it would be a great error to send the "warm brothers" to prison. He found it unthinkable that "the most honored carriers of state recognition, aristocrats from the oldest

lines, millionaires and the chiefs of the most significant major firms"
would actually be prosecuted for their homosexual acts. Though the
countess wrote on sweetly perfumed paper, now there was a whiff
of threat. Admitting that the Viennese elite was "warm," he pointed
out that this meant that "the warm brothers" would look after one
another. Even, was the suggestion, if things got hot.[20]

All of this was mere prelude to the Redl Affair of 1913, which
linked homosexual love to fears of espionage for the rest of the
twentieth century. Colonel Alfred Redl, the ninth son of a railway
clerk, had risen to the powerful position of head of Habsburg military counterintelligence. A flamboyant lover of men, he wore
dresses and subsidized dozens of lovers. Like many officers, he led a
life he could not afford, if perhaps more extravagantly so than most.
His brother officers saw debt as a predictable part of life and love
between men as a private matter between adults. Redl paid for his
lifestyle by selling secrets to the Russian Empire. In May 1913 he
was unmasked and committed suicide. The details of the affair were
smothered by the Habsburg army and court. Most likely Stefan, as
an archduke and by then a naval admiral, knew the whole story. He,
Maria Theresia, and Willy were in Vienna at the time the scandal
broke. They had brought Willy from Hranice so that he could finish
his studies with private tutors in a calmer environment. Redl's bullet to the brain, fired as Willy was preparing for examinations, was
a final lesson.[21]

In these misty years of adolescence, as his Polish crown receded into
a distant future shrouded further by the present torments of education, Willy consoled himself by dreaming up a kingdom of his very
own. He found that the skills meant to prepare him for a Polish destiny could be exploited to achieve other ends. Back on the island of
Lošinj, his Polish lessons had been, quite literally, a walk in the
park, instruction separated from any Polish reality by a thousand
kilometers. The language, although quite difficult, must have
seemed pure and abstract. In Galicia, Willy would have heard Polish everywhere he went: Poles governed the province, and it was the
language of schools, courts, and, in most cities, of the streets.

Yet Galicia was home to other peoples as well, as Willy must dimly have understood. In truth, Ukrainians were not far away. The mountains around his father's castle were inhabited by highland shepherds and hunters, divided into clans. Some of these spoke dialects of what was recognizably Polish; others spoke something else, something gentler. Willy seems to have learned a few words of this other language from local children, perhaps without knowing at first what it was. His mother Maria Theresia liked the soft sounds of the language, which she knew was Ukrainian. It reminded her of her native Italian, a language she used every day when the family lived on the Adriatic and that she now missed in the mountains.[22]

Willy was learning, from Polish literature, that Poles and Ukrainians stood in an ancient competition for they lands they both called home. In the novel *With Fire and Sword* by Henryk Sienkiewicz he had read about the great rebellion of the Ukrainian Cossacks against the Polish aristocracy in Ukraine in the seventeenth century. Though Sienkiewicz, the most popular Polish novelist of all time, wrote in a key distinctly sympathetic to Poland, he did not deny the Cossacks a certain wild dignity. Willy was not the first or the last reader to feel a subversive affection for the Ukrainians of the story. This opposition of civilized Polish nobles and barbarous Ukrainian Cossacks, familiar from literature, came to life in Willy's conversations with his brothers-in-law. These Polish aristocrats were scions of families who had once owned tens of thousands of Ukrainian serfs. They told Willy that Ukrainians were a race of savage bandits. Such remarks "interested" Willy and "drew my attention." Now that Willy knew Polish aristocrats well enough to dislike them, he could easily take the Cossacks as his heroes.

At some point, probably in 1912 when he was seventeen, Willy decided to find the stronghold of the bandit Ukrainian nation. His imagination inflamed, Willy studied the family map of Galicia, wondering where he would find the barbarians. That summer, Willy set off eastwards on his own. He traveled, son of his father, "incognito" in a second-class carriage to Vorokhta in the Carpathian Mountains. He marched all by himself through the green pines. He found Ukrainians of the Hutsul clan, free people who lived from hunting and farming, though not the wild men in skins he was expecting. He enjoyed their hospitality and their songs. He spoke to them in Polish, a language very close to Ukrainian, and took the opportunity to learn more Ukrainian words. Willy was gifted with languages, and it is difficult for a native speaker of Polish not to understand a great deal of Ukrainian. Willy returned to Żywiec "as a different person." He had found a people without a kingdom. He had watched *The Emperor's Dream*, a vision of peoples revering their sovereign. He had participated in his father's national dream, that Poland would have Habsburg rulers within the Habsburg monarchy. Why should Ukrainians not have their own Habsburg ruler?[23]

To embrace the Ukrainians, as Willy did that summer, was to see Galicia anew. The optic of nationalism always brings one group into focus while occluding others. Willy's father and brothers-in-law saw Galicia as a Polish land. In fact, it was also home to Ukrainians and Jews, and indeed to many others. The smallest disturbance, a twitch of the lens, and they came into focus. Żywiec itself was a Polish trading town with a proud baroque Catholic church and few Jews or Ukrainians, but some nearby villages boasted beautiful wooden Ukrainian churches, with onion-shaped cupolas adorned with ornate metal crosses. As Willy moved away from his father's plans and the Polish in-laws they generated, he found his own Ukrainian vision of Galicia. By seeing what his father did not, by identifying himself with the nations the Polish princes scorned, he was elevating himself within his family, and indeed the dynasty. He was the youngest child of a peripheral branch of the House of Habsburg. Yet there was no Ukrainian Habsburg. He could be the first.[24]

Willy's subconscious drives to join a community, to "be closer to people," felt like rebellion. Galicia was run by the Polish nobility, to the detriment of its heavily Ukrainian peasantry. Polish nationalists denied the existence of a separate Ukrainian nation, believing that Ukrainians were simply raw material that could later be assimilated into a growing Polish nation. Yet Willy's Ukrainian identity was not disloyal to the Habsburg dynasty. On the contrary, a Ukrainian Habsburg might be a useful asset in the complicated national politics of the monarchy.[25]

As the monarchy's politics became steadily more democratic, the voices and the votes of peoples such as the Ukrainians counted for more. Speakers of Ukrainian were reckoned to be about 13 percent of the population of the Austrian part of the monarchy by the census of 1910; Ukrainian politicians held 6 percent of the parliamentary mandates awarded after the elections of 1907, the first held according to the principle of one man, one vote. Poles had been a mainstay of government coalitions in the late nineteenth century, but the electoral weight of Ukrainians was increasing. In future free elections, surely Ukrainian parties would claim still more seats in parliament. In this situation, Willy might correctly have supposed, his own dynasty would not eschew a Ukrainian member.[26]

The Habsburg dynasty had to consider Ukraine for reasons of foreign as well as domestic policy. Like the Polish and Yugoslav questions that Stefan had sought to master, the Ukrainian question concerned not only the Habsburg monarchy but also its imperial neighbors. Wilhelm heard Ukrainian in the Carpathian Mountains, but the same language was spoken, in different dialects of course, two thousand kilometers to the east, deep in the Russian Empire. This was the great era of east European ethnography, the science that came to be known as anthropology. Ethnographers travelled great distances to demonstrate the existence of a common language and culture across political boundaries. They were seconded by demographers, who counted millions of Ukrainians in the Habsburg monarchy, but tens of millions more in Russia.[27]

Nationalism made it impossible for empires to be conservative. Once peoples were seen to extend across imperial boundaries, imperial policy had to contemplate gains or losses. Stability looked impossible. The Ukrainian national question could either weaken or strengthen the Habsburg monarchy; it could not be neutral. If a Ukrainian entity came into being, it would have to take territory from the Habsburg monarchy, the Russian Empire, or both. So Vienna and Petersburg both worked to ensure that any shift would be in their favor, to allow some kind of national unification under their rule, with their sponsorship. The Russian Empire tried to persuade speakers of Ukrainian in the Habsburg monarchy that they were members of an Orthodox family of nations beholden to the tsar. The Habsburgs supported a separate church for their Ukrainians, the Greek Catholic Church. Its Ukrainian leader, the brilliant Metropolitan Andrii Sheptytsky, wished to convert the Russian Empire. Neither Russia nor the Habsburg monarchy contemplated losing its Ukrainian territories, but both could imagine resolving the Ukrainian national question by absorbing the territories of the other.[28]

Habsburg princes far more important than young Willy studied the Ukrainian question. Crown Prince Franz Ferdinand had a Ukrainian political advisor. Emperor Franz Josef found himself drawn by fears of a coming war to devote some attention to Ukraine. In 1912, the summer when Willy made his journey, war was raging in the Balkans. The Ottoman Empire was collapsing, and the Habsburg monarchy had to compete with Russia for control of the Balkans. Although the Balkans was the scene of the anticipated contest for power between Vienna and Petersburg, the Habsburg monarchy and the Russian Empire had no common border there. Their shared frontier was the eastern border of Galicia. Any war with Russia would thus be fought along a Ukrainian front, with Ukrainian territory certain to change hands.[29]

A war for Ukraine was an uncomfortable prospect for the Habsburgs. The army was impressively multinational and multilingual, but the older noble nations were overrepresented in the officer corps. Only about one in every five hundred officers was a native speaker of Ukrainian. It made sense, anticipating an eastern front in Ukraine, to train a Ukrainian officer who would also represent the House of Habsburg. Emperor Franz Josef turned to the one plausible candidate. He asked Willy to study the Ukrainian question in autumn 1912. The next year, Willy enrolled at the imperial military academy at Wiener-Neustadt to train as an officer.[30]

Willy's seeming rebellion led straight to an imperial mission. As a cadet at the academy, he continued his studies of Ukrainian language and culture. Despite the additional coursework, in most respects Willy was simply another cadet, as his father intended. He shared the routine of the other young men of his class at the academy: reveille at 5:00 each morning, and lessons between 6:00 and 1:00 and again between 3:00 and 6:00. Willy liked geography and law. He had high grades, near the top of his class, although it is hard to know what that meant. Habsburg archdukes sometimes received degrees, but they did not always study. The predicament of teachers forced to examine archdukes was a source of humor in the Habsburg domains; a sample examination question for archdukes, according to one cabaret wit, was "How long was the Seven Years' War?"[31]

Willy seems to have enjoyed the academy at Wiener-Neustadt more than his preparatory school at Hranice. Willy and some comrades borrowed the headmaster's auto for nine nights in a row. He loved the riding and the swordplay and the swimming. Like his previous school, Wiener-Neustadt was homoerotic, although perhaps less aggressively so. Older boys were permitted to choose their favorites from the younger; the warden was bribed to allow two boys to spend time together in the punishment cell. If Willy was displeased by anything about his new school, he found, as a young man of eighteen, practical ways to express his discontent. Vienna had much more to offer than Hranice, and his brother Leo entered the academy in the same year. The brothers had leave on Sundays, which they could use to see their parents. Stefan and Maria Theresia now spent much of the year in Vienna, in Stefan's palace on 61 Wiedner Hauptstrasse. This residence was a short ride by fiacre to the Hofburg, the palace of Emperor Franz Josef. Willy was also reunited with his favorite sister, Eleanora. When Eleanora visited from Istria, she and Willy would take long walks together in Vienna.[32]

These walks were an important part of Willy's education. He was now a young man capable of noting social difference, passing the time with a beloved sister who had married a man of a much lower class. The city Willy and Eleanora observed together was a gargantuan metropolis, home to two million people. As brother and sister walked south from their father's palace, away from the Hofburg and the Ring, they would quickly reach Margareten and Favoriten, neighborhoods flooded with a growing working class. Willy began to read, on his own time, the works of the Austro-Marxists. This was a peculiar group within the socialist movement, whose approach to the national question suited Willy. Austro-Marxists hoped that the empire would become a nationally tolerant social welfare state as the result of legislation passed by a democratic parliament. Willy applied the socialist program to his own favored people, the Ukrainians, one of the poorest and most agrarian peoples in the empire.[33]

As Willy committed such small transgressions, his energies were channeled within a larger system. It was precisely his minor rebellions that provided him with just the energy he needed to become a young man with skills that might one day serve his empire. He was being watched and cultivated. He was no longer one of several potentially Polish archdukes, but the only possible Ukrainian prince among the Habsburgs. He was no longer last in line for a Polish mission, but first in line for a Ukrainian one. An archduke was aligned with a peasant people, an old dynasty with a new nation. At the right moment, Wilhelm and his chosen people might bring youthful vigor to an ancient empire.

In his novel *The Man without Qualities*, Robert Musil describes a committee that must plan the jubilee of seventy years of Franz Josef's rule. After intricate affairs among blood relatives, long considerations of the influence of father figures, and extended digressions on the philosophy of politics, this comes to no practical conclusion—but does provide the single example in world literature of committee meetings convincingly presented as the place to understand reality. A professional diplomat tries to explicate the essence of diplomacy: do not do the thing that you want to do. The novel's hero defines action: not what you are doing at the moment, but the next thing that you will do. Musil is struggling to reveal something of the Habsburg sense of time: an unceasing present that cannot be controlled in its every detail but can be mastered in its totality, so long as one is tactful, deft, and unconcerned about the world except as a representation of family power.

Timelessness in Musil's novel is conveyed by the duration of Franz Josef's reign, so unusually long that it lent the dynasty an aura of eternity. By the twentieth century, most Habsburg subjects could remember no other emperor. Yet this was timelessness by individual stubbornness, rather than by dynastic confidence in the merits of generations to come. Franz Josef had thus far declined to die, but his heir, Franz Ferdinand, was impetuous and unpopular. The empire itself had been driven from its global mission into central and eastern Europe, where its rulers increasingly felt cornered by powers that grew rather than shrank with time.

The sense of eternity was in competition with a sense of catastrophe. In the early years of the twentieth century, the Habsburg monarchy had become enmeshed in a European alliance system, a competition between two groups of states arming for war. Habsburg diplomacy, usually lithe if rarely brilliant, had lost all room for maneuver. After the unification of Germany, France sought an ally to the east, and found Russia. As the nineteenth century ended, the Habsburg monarchy and Germany were aligned against Russia and France. In 1904 Britain joined France in an Entente, designed to avoid disagreements over imperial possessions, but auguring closer political cooperation. In 1907 Britain signed a similar accord with Russia. These agreements created an informal but visible alignment of Britain, France, and Russia. Germany was powerful, but not powerful enough to resist such a coalition. Germany had begun a naval arms race with Britain, which it lost, then shifted to a conventional arms race in 1911, which brought in its Habsburg ally.

As these five states made their alliances, a sixth traditional power was fading from the continent. The Ottoman Empire was losing its European possessions. When Ottoman army officers staged a coup in the name of reform in July 1908, the Habsburg monarchy replied by annexing Bosnia and Herzegovina that October. Thirty years earlier, the Habsburgs had been granted, by treaty, the right to occupy these provinces, which legally belonged to the Ottoman Empire. Now the Habsburgs unilaterally asserted the right to annex them. The Ottoman Empire had been in decline for a couple of centuries, but the other powers had agreed among themselves regarding the redistribution of territory. So one great power, the Ottomans, was disappearing, and another, the Habsburgs, was breaking the rules by proceeding from occupation to outright annexation. Russia, which had an interest in the Orthodox peoples who inhabited Ottoman

Europe, felt the insult. Russia drew closer to Serbia. Serbia saw Bosnia as part of its own sphere of interest and, indeed, as part of a future and expanded Serbian state.[34]

Then the initiative in Balkan politics, and thus European politics, slipped from the hands of the great powers. In 1912, an alliance of four Balkan national monarchies, Serbia, Montenegro, Greece, and Bulgaria, attacked the Ottoman Empire and seized much of its remaining European territory. This conflict, the First Balkan War, showed that Europe could be remade by the small nations, and that nationalism could destroy empires. The Balkan states then fell upon each other in the Second Balkan War of 1913. When the dust settled, the main victor was Serbia, which doubled in size and increased its population by 50 percent. The Habsburg army's general staff insisted on a preemptive war against Serbia. If the monarchy did not act soon to rid itself of national pests such as Serbia, went the reasoning, the Habsburgs would meet the same fate as the Ottomans. The general staff was tired of the monarchy being Europe's patient pivot. If power had to be balanced, they preferred the high-wire act of tactical war. The man walking the high wire at least has the sense of forward motion. And he carries a stick. In 1913 and 1914, the chief of the general staff recommended war against Serbia no fewer than twenty-five times.[35]

Back in the 1890s, in gentler times, Franz Ferdinand and Stefan had discussed Balkan politics as they sailed together in the Adriatic. During the Bosnian annexation crisis, the two men exchanged correspondence, fearing war. Franz Ferdinand did not believe that war could resolve the Balkan question. The addition of Serbia to the Habsburg domains, he decided, could bring only problems. Serbia would contribute only "murderers and rascals and a few plum trees." Stefan had spent two decades on the Adriatic, and felt closer to the Balkan peoples than did Franz Ferdinand. He had named one of his sons after Cyril and Methodius, the most revered saints of those Orthodox lands. Yet his thoughts were taking a similar course. In 1907, a year before the annexation crisis, he had left the Balkans and his imagined Yugoslavia in favor of Galicia and his imagined Poland.[36]

Willy understood his father's design, and was no less imaginative and mercurial than his father. His father's generation might not see the Ukrainians as a nation, but the definition of the nation was changing. It was an era of democracy, when population numbers began to count as much as wealth; of ethnicity, when culture could take the place of tradition; and of science, when demography could reckon national populations with seeming precision. Willy could regard the Ukrainians as a nation with the same status and rights as the Poles. The populist character of their politics could only attract a young man who saw himself as a friend of the common people. That Ukrainians were an "unhistorical nation," as people said at the time, attracted his youthful spirit. Ukrainians are a natural people, Willy thought, a people of spring, a sapling that can bend with the wind. Poles belonged to a civilization of rot. As he put it a couple of years later: "Poland! Yes, Poles were once a people of high culture, I must indeed concede that, but now their autumn has come. Now comes a culture of superabundance, now comes decadence."[37]

The history of the Habsburgs shows that decadence can last for a very long time. Some three centuries earlier, Willy's forebear Emperor Maximilian II had funded Arcimboldo's famous renderings of the four seasons: spring as composed of fruits and vegetables in greens and reds, autumn as an overflowing late harvest of gourds, tubers, and grapes, both in the shape of men. There is no more delightful and decadent rendering of the passing of time. Yet for all the individuality of the portraits, they represent time as an endless cycle of seasons. Yet the Habsburgs really had reached a turning point, a tangent on a circle, a moment when eternal dynastic time would yield to drastic visions of catastrophe and rescue.

The summer of 1914 would separate spring from autumn, father from son, one era from another, as the Habsburgs began the war that would end the old Europe. But in 1913, the choices of Stefan and Willy expressed neither enmity to each other nor disloyalty to their dynasty. If, as the general staff desired, the Habsburg monarchy fought a war of conquest against Serbia, its armies would have to engage Russia as well. A victory over Russia would likely increase the Polish and

Ukrainian populations within the Habsburg domains, from millions to tens of millions. If the Habsburgs won such a war, and expanded to the north and east, archdukes might indeed rule great Polish or Ukrainian crownlands, as loyal regents of their emperor.

Stefan and Willy took actions that made sense in two epochs, their own and the one that was yet to come. As they did so, they implicitly accepted a new kind of time: not the idea to which they were born, that time provides the dates and the details of the dream pictures of an eternal dynasty, but the idea to which they raised themselves, that years bring progress to a nation. Stefan became Polish in anticipation of the creation of new crownland. Wilhelm became Ukrainian in anticipation of the rise of a new nation. Yet the very skills and reputations that would allow them to aid the monarchy also prepared them for a Europe without empire, in which Poland and Ukraine had become independent states. Though Willy and Stefan did not speak of the fall of the Habsburg monarchy and the rise of independent Poland and Ukraine, their Polish or Ukrainian followers inevitably would, and did.

Willy, eighteen years old in 1913, was unable to disentangle his own ambitions from the family's grandeur. At once innocent and jaded, he had the luxury of rebelling against the very traditions he embodied. His father had made him Polish, so he decided to become Ukrainian. His father had wanted him to be an officer, and now he was a cadet preparing for a self-destructive war. Stefan had foreseen a world of nations, and now that world was upon them. Willy had chosen his own people, known only from play, travel, and books, a nation as young and green as himself.

The two of them, father and son, were as prepared as any Habsburg could be for what came next.

RED

~

Prince at Arms

CROWN PRINCE FRANZ FERDINAND von Habsburg had an anniversary to celebrate in Sarajevo on 28 June 1914. Fourteen years earlier to the day, the emperor had permitted him to marry his beloved, Sophie Chotek. Sophie had been a lady-in-waiting of the woman Franz Ferdinand was supposed to marry; since the match was unequal, the crown prince had to renounce his successors' rights to rule. The marriage was awkward for Sophie. Even as the consort of the heir to the throne, her rank was lower than that of all of the archdukes and archduchesses, including children. She entered the halls of the Hofburg after little boys and little girls. The Hofburg was drafty in the best of times, but Sophie felt a special chill. During state ceremonies in Vienna, she and her husband had to ride in separate automobiles. In Sarajevo, in the newly Habsburg province of Bosnia, these rules could be bent. Franz Ferdinand had taken Sophie with him to observe military maneuvers. In this Balkan land, Franz Ferdinand could show that he was proud of his wife. They rode together, that day, in an open car.

Serbian nationalists had their own anniversary to commemorate in Sarajevo. Exactly five hundred and twenty-five years earlier, the armies of the Ottoman Empire had defeated a coalition of Balkan princes on the Kosovo Field. Serbian nationalists recorded the Battle of Kosovo as the martyrdom of their heroic nation and the beginning of its subjugation to tyrannical foreign rulers. The twenty-eighth of June was also the feast day of St. Vitus, celebrated by Serbs as a national holiday. Serbs had political grievances, too, of course. Little more than five years had passed since the Habsburgs had annexed Bosnia. The dynasty favored the province's Catholic Croats, governed through Muslim Bosnian landowners, and distrusted the Orthodox Serbs. For Serbian nationalist students, such as Nedeljko Čabrinović, the visit of Franz Ferdinand was a wanton provocation. A day that should have memorialized the Serbian struggle against foreign tyrants was instead being devoted to welcoming one.

Čabrinović, like other Serbian nationalists, believed that Bosnia and Herzegovina should be separated from the Habsburg monarchy and attached to Serbia. He and a few like-minded people sought help from the Black Hand, a conspiratorial group of nationalist terrorists within Serbia. It was led by Colonel Apis, head of intelligence for the Serbian general staff. Apis, nicknamed after the Egyptian bull god for his immense physical strength, had taken part in the regicide that had brought the current, anti-Habsburg dynasty to the Serbian throne. Apis, who did not like Habsburgs in general, had a particular ax to grind with Franz Ferdinand. He saw the crown prince as a virile future commander in chief of Habsburg troops and believed that Franz Ferdinand wanted to annex Serbia and create an Austria-Hungary-Yugoslavia. When nationalist students approached him with a plan to murder Franz Ferdinand, he was happy to oblige. The Black Hand provided guns and bombs.[1]

On 28 June 1914, Čabrinović had a bomb. As Franz Ferdinand and Sophie proceeded slowly along the quay in their open automobile, he threw it at their car. Their driver, seeing something flying through the air, accelerated. The bomb hit the roof of the car and bounced backward. It exploded, wounding officers in the next car in the procession and bystanders along the street. A bit of shrapnel grazed Sophie, drawing blood.

The early twentieth century was an age of political terrorism, and assassination attempts were the order of the day. Five had been made on various Habsburgs in the previous four years. King Alfonso of Spain, a Habsburg on his mother's side, was personally the subject of five further assassination attempts, one of them on his wedding day. Spain was so prone to terrorism that its king made a sport of being attacked; Alfonso rode down one would-be assassin with a polo maneuver. Yet it was an era of regal bravado rather than security precautions. Franz Ferdinand reacted in the expected way—he ordered his driver forward. There was no contingency plan. He and Sophie continued along the quay to the town hall as planned, where he made a speech. Then he decided to visit the officers wounded by the bomb. From the town hall his car was meant to take an alternative route to the hospital, avoiding the quay. It did not. At one point his driver, confused, stopped the car and put it into reverse.

A second Serbian student, Gavrilo Princip, stepped from the crowd. He had a gun. Standing directly in front of the car, Princip shot Sophie and Franz Ferdinand from close range. Each of them, mortally wounded, thought of the other. Sophie asked Franz Ferdinand what had happened to him. Franz Ferdinand begged Sophie to live for the sake of their children. One bullet had penetrated her corset and abdomen, another had pierced his jugular vein. He slowly pitched forward, bleeding heavily. His hat fell from his head, its green feathers mingling with red blood on the floor of the auto. His last words were: "it is nothing." The doctors examining his corpse had to remove from his neck seven amulets of gold and platinum, which had failed to ward off evil. High on his left arm was a tattoo of a Chinese dragon, in every color of the rainbow.

That day, a Sunday, was the last day of the social season in Vienna. On the Prater Park, the orchestras played on. Horse-drawn carriages made their rounds, friends exchanged gossip. The death of a crown prince need not have meant the end of a world. Franz Ferdinand was mercurial, emotional, and unpopular. Archdukes had died before in spectacularly violent fashion, and the dynasty and the realm had endured. Emperor Franz Josef was in good health, at least as far as anyone in Vienna knew. His grand nephew, the popular Archduke Karl, now became crown prince. Karl was the son of the notorious Otto Franz, who had already died, quite appropriately, of syphilitic degeneracy. Yet Karl was a handsome and sympathetic man whose energetic and beautiful wife, Zita, had already borne him a brood of eligible children.[2]

Public opinion remained calm and the dynastic succession remained clear, but Princip's bullets had struck home. The goal of Princip and his fellow terrorists was to provoke the Habsburgs to overreact. Like terrorists in all times and places, they wished to use weakness to their advantage, inducing a great power to do something contrary to its own interests. They hoped to bring about Habsburg repression in Bosnia, which, they anticipated, would create support among the Serbian population there for their nationalist cause. Their provocation succeeded beyond their wildest dreams. Franz Ferdinand, who had actually been an opponent of war in the Balkans, was now removed from the scene. The Habsburg general staff, which had been planning a preventive war against Serbia for years, now had its decisive argument. The Habsburgs' German ally, meanwhile, had been nursing grievances against the colonial powers Britain and France, and expecting a general war in Europe that might permit Germany to win its place in the sun. The crisis provided the occasion. The Habsburg monarchy issued an ultimatum to Serbia on 23 July. Serbia's reply was equivocal, and Vienna declared war five days later. The next morning the Habsburg navy bombarded the Serbian capital, Belgrade.

So it began. Encouraged by France, Russia mobilized its army in defense of Serbia. Germany demanded that Russia cease its preparations for war. When Russia did not, Germany declared war on Russia on 1 August. This made war between France and Germany inevitable. France and Russia were allies, encircling Germany. German war plans required a quick defeat of France to avoid a two-front war. The invasion route to France passed through neutral Belgium. The German violation of Belgian neutrality brought Great Britain into the war on 4 August. In a matter of a few weeks, an assassination had brought about a regional war for the Balkans; in a matter of a few days, that regional war became a European war for control of the continent.

The First World War was not the conflict the Habsburg generals had planned. They imagined that they could strike quickly and control the political consequences. They foresaw that they would humble Serbia in a matter of days. Yet the Habsburg offensive failed. Serbian troops, hardened by two Balkan wars and commanded by intelligent generals, put up an obstinate defense, defeating Habsburg forces at the Battle of Cer on 19 August. Having attacked Serbia, a small state to its south, the Habsburg monarchy now found itself at war with Russia, an enormous empire to its northeast. Habsburg troops passed each other on railways, some going from the Serbian front to the Russian, others from the Russian to the Serbian. It did not help that Russia was in possession of Habsburg mobilization schedules and war plans, thanks to the treason of Colonel Redl, who had sold them for the money he needed to maintain his male harem. The monarchy's declared war aim, the defeat of Serbia, slipped from its grasp.

To certain imaginative spirits in the Habsburg monarchy, both the southern and the eastern fronts had promised resolutions to national questions. A defeat of Serbia would allow the monarchy to expand southwards, embracing the south Slavs of the Balkans and allowing them to realize their national life together, but under the Habsburgs. A victory over Russia would allow the monarchy to expand to the northeast, and thereby resolve its Ukrainian and Polish questions. If the Habsburgs could take sufficient territories from Russia, new Polish and Ukrainian crownlands could be created to satisfy Polish and Ukrainian national claims. Conflicts between Poles and Ukrainians within the Habsburg monarchy would be resolved by the defeat of Russia: so the Austrian prime minister assured Poles and Ukrainians alike.[3]

Ukrainian and Polish politicians, accustomed to cramped quarreling over the single province of Galicia, heard that they would soon be dividing vast lands taken from Russia. It was a tempting prospect, and it was backed by policy. The Habsburg monarchy had permitted the creation and training of a Polish paramilitary, which it now, in August 1914, renamed and sponsored as the Polish Legions. At the initiative of a Ukrainian National Council formed that same month, a Ukrainian Legion was also recruited. Like the Polish

Legions, the Ukrainian Legion served a political purpose. These units were meant to demonstrate to Habsburg subjects that the emperor was concerned about his nations, and to Russian subjects that they could expect national liberation at the hands of the Habsburg armed forces.

Yet this national policy required military victory, which in the early weeks of the war was not to be had. Even as Habsburg forces were halted in Serbia, Russia invaded Galicia. Panicked Habsburg soldiers resorted to the summary trial and execution of Ukrainian civilians believed to be disloyal. In this situation, the Habsburgs forgot about resolving national questions. The task at hand was suddenly to stop the Russian advance. As the bulk of the German army invaded France, the Habsburg monarchy found itself fighting numerically superior Russian forces on the eastern front. Habsburg generals were frustrated by a perceived lack of German support. Yet it was the Germans, not the Habsburgs, who scored the first major victory. Generals Erich Ludendorff and Paul von Hindenburg, given command of the German Eighth Army, took credit as it defeated the Russian Second Army at Tannenberg. Though they had little or nothing to do with the battle plans, made before their arrival, Ludendorff and Hindenburg became German national heroes, and the Habsburg monarchy's bloody defenses in the first weeks of the war were forgotten.[4]

Yet Germany could achieve no such decisive victory in the west. Just as the Habsburg monarchy had counted on removing Serbia from the war quickly, so Germany had counted on crushing France. Yet German forces were defeated soundly at the Battle of the Marne in September 1914. Plans for quick preventive strikes had failed. Germany and the Habsburg monarchy would have to fight a long war, facing enemies on all sides, isolated by a British naval blockade. The modern Habsburg fleet was bottled up in the Adriatic. Britain's Royal Navy was overwhelmingly strong, and London's French ally had a Mediterranean fleet of its own. The same was true of Italy, which the following year would renounce an alliance with the Habsburgs and declare war. Meanwhile, the monarchy's peacetime army had been destroyed by the Russians and the Serbs in the first months of the war. By Christmas 1914, some 82 percent of the original infantry complement of the Habsburg armed forces were casualties. About a million men were dead, wounded, or sick. The rest of the war would be fought by reserves, civilians, and officers just completing their training.[5]

One of these officers was young Archduke Wilhelm. In autumn 1914, Wilhelm began his second and final year of studies at the military academy. He later remembered that his classmates expressed enthusiasm about the outbreak of war; he did not. His closest friend at the academy was killed in action. Still, it was understood that Wilhelm would go into the field as soon as his studies were complete the following spring. A confidential report from his final semester describes him as someone who "demonstrates at every possible occasion the intention to take the initiative as a soldier and as an officer." His family expected no less. Upon reaching the Habsburg age of majority, twenty, in February 1915, Wilhelm was inducted into the Order of the Golden Fleece as well as the upper house of parliament. He was now a man, and would be expected to comport himself as such in time of war.[6]

Service during wartime was the destiny of Habsburg archdukes. Wilhelm's father Stefan, promoted to admiral in 1911 despite his retirement from active duty in the navy, was charged with tending the war wounded of the entire monarchy. (Maria Theresia assisted her husband by working "incognito" as a nurse in hospitals.) One of Wilhelm's uncles, Archduke Friedrich, was the commander in chief of the Habsburg armed forces. The other, Archduke Eugen, commanded Habsburg troops in the Balkans and then in Italy. Wilhelm's brother Albrecht served in artillery, first on the Russian and then on the Italian front, advancing to the rank of colonel. His other brother, Leo, was also completing his studies at the military academy. Wilhelm and Leo graduated on 15 March 1915.[7]

Now a second lieutenant, Wilhelm asked for and received the command of a platoon within a predominantly Ukrainian regiment. He joined his unit on 12 June 1915 and began political action among the men. He asked them to call him by the Ukrainian name

"Vasyl." He spoke Ukrainian to his soldiers. He took to wearing a Ukrainian embroidered shirt under his officer's uniform. Its pretty collar, snug around his neck, sent a message decipherable to all Ukrainians—if bewildering to everyone else. He gave his men armbands of azure and yellow, the Ukrainian national colors. Not surprisingly, Polish officers and Polish authorities in Galicia resisted these initiatives. It was they who first took to calling Wilhelm "the Red Prince." He did not mind the association with socialism; any support of Ukrainians, one of the poorest peoples of the empire, had to involve some concern for social justice. As Wilhelm recalled, his respectful treatment of peasant soldiers was more than enough to convince his Polish rivals that he was a dangerous radical.[8]

Wilhelm had missed the horrible Carpathian campaigns of the previous winter. Russian forces had moved deep into Galicia, even taking the fort at Przemyśl where Wilhelm's uncle Friedrich commanded. After the fort was retaken in May 1915, Friedrich oversaw a massive counteroffensive. As Wilhelm took up his command, Habsburg forces were on the march, moving east, driving the Russians from Galicia. On 16 June 1915, four days after Wilhelm entered active service, the Habsburgs retook Lviv, the provincial capital.

In the ensuing struggle for the rest of Galicia, Wilhelm took pride in his men, regarding Ukrainians as the best of soldiers. He protected them from persecution by local civilian authorities, who were usually Poles. He could not, of course, protect them from Russian bullets. Wilhelm did not like war. "My impressions of battle are such: above all it is false that one can get used to them. The first one is the least troubling." "My battles," he wrote in a memoir five years later, "would have given satisfaction, except for the loss of people to whom one had become attached."[9]

As Russian forces drew back to the east in summer 1915, the Ukrainian question was once again posed. Wilhelm was leading a Ukrainian unit across Galicia, helping to liberate the Habsburg province from Russian rule. Before the war had begun, Galicia had been administered by Polish elites. Then it had been ruled by Russian occupiers. Now that Habsburg power had returned, who would control the province? Poles, as before, or perhaps Ukrainians?

THE
EASTERN FRONT
1914-1918

Jonathan Wyss, Topaz Maps

Baltic Sea

LITHUANIA

Königsberg

Vilna

Danzig

Smolensk

GERMANY

Tannenberg

Minsk

Białystok

Vistula

Posen

Bug

RUSSIAN

Warsaw

Łódź

POLAND

EMPIRE

Breslau

September 1914

Summer 1916

Kiev

Cracow

Lviv

Dniepr

AUSTRIA

GALICIA

Buchach

UKRAINE

HABSBURG MONARCHY

Vienna

Bratislava

Danube

Budapest

Dniester

BESSARABIA

HUNGARY

Odessa

(Brest-Litovsk Treaty Line)
March 1918

ROMANIA

BOSNIA-
HERZEGOVINA

Belgrade

Bucharest

Danube

Black Sea

SERBIA

MONTENEGRO

BULGARIA

Sofia

The Polish and the Ukrainian questions were inextricably linked, and Habsburg policy had to account for the Germans and their preferences. As the Russians were retreating before Habsburg forces in Galicia, they were also retreating before the Germans in other lands of historic Poland. By August 1915 the Germans held the historical Polish capital Warsaw, which for the past century had been a major city of the Russian Empire. As the military balance shifted in favor of Vienna and Berlin, the allies would have to decide what to do about Poland and Ukraine. The two countries did not of course exist, but the empires needed to exploit national feeling. Unfortunately for them, it was hard to use both nationalisms at the same time, since Ukrainian and Polish patriots had a tendency to claim the same territories.

Vienna had a plan: Polish territories taken from Russia would form a Polish kingdom that would join the Habsburg monarchy. Berlin initially accepted this "Austro-Polish" solution. If Poland was to be a kingdom, however, it would need a king. Archduke Stefan was the obvious candidate: as the founder of a Polish royal family, as a member of the Habsburg dynasty, and as a friend of the German emperor. Local assemblies of Polish nobles met to elect him, in imitation of ancient Polish tradition. Rumors flew through occupied Poland that he had already been crowned king. Yet the Austro-Polish solution was meant to make Emperor Franz Josef king of Poland, not one of his relatives. A Habsburg regent who seemed too close to the Germans did not seem reliable enough. Stefan had prepared himself well, his emperor perhaps less so. Franz Josef, now eighty-four years old, hesitated. The Habsburgs missed their best chance to occupy a Polish throne.[10]

By 1916, the German position on Poland had changed, much to the dismay of the Habsburgs. Germany's role as the dominant ally was confirmed on the battlefield. Meanwhile, the German military asserted increasing control over German foreign policy. Germans began to see a dependent Poland as part of a much larger German sphere of influence in Europe. For some, this sphere would include the Habsburg monarchy as well. Germany was coming to see the monarchy as an element of Europe that was to be altered by the war, rather than simply a military ally.

Germany wished for the Habsburg monarchy to become a state dominated by its German minority. This preference militated against the Austro-Polish solution. If the Habsburg monarchy were enlarged to include a Polish kingdom, the role of the Slavic subjects in the empire would increase and the role of the German subjects would decrease. Whereas the Habsburgs' solutions to their own national problems required territorial enlargement precisely in order to satisfy the national demands of Slavs, Germany's interventions in Habsburg affairs tended to enforce the territorial status quo in order to maintain the position of Germans. Naturally, this difference produced tension.[11]

Habsburg-German disagreements left Stefan in an awkward position. The character of a future Poland was a matter of strife between Germany and the Habsburg monarchy, and he was in the middle. Although he was a Habsburg, the Germans believed that he would serve their vision of Poland. In June 1916, Berlin proposed Stefan as the regent of a future Polish kingdom. This made Stefan all the more suspicious to Emperor Franz Josef, who declined the proposal. The Habsburgs tried to persuade Germany to accept an intermediate solution, perhaps a Polish constitutional monarchy.

The confusion continued even after Germany and the Habsburg monarchy proclaimed a Kingdom of Poland in November 1916. The Habsburgs proposed a regent who would report to both Berlin and Vienna. Further stirring the pot, Vienna proposed Stefan's son-in-law Olgierd Czartoryski for this role. Of Stefan's two sons-in-law, Olgierd was seen as the more pro-Habsburg. The other, Hieronymus Radziwiłł, had property in Germany and a father active in German politics. If this proposal was an attempt to divide the emerging Polish royal family, it did not work. Stefan had the wisdom never to betray a preference for himself over his sons-in-law. Meanwhile, a press campaign in Poland generated support for Stefan. People in Warsaw hung signs proclaiming that they wanted him as king. For the time being, however, Stefan seemed unwilling to accept a Polish throne unless his authority were clearly defined. He probably wished to avoid the impression that he was nothing but a German puppet. As Wilhelm noted in a letter of December 1916, "they're telling him that perhaps he'd like to go and rule, but Papa refuses flatly."[12]

The proclamation of a Kingdom of Poland in November 1916 began a new stage of Wilhelm's political education. He had made himself into a Ukrainian of sorts, and he had made friends with his Ukrainian soldiers. He had tried to exercise some influence on Ukrainian policy, but at a purely personal level. He had written his uncle Friedrich, commander of the Habsburg armed forces, about the Ukrainian question. He apparently had an audience with Emperor Franz Josef in the matter of the decoration of a Ukrainian soldier. While at the front, however, he had had little opportunity to think politically about the future of Ukraine. His perspective on Ukrainians, as one Ukrainian politician put it, was "ethnographic," or, as we would say, anthropological. He was fascinated with the lovely baubles of intellectual childhood, the songs and the stories, the costumes and the journeys. Yet there is a leap from anthropology to political action, a leap he was preparing himself to make.[13]

As Russian forces counterattacked in Galicia in 1916, Wilhelm was brought away from the front, promoted to first lieutenant, and given safer assignments. He began to make contact with Ukrainians who were his intellectual superiors, political activists from whom he could learn. One of these was Baron Kazimir Huzhkovsky, a major in the Habsburg army. Wilhelm shared with Huzhkovsky his simple pleasures: spending time with his men, singing their songs, speaking their language. He wrote of going to sleep at night knowing that one day "dreams would become reality," and Ukraine would be free. Until late 1916, he had not yet begun to think about how that might happen. Then came the proclamation of the Kingdom of Poland, like "a bolt from a clear blue sky," clarifying the need for political thought. Like the Ukrainians who were becoming his advisors, Wilhelm feared that the new Kingdom of Poland might later embrace all of Galicia, thereby leaving the Ukrainians of eastern Galicia at the mercy of a Polish king.[14]

Conveniently for Wilhelm, that king seemed likely to be his father, whom he could see in Vienna. Wilhelm took sick leave in December 1916 to treat his tuberculosis and spent four months living in his father's palace at 61 Wiedner Hauptstrasse in Vienna and in nearby Baden, taking a cure. It was the first time Wilhelm had resided in Vienna as an adult, and he received the honors due his rank. As a member of the upper house of parliament, he met archdukes, archbishops, and heads of landholding families. At every house where he paid a call, the doorman would ring a bell three times, a distinction due only to archdukes and cardinals. In the capital, Wilhelm began to consider the liberation of Ukraine not as the dramatic result of battlefield victories and good intentions but as a project requiring initiative and tact.

The proper approach, he decided, was to work within the Habsburg system. The best way to protect Ukrainians from the Kingdom of Poland would be to create a new Ukrainian province, made up of the eastern half of Galicia as well as the entire province of Bukovina. If such a province were created, western Galicia could be joined to the Kingdom of Poland with no harm to Ukrainians. Wilhelm apparently got the agreement of his father for such a plan in late December 1916. He could then begin to imagine the disposition of eastern Europe after a Habsburg victory over the Russian Empire. He proposed a Habsburg monarchy composed of Austrian, Bohemian, Hungarian, and Polish kingdoms, as well as a "Principality of Ukraine." An archduke would be the regent of each of these kingdoms. The regent of the Polish crownland and the prince of Ukraine would, of course, be Stefan and Wilhelm. Wilhelm could be pleased with himself. As 1917 began, Wilhelm could see the outlines of a Europe in which he could match his father, without having to defy him.[15]

Emperor Franz Josef died on 21 November 1916, and was succeeded by Karl. With the help of his Ukrainian comrades, Wilhelm prepared himself to approach a new emperor with these plans. Franz Josef had encouraged Wilhelm to learn Ukrainian and become a Ukrainian officer, but his general orientation had always been rather too pro-Polish for Wilhelm's taste. In his one meeting with Franz Josef during the war, Wilhelm had felt that he could not raise questions of high politics. Now Ukrainian politicians saw Wilhelm as their point of access to Emperor Karl. Karl was only eight years older than Wilhelm, and the two had known each other since childhood. Baron Huzhkovsky introduced Wilhelm to Ukrainian politicians of noble origins, such as Mykola Vasylko, a leading parliamentarian and school friend of the foreign minister, and Ievhen Olesnytsky, who had been an advisor to Franz Ferdinand. At their request, Wilhelm was to present a petition to Emperor Karl for the creation of a Ukrainian crownland within the Habsburg monarchy.

When Wilhelm met Karl on 2 February 1917, he was invited to sit down at a table, which Wilhelm understood to be a sign of particular favor. Franz Josef had stood at all of his appointments, which forced his interlocutors to stand, which had the happy consequence of keeping his meetings short. At the end of long consultations, Wilhelm was convinced that Karl understood the Ukrainian national question, that there was no chance that eastern Galicia would be joined to Poland, and that a Ukrainian crownland would indeed be created at some future time. From Karl's point of view the encounter was also an interesting one. He probably knew that Wilhelm had been educated to lead Ukrainians but was likely surprised at how far the experiment had progressed. Wilhelm was a Habsburg archduke and a Ukrainian officer at a time when the Habsburg armed forces were driving into parts of the Russian Empire inhabited by Ukrainians. A few days after their meeting, Karl took personal command of the Habsburg armed forces. Wilhelm would be one of his contacts within the army, a known quantity with clear political possibilities.[16]

Wilhelm moved in these circles of high politics while he was supposed to be sick in bed. Wilhelm was treated in a hospital by a Jewish doctor whom he remembered fondly as a "very intelligent man." At about the same time, he chose to make the acquaintance of another Jewish doctor, Sigmund Freud. Freud was giving a course of lectures in winter term 1916, which lasted through March 1917. Wilhelm likely attended some of the last lectures after he was declared cured in Baden but before he returned to his command in April 1917. Freud regarded civilization as the result of an unavoidable state of tension between the sex drive and its repression. Whether any of this made an impression on Wilhelm is hard to say. He was a young officer who loved his men; he was a Habsburg who saw a place for himself in the family's historically nuptial empire. If there were contradictions between his closeness with his men and his destiny to continue the Habsburg line, perhaps these were not yet clear. The conquest of Ukraine, in any event, was to be martial, not marital. Ukraine was to be conceived not in a marriage bed but in a peace treaty after a victorious war.[17]

If the Habsburg dynasty was to flourish in Ukraine, however, Russia's Romanov dynasty had to fall. And fall it did. In early March 1917, a revolt in the Russian army spread from the front lines to units in the capital, Petersburg. Soldiers sent to put down food riots among civilians instead joined the demonstrations. Tsar Nicholas II abdicated, his brother declined to succeed him, and the Romanov dynasty came to an end. Russia was ruled by a provisional government. France and Britain, Russia's allies, exerted all the pressure they could to keep the Russian army in the field. Russia's new government, formed on 14 March, placed all of its hopes on one last offensive.

Meanwhile, the new Russia struggled to deal with the legacy of an enormous continental empire, of which Russians were no more than half the population. Throughout the west and south of the old empire, political parties tentatively declared their rights to decide the future of the non-Russian nations. In Kiev, a Ukrainian Central Council was established on 20 March. This was the moment that many Ukrainian politicians in the Habsburg monarchy had awaited. Ukrainian lands seemed to be on the brink of national independence. Just a nudge was needed, and they might be the people to provide it. If the Habsburg army could enter Ukraine, they might just escape the confines of Galicia and create a great Ukrainian state.

At this moment full of expectation, after the death of Franz Josef, after the fall of the Romanovs, Wilhelm returned to the battlefield. He left Vienna for Lviv on 3 April 1917. He rejoined his men two days later, having sent them beer and liquor from the capital. He had a knack for pleasing his soldiers; by now he had also learned something about politics. He had come to understand Ukraine's political dilemmas, and had negotiated with his father and with Karl. He was on the unpredictable eastern front again, but he was calmer about politics. When important news came from Poland, he was no longer disoriented. In April 1917, Berlin and Vienna agreed in principle that Stefan would be king. On 1 May 1917, the Polish Regency Council, established by the occupying powers to appoint a monarch, made the appropriate motion. Later that month, Emperor Wilhelm II awarded the Iron Cross to Wilhelm. Despite the honors bestowed upon father and son, the political disposition of Poland and Ukraine was far from final, as both Stefan and Wilhelm understood.[18]

Back in Vienna, Wilhelm's Ukrainian friends had found a new way to exercise influence. Emperor Karl had decided to reopen the parliament. His Austrian domains had been ruled as an imperial military dictatorship since almost the beginning of the war, without meetings of the legislature. On 30 May 1917, the lower house of parliament met for the first time since 1914. Ukrainian political parties called for the creation of a Ukrainian province in the monarchy, and expressed their support for Ukrainian national self-determination in Russia. Yet it was the Polish parties, not the Ukrainian ones, that provided the new coalition government with the votes it needed to pass legislation. In such a situation, with pressure coming from both Ukrainians and Poles, the Habsburgs needed to win the war abroad just to keep the peace at home. The only sure way to satisfy both Poles and Ukrainians was to annex Russian territories, which could be divided between new Polish and Russian crownlands.[19]

So as Ukrainian and Polish parliamentary deputies debated in Vienna, they all looked east to the only real solution. Wilhelm, fighting his way across Galicia and into formerly Russian territory, was making a reputation for himself as a Ukrainian patriot. He still spoke in idealistic terms, writing to a Ukrainian friend that "the goal of his life was to make the people happy." But he also promoted himself quite self-consciously, asking his Ukrainian contacts to inform one another of his exploits. For the short term, Wilhelm now believed that the best solution to the Habsburg monarchy's national problems was the creation of an Austria-Hungary-Poland from the Habsburg lands, with east Galicia attached to Austria rather than to Poland. As a Habsburg and as a Ukrainian, he took for granted that the resolution of the Ukrainian question would benefit both his family and his nation.[20]

His emperor knew that matters were not so simple. Karl had to do something to rally Ukrainians to the Habsburg cause. Wilhelm was the obvious instrument. Karl placed a telephone call to Wilhelm— something his predecessor would never have done, as Franz Josef never used a telephone—and asked him to join him on a whistle-stop tour through Galicia. The two men met at a Vienna train station, Emperor Karl greeting his cousin most graciously: "You know, dear Wilhelm, I have taken you with me so that the Ukrainians have a visible sign of my interest for the land and people." As the two young Habsburgs traveled together through eastern Galicia in July and August 1917, Karl promised that Ukrainians would be treated fairly by Habsburg troops and the reestablished Habsburg administration.[21]

A few weeks later, Karl summoned Wilhelm for another Ukrainian political mission. Wilhelm was to make the acquaintance of Andrii Sheptytsky, the metropolitan of the Greek Catholic Church, the Ukrainian national church in Galicia. Sheptytsky's cathedral was in Lviv, the main seat of his church, and he had been arrested when the Russians occupied Galicia early in the war. This was no surprise. The Russians had known that Sheptytsky hoped for a Habsburg victory that would allow the Greek Catholic faith to spread from Galicia throughout the Russian Empire. Now, after the February Revolution, Sheptytsky was released from prison. He was making his way back to Galicia, to Lviv and to his cathedral. Because the Habsburgs needed Ukrainian support, Karl wished to make a gesture of welcome. He dispatched Wilhelm to Lviv to greet the illustrious Ukrainian churchman.

Wilhelm arrived at the Lviv train station in the early afternoon of 10 September 1917, in a car bedecked with flowers, at the head of a greeting party and a band. He greeted Sheptytsky in Ukrainian as well as German, to the delight of Ukrainian onlookers and the metropolitan himself. Sheptytsky had not met Wilhelm previously. Now

St. George's Cathedral,
Lviv

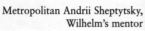

Metropolitan Andrii Sheptytsky,
Wilhelm's mentor

suddenly before him stood a young and handsome archduke, speaking decent Ukrainian, greeting him before a gathering crowd in the name of their sovereign. Under Wilhelm's uniform, as the metropolitan and the crowd could see, was an embroidered Ukrainian shirt. "Vyshyvanyi," the onlookers called out, the Ukrainian word for such embroidery. This became Wilhelm's Ukrainian last name. Suddenly he had a full Ukrainian identity—Vasyl Vyshyvanyi.

Sheptytsky became Wilhelm's new patron and guide. Sheptytsky began to see Wilhelm as an agent of his own plans for the liberation of all of Ukraine. Sheptytsky had hoped, at the beginning of the war, that a Habsburg officer could be found who might rule Ukraine for the Habsburgs. Now he had a Habsburg officer who was not only Ukrainian by choice but also an archduke by birth. A better candidate for king was hard to imagine.[22]

Even as Emperor Karl dispatched Wilhelm to handle Ukrainian matters, he was thinking about the larger question of a European peace. War had brought down the Romanov dynasty in Russia. While this was good news for the Habsburgs in the short run, it was a poor sign for European dynasties contemplating further years of war and hunger. Karl feared that continued war would bring further revolutions and abdications. His foreign minister, in a note that Karl passed to Emperor Wilhelm II, wrote in April 1917 that if "the monarchs of the Central Powers are unable to conclude peace in the next few months, the peoples will do so over their heads, and then the waves of revolution will sweep away everything for which our brothers and sons are still fighting and dying today."[23]

Yet Germany was the senior ally, and Wilhelm II did not wish to end the war. German policy, in any event, was now in the hands of the two generals, Ludendorff and Hindenburg. They held Germany and its allies hostage to a certain logic of war: making peace was senseless at any given moment since the next could bring a battle-field victory and thus better terms. Failing to persuade the Germans to make a general peace, Karl sought at least a political settlement regarding Poland. In October 1917, the two governments agreed that Karl could rule Poland in exchange for closer economic and political ties between Vienna and Berlin. Ludendorff and Hindenburg overruled this arrangement. They sought a satellite Poland whose men could be exploited as cannon fodder. Germany's candidate for the king of such an entity was Stefan. By endorsing him, the Germans seemed to be accepting the Austro-Polish solution. In fact, the generals meant to keep the crown away from the Habsburg emperors, and exploit Poland as they saw fit.

In November 1917, it might have seemed that Germany was right to be so uncompromising with its ally, and to expect the great breakthrough that could win the war. That spring the German foreign ministry had hit upon the idea of sending a Russian exile named Vladimir Lenin to his homeland in a sealed train. Upon arrival he declared, in his April Theses, that Russia should withdraw immediately from the war. Lenin and his Bolsheviks overthrew the Russian provisional government on 8 November, and replaced it with a new communist order. Russian troops turned on their officers, and Habsburg and German forces easily advanced.

The Bolshevik Revolution was the desired result of German policy, but the Habsburgs still had a card to play in Russia: the Ukrainian national movement. Wilhelm, who was promoted to captain that November, was on the edge of a great victory. The Ukrainian Council in Kiev declared in January 1918 that Ukraine was an independent state. Wilhelm, advised by Sheptytsky, saw that the new Ukraine would require help to survive a coming attack of the Bolsheviks' Red Army. It was thus crucial that the new state be recognized by the Central Powers. Wilhelm could win his Ukraine if he could shift from battlefield commander to stealthy diplomat. Wilhelm celebrated eastern-rite Christmas with his men on 7 January, took leave from the army on 12 January, and henceforth turned his full attention to the diplomacy of Ukrainian independence.[24]

Negotiations among Germany, the Habsburg monarchy, and their two eastern partners began in Brest-Litovsk in the first days of 1918. One eastern partner was the Bolsheviks, whose withdrawal of Russia from the war served German and Habsburg interests. The second partner was the new Ukrainian National Republic, which sought protection from those very Bolsheviks. Wilhelm and an ally, the Galician Ukrainian politician Mykola Vasylko, made Ukrainian diplomats from Kiev understand that their country's reputation as a strong agricultural economy made their negotiating position stronger than it appeared. The Habsburg monarchy was desperate for food. A British naval blockade was starving the country, and the monarchy's output of wheat had fallen by almost half during the war. On 20 January 1918, during the negotiations, 113,000 workers were striking in Vienna, demanding food. The next day, the Habsburg general staff wrote that the army "was living from hand to mouth."[25]

This knowledge emboldened Ukrainian diplomats to make two demands. One was that their independent Ukrainian state include a certain westerly region that Poles regarded as Polish. The second was that the Habsburg monarchy recognize a separate Ukrainian province. On 22 January, the Habsburg foreign minister presented these two points in Vienna. The government, in a desperate position, accepted. On 9 February 1918, German, Habsburg, and Ukrainian diplomats signed an accord known as the Bread Peace. Germany and the Habsburg monarchy agreed to recognize the Ukrainian National Republic, and the Habsburg monarchy, in a secret protocol, promised to create a Ukrainian crownland from eastern Galicia and Bukovina.

Meanwhile, war between Bolshevik and Ukrainian forces was raging. On the very day the treaty was signed, the Red Army took Kiev, the city that was supposed to be the capital of independent Ukraine. The Ukrainian delegates had gained international recognition for a state that could not defend itself against the Bolsheviks, within borders that were bound to offend Poles, and with the right to intervene in the internal affairs of the Habsburgs. All of this was in exchange for the promise of food that the Ukrainian state lacked the infrastructure to deliver. This appeared to be quite a diplomatic coup, and Wilhelm was pleased. Every major Ukrainian political demand was satisfied. He had helped to create the basis for two Ukrainian political entities, the independent Ukrainian National Republic to the east, and the Ukrainian crownland within the Habsburg monarchy. He no doubt hoped that the two units might one day be joined into one, perhaps into his "Principality of Ukraine." A principality, after all, would need a prince. Given the revolutionary mood in the east, the prince ought to be red.

For Wilhelm, the signing of the Bread Peace was "for me as a Ukrainian, and I do feel myself to be a Ukrainian, one of the most beautiful days of my life."[26] In the poetry that Wilhelm wrote about the war, he claimed romantically that the future of Ukraine could be seen through "a drop of red blood," through the suffering of his men. His soldiers had certainly helped make him the Ukrainian officer he was, teaching him songs and stories, giving him an object of loyalty and love. His triumph at Brest-Litovsk, however, had more to do with the political education he had acquired from Ukrainian politicians, Habsburg emperors, and his own father. The Ukrainian National Republic recognized in February 1918 was Wilhelm's triumph as a young diplomat. It was far larger than the Kingdom of Poland proclaimed in November 1916, it was legally an independent state, and it seemed to have more secure backing from Vienna and Berlin.

Wilhelm had surpassed his father, without ever yet having to confront him.

GREY

~~~

Shadow Kings

THE UKRAINIAN NATIONAL Republic was a protectorate from the beginning. Germany and the Habsburg monarchy, having recognized its government at the Bread Peace of 9 February 1918, then had to clear its territories of Bolsheviks. At the invitation of the Ukrainian government, German soldiers crossed the Ukrainian border on 18 February. Habsburg forces entered Ukraine ten days later. With the two allied armies hurtling eastward across Ukraine toward Russia, the Bolsheviks had to make peace. By the terms of the treaty they signed with Germany and the Habsburg monarchy in March 1918, they conceded the territories of Ukraine. The war was over in the east, and Berlin and Vienna had won.

Yet the victorious allies were in disaccord. Germany had entered Ukraine without waiting for the Habsburgs; the Habsburgs had followed to make sure that Germany did not take everything for itself. German and Habsburg troops brushed up against each other, leading to misunderstandings and strife. More than a month passed before the German and Habsburg general staffs could agree upon occupation zones. Germany would occupy Kiev and the north, the Habsburg monarchy, the south, and both powers would control the Black Sea ports, such as Odessa. Both Germany and the Habsburg monarchy set up diplomatic posts in Kiev.[1]

Berlin and Vienna took fundamentally different approaches to Ukrainian policy. The Habsburgs wanted the Ukrainian state to become politically self-sufficient, so that it would be their ally—against revolutionary Russia now, but also against Germany later. The Habsburg occupation of southern Ukraine was therefore meant to be creative. Even though the peoples of the Habsburg monarchy were hungry, procurement of food was not the first priority of Habsburg soldiers in Ukraine. Their main goal, according to the army chief of staff, was "the strengthening of national Ukrainian separatist thought." "The awakening of the national Ukrainian orientation during the war," wrote the Habsburg envoy in Kiev, "was certainly a correct and successful move" against Russia. Now the same policy was to be continued, to weaken the Germans. Ukrainian nationalism should be supported, and Ukrainian institutions built, as a bulwark against the Habsburgs' current ally. As the Habsburg military intelligence officer responsible for Ukraine put it: "We, as the creators of the first Ukrainian military unit, are called upon to enter Ukraine as leaders—against Germany!"[2]

Germany had its own, much simpler, policy. For Berlin, Ukraine was a source of food, and Ukrainians were peasants who grew crops for Germans. That was about as deep as Germany's Ukrainian policy went. While the Habsburg monarchy saw the new Ukrainian state as a strategic gain, Germans regarded it as an instrument for the gathering of grain. If a given Ukrainian government failed in this mission, went the German thinking, it could be replaced with another. While the Habsburgs believed that the promotion of Ukrainian nationalism served their own interests, Germans were just as happy to find allies and agents in Ukraine among Russians, Poles, or Jews. The Habsburgs also feared that their German allies, rather than seeking peace after the victory in the east, wished to use Ukraine to reach the oil fields of the Caucasus and Iraq, which would allow them to continue the war in pursuit of world power.[3]

In general, the Germans prevailed. The Habsburg armed forces had to accept an overall German command. On 29 April 1918, the Germans dissolved the Ukrainian government with which both powers had just negotiated. The authorities of the Ukrainian National Republic had certainly been incompetent: the president, a historian, had the habit of taking his phone off the hook so that he

could correct the proofs of his books without interruption. Yet it had at least been legitimate, composed of a range of political parties with aspirations to represent the peoples of Ukraine. After the coup, Ukraine remained a formally independent state, but one whose government was selected by a foreign power. The Germans established a puppet military dictatorship under Petro Skoropadsky. He took the traditional Ukrainian title "hetman," and his regime was called the Hetmanate.[4]

The creation of the Hetmanate was an entirely German policy, a step taken without the Habsburgs. Yet the Habsburg monarchy was not as weak as it might have appeared. Emperor Karl had one trick left.

On 18 February 1918, the day that the German army crossed into Ukraine, Karl had summoned Wilhelm to Vienna by telegram. Karl told Wilhelm that he had created a "Battle Group Archduke Wilhelm," which incorporated about four thousand Ukrainian soldiers and officers. It included the Ukrainian Legion, the special unit created for intelligence and propaganda purposes at the beginning of the war. Its troops were immediately sent east to Ukraine, where Wilhelm was to join and lead them. He was to be Karl's eyes and ears, reporting to him on Ukrainian affairs as one Habsburg to another.

Wilhelm was also to support the Ukrainian national cause, by his presence and by his actions, in any way he saw fit. As Wilhelm wrote, "His Majesty was *most gracious* and assigned me the task to work in Ukraine not only militarily but politically, and in this connection granted me *unlimited* liberty of action as a mark of his trust."[5]

Wilhelm later claimed that the two men never spoke of a Habsburg being crowned king of Ukraine, and this is probably true. For the two Habsburgs, such a discussion would have been superfluous. It would have been utterly obvious to both of them that opportunities for dynastic expansion were to be prudently considered.

In late March 1918 Wilhelm set out to join his troops, sailing across the grey waters of the Black Sea to Odessa. He rushed from the port to the hinterland, to the Ukrainian steppe, northeast to his Ukrainian Legion. He found them just outside the ancient city of Kherson, on 1 April 1918. Although the Ukrainian Legion was recruited from men either too young or too old for regular army service, and included a large number of bespectacled junior officers, Wilhelm chose to see his men as "beautiful, healthy, young boys, exhibiting great discipline, better than in the Habsburg army." He and they were all delighted to be in Ukraine. With Wilhelm now in command, and the Legion incorporated into his larger Battle Group, the troops made their way from Kherson to the place in Ukraine most redolent with national symbolism: the site of the ancient Cossack fortress known as the Sich.[6]

The Cossacks, free men who lived by warfare, fishing, and farming, were the pride of Ukrainian history. For Orthodox Ukrainian peasants, the vast majority of the Ukrainian population, the Sich had once meant freedom. For centuries, peasants essentially had two life possibilities: serfdom at the hands of Polish landlords and their Jewish trustees, or enslavement at the hands of Muslim Tatars if they tried to escape. The only refuge was the Sich, where a peasant might become a Cossack. In the middle of seventeenth century,

Harvard Ukrainian Research Institute

Wilhelm in Command, 1918

the Cossacks had risen against Polish rule. That revolt led to the bloody death of much of the population of Ukraine, and brought about the subjugation of the Cossacks by Russia. Yet the myth of courageous Cossacks challenging decadent Polish nobles, so attractive to Wilhelm personally, was irresistible to Ukrainian patriots generally. The Ukrainian Legion even called itself, in historical tribute to this legend of Ukrainian independence, the "Ukrainian Sich Marksmen."

That Cossack past was distant not only in time, but in space. The Legionaries were Galicians, and there had never been any Cossacks in Galicia. Their reverence for the Cossack past, until this very moment, had always been entirely theoretical. Back in the Habsburg monarchy, in that other world of cafés, universities, and government offices, the founders of the Ukrainian Legion, intellectuals all of them, had quite consciously referred to Cossack heroism as a way to build pride in a Ukrainian nation they wished to create. Now the

Legionaries were in Ukraine, at the Sich, making camp with the ghosts. Wilhelm wrote of the "great joy among us that it was we who had the good fortune of occupying these famous lands." He and his Legion made sunset visits to the site of the ancient fortress, and erected crosses upon the hills. The men fell easily into the romantic ideas that the past could be resurrected, and that a people lost to history could be restored.[7]

Their commander, Wilhelm, knew that history was not enough. Habsburg policy was to build a Ukrainian nation, and that meant action in the here and now. Wilhelm was at the Sich to turn peasants who spoke Ukrainian into Ukrainian peasants, in a policy that he called "Ukrainization." As he put it: "There are only two possibilities: either an opponent will be able to send me away and russify, or I will be able to remain here and ukrainize." This Ukrainian nation was not the same thing as the Ukrainian state that currently existed, a puppet of the Germans that relied upon Russian officials. It was rather a vision of a future in which a whole vast country would resemble the small area occupied by Wilhelm and his troops. In that small zone, around the Sich, Wilhelm had to build Ukraine, and quickly.

Wilhelm's policies were like those of nation-builders in all places and times: affirmative action, press propaganda, and historical romance. He screened officials by ethnicity, staffing the village administrations with Ukrainians. He used the press to spread the message of national liberation, founding a newspaper with a Ukrainian national tone. He believed that the next generation should see the world differently than its parents had, and so sent his officers to teach in schools. His Legion fraternized with the local peasants, drawing them toward a political identification with Ukraine. The fraternization took many forms, some of them scripted. Wilhelm's men spent much of their time writing and acting in plays performed for local audiences in the available venues. Every other week they performed in a local stable. As Wilhelm recalled, "our boys frolicked to the early hours with the local girls."[8]

So Ukraine was born in a stable, but then again so was Christianity. Even as Wilhelm spread the idea of a Ukrainian nation embracing people on both sides of the old Habsburg-Russian border, he played a part in a policy designed to end the ancient Christian schism. Ukraine, long a borderland between east and west, Catholic and Orthodox, was a traditional testing ground for church union. A sixteenth-century attempt yielded, instead of union, a third, "Uniate," church, one subordinate to the Vatican but using a liturgy like that of the Orthodox Church. In the nineteenth century, the Habsburgs had made this Uniate Church their own, educating its priests and naming it the Greek Catholic Church. By the twentieth century, Greek Catholicism had become the national religion of Ukrainians in the Habsburg monarchy.

It was Metropolitan Andrii Sheptytsky, whom Wilhelm had welcomed a few months earlier in Lviv, who had made of the Greek Catholic Church a Ukrainian national institution. Now, in 1918, Sheptytsky had a grand plan. He would convert the Orthodox of the former Russian Empire to Greek Catholicism, thereby bringing them under the Catholic Church, and thus ending the schism. If the Ukrainians of the Russian Empire converted from Orthodoxy to Greek Catholicism, this would also help the Habsburgs control Ukraine, since the seat of Greek Catholicism, Lviv, was in the Habsburg monarchy.

Sheptytsky provided Wilhelm with a chaperone, the Belgian Redemptorist priest François-Xavier Bonne. Bonne, like several other Redemptorists, had accepted the Greek Catholic rite and a Ukrainian national identity. He was Wilhelm's constant companion in Ukraine. The two of them quickly realized that there was no sense taking hasty action to propagate Greek Catholicism. In eastern Ukraine, Orthodoxy was the Ukrainian faith, and notions of Catholicism or Greek Catholicism brought confusion. Wilhelm and Bonne found that local Ukrainians, rather than expressing interest in the religions of the west, wanted to convert Wilhelm to Orthodoxy![9]

They also found that Ukrainians followed Wilhelm despite his Catholic religion, because he represented just the kind of revolutionary leadership that they wanted. Property was more important to Ukrainian peasants than religion or nationality, as Wilhelm seemed to understand. In Wilhelm's personal occupation zone, peasants kept the lands they had taken from their landlords during the revolutionary year of 1917. He prevented the Ukrainian state from restoring land to previous owners, giving local noblemen the back of his hand as necessary. He even stopped the Habsburg armed forces from carrying out food requisitions. Peasants who resisted requisitions in neighboring areas began to arrive in Wilhelm's zone. Wilhelm even gave shelter to partisan leaders who defended peasants from the Habsburg armed forces.[10]

Wilhelm's attitude to peasant property made him a legend all across Ukraine, a royal Robin Hood. Habsburg authorities in Kiev noted with alarm that Wilhelm's Sich had become "the destination of all the dissatisfied elements of Ukraine." They noted the "attraction" that he exerted upon everyone dissatisfied with the occupation. The military was concerned that "serious circles" among Ukrainian politicians regarded Wilhelm as a candidate for king of Ukraine. The Germans, too, were agitated by the "growing popularity of Archduke Wilhelm, known to the people as Prince Vasyl."[11]

Germany unwittingly helped Wilhelm gather more Ukrainian soldiers at the Sich. The German army, occupying the strategic Crimean Peninsula in the south in March and April 1918, ordered the Ukrainian unit known as the Zaporizhian Corpus to go elsewhere. In the wake of the Skoropadsky coup of 29 April, the commanders of the Corpus feared that their unit could be dissolved by the Germans. They made for the Sich. Like the Galicians of the Ukrainian Legion, the officers of the Zaporizhian Corpus were devoted to Cossack traditions. "Zaporizhian" means "beyond the rapids," a reference to the Sich. The Zaporizhians, with their shaven heads and curved swords, were a more fearsome lot than the Galicians, with their spectacles and schoolbooks. The Zaporizhians wore their swords to church, and even took them to confession. They explained that their blades had much to confess, which was probably true enough.[12]

As May 1918 began, the Sich provided the mythical backdrop for an extraordinary encounter of Ukrainian soldiers from the east and the west. Early that month, the Zaporizhians invited Wilhelm and his Legion to a banquet. Colonel Vsevolod Petriv recalled the first meeting of his east Ukrainian soldiers with the comely archduke: "It was quite a gathering: our massive boys, typical chock-a-block Ukrainian faces, and among them popped up the visage of the archduke, a slim youth, with reddish hair and no mustache, in an Austrian uniform with a Ukrainian shirt underneath." Wilhelm made a fantastic first impression. The men told Petriv that he took the initiative to speak to them, that he shared their concerns about politics, that he knew their country, that he spoke their language. Most remarkably, they felt that he was of the people. "He's a simple man, like us!" they exclaimed, astonished, but believing. They were not entirely wrong. Wilhelm was charming and tactful, but entirely free of guile or duplicity.[13]

A second party followed, with the Ukrainian cavalry impressing Wilhelm with feats of horsemanship. The Zaporizhians saw themselves as Cossacks, and maintained Cossack traditions of horsemanship. The standard trick was to pick up a cap from the ground while riding at full speed. Cossacks could ride on the side of a horse to simulate death or to dodge arrows or gunfire; some of them could even ride underneath. They could reverse their position on the saddle, from facing forward to facing backward, while their horses ran at full gallop. Wilhelm, who had been taught to ride by a fat Pole in the enclosed parks of his father's castle, had never seen anything like this stunt riding on the open steppe. Again, Wilhelm mixed easily with the soldiers and happily drank beer with the local peasants.

By showing the Ukrainians that he was one of them, Wilhelm was showing that he might rule them. The Ukrainian soldiers drew this conclusion for themselves. At one of these gatherings, they placed Wilhelm on a throne that they had brought back from the Crimea, and carried him about, calling out "Glory!" At another, Wilhelm was given a Cossack cap and the long felt cloak that the Cossacks called a *burka*. Like much of Ukrainian culture, the word *burka* has Muslim origins. While for Arabs a *burka* is the all-covering outer garment worn by women, for Ukrainians it is the national coat worn by warriors and leaders. Dressed in a *burka* and a fur cap, Wilhelm had become, as he had long wished, a prince of the European Orient. His childhood dreams of the East, and his youthful ambitions for a

Ukrainian throne, seemed close to fulfillment. Seeing Wilhelm so dressed, the men spoke lightly of Wilhelm's "coronation."[14]

A proper coronation was just what Colonel Petriv's colleague, Colonel Petro Bolbochan, had in mind. After a meeting with Wilhelm, Bolbochan proposed to Petriv that they use Wilhelm as a way to overturn the German-sponsored Hetmanate. "Wouldn't it be just the thing," he asked, "to make a little putsch and proclaim Vasyl Vyshyvanyi hetman of all Ukraine?" He proposed a constitutional democratic monarchy. Wilhelm would sign a monarchist constitution, which would expire when democratic elections could be held.

The two east Ukrainian colonels proposed this plan to Wilhelm. Wilhelm gave them an ambiguous reply, and cabled Emperor Karl for guidance on 9 and 11 May. Karl wired back that he wished for Wilhelm to continue his pro-Ukrainian policies, but to do nothing that would endanger the alliance with Germany or risk the delivery of food supplies. Wilhelm was not to act precipitously. If a Habsburg were to assume the throne and then lose it, this would discredit the whole dynasty. The crucial thing was to choose the right moment. Wilhelm was not to take "decisive steps"—at least "for the time being."[15]

Beyond Wilhelm's small theater, the Habsburg occupation of southern Ukraine was a disaster. Wilhelm was able to present himself as a Ukrainian, and to protect the peasants. No other officer was so lucky. In general the army had no methods to demonstrate its good will, and an urgent need to collect as much food as possible. Habsburg soldiers, greeted at first as liberators, were soon seen as plunderers. Peasants did not want Habsburg currency for their grain and livestock, and the Russian ruble was worthless. Peasants hid their grain in holes in the ground. Railway workers went on strike. Habsburg soldiers ordered Ukrainian policemen to burn down villages where peasants resisted requisitions. Hungry themselves, soldiers ate most of the food they collected. By the terms of the Bread Peace, Ukraine had promised the Central Powers one million tons of food by summer. Less than a tenth of that arrived. Since the Ukrainian government could not keep its promises, the Habsburgs did not keep theirs. The secret protocol to the Bread Peace, promising a Ukrainian crownland in the Habsburg monarchy in return for the grain, was burned in the German foreign ministry.[16]

The burning of villages and documents hardly brought Ukraine under control. Peasant rebels found leaders, some of them Bolsheviks, who taught them partisan tactics. A rather typical Habsburg report of June 1918 describes the murder of two gendarmes in a village, and the retaliatory execution of thirteen villagers by hanging. In July, a railway official was robbed, tied up, and left on the tracks. Habsburg and German troops could not find the culprits. That same month, Habsburg soldiers used artillery to pacify a village. They could no longer distinguish partisans from the rest, and their retaliations against civilians simply drove more young men to the forest to fight the occupiers. By August, Habsburg military intelligence recorded that the "murder of landowners, policemen, and officials and other enemy acts of terrorism against the troops of the Central Powers were the order of the day."[17]

Some of the confrontations with partisans were truly grotesque, as in the village of Hulai Pole on the last day of May. Habsburg troops, surrounded and outgunned, took shelter in a few houses. One soldier was sent out to surrender. He was beheaded and his body cut to pieces in view of the others. Then the remaining soldiers were taken at gunpoint from the houses and executed. The Habsburg punitive expedition killed forty-nine people, who may or may not have had anything to do with the incident. Habsburg officers had little idea of local politics, and could rarely identify their adversaries with certainty. In this case, they believed that the partisans were Bolsheviks, although Hulai Pole was in fact the stronghold of an anarchist band.[18]

Habsburg officers regarded Ukraine as a volcano before an eruption. Remaining in Ukraine would generate more discontent; leaving it would provoke mass violence. They feared that landowners and Jews would be murdered en masse if the Central Powers withdrew. Wilhelm's policy seemed only to worsen this fearful predicament. He sheltered peasants from requisitions, and helped partisans resist his own army. He was even sympathetic to the murderous anarchists of Hulai Pole, musing that his ancestor Emperor Rudolf had founded the Habsburg dynasty with similar methods. Habsburg occupation authorities had to wonder exactly what the young archduke was doing. In mid-June, the commander of Habsburg forces finally just put the question to him directly, but Wilhelm declined to answer. Habsburg diplomats also wrote to the emperor, pleading that he recall Wilhelm from Ukraine.[19]

The German allies were distressed. The very day that they had entered Ukraine, they had received their first intelligence report of a plot to put Wilhelm on a Ukrainian throne. They discounted that possibility at first, but could not fail to note the growing evidence. In March, before Wilhelm arrived on the scene, German diplomats concluded, correctly, that the Habsburgs were "pursuing wide-ranging political goals in southern Ukraine." On 13 May, the German military noted that "the thought of a personal union with Ukraine"— that is, a Ukrainian kingdom ruled by a Habsburg as king—"haunts various Austrian heads." That same day, German diplomats reported that Wilhelm would be happy to become the successor to their hetman—who had been in power for only two weeks.[20]

The Germans were surprised by the threat posed by Wilhelm. He was a red prince, a member of the ruling class who seized the revolutionary moment to implement a radical social and national policy. They understood, of course, that the Bolsheviks, whom they had driven from Ukraine, could draw support from those who resisted Germany's exploitative policies. They could listen to as much Bolshevik radio propaganda as they liked. They could also read the Bolsheviks' telegrams, since political commissars, including one Joseph Stalin, did not bother to use code. Bolshevism was no surprise. Yet the Germans were not prepared for a monarchism of the left, for a Habsburg who delivered, at least on a small scale, what the Bolsheviks also promised to a country tired of war and occupation: land, peace, and national freedom.[21]

Frustrated Germans told one another that Wilhelm, "like his father," was something of a "fantasist." This was true, but it was small consolation. Unable to persuade Karl to remove Wilhelm from Ukraine, they had to content themselves with sending agents to the Sich to observe his doings. The news was not good. Wilhelm was, as one spy reported, "much loved in his Ukrainian milieu." He was "considered by everyone who knows him to be a future hetman or king." "By his amiability, his tact, and his Ukrainian sympathies, as well as by the extreme simplicity of his private life," reported another informant, "the archduke has been able to win a very great popularity, not only among the people in his immediate surroundings, but also among large circles of the Ukrainian population." That agent continued: "Legends of all kinds are recounted from one end of Ukraine to the other about this adventurous prince, this friend of Ukraine, who came to establish himself at the ancient Sich." The conclusion was inevitable: "The very popularity of Archduke Wilhelm is a great danger for the future of our state"— meaning the puppet regime of Hetman Skoropadsky.[22]

Disinclined to admit any anxieties to their Habsburg ally, the Germans preferred to speak of the fears of their puppet ruler, Skoropadsky. They explained that Hetman Skoropadsky, "nervous by nature," regarded Wilhelm as his "běte noire." This was true enough. Skoropadsky, a proud and suspicious man, believed that Wilhelm was a pretender to the throne. He supposed, correctly, that Wilhelm had the backing of the Habsburg court and the Greek Catholic Church. The Germans tried to calm Skoropadsky by removing the military basis of Wilhelm's power. By June they had dissolved the Ukrainian troop concentration around the Sich, ordering the Zaporizhian Corpus to take up new positions to the north. Wilhelm was left then with only the four thousand men of his Battle Group. Yet by that time great damage, political and psychological, had already been done. In July someone carried out a media hoax, placing articles in European newspapers with the false story that Skoropadsky had resigned as hetman in favor of Wilhelm. At about the same time, a Bolshevik assassinated the commander of German forces in Ukraine. Skoropadsky was furious, and his German patrons were beginning to worry.[23]

Emperor Karl, however, was loath to remove Wilhelm. Worrying the Germans and infuriating Skoropadsky were probably among his goals. If the Germans botched the occupation badly enough, as indeed they were doing, they might in the end require the help of the Ukrainian Habsburg. In the meantime, Wilhelm's presence in Ukraine was one of the few ways that Karl could get the attention of the dominant German ally. In July 1918, Karl pretended to yield to all the pressure, writing to Emperor Wilhelm II of Germany that Wilhelm would come to the western front and explain his actions personally.

In fact, Karl was determined to continue his personal eastern policy, and to use the occasion to press his general policy of peace. The Germans, as he saw matters, were exploiting Ukraine for its foodstuffs and Poland for its recruits, without offering either country the requisite political autonomy. Karl certainly thought that the Habsburgs could rule both Poland and Ukraine with a softer touch than the Germans, and clung to the end to his idea of a Habsburg crown for at least the first, and perhaps also the second. More pressingly, Karl wanted the Germans to end the war while Vienna and Berlin still had territory that they could dispute. In his view, each month brought more risks than opportunities, and the time for an armistice had come.

It was in this mood that Karl summoned Wilhelm to Vienna, gave him a stack of denunciations sent from Ukraine and a personal vote of confidence, and sent him on his way to speak to Emperor Wilhelm II at German headquarters in Belgium. There Wilhelm could explain Karl's position and, if he liked, his own. Wilhelm accepted the emperor's mission, burned the denunciations, and was on his way west.[24]

In journeying from Ukraine to Belgium, from the eastern front to the western, Wilhelm was following the paths of hundreds of thousands of German soldiers. The peace treaties signed with Ukraine and Bolshevik Russia in February and March 1918 had allowed the Germans to transfer forty-four divisions to the west and mount five major attacks in France in spring and summer 1918. By June the German army was within forty miles of Paris, which it shelled. Yet the French and the British kept fighting, and the Americans were coming. The Germans took one million casualties in this offensive, soldiers they could not replace. Meanwhile one million Americans arrived in France.

On the eighth of August 1918, Wilhelm arrived at Spa to speak with the German emperor. It was, from the German point of view, the worst day of the entire war. That morning the armies of France, Britain, and the United States had launched a massive attack at the French city of Amiens, about 120 kilometers north of Paris. This was the largest tank battle of the First World War—and Germany's enemies had all of the tanks. By afternoon, when the German emperor greeted Wilhelm in his tent, the Germans had taken tens of thousands of casualties and retreated eight miles. The mood at German headquarters on that bitter day was anger that the Habsburg monarchy was doing little to help on the western front.[25]

Wilhelm had come to Spa on a delicate Habsburg mission on a day when the Germans were eager to blame the Habsburgs for their own problems. Amiens showed that Karl had been right to seek peace—but the Germans could not admit this, not at such a moment. German officers dissuaded Wilhelm from mentioning Karl's desire for a general peace. Wilhelm did speak to the emperor about his military command in Ukraine, and received his blessing to return. The emperor's staff thought that Wilhelm compared favorably to the rest of the Habsburgs. The German emperor himself wrote that such an appealingly "young and fresh" officer should be back on the lines with his men. He seemed glad to have found an attractive Habsburg who was eager to fight.[26]

Five days later, Emperor Karl arrived in Spa to plead for an immediate peace. The day before, the Battle of Amiens had ended, a major defeat for the German army. Few senior German officers believed that the war could be won. Emperor Wilhelm II, who was kept ignorant of the true details of the fighting, tried to bully Karl about Poland. Karl gave no ground. The question, however, was moot. Eastern affairs were now essentially irrelevant. The war was decided on the western front. The Germans were falling back, day after day. For the first time in four years of war, German soldiers were capitulating in large numbers. No Ukrainian food or Polish soldiers would make any difference. The Germans wanted Habsburg help in the west, but the Habsburgs needed the army to keep the peace at home as hungry civilians rioted. The two emperors could only agree that further decisions would be taken after the next success on the western front. There would be no next success on the western front.[27]

As the emperors spoke, Wilhelm was on his way back to Ukraine, confronting bureaucratic hindrances at every step. German and Habsburg diplomats and officers tried to delay Wilhelm at every point—at Spa, at Berlin, at Vienna. Everyone knew, claimed the Germans, that Wilhelm wished to be king of Ukraine. When Habsburg officials appealed to their own emperor to prevent Wilhelm's return to Ukraine, Karl replied that Wilhelm II's endorsement had settled the whole issue. His officials instructed him that declarations from the German emperor meant nothing. No German or Habsburg official could challenge the legitimacy of monarchical rule, but, as the war went on, the monarchs themselves were not always taken seriously. Imperial authority had been hollowed out by four years of bloody and purposeless war.[28]

German and Habsburg officials feared that Wilhelm's presence in Ukraine could bring down the Hetmanate and lead to complete chaos throughout the country. Habsburg diplomats explained that "every single person in Ukraine regards the archduke as our candidate for the throne," and that Wilhelm's return would be a "death blow" for the hetman. Wilhelm returned anyway, rejoining his troops in early September. Knowing of the hetman's anxieties, he volunteered to come to Kiev to explain himself. Habsburg and German diplomats, seeing such a visit as the pretext for a coup, agreed that this was a "most unfortunate idea." The Germans announced that, were Wilhelm to arrive in Kiev, he would be treated according to his military rank (of captain) rather than as an imperial and royal archduke of the House of Habsburg. Governments were not taking the dynasties very seriously.[29]

Yet even as the Germans worked to keep Wilhelm away from Kiev, they were trying to induce his father Stefan to come to Warsaw. On 28 August, as one German diplomat protested Wilhelm's plan to visit the Ukrainian capital, another was presenting Stefan the German conditions for taking a Polish throne.

Polish State Archives, Żywiec

Portrait of Stefan, 1918

It was a hard case to make. By endorsing the Ukrainian National Republic, Germany and the Habsburgs had alienated Polish politicians. Polish troops in the Habsburg armed forces had mutinied, and Polish soldiers refused to join the army that Germany wished to raise. The leader of the Polish Legions created by the Habsburgs, Józef Piłsudski, was in German prison for refusing to swear a loyalty oath to Germany. Stefan saw that any such Polish kingdom, at this point in the war, would be nothing but a German colony. He spent the war collecting and distributing money to care for Polish war wounded; he had no desire to see more Polish boys killed and maimed for the German cause. German commanders planned to take territory from Poland's west, strip property from landowning Poles resident there, and deport them. This was not a policy that a self-respecting Polish monarch could contemplate. Stefan discussed the matter with Emperor Karl, who instructed him not to take the Polish crown.[30]

In September 1918, Hetman Skoropadsky went to German head-quarters himself, and extracted a promise from the German commanders that Wilhelm would leave Ukraine. Yet even then Karl did not concede to German pressure. The German commanders, Ludendorff and Hindenburg, had blocked Karl's efforts to become king of Poland, but they could not force him to abandon dynastic hopes in Ukraine. The commander of Austrian forces in Ukraine did finally find the argument that would convince his sovereign to reassign Wilhelm. On 23 September 1918, he told Karl that, in the prevailing revolutionary conditions, he could no longer guarantee Wilhelm's personal safety. On 9 October, Wilhelm and his men sailed from Odessa, from a Ukraine they had done much to create.[31]

Ordered to Chernivtsi, the capital of the Austrian province of Bukovina, Wilhelm fell ill and was confined to his bed. He was greatly worried about the future of the Ukrainian National Republic. Wilhelm feared that his withdrawal was the beginning of the end, that Ukraine would be overcome by the Bolsheviks. Now that the red prince had to go, he foresaw a Bolshevik Ukraine, and a communist threat to all of Europe. He was no less disquieted by the prospects for the Habsburgs. He spent his evenings speaking to the local governor about the future of the monarchy. The newspapers, which they read together, brought much to discuss. Wilhelm, short on cash, borrowed some money from the local governor. He also managed, somehow, to procure himself an automobile.[32]

The Germans were now negotiating directly with the Americans, on the basis of President Woodrow Wilson's peace terms, known as the Fourteen Points. Wilson had proclaimed the principle of national self-determination, that peoples should choose the state of which they would be citizens. The Germans generally believed that this idea could bring them an honorable and acceptable peace. Wilson's Point Ten was autonomy for the nationalities of the Habsburg domains. The Habsburgs had always believed they could comply with this demand if necessary. The American standards for autonomy were surely not too high. After all, when Wilson first pronounced his Fourteen Points before a joint session of the U.S.

Congress, none of the assembled representatives or senators was African American. Karl, on the other hand, had a parliament that forced his hand on minority policy, so much so that national liberation had to be a Habsburg goal during the war itself.

Now Karl complied with one of Wilson's demands. On 16 October 1918, he decreed that his Austrian domains be reconstituted as a federation of national provinces. Still on his sickbed in Chernivtsi, Wilhelm supported this initiative, believing that a Ukrainian crownland federated within the Habsburg monarchy could be saved from Bolshevism, regardless of what happened in the revolutionary east. Hearing of plans to declare an independent west Ukrainian state in Lviv, he wrote to Ukrainian leaders to try to dissuade them from seceding from the monarchy. Believing that a disintegration of the Habsburg monarchy was "unthinkable," he proposed on 18 October that any new Ukrainian state petition to join the monarchy as a crownland. He was out of step with events. The Habsburg version of self-determination—national crownlands loyal to a Habsburg emperor—was no longer possible. Wilhelm, who had made himself the intermediary between the eternal dynasty and the young nation, was no longer necessary.[33]

That same day, 18 October, Woodrow Wilson responded to Karl's federation by urging the nations of the Habsburg monarchy to declare their full independence. Pressing now for the destruction of the monarchy, Wilson had gone where Wilhelm could not. The Ukrainian conspirators in Lviv had thus far considered Wilhelm to be the natural leader of their army. Seeing that he still supported the monarchy, and that the monarchy would not survive the war, they changed their minds. An officer sent to Chernivtsi to recruit Wilhelm returned instead with someone else. Wilhelm neverthless helped divert Habsburg resources to the cause of Ukrainian independence. In these last days of October, likely with Wilhelm's connivance, two Habsburg regiments with a majority of Ukrainian soldiers were ordered to Lviv. They joined a large number of officers who were veterans of the Ukrainian Legion. On 1 November, Ukrainian troops gained control of Lviv and declared an independent West Ukrainian National Republic.[34]

Wilhelm made a last important gesture. He ordered his troops from Chernivtsi to Lviv to fight for the Ukrainian cause, rising from his hospital bed to see them off at the train station. This decision was his own; the men, not realizing that the issue of Ukrainian statehood would be decided in Lviv, wanted to stay in Bukovina. Wilhelm was seeing his men for the last time, knowing that they would be fighting for a cause that no longer seemed to need him. The soldiers arrived in Lviv a few days later, no longer members of the Battle Group Archduke Wilhelm, but soldiers of a West Ukrainian National Republic. They should have arrived a bit sooner. Trained for the political mission of Ukrainization, they could not resist stopping at train stations to replace Polish signs with Ukrainian ones, just as Wilhelm had taught them.[35]

Wilhelm had helped to build a nation, but that nation's leaders were acting without him. They had learned from him, then rebelled against him. His Europe was ceasing to exist, and his dynasty was in danger. The war had gone on too long—for Wilhelm, for Karl, for all the Habsburgs, and for their monarchy.

As late as August 1918, when Wilhelm and Karl had visited the German emperor at Spa, the Habsburgs might have emerged victorious, or at least satisfied. There were no foreign soldiers on Habsburg soil, and the monarchy occupied much of Ukraine, Serbia, and northern Italy. Had the Germans heeded Wilhelm and Karl's August appeals for an armistice, the Habsburg monarchy might, just possibly, have survived. Autumn brought only disaster. In September the Serbs regrouped and liberated their capital Belgrade. In October an Italian counterattack destroyed the Habsburg forces in the Alps. In November Romania reentered the war, invading the Habsburg province of Bukovina and taking its capital Chernivtsi.[36]

Wilhelm fled the Romanian advance. As his secretary Eduard Larischenko drove him from Chernivtsi just before the Romanians arrived on 9 November, the Habsburg monarchy still existed. When they arrived in Lviv a few days later, it did not. In the meantime, a general strike had broken out in Germany; the German emperor chose not to return home from Belgium. His empire became a republic, signed an armistice, and began preparations for peace negotiations. In the Habsburg monarchy, national leaders had taken over local organs of administration. With defeat added to hunger, tedium, and suffering, national rebellion finally undid the multinational monarchy. New national states were declared across its entire territory. Habsburg power was broken, after eight hundred years. On 11 November, Karl withdrew from the affairs of state and retired to a hunting lodge. By the time he did so, he had no army, not even an honor guard. Cadets from the military academy were his only escort.[37]

Dynasties suddenly counted for nothing, for less than nothing. Ukrainians in Lviv had founded a republic, whose president informed Wilhelm that his services were not required. In Warsaw, the regency council of the Kingdom of Poland, formed to make Stefan a Polish king, instead transferred its authority to Józef Piłsudski. He founded a republic. Stefan's Polish career, like those of his Polish sons and sons-in-law, was suddenly over. The Polish national question had finally been answered, against the Habsburgs. Poland claimed all of Galicia for itself. In Ukraine, the Skoropadsky regime was brought down by military officers, some of whom had once asked Wilhelm to make a "little coup" and rule them. Wilhelm had never made his move. Wilhelm had, at Karl's instructions, deferred his dream of taking power in Ukraine—"for the time being."

As of 11 November 1918, armistice day, there was no more "time being"; imperial time had ceased to be. For centuries, Christians had regarded the Holy Roman Empire, ruled by the Habsburgs, as the opposite of a sign of the apocalypse: so long as it existed, the world would not end. In the early nineteenth century the Holy Roman Empire had been dissolved, but the Habsburgs, under Franz Josef, had recovered and endured, throwing a grey cloak of timelessness over the shuddering body of a continent changing itself from within. Now, with empires destroyed and dynasties dethroned, progressive time began. It was socialist time, the promise of new beginnings for oppressed classes at the end of a feudal age; national time, the conviction that peoples could move forward from a dark past of imperial oppression into a brighter future of state independence; or liberal time, the confidence that new republics would create the conditions for lasting peace in Europe and the world.

In central and eastern Europe, kings ruled only shadows, and pretenders sought refuge where they could. Stefan retreated to his castle in Żywiec, which was promptly confiscated by the Polish Republic. Skoropadsky fled from Ukraine to Germany on a German troop train, disguised as a doctor amidst the real war wounded. As Polish troops entered Lviv, Wilhelm slipped from the city and made for the shelter of a monastery in an east Galician town. He would hide there amidst the monks.[38]

An eternity was over. Wilhelm was twenty-three years old.

WHITE

~

Agent of Imperialism

SUDDENLY THE WORLD seemed to be conspiring against Wilhelm's beloved Ukraine, and there was nothing he could do. As the victors of the First World War convened in Paris in January 1919 to decide upon the future of Europe, Wilhelm was hiding in a monastery in the east Galician town of Buchach. The British, French, Americans, and their allies designed the postwar order, while the defeated powers, excluded from the peace conferences, could only send written protests.

The historical monarchy of the Habsburgs, defeated on the battlefield, would be dismantled. The American president, Woodrow Wilson, had announced the principle of self-determination, that nations should be allowed their own states. As states were created or enlarged from the territories of the Habsburg monarchy, Wilson's standard was applied, but very unevenly. Czechs, Poles, Serbs, and Romanians, seen by the victors as allies, were entrusted with massive national minorities. Hungary, seen as an enemy, was reduced to a third of its previous size. Austria was made into a small republic of speakers of German, most of whom probably wished to join Germany. This the victors forbade, even though it is what self-determination required.[1]

The victors decided who was a nation, and who was not. Thus Ukraine was not a nation, and had no right to self-determination. Insofar as the Americans, British, and French had any notion that Ukraine existed, they regarded it as an artificial creation of Berlin and

Vienna. Ukrainian politicians, who had counted on Germany and the Habsburg monarchy, had few friends in London, Paris, or Washington. Now that the war was over, Wilhelm's friends hurried to correct the imbalance. Sheptytsky and Bonne, so recently his patrons in Habsburg Ukraine, now rushed to persuade the victors that the Ukrainian people deserved self-determination. They faced a difficult task.[2]

Wilhelm, hidden away in a Galician monastery as 1919 began, was far from the Paris peace talks. Ukrainian politicians thought this was for the best. His character and achievements, so attractive just weeks before, could now only weaken the precarious Ukrainian cause. The idea of a red prince, a powerful intoxicant during the war, now became a fatal potion. Wilhelm represented both Habsburg power and social liberation in eastern Europe, at a time when the victors wished to prevent Habsburg restoration and Bolshevik revolution. In spring 1919, as Hungarian Bolsheviks fought a war to regain the traditional crownlands of the Hungarian kings, this combination of modern and traditional ideology was a genuine threat.

Poland, Wilhelm's enemy, knew how to play the Ukrainian card to its own advantage. Outmaneuvered by Wilhelm in February 1918, during the negotiations of the Bread Peace, Polish politicians now took their revenge. As Poles fought a Ukrainian army for control of the Habsburg province of Galicia, they portrayed their struggle as a continuation of the First World War. Poland was among the victors, and Ukraine, so they argued, was a creation of the enemies that had to be defeated for the war to be truly over. Polish diplomats presented the Ukrainian nation as a Habsburg plot, "personified" by Wilhelm. The charming Polish pianist Ignacy Paderewski told the Americans that Wilhelm had 80,000 troops at the gates of Lviv. Wilhelm wrote personally to President Wilson, trying to explain that Ukraine was a nation deserving of self-determination, but to no effect.[3]

Wilhelm had lost a war, and an argument, and now had to look after his fragile health. On 6 May 1919 Wilhelm left the monastery, and took to the mountains in his automobile. Suffering from tuberculosis, he wanted less cramped conditions; perhaps the monks wanted the same. Wilhelm was used to the companionship of men in close quarters, from school, from the military academy, and from the army. He and his secretary Eduard Larischenko perhaps liked the cloisters all too well. However that may be, Wilhelm and Larischenko sought the mountains and the Ukrainian mountaineers he had loved so much as a youth. But there he found no repose. On 6 June he was captured by the Romanian army, taken to Bucharest, and interrogated. He was imprisoned in a monastery outside the capital while Romanian authorities essentially demanded a ransom from Austria for his return. Presumably the Romanians took his car.[4]

Wilhelm's health did seem to improve in Romania, and after three months he was rescued by representatives of the Ukrainian National Republic. He was showing signs of life, as was the state he had helped to create. The Ukrainian National Republic, once a protectorate of Germany and the Habsburg monarchy, had found its way to true independence. With the withdrawal of German and Habsburg forces, a coterie of Ukrainian politicians called the Directory had replaced the German puppet government. This new regime brought Wilhelm from Romania to Ukraine, and enlisted him as chief of foreign relations for the army.[5]

The Ukrainian state no longer had any powerful protectors, and neither did Wilhelm. On 10 September 1919, Wilhelm was back in Ukraine, at army field headquarters at Kamienats Podils'kyi. He found himself interrogated by his new colleagues, forced to explain just how he had become Ukrainian. He promised them that he would fight for Ukraine so long as he had strength in his limbs. Once he was accepted into the ranks of the army of the Ukrainian National Republic, he could survey the position of his new patron.

The news on the front was not good. Kamienats Podils'kyi, in southwest Ukraine, was the site of an ancient fortress that once defended old Poland from the Ottoman Empire. It was where desperate Ukrainian governments and armies sought shelter in 1918 and 1919 when Kiev, their capital, was controlled by other powers. This was rather often. During the wars for Ukraine that followed the First World War, Kiev was occupied a dozen different times. The Ukrainian National Republic faced three powerful rivals: the Red

Army of the Bolsheviks, a White Army of Russian counterrevolutionaries, and the Polish Army of Józef Piłsudski.

The territory of Ukraine, after five years of war, was wracked by banditry and pogroms. The army of the Ukrainian National Republic, like the armies it fought, included within its ranks local commanders who were more interested in robbing and killing Jews than in liberating the country. Wilhelm was in no position to help. A year earlier, he had been seen, by some of the officers of this very army, as a likely monarch. But he had missed his chance, and had ended the war in miserable isolation from any source of power. He was still a legend in the Ukrainian countryside, but the Directory had no intention of loosing a potential rival upon the country at large. Wilhelm was to work with his languages in his tent. In his new and relatively humble position, he had little to offer. He spoke English and French, but the Americans, the British, and the French could not be persuaded to support Ukraine. The victors feared the Bolsheviks but saw Poland, rather than Ukraine, as the barrier that would keep communism from Europe.

Along with his fellow officers, Wilhelm could only observe as Poland intelligently exploited the situation. Poland's head of state and commander in chief, Józef Piłsudski, watched and waited as rivals for Ukraine weakened each other over the course of 1919. The White Army, whose leaders wished to re-create an imperial Russia that included Ukraine, dislodged the army of the Ukrainian National Republic from Kiev in summer 1919. Then the Whites were overmastered by the Red Army of Lenin and Trotsky, who aimed to spread an international communist revolution first to Ukraine, and then to Poland and Europe. In autumn 1919, the army of the Ukrainian National Republic regrouped to battle the Red Army, but with little hope of success. In desperation, the Ukrainian National Republic had to ask Poland for help. The Reds and the Whites wished to destroy the Ukrainian state. Poland, at least, claimed that it wanted Ukraine as an ally.[6]

As Wilhelm understood, an alliance with Poland, though the only option, was a moral trap for Ukrainians. It required that some Ukrainians betray others in the name of the survival of Ukraine. Poland had just defeated, in July 1919, the army of the West Ukrainian National Republic, the Ukrainian state formed from the eastern part of Habsburg Galicia. Poland now held these formerly Habsburg territories, and in exchange for an alliance would demand that the Ukrainian National Republic formally renounce them. One Ukrainian state would have to betray another, and the Galician lands where Wilhelm had found his Ukrainian identity would have to be incorporated by Poland. Wilhelm, disgusted, left the service of the Ukrainian National Republic after only two months, in November 1919.[7]

Some Ukrainians were willing to risk an alliance with Poland, but Wilhelm was not among them. He thought that the price was too high. He was not above making compromises to aid the Ukrainian cause, but he could not bring himself to take orders from Warsaw. That would have undone the logic of his entire political life, in which his embrace of Ukraine was a rebuff to his father's Poland. Wilhelm would try to find support for an independent Ukraine from other quarters. These were his musings as he left Ukraine and made his way westward with Larischenko. Wilhelm was struck down by typhus, and forced to halt in, of all places, Romania.

As Wilhelm contemplated the new year from a sickbed in Bucharest, his reasons for despair were the same as his reasons for hope. Ukraine had become the showpiece of the fiasco of the victors' Europe. The allies wished for a Europe of national republics. The Ukrainian National Republic was precisely that, and yet its fate was constant bloodshed. The Ukrainian National Republic was allied with Poland, and Poland would take from Ukraine what it wished. The dilemma, however, was more general. Germany, Austria, and Hungary had also been denied national self-determination. Leaders who had believed that they would make peace on the basis of Wilson's Fourteen Points had been brutally deceived.

The Europe of 1920 was thus a hotbed of revisionism. Germans, Austrians, and Hungarians wished to alter, or "revise," the postwar settlements. Some of them were monarchists, some were authoritarians, and some had no clear political commitments. They were united by the conviction that their countries had been visited by a great injustice, and by their hostility to the new or enlarged states supported by the victors. Poland, Czechoslovakia, and Romania, states that had taken territory from the German Empire and the Habsburg monarchy, seemed like inviting targets. The revisionists feared the Bolsheviks, who aspired to bring their revolution to the rest of Europe. At the same time, they realized that the Red Army, if it came west, might bring them their great opportunity to revise borders.

The revisionists wanted to enlarge some states, and reduce or even eliminate others. Their hope was that a revolution from the left would enable a revolution from the right. This passage from communism to authoritarianism might have seemed a desperate fantasy, had it not already happened twice, in the German province of Bavaria, and in Hungary.

Bavaria, in accordance with the German federalist system, had its own government. Its parliament had been dissolved, however, after a revenge shooting in its chambers. In April 1919, a young playwright, Ernst Toller, declared a Soviet Republic of Bavaria. Toller announced that the university in Munich was open to all applicants, except those wishing to study history, which was to be abolished as a threat to civilization. His foreign minister telegraphed the Bolsheviks in Moscow to complain that there were no keys to the bathroom in the foreign ministry. The Bolsheviks had serious answers to frivolous questions. Their own people took direction of the Bavarian revolution and began to take hostages. The German government, though itself Social Democratic, panicked at this point. It sent in right-wing militiamen, mostly war veterans, to quell the revolution. The Bolsheviks killed the hostages, and the militiamen killed the Bolsheviks and many others. On 1 May 1919, the communists were defeated, and the counterrevolution began.

Hungary, like Bavaria, had undergone a communist revolution in 1919. The victors had to send in Romanian troops to restore order. As the Romanians departed, power was taken by a former Habsburg admiral, Miklós Horthy. Riding into the capital on a white horse, he chastened Budapest for having clothed itself in the red rags of revolution. In these conditions, France, Britain, and the United States had to settle for Horthy's conservative counterrevolution rather than hope for the creation of a republic. The victorious powers made Hungary accept its borders, even though the entire Hungarian political class rejected them. Hungary became the most openly revisionist country in Europe, its political slogan "no, no, never" signifying its total rejection of the postwar order. Perhaps if Hungarians could find allies among Germans and Austrians, they could remake Europe to their liking.

As Wilhelm now had time to understand, the mayhem created by weak but ambitious revisionists in Germany and Austria might yet give Ukraine a chance. Indeed, Ukraine might prove to be the ally the revisionists needed as they sought a new power balance on the European continent. As it happened, even as Wilhelm lay sick in Romania, an old Hungarian acquaintance of his family was preparing the model for a new European order, one that just might require a man of Wilhelm's talents. Trebitsch Lincoln, perhaps more than any other individual, embodied the chaos of possibility of the Europe of 1920.

Wilhelm's trio of identities—Habsburg, Polish, and Ukrainian—was paltry stuff in comparison to the many lives of Lincoln. A petty thief in Budapest, he had fled the police of his native Hungary for England. A Jew, he took up with Christian missionaries in London, and was engaged by the Quaker industrialist and temperance advocate B. Seebohn Rowntree. In 1910 he won a seat in the British House of Commons. With this credential, he appeared a credible backer of schemes for investment in the Galician oil fields. In 1911 Lincoln recruited Wilhelm's brother-in-law, Hieronymus Radziwiłł, to the board of directors of a company called Oil Pipe Lines of Galicia. The company went under.

Lincoln, a leopard who could change his spots, saw a new opportunity in the First World War; he decided to become a spy. He sold his services to the Germans and was pursued by the British. He made his money by selling dramatic accounts of his career as a spy to the American tabloid press. The British, unsurprisingly, revoked his naturalization as a British subject in December 1918. Lincoln went to Germany, where he made a name for himself the following summer as an anti-British, right-wing journalist. He had arrived in Germany just as the population was shocked by the terms of the Treaty of Versailles, signed on 19 June 1919, which seemed to guarantee that the country would remain weak and dependent forever. Germany lost territory, population, and the right to field a mass army. Lincoln used his talents to fan German popular outrage.[8]

By autumn he had befriended a German colonel, Max Bauer. Bauer was an authoritarian nationalist who believed that only dictatorship could save Germany from the perils of anarchism and Bolshevism. During the war he had been a close aid to the German commander Erich von Ludendorff, Bauer's candidate for dictator. Ludendorff had resigned from his functions in October 1918, just before the armistice. Although he bore the responsibility for Germany's conduct of the war, Ludendorff felt free to blame others for the defeat. He fled at the war's end to Sweden under false whiskers and on a Finnish passport. He developed there the theory of "the stab in the back": that Germany had been defeated not by its enemies on the battlefield, but rather by alien conspirators at home. These traitors were in league, as he saw matters, with the vengeful victors, Britain, France, and the United States. Germany's new republic and its socialist government were illegitimate consequences of this dark plot. They were to be destroyed.[9]

Returning to Germany, Ludendorff gathered Colonel Bauer and some other old allies in Berlin. Bauer introduced Ludendorff to Lincoln, who joined their conspiracy with ardor. On 13 March 1920, their clique overturned the government of the young German republic. With the support of German soldiers returning from the eastern front, Ludendorff and his confederates took power in a quick putsch. They proclaimed themselves to be Germany's sole hope of rescue from communist revolution and from an imposed peace that deprived Germany of its status as a great power. Lincoln became the new government's press secretary. Thus a Hungarian Jew and onetime British subject occupied the most visible function of a German nationalist government. A young Austrian war veteran named Adolf Hitler, an early admirer of the putsch, concluded that it "could not be a national revolution" since "the press chief was a Jew."[10]

The putsch won the support of the army, but not of the population. When the legitimate authorities ordered the army to suppress the revolt, they were flatly refused. They then called upon the working class to begin a general strike, which was more effective. After four days in power, the conspirators left Berlin on 17 March 1920. As the German republic was restored, Lincoln, Bauer, and other plotters hastened to Bavaria.

Bavaria was a safe haven within Germany for nationalists and counterrevolutionaries. It was in the south, far from northerly and rather socialist Berlin. It was heavily Catholic, whereas most of the country was Protestant. And by now it had already passed through its own cycle of communist revolution and counterrevolution, with right-wing militias and authoritarians victorious in the end. The conservative architecture of its capital, Munich, which Hitler would come to admire, offered a reassuring vista to men of the right. The heir to the Bavarian dynasty, Crown Prince Rupprecht, offered his personal support. Now that Germany was a republic rather than an empire, the crown prince had few hopes of ever becoming king. He, too, would need a counterrevolution, thus his warm welcome to the putschists.

The conspirators, after the Berlin disaster, turned their minds in Munich to more brazen schemes involving the entire postwar order. By summer 1920, the Paris peace talks had produced treaties regarding Germany, Austria, and Hungary, all of them deeply unsatisfactory to many of the people concerned. Germany lost some territory and a good deal of sovereignty; Austria came into existence despite the preference of its population to join Germany; Hungary lost most of its territory and population. More and more politicians and veterans embraced revisionism.

Meanwhile, in eastern Europe, beyond the reach of the victors and their peace treaties, Poland had undertaken the mission of defeating the Bolsheviks. The Polish army, allied with the Ukrainian National Republic, reached Kiev in May 1920, only to be expelled by the Bolsheviks in June. The Red Army now began a march west to Europe. The Polish incursion seemed to have released a general Bolshevik invasion. The Red Army would now advance west until forced to halt by some greater force. As the German conspirators in Munich could see, Europe was fluid not only because the defeated states were dissatisfied, but also because its eastern half was still a battlefield. This line of thought led them toward Ukraine.

Lincoln wanted to form a "White International": an alliance of German, Austrian, Hungarian, and White (anti-Bolshevik) Russian revisionists, directed against the Entente Powers, Poland, and Bolshevik Russia. Ukraine, lying between Poland and Russia, was the natural enemy of both, and thus a natural ally of the revisionists. Even though the Ukrainian National Republic was now Poland's ally against the Bolsheviks, the war was unlikely to end with the creation of a durable Ukrainian state. In the best case, a victorious Poland would incorporate lands that Ukrainians saw as western Ukraine. As the Red Army stormed westward in July 1920, a Polish victory seemed unlikely. A victorious Bolshevik Russia would take Ukraine in the name of revolution. Regardless of what happened, many Ukrainians would be dissatisfied. They would be revisionists, and so they could be allies.

During that summer, Lincoln and his fellow putschists saw how the strategic situation might soon turn in their favor. Two of their enemies seemed to be destroying each other. Poland, the largest state created by the hated Paris peace settlements, was at war with Bolshevik Russia, the embodiment of their communist nightmare. Once it became clear which side would win, the White International could move into action. In the meantime, they contemplated the Ukrainian question.[11]

No Ukrainian was better known to them than Wilhelm. The red prince had been a great irritant to the Germans in 1918, precisely because he was so popular in Ukraine. He had been a rival to the Germans' chosen leader, Hetman Skoropadsky, and a threat to their domination of the country. General Ludendorff, deeply involved then in Germany's expansionist plans in Ukraine, was well aware of Wilhelm's monarchist pretensions. If Ukraine was to be a revisionist ally of Lincoln and his White International, the revisionist alliance would need someone who had a record in Ukraine and was still popular there. This logic led the White International to search for Wilhelm in Vienna.

In that summer of 1920, Wilhelm, like Lincoln, was in a watching and waiting mood. He had reached Vienna from Bucharest in March, tired, poor, and probably more than a little confused. He could no longer reside, as he had in the past, in his father's palace on the Wiedner Hauptstrasse. He was not in touch with Stefan; and the building in any event had been nationalized by the Austrian Republic. Wilhelm had no citizenship in this new Austria, and indeed no right to attain it. One of the very first acts of the republic was to ban members of the former dynasty from Austria unless they renounced their claims of succession to the monarchy. This Wilhelm never did—and yet he installed himself in Vienna. Both Vienna and Austria were governed by Social Democrats at the time, and the authorities left him alone. Perhaps he was still seen as red by some, and as a prince by others.

Wilhelm took some time to find his way. He lived on the modest pension he still received, despite his retirement, from the Ukrainian National Republic. No one seemed to know where he passed his nights, but he lunched almost every day at the Café Reichsrat—a few feet from the parliament that had passed the law forbidding his presence. He passed his time quietly, in a corner, waiting for propositions. He had hardly been forgotten. Gossip swirled around him, a Habsburg prince and a Ukrainian pretender, a champion of two causes whose time, it seemed, had passed. Though Wilhelm spoke little about his own plans, more than a few of his fellow Viennese were happy to remind journalists of his recent exploits. As a foreign journalist recalled at the end of March, writing of Wilhelm's Ukrainian dream: "the man had ideas!"[12]

That summer, Wilhelm in Vienna was reaching the same conclusions as Lincoln and the German conspirators in Munich. They were all awaiting the outcome of the Polish-Bolshevik War, with the thought that the disruption of the Red Army could be used to provoke a counterrevolution from the right. After the experiences of Hungary and Bavaria, this plan could not be called irrational. It required a catastrophe, but after the slaughter of the First World War, with its twenty million dead, another disaster was easy to imagine. By August 1920, the Red Army was at the gates of Warsaw, the Polish capital. For the White International, as for Wilhelm, this was a moment of desperate hope. Colonel Bauer reasoned that the moment the Red Army destroyed Poland the White International should launch a counterattack against Russia from Germany, Austria, Hungary, and Ukraine. He worked frantically to bring Wilhelm into the conspiracy.[13]

More than the Germans, Wilhelm was in a conflicted position. The White International plot could only work after the defeat of the Polish army, the destruction of the Polish state, and the likely execution of his family. If the Bolsheviks took Poland, Habsburgs would be killed as class enemies. His brothers Albrecht and Leo, veterans of the Habsburg army, were now serving in the Polish army. They could be murdered by Bolshevik irregulars for that reason as well. If Poland was doomed in any case, Wilhelm seems to have reckoned, at least an independent Ukraine might arise. He was willing to take that chance. In August, as his brothers defended Warsaw, his secretary Eduard Larischenko told the Germans that Wilhelm's services were available. Then, to Wilhelm's surprise, the Polish army achieved a miracle. A daring counterattack at Warsaw drove Bolshevik forces from Poland. This Polish victory was the most important turning point in European history since the beginning of the First World War. In a sense, it was only at the gates of Warsaw in August 1920 that the First World War came to an end. War had brought revolution, and revolution had brought more war. Only with the Polish victory at Warsaw did the revolutionary war of the Bolsheviks lose its impetus, and only there did the new European order, represented by new republics such as Poland, successfully defend itself.[14]

The Red Army would spread no revolution across Europe, as Lenin and the Bolsheviks had hoped. Without revolution, there could be no counterrevolution. The White International collapsed. Trebitsch Lincoln abandoned his friends in September 1920, stealing the organization's archive and selling choice documents to the press.

Poland would survive. Wilhelm's family would survive. His brothers could celebrate peace and victory. After five years of war, as Habsburg and then Polish officers, Leo and Albrecht could return to their father's estate. They had proven themselves as Poles in the clearest way possible, risking their lives on the battlefield. Now Wilhelm's eldest brother, Albrecht, could make good on his plans to take a Polish wife.

Albrecht's fiancée was Alice Ancarkrona, the daughter of the Swedish king's master of the hunt. Like Albrecht, she was a Pole by choice.

Alice had come to her Polish identity through her first husband, some ten years before. At a ball in Stockholm, she had met the Pole Ludwik Badeni, a rich and handsome Habsburg diplomat. Knowing her to be an excellent rider, Badeni asked her how to gallop across ice. It was the perfect question, since she sought throughout her entire life to unify grace and daring. They were married in 1911, sailing for a honeymoon through the fjords on a boat bedecked with flowers. She bore him a son. But Ludwik then fell ill, lost his mind, and was consigned to an insane asylum.

In 1915 in Vienna, dressed informally and carrying toys for her little boy, Alice was introduced to Albrecht, at a tea. It was love at first sight. A man and a woman who had chosen Poland chose each other. Yet they could not court; Albrecht had to return to the front, and Alice's husband was still alive. After Ludwik Badeni died in 1916, Alice decided to move to her late husband's estate in eastern Galicia.

In autumn 1918, as the tides of war were turning, Albrecht prevailed upon her to return to Vienna. He knew that Wilhelm's comrades were planning to claim eastern Galicia for an independent Ukrainian state. She got as far as Lviv, where she was trapped by the Ukrainian uprising of 1 November. Alice managed to slip back to her Galician estate, which was soon surrounded by Ukrainian partisans. Alice knew how to talk to Ukrainians, and indeed liked them a great deal. With no one to help her but an English governess, she negotiated with the men who had appeared at her doorstep with the thought of seizing, at the very least, her possessions. She lost some of these, but she and her young son survived. In 1919 Albrecht found her and her boy, and took them both to the safety of Cracow.[15]

By then Albrecht was no longer a Habsburg but a Polish officer, fighting in the Polish-Bolshevik War. Alice was to be his reward; when the war was over, the two of them could marry. Alice was by no means of royal origin, so the match was unequal by Habsburg rules. Yet by now the Habsburg monarchy was no more. She was a noblewoman who had become Polish, but she was no Polish aristocrat, so the marriage also fell foul of Stefan's political principles. By 1920, however, Stefan had no hope of claiming a Polish crown. He was simply happy that his new daughter-in-law spoke perfect Polish.

Alice Ancarkrona

Identity had transcended ambition. The man wanted Polish grandsons. Alice and Albrecht were married on 18 November 1920 at the castle at Żywiec, he in his Polish officer's uniform, she in a dress of white and grey.[16]

Albrecht was now, beyond any doubt, the good son, the most Polish of the children. He was the only son to find a Polish bride (of sorts), and thus the only one who might continue the line of the Polish Habsburgs. Leo, too, had served with great distinction in the Polish Army, and wished to marry; but his fiancée was Austrian, the noblewoman Maria Montjoye, known as Maja. He would marry her two years later, in October 1922, at St. Stephen's Cathedral in Vienna. This marriage was acceptable, but no cause for celebration. Wilhelm was Ukrainian, and had been seen with Ukrainian women. In Vienna a young musician named Maria was thought to be his girlfriend. But Wilhelm seemed not to be the marrying type.

A break was coming. Stefan the Polish father and Wilhelm the Ukrainian son could live in harmony in a Europe of multinational monarchy, but not in the new Europe of national republics. Wilhelm's ambitions could be reconciled with those of his father so long as the Habsburgs had reigned and a Habsburg emperor dreamed of Polish and Ukrainian crownlands. When the monarchy was shattered, Wilhelm and his father found themselves, suddenly, representing the irreconcilable interests of nations at war for territory. In late 1918 Wilhelm had sided with the Ukrainians in a war with Poland for eastern Galicia. In late 1919 he had left the Ukrainian National Republic because it planned to ally with Poland. Then, in summer 1920, he had staked his own political future upon the complete destruction of Poland, and quite likely the death of his family, at the hands of the Bolsheviks. Wilhelm had not been home since 1918, and he had not spoken to his father.

Wilhelm did not attend Albrecht's wedding. He must have felt weak and humiliated. His Ukraine had fallen into the disgrace of an alliance with Poland. His brother Albrecht's Poland was victorious, and, as Wilhelm had predicted, in its victory had betrayed its Ukrainian ally. Poland had built no independent Ukraine after its defeat of the Bolsheviks. Instead, it had settled for an armistice, and would soon place the Ukrainian soldiers who had defended Warsaw in internment camps. Wilhelm, in allying himself with the losing side, had placed himself beyond the family succession. He must have seen that the Polish children from the marriage of his Polish brother to a very beautiful woman would be his father's heirs. He had rejected his father's political legacy and now found himself on the margins of the family itself, alone in Vienna, as his family gathered in Żywiec. He took aim at Poland, and at his father.

In an interview in a Viennese newspaper on 9 January 1921, Wilhelm presented Poland and Poles as behaving dishonorably. "Megalomania," he said, "seems to have become endemic in that country." Pointing to a pogrom of Jews in Lviv that took place under Polish occupation, he asked whether "a civilized country would do such a thing?" He spoke of eastern Galicia, whose occupation by Poland had been accepted by the Entente, as a "purely Ukrainian land."[17]

Stefan's response was swift and dismissive. On 31 January 1921 he drafted a newspaper article for several European newspapers, declaring that Wilhelm's "relations with home had been broken." In a reply of 18 February, Wilhelm expressed his astonishment that his father had aligned himself so closely with Poland, a country that had betrayed the dynasty to whom it had pledged loyalty (he meant the Habsburgs) as well as the country whose fate was in its hands (he meant Ukraine).[18]

Wilhelm's father was truly offended. Before the war, Stefan and Wilhelm's sense of honor had been invested in the Habsburg dynasty, even as they took steps to improve their own position in it. During the war they had discussed the boundaries of Poland and Ukraine, as good Habsburgs, as father and son. Now, in a Europe of nations, the interests of Poland and Ukraine were truly distinct, as were the commitments of father and son. The nation, not the dynasty, was suddenly a matter of honor. Wilhelm had chosen to call his father's honor into question. He could not expect to be welcomed again, so long as his father lived, at the castle in Żywiec.

More was at stake, though, than love and honor. A family fortune also hung in the balance. When Albrecht married Alice in November 1918, the castle and the entire family estate were legally the property of the Polish state, which had nationalized everything. As Stefan and Albrecht worked furiously to regain the property, Wilhelm's Ukrainian record was a constant hindrance. Stefan had to distance himself from his renegade youngest son if he wanted to have any hope of keeping his property. In a petition to the Polish government, he wrote that "no one can say that he took any moral or material part in the alleged activities of his youngest son Wilhelm." Albrecht claimed in some self-published family propaganda that "both sons" were Polish officers (conveniently denying Wilhelm's existence) while "both daughters" had married Poles (conveniently denying the existence of Eleanora, who had married Kloss, an Austrian).[19]

In the end, the Polish Habsburgs struck a deal with the new Polish authorities. Stefan and Maria Theresia and the four children resident in Poland were granted Polish citizenship in August 1921. Stefan gave 10,000 hectares to the Polish state in 1923, and was granted the remaining 40,000 hectares by presidential decree in

1924. His sons Albrecht and Leo and their families could live in prosperity in independent Poland. His daughters Renata and Mechtildis, married to Polish aristocrats, also enjoyed enviable positions. Even Eleanora, who had married a commoner, was not excluded from the family wealth, at least not by her father. Italy had seized Stefan's yacht as war booty, and his villas in Istria as the property of the defunct dynasty. In order to keep the Italian possessions in the family, Stefan attempted to deed them to Eleanora and her husband Alfons Kloss. Kloss, once the captain of Stefan's yachts, now had frequent occasion to write to his father-in-law. His letters invariably began: "Dear Papa."[20]

Wilhelm wrote no letters to his papa. At the age of twenty-five, he severed himself from all paternal authority. During Wilhelm's years at war, his father's authority had been eclipsed by that of a series of Ukrainian father figures. Now, even as he broke with his father, he lost them all. Baron Huzhkovsky, his first Ukrainian mentor, had died in 1918. Father Bonne, his Catholic companion in Ukraine, had moved to Rome in 1919 to serve as the envoy of the Ukrainian National Republic to the Vatican. Metropolitan Sheptytsky, his most important collaborator, journeyed west in early 1920 to gain funds for the Ukrainian cause.

The very same newspaper article that provoked the family quarrel also alienated Wilhelm from the Ukrainian National Republic, the Kiev state Wilhelm had briefly served in autumn 1919 and then abandoned. He was formally still an officer in its army when he publicly criticized its alliance with Poland, which he called "unnatural." Mykola Vasylko, Wilhelm's ally at the Bread Peace negotiations, asked Wilhelm to recant. When Wilhelm refused, he lost contact with Vasylko and his position in the Ukrainian National Republic. He had now lost all of his prominent Ukrainian friends, and his only official Ukrainian position. As of March 1921, he no longer received a pension. He now had no source of income.[21]

The final candidate for paternal authority was a former rival: Pavlo Skoropadsky, the former hetman of Ukraine who in 1920 founded a Ukrainian monarchist movement. Wilhelm saw an opening. Everyone knew that Wilhelm had been more popular than Skoropadsky in Ukraine in 1918. If Skoropadsky wanted to trade on his record of 1918 to gain further support from Germany, he would have to deal somehow with Wilhelm's legacy. Wilhelm, for his part, had reasons to come to terms with Skoropadsky. The former hetman had relations with important Germans, whom Wilhelm wanted as allies. In May 1920, the two men began to speak about a future division of authority in a future Ukraine.[22]

In January 1921, the two Ukrainian pretenders struck a deal. In a future Ukraine, Skoropadsky would be hetman of central and eastern Ukraine, eastern Galicia would be an autonomous district, and Wilhelm would be king of the whole country. The terms were perhaps less strange than they seemed. The Ukrainian cause had been hurt in 1919 by the division of the country into two entities: the Ukrainian National Republic (formed from lands of the former Russian Empire) and the West Ukrainian National Republic (created from former Habsburg territories). The creation of a Ukrainian monarchy under Wilhelm would be one way, at least notionally, of bringing the country together, of overcoming the old border between the Habsburg and Russian empires, of imagining Ukraine as one vast and unified state.

The scheme did have some German backing. Certain German politicians and military officers believed that Ukraine could again become what it had been during the war, a barrier to Bolshevism and a way to keep Poland small, weak, and dependent. Wilhelm met with Skoropadsky's representatives and officers of the German general staff in Vienna in March 1921. The German officers proposed that the Ukrainian General Council, an organization Wilhelm had formed in Vienna, be transformed into a proto-government. They gave clear hints that Germany would support a movement to create an independent Ukraine.[23]

Wilhelm had returned to center stage, which he seemed unable to share. He needed father figures, people to imitate and adore, but he also needed to be the dashing young man in charge. Skoropadsky, a proud and jealous man, had little sense of how to pacify his younger ally. Wilhelm broke with Skoropadsky in April 1921. He had come to believe, falsely, that Skoropadsky's followers were secretly supported by Poland. He maintained, perhaps sincerely, that he found Skoropadsky's monarchism insufficiently democratic. Wilhelm imagined that a king would be needed until the will of the people could be ascertained. Of course, Wilhelm thought that the Ukrainian people, given a chance, would proclaim him their king. So once again the two men were rivals.

In that spring and summer of 1921, as Ukrainian patriots had little cause for hope, they clutched at every straw. Wilhelm and Skoropadsky represented the two Ukrainian monarchies, the shabby Hetmanate of recent reality and the fanciful Habsburg realm of dreams. Ukrainian veterans of all the lost wars spread rumors of the two pretenders' reconciliation through Vienna: Wilhelm was to marry Skoropadsky's daughter and found a Ukrainian dynasty. Those who knew Wilhelm understood that such a marriage was unlikely. Though he had a Ukrainian girlfriend of sorts, his closest companion remained his secretary, Eduard Larischenko. It was Eduard, according to the Austrian police, who played the "leading role" in monarchist propaganda proposing Wilhelm as the king of Ukraine.

Wilhelm now seemed uncertain how to proceed. He had his Ukrainian General Council, and he had founded a veterans' organization. Yet was this a gesture towards the future, or towards the past? He wrote to friends of emigration, and spoke of living in the United States. His separation from all previous guides had left him unsure of his course.[24]

Fortunately for Wilhelm, nothing worked better in Ukrainian politics than rebellion; and in 1921, Wilhelm's refusal to collaborate with Poland brought him new popularity among Ukrainians. As Wilhelm had expected, Poland disappointed the soldiers of its Ukrainian ally, the Ukrainian National Republic. In the final peace treaty after the Polish-Bolshevik War, made at Riga in March 1921, Poland divided Ukrainian territory with the Soviets, leaving Ukrainian soldiers who had defended Warsaw in internment camps. In their misery, many of these soldiers then remembered Wilhelm, who now looked like a political thinker of realism and foresight. Perhaps

Wilhelm was indeed the man who could wash them clean of the stain of the Polish alliance, and bring them victory in a new war with the Bolsheviks.

In April 1921 a Ukrainian intellectual, Ievhen Chykalenko, developed the appropriate ideological justification for crowning Wilhelm king of Ukraine. The fiascos of the past few years, he argued in the Ukrainian émigré newspaper *Volia,* had shown that Ukrainians were unable to produce their own leaders. Chykalenko noted that the Ukrainian capital of Kiev, and its associated medieval civilization, had been founded by Vikings from Scandinavia, known traditionally as "Varangians." What Ukraine now needed, he wrote, was another foreign ruler, a new "Varangian," to begin a new ruling dynasty. Every reader knew that the dynasty was to be the Habsburgs, and that the new Varangian was to be Wilhelm.

Rumors flew of a Habsburg Ukraine. A new dynasty could arise, Ukraine would be the fatherland of the fatherless, and Wilhelm could compensate for his alienation from his Polish family by beginning a Ukrainian line. Wilhelm had hope, he had support, he had a goal: an independent Ukrainian monarchy. Every other Ukrainian leader had failed; perhaps it was, after all the disappointment, his destiny to succeed.[25]

All he would need was a powerful backer. For a glittering moment, it seemed that this might be Emperor Karl, restored to the Habsburg thrones.

Like an awaited echo, not quite the past and not quite the future, the Habsburg name still quickened the senses of leaders of the new Europe of republics, as a promise or as a threat. Many of those who imagined Wilhelm as ruler of a Habsburg Ukraine in spring 1921 also expected a Habsburg restoration in central Europe generally, a hope that hung on the recently dethroned Emperor Karl. He was alive and well, still full of ambition and vigor, and had never formally abdicated any of the Habsburg thrones. From his place of exile in Switzerland, he considered not so much whether to try to restore himself to the thrones, but rather with which of them to begin. Austria, the obvious choice, had become a republic. Its constitution forbade a restoration of the monarchy, and indeed banned Habsburgs who did not renounce their claims to the succession from entering the country. Karl's thoughts turned then to Hungary, which was still a kingdom, one seemingly awaiting its king.

Karl made his move in March 1921. Leaving his family in Switzerland, he made his way to Strasbourg, France. There he met a confederate, who furnished him with a rail ticket and a Spanish passport. On Good Friday, Karl, dressed in a plain suit and carrying a walking stick, took a place in the Vienna express. The next day he was met by another accomplice at the Westbahnhof. The two men took a taxi to a Vienna residence. Karl left his walking stick in the cab. By the time the Viennese police identified its owner, Karl was across the Hungarian border.

Holding power in Budapest as regent was Admiral Miklós Horthy, a man who owed everything to the Habsburgs. He had sailed around the world at the orders of Archduke Maximilian, served as aide-de-camp to Emperor Franz Josef, and sailed to Spain with Archduke Stefan. During a naval mutiny of 1918, Stefan had recommended to Karl that Horthy, then only a captain, be promoted to admiral and placed in command of the entire Habsburg fleet. This Karl had done. After defeat had destroyed the Habsburg monarchy, Horthy had returned to his native Hungary. Now regent of Hungary, he was gracious to the man who had been his sovereign and had made his career. Horthy promised not to rest until he had restored Karl to his Hungarian throne.

On Easter Sunday, 1921, Karl reached the Royal Palace at Budapest, where he was received by Horthy. The greeting was not what he expected. "This is a calamity," announced Horthy. "Your Majesty must go away at once." Karl had little choice. Horthy claimed that a restoration in Hungary would bring an invasion from the countries that had gained Hungarian territory at the Paris peace settlements, Czechoslovakia and Romania. Karl tried again in October 1921, this time with his wife Zita and the support of some Hungarian soldiers, and was again defeated. Karl and Zita then sailed down the Danube, across the Mediterranean, through the Straits of Gibraltar, into exile on the Atlantic island of Madeira.[26]

Wilhelm remained a seeker of power, the lone Habsburg who could yet hope to rule a kingdom. Having observed Karl's first failure from Vienna, Wilhelm understood that any further attempt to revise the postwar order would need rich and powerful partners. In June 1921, he believed that he had found some in Bavaria, amidst a German revisionist triangle. On one side were Colonel Bauer and General Ludendorff, the authoritarian officer and his wartime master, still wearing their uniforms and spiked helmets. The two men were what was left of the White International, still conspiring, without Lincoln, in Munich. In summer 1921 they regarded Ukraine as the weakest point in the European order, where a timely blow might start a general counterrevolution.

On the second side of the triangle were the German militias, the outlaws and orphans of the postwar peace treaties. The Versailles Treaty limited the number of men Germany could legally keep under arms, which forced the German government to try to disarm the various paramilitary organizations formed by dissatisfied veterans. When the militias were banned, Bavarian militiamen had gone underground to join the shadowy Pittinger Organization. Otto Pittinger and his backers were the third side of the triangle. Pittinger, an important figure in Bavarian politics, was able to raise a good deal of money by promising to revise the postwar settlements. Some of his investors saw this revision as the unification, or *Anschluss*, of Germany and Austria; others believed in the destruction of Bolshevik Russia and the creation of a Ukraine friendly to German investors.[27]

In July 1921, Wilhelm began to take money from the Pittinger Organization. Bauer moved to Vienna the following month, to mediate between the Bavarian money and Ukrainian ambition. He and Wilhelm became friends. Wilhelm was to use his monthly subsidy of 130,000 marks from the Bavarians to improve his own political standing among Ukrainians. He began by distributing aid to needy Ukrainian veterans. Then he established a new Ukrainian paramilitary based in Vienna, the Free Cossacks, whose members were meant to endorse a military resolution to the Ukrainian question, without being too curious about the political details. The Austrian police estimated that forty thousand Ukrainians joined the group. This figure, although cited ever since, is very likely inflated. Nevertheless, it conveys Wilhelm's popularity as a military commander, and the fears he aroused among the forces of order.

In October 1921, Wilhelm founded his own newspaper, whose masthead featured a Ukrainian peasant with a hammer and sickle proclaiming, "Ukrainians of All Lands, Unite!" Wilhelm, still a socialist, was consciously echoing the call of Marx and Engels in their *Communist Manifesto*, "Workers of the World Unite!" With these gestures, he made it clear that his monarchism was of the left and communicated that his vision of Ukraine included not only the lands controlled by the Soviets but also east Galicia, occupied by Poland. Through the newspaper, Wilhelm proclaimed the same political program as ever: that a liberated Ukraine would call a constituent assembly to decide upon the form of the Ukrainian state. Democracy could and should, however, lead to a monarchy. His newspaper argued that a European state ruled by a "modern monarch" held more promise for durable democracy than a republic.[28]

Wilhelm's German backers thought they knew how to get the modern monarch into Ukraine. Even as Wilhelm indulged in communist imagery, they made plans that smacked of the most brazen capitalist imperialism. The model was a German syndicate known as Aufbau, the creation of Max Erwin Scheubner-Richter. Aufbau's business plan was to sell investors shares that could only yield returns after a future war. Their money would finance an invasion of Bolshevik Russia; the invasion would create new political regimes, which would then offer investors trade concessions. Taking Aufbau as the model, Wilhelm founded a Ukrainian syndicate. He sold shares against the promise of future preferential trade access to Ukraine. The money raised by selling shares was meant to finance the army that would liberate the country.[29]

Wilhelm pursued this scheme with energy. He had little head for numbers, but he did know how to promise everything to everybody. He made the rounds in western Europe, seeking investors. He sought publicity for his scheme, and had no trouble finding it. His was a famous name, and he knew how to get attention. The press reported that he told American Jews that his future Ukraine would be a "promised land" of east European Jewry. Wilhelm had something of a philosemitic past. His favorite teacher at the military academy in Wiener-Neustadt had been Jewish, as was his favorite doctor during the war. He had broken with the Ukrainian National Republic during the worst of the pogroms in Ukraine, and he had criticized Poland for a pogrom in Lviv. Still, one might wonder at the audacity of a man who took money from Bavarian anti-Semites to bring Zion to Ukraine.[30]

The Ukrainian syndicate was subordinate to the Bavarian scheme. Wilhelm was doing his part to raise men and money, but the Germans saw his efforts as part of a larger multinational alliance subordinate to German leadership. In autumn 1921, the German plotters imagined that Ludendorff would be the overall commander of an invasion force made up of militiamen of various nationalities. Ludendorff deluded himself that two million men, Germans, Ukrainians, and other revisionist allies, would somehow fill the ranks of this army. The army, when formed, would invade Bolshevik Russia, eliminate communism in Europe, remake the postwar order, and create a Ukrainian state. Ludendorff imagined Wilhelm as a future leader of Ukraine. It appears that the two of them cooperated in the smuggling of arms to Ukrainians in eastern Galicia.

Wilhelm spent the autumn and winter of 1921 recruiting soldiers to invade Ukraine the following spring. He traveled from internment camp to internment camp, from city to city, offering Ukrainian soldiers another chance at liberating their country. He spoke of a "Green International," a socialist Ukraine of workers and peasants, ruled by a monarch. Once they were issued a horse, a rifle, and the clothing needed to disguise themselves as foresters, recruits were sent to Bavaria for training. Wilhelm was also in touch with German colonists in Ukraine, who promised to help liberate "our dear fatherland" the coming spring.[31]

It was hard to recruit thousands of men for a springtime invasion of Bolshevik Russia without attracting a certain amount of attention. The Austrian press wrote of Wilhelm as the man of the future in Ukraine. French intelligence called him the unquestioned leader of Ukrainians. The Bolshevik secret service noted his successful recruitment of Ukrainian veterans in Czechoslovakia. Czechoslovak spies, going a bit over the top, reported that Wilhelm was part of a grand monarchical plot backed by the Vatican. Polish intelligence, perhaps the best informed, saw in Wilhelm a viable candidate for a Ukrainian throne, and knew that he would have support in eastern Galicia. Those who had reason to know and care saw a return of Wilhelm to Ukraine as a real and frightening possibility.[32]

The Ukrainian National Republic saw Wilhelm as a rival. After its failure to liberate Ukraine in alliance with Poland, the Ukrainian National Republic was nothing more than a government in exile in Poland, dependent upon Polish funding. Its leaders, too, wanted to organize a military intervention in Soviet Ukraine, to restore themselves to power. Their Polish orientation made them impossible allies for Wilhelm. He also clearly wanted to be a Ukrainian monarch, a goal that was incompatible with the establishment of a republic. In September 1921, Wilhelm rejected an offer of collaboration from the Ukrainian National Republic. Its leadership then decided to discredit him abroad. The order went out to tell western governments and investors that Wilhelm was "an unknown figure," precisely because the opposite was true. Wilhelm's Ukrainian rivals knew that Ukrainian veterans paid more attention to him than to any other commander.[33]

The leaders of the Ukrainian National Republic then did the one thing certain to discredit the idea of a covert plan to invade Bolshevik Russia: they executed one themselves. With the aid of the Polish and Romanian governments, a few thousand Ukrainians slipped east across the border on 4 November 1921. In Soviet Ukraine, they found a local population weary of war and hungry after a year of famine, and a Red Army waiting fully prepared for their arrival. Bolshevik agents had uncovered their plans. The Ukrainian forces were cut to pieces in a series of brief battles. The Bolsheviks executed the prisoners of war, burned down some villages, and claimed the easy victory.

The Ukrainian National Republic had not meant to undermine Wilhelm, only to anticipate his next move. After the fiasco of November 1921, however, Bavarian investors no longer believed that the Bolsheviks could be defeated by a military incursion. Pittinger, still in Munich, ceased his payments to Wilhelm in February 1922. Wilhelm's newspaper closed down in May, and his Free Cossacks split into factions. Wilhelm's alliance with the Germans came undone.[34]

Without their Ukrainian allies, the Germans quarreled among themselves. Bauer, who believed that the Ukrainian project had a future, was enraged at Pittinger. Wilhelm did indeed have support among Ukrainian partisans, and would for some time. Bauer wrote to Ludendorff that the end of the Bavarian subsidy to Wilhelm was "crushing, since the entire Ukrainian undertaking, with its ever more remarkable journal, its press service, and its connections to Ukraine were built only with and were entirely dependent upon Bavarian help." He complained to Ludendorff that the Ukrainians would remember "German perfidy."[35]

The German nationalists then went their own ways, Pittinger concentrating on Bavaria, Bauer supporting an Austrian monarchist movement, and Ludendorff moving closer to the German National Socialist movement—the Nazis. In April 1922, Germany signed a treaty with Bolshevik Russia. Ukrainian hopes for national liberation, increasingly desperate, were now exhausted. The Germans and Habsburgs had abandoned the Ukrainian National Republic in 1918. The victorious allies had not brought self-determination. Poland allied with the Ukrainian National Republic in 1919, but had not brought independence to any part of Ukraine. Then came the last throw, cooperation with Germans against Bolshevik Russia. By now the revisionists had abandoned their invasion plans, and the German state had accepted the reality of Soviet power.

What would Wilhelm do? He had completed his rebellion against authority, breaking with his father to found his own monarchy, then striving for restored Habsburg power in implicit rivalry with his former sovereign Karl. Wilhelm had struck out on his own, and made his own compromises. By the time he was done, there was no one left to judge him, no one against whom to struggle. He had forced his way through an unlocked door, to find only emptiness on the other side. His former sovereign Karl, who had given Wilhelm his chance in Ukraine, fell ill and died in exile on Madeira in April 1922. His father Stefan, who had raised Wilhelm to be a ruler of Poland, suffered a terrible stroke in 1923. He lost the use of his legs, and then his ability to read and write. Wilhelm could no longer make amends with his father, even had he so wished. Along with the Habsburgs had fallen their ambitions. Ukraine was Soviet; Poland was a republic; Austria was stripped of empire; Hungary had rejected its Habsburg king.

Who would Wilhelm be? It was not easy to be a young Habsburg at this moment. Wilhelm had come of age in an age that would not come to him. The past was suddenly illegible, the future unknown. Wilhelm had lost the easy assurance that time was an eternity of royal blue—or at least a green maturation to power, or a bloody red march to victory. He had learned to think instrumentally, and had become an instrument. His only success was to strengthen the white politics of the moment, a European counterrevolution that was already turning brown at the edges. In a Europe where republics could not count on the support of the west and where Bolshevism had conquered the east, the idea of Ukrainian liberation had led Wilhelm to German revisionists of the far right. Two of Wilhelm's German partners would march with Hitler in his first attempt to seize power, the Munich Beer Hall Putsch of 1923.[36]

The Nazi movement was national self-determination run wild, perverted by a defeat misunderstood, poisoned by racial mysticism. Hitler failed to come to power, but a year earlier Benito Mussolini had brought his fascist movement to power in Rome. Italy was actually a victor in the First World War, but his fascists claimed that it needed more territory nonetheless. National self-determination was no longer a principle to be applied once at war's end by the victorious powers, but rather the continuous struggle of Nazis and fascists to remake their nations in the turbulence of mass mobilization and the violence of new war. Though the victors would never admit this, self-determination had been corrupted from the beginning by considerations of power. Now fascists or Nazis would seek the power they needed to remake Europe as they saw fit, speaking of national justice and national rights all the while.

Self-determination was murky not only in practice but also in principle. It assumed that nations were like individuals, with rights that could somehow be fulfilled. But then what about the actual individuals, and their individual rights as such? Wilhelm was an especially colorful character, but he was one of millions of east Europeans whose nationality could not easily be defined. A Habsburg, he represented a complex social reality that self-determination denied. The old Europe of multinational empires had left much room for ambiguity about national identity, an ambiguity that allowed for a certain kind of human freedom. If national identity is conferred by birth or by the state, it hardly liberates the individual. If nationality is instead recognized to be a matter of evolution or conviction, it can permit the individual to grow and change. Nationality, then as now, was a messy business, very often a choice personal as well as political, sometimes wet like young bodies full of life, sometimes dry like the ink of signatures on treaties.

In summer 1922, when all of his allies had gone, Wilhelm could no longer sit at the Café Reichsrat and wait for propositions. He had accepted too many already. Bauer had given him some money at the end of the Bavarian adventure. Wilhelm, with no profession and no relations with his rich father, perhaps thought it most judicious to leave Austria while he had some cash in his pocket.[37] He had no citizenship, no legal identity, and no passport. He procured a blank Austrian passport and made a certain decision. In November 1922, he left the country under his Ukrainian name, Vasyl Vyshyvanyi.

LILAC

~

Gay Paris

ITH NO FUNDS and no army to fight the Bolsheviks, in
November 1922 Wilhelm made for Madrid, where he could
expect a warm welcome from his extended family. The king of
Spain, Alfonso XIII, was a Habsburg on his mother's side, and Wilhelm's first cousin. Maria Christina, Alfonso's mother and Wilhelm's aunt, had ruled as regent during Alfonso's childhood. In
Spain, Wilhelm could reassure himself that he belonged to a family
that could still rule. He would hope to make some money, conspire
if possible in a Habsburg restoration, and try, somehow, to sustain
his Ukrainian dream.

Not long before Wilhelm, Empress Zita had arrived in Madrid.
Emperor Karl's death had left her without a husband, without an
empire, and without a home, exiled on Madeira with seven children
and pregnant with an eighth. King Alfonso of Spain took Zita under
his care. He sent a Spanish warship for Zita and the children and
met them at the train station in Madrid. Zita was thirty, and Wilhelm was only twenty-seven; these two Habsburgs still had a future
to imagine for themselves, even if the recent past had brought great
sadness.

Alfonso and Maria Christina were gentle hosts, soothing spirits
at a time of heartbreak. Zita had lost her husband and her empire.
Maria Cristina, whose favorite pastime was gathering lilies and violets, admired Zita's brood of young archduchesses and archdukes.

Wilhelm had lost his Ukrainian dream and his close relationship with his father. Alfonso tried to make peace within Wilhelm's branch of the Habsburg family. Understanding that Wilhelm's Ukrainian career had put Stefan's Polish property at risk, Alfonso intervened with the Polish government on Stefan's behalf, promising a friendly Spanish policy to Poland if Stefan were allowed to keep his estate.[1]

Here in Madrid, the exiled Habsburgs might find respite, and plan some kind of restoration of their monarchy. Yet, even as Wilhelm and Zita watched, monarchism came under threat, even in conservative and Catholic Spain. In 1923, General Miguel Primo de Rivera overthrew the Spanish parliamentary system. Alfonso supported the coup and continued to reign, although Primo de Rivera and his associates held real power.

Like Benito Mussolini in Italy the year before, Primo de Rivera preserved the monarchy, but created an authoritarian regime to govern the country. In Italy the transformation of monarchy was legitimated by the idea of fascism, a cult of Mussolini as leader and a worship of the nation, in Spain by a collective military dictatorship that promised reform and a future return to normality. What united Spain and Italy was the displacement of royal authority by military force and individual charisma, by men of the right, without the abolition of the monarchy. Monarchs lingered in the background, hiding their uncertainty about the future behind bravado or propriety.[2]

Wilhelm, who had charm and tact but little strategic sense, did not see the contradiction between dictatorship and monarchy. He assumed that his authoritarian benefactors would somehow become his inferiors after he became king. His allies in the Ukrainian syndicate and the Bavarian invasion plan had taken the opposite view. Colonel Max Bauer, his close associate in Vienna, believed that the role of monarchs was to prepare the way for dictators.

Wilhelm and Bauer remained friendly; at Wilhelm's suggestion, King Alfonso invited Bauer to Madrid in 1924 to reform the Spanish army. With Bauer came Josef Piegl, a monarchist Austrian engineer who had once helped Wilhelm raise money in Vienna. Another member of their organization, Friedrich von Wiesner, remained in

Vienna. Wiesner, a lawyer and a diplomat, had been a trusted servant of Emperors Franz Josef and Karl. He founded, in Vienna, an organization to prepare the way for the replacement of the Austrian republic with a monarchy. Under Alfonso's care, adventurous relations joined Wilhelm in Madrid. One of these was the Infante Fernando, who was a first cousin to both Alfonso and Wilhelm and whom Wilhelm called "Nando."[3]

At a certain point, royal insouciance gives way to human frivolity. Wilhelm liked carousing with Nando and Alfonso, but a shadow hung over his plans. Trebitsch Lincoln, who had disappeared in 1920 with the archive of the White International, had another trick to play on Wilhelm.

After his stint as a German nationalist, Lincoln had made his way to China, where he sold arms and advice to local warlords. Lincoln had somehow convinced Bauer that China was the coming market for firearms and reactionary politics. Bauer left for China in 1927, and Piegl followed in 1929. In this way, men who were first dedicated to a German dictatorship and then to a Habsburg restoration found themselves in Beijing advising the Chinese nationalist leader Chiang Kai-Shek. Bauer died in 1929, and Piegl disappeared from the scene. Lincoln himself had one more life left. He was ordained as a Buddhist monk in 1931, and spent the rest of his days collecting European and North American acolytes—and their worldly possessions. He died of natural causes in Manchuria in 1943.[4]

Needing money, Wilhelm had a go at exploiting the booming Spanish economy of the late 1920s. Wilhelm was a relative of the Spanish king, and Alfonso was himself the backer of a great deal of state investment. Wilhelm and his cousin Nando seem to have brokered some arms deals—perhaps selling the surplus that remained after Wilhelm's failed plan to invade Bolshevik Russia. Wilhelm sought to broker a loan for the construction of a dam in Austria, but without success. He and Nando took an interest in the aeronautics industry, trying to mediate in an arrangement whereby German civilian aircraft would be converted to military use by German engineers in Spain. This scheme would have enabled Germany to circumvent limitations on rearmament imposed by the Treaty of

Versailles. Wilhelm also sought foreign investment for Spanish road-ways, mines, and real estate development.[5]

Something scuppered almost every deal. Usually the problem was Wilhelm himself. His only business assets were his good looks, dress sense, and last name. His only business skill was acquainting capital with investment propositions. He was usually unable to formalize his role in any transactions that followed. His letters reveal no incli-nation to make calculations or consider risks; he reckoned people as rich or very rich, propositions as promising or very promising, and so on. Never having had to think about money before, he lacked fi-nancial discernment, or really even the sense that economics has laws beyond those of human personal relations.

Wilhelm's business methods revealed much about his priorities. Once, for example, he brought a group of rich American speculators to Madrid to invest in a real estate project. He was absolutely fas-tidious about the lodging arrangements (the Ritz and the Savoy) but totally unreliable about everything else. His first priority upon his arrival with the group was spending time with Maria Christina and Nando. Then he suddenly went off to Barcelona with some friends, gave an incorrect forwarding address, and left his associates and the Americans to pick up the pieces.[6]

By the late 1920s, Wilhelm was going back and forth to Madrid from Enghien-les-Bains, a resort town not far from Paris. In 1926 he had bought himself a small villa on 5bis, rue Péligot, apparently with money that he borrowed from wealthy Hungarian aristocrats, the brothers Thomas and Moríc Esterhazy. Moríc, once a prime minister for Emperor Karl, was a monarchist. The brothers might have believed that they were supporting a candidate for some future throne. What they were allowing, at least for the time being, was a comfortable lifestyle for a Habsburg political exile.[7]

Wilhelm lived "incognito" in Enghien, just as his father had taught him, using his Ukrainian name with the French authorities. He did send telegrams to Madrid under his own name, because he had to impress people; so postal employees knew who he was, which meant that the police also knew. Although his official papers (his Austrian passport and French visa) were in his Ukrainian name, Wilhelm was known to the French authorities as a Habsburg arch-duke. His great pleasure was a little automobile. Though he never spoke to his father, the car must have been a reminder of Stefan's en-thusiasms and Wilhelm's childhood. The local police followed him from time to time as he took pleasure jaunts to Paris.[8]

Wilhelm did maintain contact with Ukrainians in Paris, among whom he was quite popular. He remained especially close to Eduard Larischenko, his personal secretary since 1918. Larischenko had been involved with the Ukrainian syndicate in Vienna, and then with Wilhelm's Madrid business. He was one of the two important men in Wilhelm's life. The other was Wilhelm's valet, a Latvian called Constant Kroll, who served in Wilhelm's Enghien household from 1926 to 1928. As the French police put matters, more or less tactfully, Wilhelm exhibited toward Kroll a "sympathy that left no doubt about the nature of their relationship." When Wilhelm trav-eled to Spain, his first concern was that his hotel room communicate directly with the room next door, and that both rooms have a bath. This was for convenient access to his male secretary. He brought a man with him when he traveled, either Larischenko or Kroll, and perhaps both.[9]

At some point Wilhelm broke with the two men. He had his rea-sons: Kroll was found guilty of handling stolen goods, and Lar-ischenko admitted to a growing affection for the Soviet Union. Wilhelm sold his house in Enghien (without paying off his debts to the Hungarian Esterhazy brothers) and in October 1931 rented an apartment in the seventeenth arrondissement of Paris, at 45, rue des Acacias. After his men left him, he lived there with his cat, which he adored.

It was a lovely neighborhood. From his door Wilhelm would have walked a few steps to the right to reach rue Carnot, and then turned left on that tree-lined boulevard to reach the Arc de Triom-phe and the Champs Elysées. Wilhelm was close to the most exclu-sive neighborhoods of right-bank Paris, a hard place to make an impression. The Paris of the day was so full of princes and pretenders that the arrival of another scarcely made a difference. Wilhelm's brother-in-law Hieronymus Radziwiłł, for example, was having a fine time in the city. Radziwiłł's presence was a bit of good fortune for Wilhelm. Once Wilhelm's brothers gained control of the family brewery from their ailing father, they made sure that Wilhelm received a twice-monthly subsidy of about 2500 French francs. Perhaps because they knew their father would disapprove, or perhaps because Wilhelm was living in Paris under an assumed name, they wired the money to him care of Radziwiłł.[10]

Many of these royals, like Wilhelm, were in exile. With time, more monarchs came calling. Radziwiłł spent his time in France playing polo with King Alfonso, who had left Spain after the declaration of a republic in April 1931. Alfonso had arrived in Paris at about the same time as his cousin Wilhelm, and cut a very fine figure among its various foreign royals. A Russian grand duke dubbed him "the manly sovereign of Europe," an opinion with which Winston Churchill was inclined to agree. Alfonso was indeed an excellent sportsman (not only polo but golf and tennis) and the sponsor of soccer clubs (among them Réal Madrid); he was also the father of ten children (seven legitimate) and the sponsor of three films (all pornographic). Like his cousin Wilhelm, he liked, as people said at the time, to motor.[11]

Friction between royal Spanish heterosexuality and prominent Parisian homosexuality led to some warm moments. On one occasion, Alfonso was in a loge of a theater with his wife and Serge Diaghilev, leader of the Ballets Russes and center of a homosexual cult of fervent admirers. Alfonso gave Diaghilev a cigar, but the ballet master, oddly enough, did not know how to smoke. He set the dress of the royal consort on fire.[12]

The man who recounted the story of the cigar was the fantastically prolific French journalist Michel Georges-Michel. A traveler and a bon vivant, Georges-Michel had known Wilhelm since childhood and counted him among his dozens of famous friends. He was friendly with all kinds of Parisian celebrities, aristocratic and *arrivés*, male and female, homosexual and less so. He was the author of countless gossipy newspaper articles, often intended to further the political or artistic careers of his favorites, as well as dozens of

INTERWAR EUROPE
1923-1938

Jonathan Wyss, Topaz Maps

books. His novels bore titles such as *The Rose of Persia*, *At Venus's Party*, *Bohemia at Midnight*, and *The Fifth Marriage of Princess Sonia*. The same sensuous tonality pervaded his work as a society columnist and travel writer.

Georges-Michel was delighted to have Wilhelm in Paris. He promoted the "Archiduc Guillaume de Habsbourg-Lorraine," as Wilhelm was known in France. It was perhaps under George-Michel's influence, or at least with an eye to the fame that the press could bring, that Wilhelm allowed his Habsburg name to be used in such articles. In Enghien he had at least made a pretense of living "incognito," under his Ukrainian name Vasyl Vyshyvanyi. In Paris he allowed himself to be a Habsburg again, and to be introduced under his own name, by George-Michel and others, into the emerging world of press celebrities. It was Georges-Michel who wrote the charming article about his friend's tattoos in 1934.[13]

The proximity of a blue anchor to blue blood, the inseparability of low appetites and high birth and breeding, were characteristic of Wilhelm and his Paris. As he left behind his attempts at political anonymity, he permitted himself sexual indiscretions of a new kind, or at least on a new scale. Wilhelm had always been a lover of men, perhaps at school, likely in the trenches, and certainly with his secretary and valet. In Paris, he risked letting himself be known for what he was.

Some of the sexual escapades involved fellow aristocrats, with whom he was seen going out for the evening from rue des Acacias wearing women's clothing (or so at least the press reported). The police noted that a frequent companion in Wilhelm's nighttime romps was a member of the Spanish royal house who called himself Fernando Ducal—almost certainly Don Fernando de Borbón y de Madan, the duke of Durcal. Although homosexual liaisons were legal in France, Don Fernando managed to get himself expelled from the country anyway. Mostly, though, Wilhelm liked to go slumming. He seems not to have frequented the better-known homosexual clubs in Paris, such as the Carrousel or Madame Arthur's in Montmartre. He was rather, according to the Paris police, a "habitué" of "maisons spéciales"—the nice French term for homosexual brothels.[14]

Wilhelm liked the common touch, as well as the oriental touch. The establishments that he attended, as the police noted, "assiduously," had Arabic names, such as Khalif. Khalif was nicely located on the left-bank rue de Vaugirard, just where it wends around the Luxembourg Gardens, about halfway between the Senate and the intersection with the rue Monsieur le Prince. In the France of the day, names like Khalif connoted not only adventure and empire but also transgressions of class and racial boundaries. Wilhelm seemed to like crossing these lines and indeed to regard his sexual explorations among the lower classes as an expression of human generosity. Wilhelm signed himself "Robert" at these establishments. At the Khalif,

Wilhelm made the acquaintance of a worker's son, whom he continued to meet. Wilhelm also engaged an Algerian as his new valet. The police regarded this Maurice Néchadi as "a pederast who exercises much influence over his master."[15]

That was probably so. Wilhelm always wanted men, either above him as father figures or below him as servants or soldiers. He wanted to rebel against the patriarchs and yield to the lackeys, which made for a complicated life. He did know how to have his way, however, with women. On one occasion a female journalist came along as he had his portrait painted, and saw fit to write about the experience. The article, "Watching His Imperial Highness Wilhelm von Habsburg as He Poses," is one long, slow sexual submission. Its author cites her own questions to the archduke, who had to sit still as she stared at him. One of these was: "Have you ever given orders, my lord, just by looking, without saying a word? Your eyes have such force." This was the effect Wilhelm had on women. He rarely sought it, and never commented on it; but it must be said that he sometimes used it.[16]

The portrait painter had made a small career painting the lovers of Paulette Couyba, a group to which Wilhelm belonged. Paulette and Wilhelm had found each other somewhere in Paris in the early 1930s, perhaps in the Montmartre demimonde where Wilhelm was going down while Paulette was coming up. She was a fraud, a bounder, a lover, something of a genius. One observer captured the two dominant opinions about her, both correct: "Certain people see her as troubled, or at least suffering from megalomania, whereas others regard her as endowed with a superior intelligence." Wilhelm liked both sides of her, and allowed himself to be seen with her, and even seen kissing her. She took to calling herself his fiancée.

Wilhelm was perfectly naïve about people, in way that only protected aristocrats can be; Paulette was unusually inventive, in a way that allowed her to meet people such as Wilhelm. His family origins were known to all; she had an interesting story about hers. She claimed to be the niece of the French politician Charles Couyba, a senator, a minister of labor, and a minister of commerce. For all the decades of his political life, Couyba led a second life under a second name, as Maurice Boukay, lefty love crooner. His youthful "Songs of Love" were published with a preface by the symbolist poet Verlaine. He was also known for his "Red Songs," his "Arabian Symphony," his "Last Virgins," and, last and perhaps least, his "Most Beautiful Love Affairs of Casanova."

Charles Couyba's fascinating life united the high and the low, the politics of the French Senate in the Luxemburg Gardens with the tawdriness of Montmartre bars. It would have been an interesting inheritance for his niece Paulette—were Paulette indeed his niece, which she was not. Her own rise to notoriety in Paris was fueled by an even more combustible mixture of state power and romantic expression. A working-class girl from the provinces, she took a job as a postal worker in 1920, then found a series of secretarial posts in the offices of government ministries. From about 1927 she was engaged as the private secretary of a series of wealthy men—that, at least, was how she defined her position when asked. She typed, charmed, and seduced her way to power and wealth.[17]

Paulette's first conquest was Joseph Caillaux, a French politician associated with scandals that made an impression, even in Paris. A flamboyant lady's man, he strutted during debates on silk tariffs because he knew so much about ladies' undergarments. He flouted his many mistresses, and even married some of them. Some fifteen years before he met Paulette in the late 1920s, his first two wives created one of the first great scandals of the mass media. After a newspaper published a love letter from Caillaux to the mistress who had become his first wife, the mistress who had in the meantime become his second wife took her revenge—not on him, but on the newspaper. Caillaux's second wife, Henriette, murdered the editor of *Le Figaro* with six shots from a Browning automatic.

Henriette Caillaux's trial, which began in July 1914, was called at the time the trial of the century. It distracted the French public from the Balkan crisis that was leading their country to war. Madame Caillaux never denied that she had killed the editor but pled innocence on the grounds that she could not control her own passion. She could not, she argued, be expected to control herself in such circumstances. The judge agreed. Henriette Caillaux was acquitted on 28 July 1914, the day the Habsburg monarchy declared war on Serbia. Joseph Caillaux began the First World War not exactly draped in honor, but he managed to worsen his reputation nevertheless. He was convicted of damaging the security of France by passing information to the Germans. But he was soon amnestied—and then placed in charge of the finance ministry.[18]

Such was the high society of interwar Paris, the world into which Caillaux introduced Paulette. He taught her much of what she needed to know about cynicism, duplicity, and the weaknesses of strong men. For him, she was an item on an inexhaustible list of lovers; for her, he was the first example of an experience that she could then repeat. After learning from Caillaux, Paulette proceeded to commence relationships with two other French politicians, according to the records of the French police. She was believed to be the secretary and lover of Anatole de Monzie, a left-wing politician, friend of the Soviet Union, and minister of education in the early 1930s. She was also thought to be the assistant and lover of Maurice de Rothschild, a prominent member of the French branch of that extraordinarily wealthy family.[19]

Paulette's connections became Wilhelm's, after a fashion. She used methods he could not have imagined to try to get him what he wanted. Wilhelm, who hoped to secure the right to live indefinitely in France, tried three times to gain French citizenship. On all three occasions, the relevant authorities received what seemed to be letters or phone calls of support from de Monzie or Caillaux. These were perhaps not the best endorsements, given that the former was openly pro-Soviet and the latter was regarded as pro-German. Then again, such were the ministers of government of interwar France. In any event the woman who presented herself as the secretary of the two politicians, and who delivered the letters and made the phone calls, was almost certainly Paulette. The police had to investigate Wilhelm's past under what seemed to be political pressure. A police chief resolved to find out "the truth about the archduke, his role, and his sentiments"—no easy task! Fortunately for the police chief, the foreign ministry intervened, recommending against granting Wilhelm citizenship. The police files reveal a long investigation of Wilhelm, including informant reports, true and false, about his past. It hurt Wilhelm's case that he had fought in the Habsburg army in the First World War. Most likely, the French foreign ministry, which had a clear policy against a Habsburg restoration, wished to deny any appearance of official French endorsement to a Habsburg who might have a political future.[20]

So Wilhelm remained a foreigner, at a time when chauvinism was on the rise. Yet his origins and his name did grant him a certain cachet, at least among members of Parisian high society who enjoyed fame and wealth but lacked what he had: a royal past. One such admirer of Wilhelm was the singer and dancer Mistinguett, at the time still the most popular entertainer in France, and the highest-paid female entertainer in the world. Her appeal was a matter of gestures of the body and tones of the voice that were almost ineffable in their time, and so all but lost when she ceased to perform. She was one of the last great entertainers of the era when live performance sufficed for fame. Jeanne Bourgeois, a girl from Enghien, had first performed as Mistinguett in 1895, the year Wilhelm was born. In 1919, when Wilhelm was plotting for Ukraine, she was insuring her legs for half a million francs. Now, in the early 1930s, they found themselves moving in similar circles.[21]

Wilhelm and Mistinguett shared the town of Enghien, where she was born and where he had chosen, for a time, to live. They shared a certain royal milieu, to which Wilhelm was born and into which Mistinguett made her way through other means. Wilhelm had known Edward VII, the king of England, since his childhood. Mistinguett claimed to be one of the king's mistresses. She was friendly with the kings of Spain and Sweden, who had intervened on behalf of Wilhelm's father to help him keep his estate in Poland.

Wilhelm and Mistinguett also shared a friendship with Friedrich Wilhelm von Hohenzollern of Prussia. While Wilhelm was a member of the ruling house of Austria who had been disowned by his father, Friedrich Wilhelm was a member of the ruling house of Germany who had watched his father waste the family treasure. His father had been known to feed his hounds sweetbreads in cream, while making the servants crawl about and bark. His wife got the riding whip if she complained about his harem of actresses. Wilhelm and Friedrich Wilhelm were, if for different reasons, in much the same position: glorious but poor. At one dinner they positioned themselves on each side of Mistinguett, competing for her favors. She seemed to prefer Wilhelm, and mused about marrying a Habsburg archduke.[22]

The princes and the singer were together on the beach in the summer of 1932, as a rumor circulated that Friedrich Wilhelm was to marry a rich American widow. After his wastrel father's death, Friedrich Wilhelm owned nothing more than a small castle in Switzerland. Lucienne Swinburne, the American widow, had been the wife of a virtuous soap magnate, and had millions of dollars. On the same day that the French press carried the announcement of her husband's death, it also reported that he had donated a castle as a clinic for poor children. It might have appeared to be a perfect match (at least to Michel Georges-Michel, who spread the rumor). After all, she had lots of money and years of being good; he had great need of money and a family tradition of being bad.[23]

Yet when the widow appeared one fine day, it was with Wilhelm rather than with Friedrich Wilhelm. She introduced him with his full titles to reporters, and he took the opportunity to invite everyone to call him by his first name. "Only in romance novels," he said, "do people still use their titles." Mistinguett, twenty years his senior, again began to wonder aloud about the prospect of marrying a Habsburg archduke, "a good one." She liked what she saw in Wilhelm. Yet her attitude about Wilhelm's pretty eyes was perhaps more cynical than that of Georges-Michel, the chronicler of these incidents. He paused to note that Wilhelm's "eyes were as blue as ever." She was a woman firmly committed to the reality of the artificial, who began her memoirs with the dictum that "the sea is never as blue as on a backcloth." Among such self-made women such as Paulette and Mistinguett, Wilhelm had many attractions but few defenses.[24]

Wilhelm's Habsburg name, apparently nothing more than a subject of idle conversation on the Riviera, still meant something more in the 1930s, at least in Wilhelm's own mind. He maintained a relationship with the most important Habsburg still active in politics, Empress Zita. She and Wilhelm had been together in Madrid; while Wilhelm had chosen France for his place of permanent exile, she had moved her large family to Belgium. One of the few things that Wilhelm did with something like discretion was visit her there. Now, in the early 1930s, she was plotting a restoration of the Habsburgs. In her plans, it seems, there was a place for Wilhelm. Wilhelm, for his part, still wished to be king of Ukraine, and saw a Habsburg restoration as the first step to the realization of his dream.[25]

It was a time when all of Europe was abuzz with the rumor of a Habsburg return. Zita, wearing only black to mourn Karl and the empire, had held the family together, raising the eight children strictly. Zita's eldest son, Crown Prince Otto, only six years old when the monarchy collapsed, reached the Habsburg age of maturity (twenty) on 20 November 1932. Wilhelm, like any Habsburg with ambitions, awaited this day with hope. In late 1932 Otto was in Berlin, carrying out research for a doctoral dissertation, and more importantly making the acquaintance of German politicians. In the German capital, Otto attracted the attention of a coming man of the right, Adolf Hitler. Hitler saw Otto as a potential puppet monarch, someone who might help him to merge Austria into Germany.

Otto, however, wanted something else: an Austria that would remain independent, restore the monarchy, and thereby begin a general Habsburg resurgence throughout central and eastern Europe. Once he had turned twenty, Otto began to frequent Paris, where he was introduced into society by his uncle Sixtus of Bourbon-Parma. It had been scarcely a decade since Karl had tried twice to restore himself to the Hungarian throne, and some Hungarians looked to his son with hope. The Hungarian press raised, on several occasions, the possibility of a restoration.[26]

Benito Mussolini, Italy's fascist Duce (or leader), tried to persuade Zita and Otto that a Habsburg restoration could be their common project. In 1932 the Italian press began, indirectly, to promote a Habsburg restoration, editorializing that the Habsburgs would be better than Hitler as masters of central Europe. Mussolini invited Zita to Rome, and told her that he wished to see the Italian crown princess married to Otto. Such a union was even announced, regularly if erroneously, in the European press in the early 1930s. Mussolini also told Zita that he hoped for a Habsburg restoration. What he likely envisioned was a merger of the Habsburgs with the Italian royal family, providing monarchical legitimacy for Italy throughout southern and central Europe and leaving the true power to him.[27]

Zita and Otto believed that a restoration would begin in Austria itself, in the heartland of the old Habsburg monarchy. It was, in the early 1930s, a land of political contradictions, a place where modern politics seemed to have led to a dead end. Politicians of the far right, Austrian Nazis, believed that their own country should not exist, that it should be united to a Nazi Germany. On the left, Social Democrats also doubted that Austria should exist, preferring unity with a future socialist Germany. The only major party that supported Austrian independence was the Christian Socials of the center-right. Yet this was a party based in the Christian, German-speaking working class, traditionally loyal to the House of Habsburg. As of 1933, then, Austria was an independent republic, but no major political force was committed both to independence and to the republic. The country fell into economic depression in the early 1930s, giving the Social Democrats reason to hope for an electoral victory. Hitler took full control of the German state in spring 1933, giving Nazis reason to hope for the takeover of Austria by Germany. Something had to give.

Otto, Zita, and Wilhelm believed that the way out of the impasse was a Habsburg restoration. Otto wanted a kind of socialist monarchy, which would attract the working class with a welfare state and with nostalgic references to grand Habsburg history. In March 1933, Austrian chancellor Engelbert Dollfuss took a different course, one that led straight to civil war. He dissolved the parliament, and formed what he called a Fatherland Front from his own Christian Social Party, a few other right-wing organizations, and the major right-wing militia, the Heimwehr. The Fatherland Front was a kind of synthesis of tradition and modernity; it was Catholic, but it accepted that the state had a major role to play in society. It was friendly to the Habsburg past, if not necessarily to the idea of a Habsburg restoration.

The Habsburgs, watching from the west, believed that the Fatherland Front could never unite the people as well as a monarchy, and perhaps they were right. The new regime led immediately to two major social and political conflicts. Once the Heimwehr paramilitary was in power, it tried to disarm the left-wing paramilitary of the Social Democrats, the Schutzbund. The Schutzbund defended itself, and on 12 February 1934 socialists called a general strike in Vienna. The government now sided with the Heimwehr against the left, as the capital city quickly became the main site of socialist resistance. Vienna was the socialists' electoral stronghold; socialist municipal governments had built a remarkable "Red Vienna" of public housing, public works, and public parks. Now socialists made their last stand in housing complexes such as Karl-Marx Hof, while government forces shelled them from surrounding hills. In this conflict of countryside with city, the countryside won. Red Vienna's population was subdued, its monuments destroyed, its Social Democratic Party banned.

Soon after Chancellor Dollfuss suppressed the threat from the left, he faced a shocking attack from the right. On 25 July 1934 a band of Nazis slipped into his offices and attempted a coup d'état. They shot Dollfuss, and then let him bleed to death, denying him medical attention and last rites. Soon they were overwhelmed by loyal government forces.

The Fatherland Front had survived a year in power, but after a civil war and a fatal coup attempt, it could hardly be called a great success. After all this violence, the next chancellor, Kurt von Schuschnigg, had to ask himself how Austria could be governed. The Fatherland Front stood for Austrian independence, but what sort of Austria did it mean to defend? Schuschnigg and his ministers spoke of Catholicism, of the unity of the people with their leaders, of a spiritual rearmament, of history. To many Austrians, this propaganda recalled the Habsburg past, and some began to imagine a

Habsburg future. Austrian towns began to grant Otto honorary citizenship. Chancellor Schuschnigg even began to speak to Otto. The terms of his return were to be negotiated, but the return itself must have seemed, at least to Otto and Zita, like nothing more than a matter of time.[28]

Lilacs bloom on old wood; dynasties know how to wait. As Zita and Otto planned a grand return to Vienna, they must have seen Wilhelm as a valuable ally to the Habsburg cause. He appeared to bring familial, financial, and political assets to Zita's plan to restore Otto to the Habsburg thrones. He was one of the few Habsburg archdukes not to have married unequally. His two brothers, for example, had married women not of royal rank and so could never father heirs to Habsburg thrones. They had in effect removed themselves from the future of the dynasty. They thus had little incentive to join in any dynastic endeavor, even were Zita desperate enough to ask their help. Wilhelm's lifestyle as a reckless bisexual playboy ensured that he never fell into the bourgeois trap of marriage for love. If one does not marry, one does not marry unequally.[29]

Nor had Wilhelm done anything so outrageous as to require an expulsion from the family chivalric order, the Knights of the Golden Fleece. The standards of outrage were fairly high, but some Habsburgs had managed to cross them. Archduke Leopold, for example, profited in America from certifying the authenticity of family jewelry that he had never seen and that did not belong to him. This in itself might not have been enough. Then he spent his ill-gotten gains in Vienna on conspicuous pleasure. That too might not have sufficed. But in January 1932, after a ball, he went to the Bristol Bar, and continued to drink and dance with the collar of the Order of the Golden Fleece hung, in some unspecified but outrageous way, on his body. When Otto came of age, he expelled Leopold from the Order.[30]

Wilhelm also appeared to be financially sound, especially after the death of his father on 7 April 1933. The family brewery was a great success in independent Poland, and the family still had tens of thousands of hectares of profitable woodlands. Wilhelm had returned home to Żywiec for the funeral and discussions of the inheritance.

Despite the differences with his brothers Albrecht and Leo, he seemed to get along with them—or, at least, to arouse their instinct to protect him, the youngest brother.

His eldest brother, Albrecht, had become Polish in a way that even their father had never quite been and that Wilhelm had never wished to be: with a Polish military record, a Polish accent, a Polish wife, and Polish children. His wife Alice was, of course, a Swede by birth. Alice had become Polish for her first husband and remained so for Albrecht. Yet she had a secret longing for Ukraine. Her first estate had been in lands populated by Ukrainian peasants, and she missed them. It was, perhaps, no accident that one of the cooks at the family castle was from Kiev. Was she was charmed by Wilhelm, her Ukrainian brother-in-law, the family rogue? Did she put in a good word for him with her husband, who held the family purse strings?[31]

Albrecht was certainly generous with Wilhelm. Though Wilhelm had been disowned by their father, Albrecht made sure that Wilhelm got his appanage, his regular cash subsidy from the family. This distribution had probably begun in the late 1920s when their father was too sick to know. Now that Stefan was dead, Albrecht set out to restore Wilhelm to financial soundness. Albrecht's lawyers made a careful survey of Wilhelm's debts and paid off his creditors in April 1934. Wilhelm owed \$94,000 and £2,100, a significant amount at the time (about \$1.5 million and £100,000 in 2008). Albrecht also, at his own initiative, agreed to pay Wilhelm as before. Wilhelm would continue to receive about 60,000 French francs a year.[32]

With Wilhelm's creditors suddenly requited, it must have appeared to Zita and Otto that Wilhelm had come into a good deal of money. The Esterhazy brothers, suddenly repaid the entire sum of their debts, might have let this fact be known to other monarchists. This appearance of wealth would have been strengthened by a one-time grant that Wilhelm received from his family for travel in May 1934, which he used to go on a pleasure jaunt to Morocco and Tunisia. Wilhelm looked rich, but in fact he was merely solvent.[33]

Zita and Otto also knew that Wilhelm had a certain Ukrainian political profile, a connection to a major European country that might join a Habsburg restoration. Even as he carried an Austrian passport and tried to gain a French one, even as he called himself a Habsburg among the French, Wilhelm still lived under his Ukrainian name and spoke Ukrainian with fellow exiles in France. The quality of his written Ukrainian actually improved while he was in exile. In 1918 he was proud to write a few lines to his mentor, Andrii Sheptytsky, in a telegram; by the 1930s, he could write long letters that, while not free of errors and polonisms, were quite expressive of his thoughts and feelings.

Often the addressee was a fellow Ukrainian aristocrat, Jan Tokarzewski-Karaszewicz, known in Ukrainian circles, where he styled himself a prince, as Tokary. The two men had different ideas about certain matters, such as the desirability of an alliance with Poland. Yet they became close friends. Both of them, after all, wanted an independent Ukraine, of the sort that would regard them as royalty. Each of them liked having a friend who knew when and how to use noble and royal titles in correspondence and conversation. Together they endured the terrible news from Soviet Ukraine, for example of the famine that killed at least three million Ukrainian peasants in 1933. That was the greatest horror of the twentieth century thus far, but only Ukrainians paid it much heed. It seemed to cement Wilhelm and Tokary's friendship.

Wilhelm's Ukrainian identity was still credible to Ukrainians generally, not just to their aspiring aristocracy. He still knew how to be one of the boys. He attended meetings of Ukrainian exiles, and gave money to Ukrainian causes. He lent his name to efforts to raise money for the victims of the famine. He grew close to the Organization of Ukrainian Nationalists, a conspiratorial terrorist organization that sought to create an independent Ukraine. It was led by other former officers of the Habsburg army, sometimes men who had served with or under him. Two of its leaders, Ievhen Konovalets and Andrii Melnyk, had served in Ukraine with Wilhelm in 1918, when they discussed staging a coup in his favor. Now they used Wilhelm's connections to gain diplomatic support for Ukraine. Wilhelm traveled on their business to London, where he sometimes saw Tokary's beautiful wife, Oksana. In June 1934, Hitler told Mussolini that Wilhelm was the liaison between the Ukrainian nationalists and the Austrian militias.[34]

It was that summer, twelve years after the collapse of his last Ukrainian plot, that Wilhelm decided to return to Ukrainian politics. He began to consult with an old accomplice, Vasyl Paneyko, about his ideas for a restoration. Paneyko was a French journalist and a former Ukrainian diplomat, hailing from the old Habsburg province of Galicia. Wilhelm had known him in Bukovina in October 1918, when the Habsburg monarchy was falling apart. Paneyko, known even then as a Ukrainian with an unusual fondness for Russia, nevertheless became one of Wilhelm's confidants. Now, in the summer of 1934, Wilhelm gave Paneyko to understand that an attempt at a Habsburg restoration was in the works.

Wilhelm told Paneyko that had he made several trips to Belgium to see Zita. Polish intelligence, working with multiple sources, believed that Wilhelm and Zita were discussing his role in a Habsburg restoration, as the ruler of an independent Ukraine subordinate to the restored monarchy. This prospect would not have seemed terribly remote. Monarchists believed that Otto's elevation to an Austrian or Hungarian throne would begin a chain reaction that would transform central and eastern Europe. Democracy had already failed in every country in the region (except Czechoslovakia). Habsburgs could easily believe that their rule would be preferable to that of the various military regimes and quasi-monarchies that now prevailed. Certainly it was preferable to domination by Hitler's Germany or Stalin's Soviet Union. In such a moment of transformation, a Habsburg Ukraine could be offered to Ukrainians who had suffered so much under Polish and especially under Soviet rule.[35]

Wilhelm visited Berlin several times while Otto was a student there, in late 1932 or early 1933. Perhaps his aim was indeed, as Wilhelm later claimed, to fly from Germany to America in a Zeppelin. But he did have occasion to speak about Otto in Berlin, and it certainly seems possible that he spoke to Otto. They certainly shared political opinions. The two Habsburgs believed that a Habsburg Europe was the only plausible alternative to a coming wave of totalitarianism. Both were appalled by the Nazi putsch in Vienna in July 1934, and both drew the conclusion that the time for action was near. After that failed coup, Wilhelm wrote to a friend that "in the matter of the recent events, I have some very interesting details, which are very shameful for the government of Hitler, that son of a bitch." Another sign of their closeness was Otto's choice of the man to lead the restorationist movement in Austria. He entrusted the mission to Friedrich von Wiesner, an associate of Wilhelm for more than a decade, and incidentally of Jewish origin—one more sign of the opposition of the monarchists to the Nazis. Wiesner quickly built up an organization of tens of thousands of members.[36]

In summer 1934, Wilhelm also seemed to be planning a trip to Rome to see Mussolini. He took Paulette Couyba to fancy shops to buy dresses to meet the Duce. In Paris he moved her into the apartment building right next to his, on rue des Acacias. It was there that he was seen kissing her in the lobby. Paulette must have thought that she somehow fit into his political plans. If she was his fiancée, as she said and perhaps even believed, than surely she would one day be his queen. Of course, no Habsburg who wanted a throne with the family's endorsement could marry a former postal worker. If Wilhelm was to take part in a restoration, he would have to become the loyal servant of Zita, and Zita alone.

Perhaps Wilhelm believed Paulette knew nothing about Zita. Perhaps he was right. Then again, perhaps not. The connections between the two women, different as they were in almost every respect, were quite close. One of Paulette's lovers, Anatole de Monzie, was one of Otto's political contacts in France. One of Paulette's neighbors on the rue des Acacias and a frequent companion of Wilhelm's nighttime romps, Count Colloredo, was Zita's emissary to Mussolini.[37]

Much as Wilhelm surely wished to keep these parts of his life separate, they were slowly coming together.

On the evening of 10 November 1934, Wilhelm crossed the Place de Vendôme on his way to dine at the Ritz. The Place de Vendôme is designed to awe. At its center stands a column portraying Napoleon as Caesar. The outside of the column is made from the melted bronze of the cannons Napoleon captured from his enemies, including the Habsburgs. Surely Wilhelm walked by without a glance. The glory of the Bonapartes was in the past, while that of the Habsburgs might yet have a future. Wilhelm had a restoration on his mind. He just needed a bit of cash. He believed that he was about to meet someone with money to spare.

Wilhelm had come to dine with Henri Deterding, the founder of Royal Dutch Shell, a man known at the time as the "Napoleon of oil." In the eyes of his many detractors, he was the instigator of a meeting with British and American counterparts to create a world cartel of oil. Wilhelm was in his element, or so he must have thought. Though the ways of capital were a mystery to him, Wilhelm had been dealing with industrialists for his whole adult life. He had met Henry Ford and J. P. Morgan. Moreover, he had an invitation from Deterding, or rather from a certain Parker, who had presented himself as Deterding's personal secretary. Deterding apparently admired Wilhelm and wished to meet him.[38]

Another very wealthy man was also expected at this dinner: Maurice de Rothschild, the maverick of Europe's richest family. He had run for election to the French parliament, arguing that, since the government was beholden to his family's money in any event, a Rothschild might as well make the laws. He was an early collector of Picasso. Yet as far as Wilhelm knew, Picasso was a small Spaniard who illustrated gossipy books in which he, Wilhelm, was one of the heroes. Picasso drew caricatures for Michel George-Michels, and it seems unlikely that Wilhelm saw his work in any other context. Rothschilds, in the experience of Wilhelm's family, were people who did not know how to sail. Stefan had once saved some Rothschilds after they wrecked their own yacht, the *Eros*.[39]

Wilhelm entered the appointed dining room in the Ritz, only to meet someone he did not expect. André Hémard owned the Établissements Pernod, distilleries that produced absinthe as well as a number of absinthe substitutes. Hémard was himself the inventor of an absinthe substitute called L'Amourette. His firm was doing very well; that year it paid its third consecutive 100 percent dividend to shareholders. All the same, Hémard, like Wilhelm, had reason to be disconcerted. Wilhelm expected Deterding, who he thought had invited him; while Hémard believed he had been invited by Maurice de Rothschild.

Two men with good manners met at the Ritz, each expecting someone else. As the archduke and the liquor magnate began to approach a state of uncomfortable awkwardness, Paulette Couyba rushed in to release the tension and explain. While Wilhelm had seemingly been invited to meet Deterding by someone who called himself Parker, it seemed that Paulette was the connection between Hémard and Rothschild. She told Hémard that Rothschild had urgent business with the French government and was meeting with ministers of state in another dining room in the same hotel. A houseboy then appeared with Rothschild's calling card. No one explained Deterding's absence. Wilhelm must have been confused, though probably not for the first time. He knew how to charm people, rich and poor alike, to make them do his bidding. Yet he had no sense for the structure of any society, no idea that a setting such as this dinner could be engineered. Most likely he saw that Paulette had some sort of plan and that he had best sit quietly and look dignified.

Paulette presented a business proposition to Hémard. She claimed that she had a blocked account in the Rothschild bank that would be released the following spring. If Hémard would give her 400,000 francs now, she would be able to guarantee a handsome profit in a few months. Indeed, she would be happy to present him with a postdated check. She intimated that she would be making a great deal of money, in the meantime, as a result of a coming restoration of the Habsburgs. Hémard, she claimed, would profit "royally" if he backed her. Just then another houseboy appeared, as if on cue, with what appeared to be a letter from a bank with Rothschild's signature. Hémard seemed convinced. He promised Paulette the 400,000 francs, if only she would meet him later that evening in his office. It was the kind of proposition to which she was accustomed. She agreed.[40]

Hémard was setting his own trap. He left the Ritz, and contacted the banks. Having assured himself that Paulette's offer was bogus, he called the police. When she appeared later that night at the Établissements Pernod, she was arrested and taken to jail.

Wilhelm, present at the scene of the attempted fraud, was vulnerable as never before in his life. For a moment, his lover remained true to him. At first, Paulette told the police she had been acting alone. Then she changed her story, saying that she was working with Wilhelm to raise money for the restoration of the Habsburgs.[41]

This revision was probably at the behest of her true coconspirator and Wilhelm's false friend, Vasyl Paneyko. It was Paneyko who had written the supposed invitation to Wilhelm from Deterding, signing himself as "Parker." It is not quite clear whether Paulette and Paneyko betrayed Wilhelm before the dinner by drawing him into a situation for which he was not prepared, or whether they betrayed him thereafter by seeking to saddle him with all of the blame. But betray him they did.

Wilhelm was suddenly in the middle of a scandal with international implications. The French press lost no time in declaring the matter "a fraud to re-establish the Habsburgs." Wilhelm appeared, somewhat sheepishly, at the Austrian legation in Paris to ask for help. A diplomat put the matter delicately in a report of December 1934: "Archduke Wilhelm was incautious enough to have become involved with a lady with a questionable past." Indeed. The embassy was flooded with other visitors with some connection to the affair. Austrian nobles who gallivanted with Wilhelm offered money to quiet the outcry. Lawyers representing people defrauded by Paulette asked to be paid off by the Habsburg family. The implicit threat, of course, was that a trial and conviction would destroy Wilhelm and thus the whole family. The legation sent all such petitioners away.[42]

The scandal touched on matters of ideology that divided France and Austria. The Austrian regime was very conservative, so much so that Wilhelm's monarchism was almost acceptable. France, however, was a republic, and its politics were moving to the left. In the summer of 1934, as Wilhelm and Zita were plotting their restoration, French parties on the left had agreed upon a new alliance. The major socialist parties and the French Communist Party agreed to form a Popular Front and to present a single list of candidates at the next elections. The participation of the communists was significant, since it reflected a change in the party line set by Stalin in the Soviet Union. Until this point, communist parties had been instructed to see socialists as class enemies who wanted only to preserve the exploitative capitalist order. After Hitler's rise to power, Stalin reversed course. Now communists were to accept socialists as comrades and band together with them to prevent the rise of fascism. The French Communist Party began to sing the "Marseillaise" and to present itself as a party of the French national interest.[43]

It was a heady moment. The parties of the Popular Front believed that they represented a majority, as in fact they did; but in late 1934 and in early 1935 France was still governed by a right-center coalition, by aged and established politicians. The joke went that France was governed by men in their seventies because the men in their eighties were all dead. So during these months the Popular Front enjoyed both great confidence in its future and a complete lack of responsibility for the present. The inclusion of the communists naturally added to the sharpness of ideological divides and political rhetoric. The Popular Front was meant to stop fascism, which for the communists and indeed many of the socialists was a very broad category. It meant Hitler's National Socialism and Mussolini's Italian fascism, of course; but it also included the Catholic authoritarianism of Austria, and perhaps even the Habsburgs. From this perspective, even though Austria's leaders opposed Hitler, and one of them had been murdered by Nazis, Austria was just one more fascist country. The Popular Front could not see Austria as an ally.

Wilhelm, whatever else he was, was a consistent opponent of communism and the Soviet Union. His life's mission, when he was not in a brothel or on the beach, was to rescue the suffering Ukrainian people from the rule of the Bolsheviks. In his vision of a Habsburg restoration, Ukrainians would choose monarchy, precisely because they had suffered so much under the Soviets. For all of his frivolity and fecklessness, he was unquestionably right about the nature of communism in Ukraine. When he had been forced to leave Ukraine in 1918, he predicted that the Bolsheviks would triumph and that their Soviet Ukraine would be murderous. His prediction had proven true, and Wilhelm had the courage to speak out about the inhumanity of communism fifteen years later, in a France where communists were very important in public life.

Wilhelm's scandal was thus made to order for this frustrated, confident, and ideological left. The newspapers of the left-wing parties made the best of it. Consider *Le Populaire* of 15 December 1934: "A tall blonde, as distinguished as a socialite dancer, who played golf, was on a first-name basis with kings, threatened to thrash his lackeys, and knew how to talk to women. How could a former employee of the post office at Cahors resist such charms?"[44]

This was laughter with teeth. A serious legal argument was being made by the press before the evidence was examined by any court, before Wilhelm was even charged with anything. A woman, went the story, had fallen for "the charms" of a man. So the man was ultimately responsible. Another joke followed: "Kings no longer marry shepherdesses, but archdukes are supported by the young ladies of the Postal Service. That's progress. And so! We will march along with it." Once again, a legal point was implied. If Paulette was supporting Wilhelm financially, then her frauds were committed on his behalf. This was the line pursued by Paulette's five lawyers, all of whom were connected to the political parties that made up the Popular Front. With the help of leaks to reporters, they created the general impression, at least among a certain readership, that a crime had been committed, that it was on behalf of the Habsburgs, and that the person ultimately responsible was Wilhelm.[45]

Wilhelm's uncle Eugen appealed to the Austrian minister of foreign affairs for an official intervention, but was refused. Count Colloredo, Wilhelm's friend and Zita's ally, volunteered to help the embassy pay off whomever necessary to avoid a scandal, and was turned away. Ukrainian veterans in Paris signed petitions vouching for Wilhelm's character, but were ignored. Wilhelm's friends tried to explore Paneyko's past, but they ran out of time.[46]

Over the course of spring 1935, Wilhelm grew convinced that the investigating magistrate believed the version of events that placed him in the worst light. He also thought that the investigating magistrate disliked him as a foreigner, an Austrian, and a Habsburg. Following the advice of his friends, who warned him that he could be sentenced to prison, Wilhelm fled the country. He made his way through Switzerland to Austria, arriving in Vienna in the middle of June.[47]

The case against Wilhelm von Habsburg (alias Vasyl Vyshyvanyi), and Paulette (alias Paule, alias Olympia) Couyba, was heard at the sixteenth Paris criminal court, sitting at the Palais de Justice, on 27 July 1935.[48]

The presiding judge began the trial with a pointed reminder of Wilhelm's absence. He claimed that Wilhelm had left a calling card in the judges' chambers, with the initials "p.p.c"—"pour prendre congé," or to take my leave, a polite way of parting and saying goodbye. This reminded everyone that Wilhelm had fled the scene, fearing the verdict of the trial. Wilhelm's state defender denied the veracity of the story, saying that the calling card had been a joke by a clerk.[49]

The tone had been set. Wilhelm and Paulette were now charged with fraud, attempted fraud, complicity in fraud, and the writing of bad checks. The accusing parties were, in addition to the French state, private individuals who claimed to be the victims of the frauds. One of these was Paneyko, who thereby cleverly inserted himself into the proceedings. He got to tell a tale, likely invented, that he had lent Paulette 20,000 francs, only to see the very same banknotes in Wilhelm's briefcase. He also had the opportunity to call Wilhelm names and generally degrade the level of rhetoric in the courtroom. He said that Wilhelm was a *souteneur* or pimp, although what he really meant was that Wilhelm was pimp, gigolo, and john: he sent Paulette to do his work for him, made love to her to get the money, then spent that money on sex with sailors. In these ways Paneyko transformed his own role from that of conspirator to victim.

It was in this light that the judge considered the other charges. Wilhelm had indeed raised money in Britain to enlarge a golf course at Cannes from nine holes to eighteen. He had given the money to

Paulette, and it had vanished without a trace. Paulette had persuaded a lumber trader to give her 140,000 francs, on the promise that he would be repaid 184,000. (Hémard, the absinthe man, had declined a similar offer.) Here the charge was attempted fraud. The porter at Paulette's building had entrusted her with his savings, which he never saw again. Finally, the dress shop where Paulette had ordered her clothing for her journey to Italy had never been paid. As the shop's owner testified, Wilhelm had indeed expressed clear opinions about the dresses, but Paulette had signed the bills. It might seem that, in every case, the initiative was Paulette's.[50]

Paulette recounted her version of events, in her own particular style. She was in love. She was a poor naïve Frenchwoman. She was no match for the wiles of the handsome Habsburg prince. She had not known what she was doing, and whatever it was, she had done it for her man. She gave him all of the money, except for that small part that she needed for the care of her elderly mother. She had to have hundred-franc notes at the ready so that he could pay sailors for sex. This, of course, had broken her heart.[51]

Paneyko's lawyer drew the conclusions. If Paulette was innocent of criminal intention, then Wilhelm was guilty. "Happily," he concluded, "we are in a position to sentence this crowned criminal before a restoration in Austria." As Austrian diplomats noted, with the world-weariness of their own unhappy perspective, the lawyers' closing arguments were "drawn from a milieu that one otherwise knows only from operettas and pulp fiction."[52]

The presiding judge accepted the tale of Paulette as victim. "The greatest part of the responsibility," he concluded, fell to Wilhelm. Paulette was motivated by "circumstances independent of her will," and appeared "deserving of indulgence." Wilhelm was sentenced to five years in prison. Paulette's sentence was suspended, and she walked free.[53]

Whatever Paulette was in this plot, she was not an innocent victim of Wilhelm's guile. She was a very intelligent woman whose defense strategy had worked beautifully. The presiding judge, and indeed the entirely male courtroom, should be counted among her victims. She borrowed her defense strategy from Henriette Caillaux, the woman whose husband she had also borrowed. Henriette, having killed the journalist who published a love letter from her husband Joseph, claimed that she could not be responsible for her own actions because she was a woman of passion. This idea of a feminine "crime of passion" rescued Paulette in 1935, just as it had Henriette in 1914.[54]

What, in fact, had Paulette been doing? Was she procuring money for Wilhelm, knowing that he would spend it on sex with men, but loving him so much that she was willing to make this sacrifice? The sex with men was an element of the story that Paneyko and his lawyer liked to emphasize. As Paneyko wrote to an acquaintance, Wilhelm "always needed lots of money, not so much to live as to support and shower gifts upon all sorts of lads, Arabs, Negros, sailors, all sorts of scum from the dregs of society." Wilhelm, according to Paneyko, led "a double life: one for the day, princely, political, and the other for the night, with the worst scum of the big cities and the ports." There was something to this depiction, although Paneyko exaggerated the details for his own purposes, pressing incontrovertible facts about Wilhelm's private life into service as stereotypes. Austrian diplomats complained that the French press emphasized the sex in order to present the House of Habsburg as degenerate. Wilhelm did spend a good deal of money on sex—but never more than he had, or could borrow.[55]

In a country where the newspapers were aligned with political parties, the Habsburg restoration was at the center of the scandal. The sexual and financial details might increase circulation, but their political significance, as reporters told the story, was the decay of the House of Habsburg. Journalists initially treated a restoration as the real reason for the fraud, then presented the fraud as a reason why a restoration would be laughable. By the end they could contrast Wilhelm's "crown of cardboard" to his "authentic shame." This transformation was a result of journalists' own work. *Le Populaire* was perhaps most artlessly explicit about the image it wished upon Wilhelm: "Habsburg! A vile being, heir to an illustrious name, born to a fortune, to honors, to soldiers, to prestige, and who finished as the lowest of Montmartre pimps, living from the money of a poor and unstable girl whom he sent to commit his foul deeds in his place!" Or perhaps *Le Populaire* was outdone by *L'Oeuvre*: "The blood of the Habsburg family, that fatal family whose cases of madness are uncountable, where murders were as frequent as natural deaths, where unhappy women were kept from sleep for years at a time! That blood fell, in 1914, on the entire world. Yesterday it only invaded the sixteenth criminal court of the Palace of Justice."[56]

Since Paulette in the courtroom was a "poor girl" or a "long-suffering woman" rather than a seasoned fraud, she could, once the trial was over, be presented as proof that any idea of restoration was absurd. She had testified that "the archduke was well placed for the restoration of the Habsburgs," which seemed ridiculous in the circumstances. She was laughed at, especially when she spoke of taking care of him, or feeding him. One reporter provided a respectful summary of Paulette's skills: "She was intelligent, ingenious, imaginative. Boasting of her future ascent to the rank of archduchess, she was able to defraud considerable sums from people too easily impressed by noble titles and the royal purple." Yet even he could not resist the comic conclusion that Paulette "looked more like a cook seized by debauchery than like an archduchess."[57]

The media had the power to render royalist politics absurd. It could hurt a figure of Wilhelm's stature. For some famous people of Wilhelm's acquaintance, such as Mistinguett, all press was good press. She asked Michel Georges-Michel to publish the rumor that she was marrying Wilhelm because any reason to be in the next day's headlines was a good one. For Wilhelm, this was simply not the case. It was not—at least not yet—a world in which any publicity for a royal was good publicity. Wilhelm circulated among the new idols of the media, the new class of celebrities, but he was not one of them. His name allowed him to enter the clubs and resorts, but it could also force him to leave. It was no longer a guarantee of success, but rather a currency that could be cheapened. He was susceptible to the media and to public opinion in a way that no Habsburg was before 1918, and he was also vulnerable in a way that his rich friends were not in the Paris of 1935. The scandal revealed this, and most painfully.

In all likelihood, Wilhelm did wish to raise money to fund Empress Zita's plan to restore the Habsburgs. This aim, and indeed the nature of the fraud, was consistent with his activities in 1921, the last time he had actively participated in politics. Never educated about or interested in the details of law or finance, he probably did not see any impropriety in his own actions. Paulette's victims, like the investors in the Ukrainian syndicate thirteen years earlier, were promised profit as the result of a political transformation that their money would help to bring about. In 1934, as in 1921, it is very likely that Wilhelm did not grasp the details. He knew that his presence made people more willing to open their wallets, and perhaps never wished to understand more.

Wilhelm had to have cash if he was not to disappoint Zita. She needed money, and was probably under the impression that Wilhelm had it. To turn this impression into a reality, he had to raise large sums very quickly, before a restoration, before Zita realized the truth. Getting one woman to raise money in order to spend it on another is always a tricky business. Wilhelm, though he probably did not grasp Paulette's schemes, certainly did understand that. After his flight from Paris, his first thought was of Zita. He asked his friends to console her: "The poor thing knew nothing of any of this and must now be suffering."[58]

The deepest truth about the politics of the scandal, like the deepest truth about the romance, will forever remain obscure. Paulette's betrayal of Wilhelm forced Wilhelm to betray Zita. Paneyko and Paulette knew of Wilhelm's cooperation with Zita in the plan to restore the Habsburgs, and they destroyed his political career and any chance he had for glory. But why?

It is certainly possible that they were working for a foreign power: for Poland, Czechoslovakia, or the Soviet Union. Warsaw knew the most about Wilhelm. Polish intelligence knew the content of Wilhelm's conversations with Paneyko, which suggests that Paneyko himself was the source and was working for Poland and that the betrayal of Wilhelm might have been a Polish provocation. Wilhelm

himself believed that the Czechoslovaks had engineered his catastrophe. As he understood, Prague had the most to lose from any
Habsburg restoration. Czechoslovakia had been carved from the
heart of the old Habsburg domains, and its leaders were hostile to
any restoration. The Soviets, of course, cannot be discounted. They
were the choice of Wilhelm's uncle Eugen. Stalin was quite good at
disposing of émigré Ukrainian politicians, although usually he just
had them killed. Three years later he would have Wilhelm's colleague, the Ukrainian nationalist leader Ievhen Konovalets, murdered by a bomb disguised as a box of chocolates.[59]

It is entirely possible that elements of the French state cooperated
with any of these powers. France was an ally of Poland and Czechoslovakia, and signed, in May 1935, a mutual assistance pact with
the Soviet Union. Most French leaders opposed a Habsburg restoration. In July 1935, as Austria rescinded its anti-Habsburg laws, a
restoration seemed quite possible. French newspapers were asking:
"Will the Habsburgs return to Austria?" The scandal made it less
likely that they would.[60]

No conspiracy is complete without love, just as no love can flourish without a bit of conspiracy. Paulette betrayed Wilhelm, but that
does not mean that she did not love him. Perhaps she had her reasons. Perhaps she understood that, if a restoration took place, the
most important woman in Wilhelm's life would be Zita. Perhaps she
grasped, even as she claimed to be his fiancée, that he could not simultaneously marry a former postal worker and found a great dynasty. Such a realization would explain the juxtaposition of
affection and treachery that the press saw fit to mock. Perhaps the
grandeur and glamour, so ripe for parody in a courtroom or gossip
column, had seemed true and tender on rue des Acacias.[61]

At the time of the trial, Paulette was thirty-seven and had already
spent several months in jail. She cannot have looked her best.
French journalists made a point of ridiculing her looks—and her
clothes. A female reporter wrote of a "face that is a bit heavy but
drawn in the best traditions of the grand century." The grand century in France was the seventeenth, when the ideal of feminine
beauty was somewhat broader than in the twentieth. A male re-

porter, raising the mailed fist of false gallantry, found her features "energetic but a touch working-class." He also pointed out that she was wearing the wrong sort of hat.[62]

Of course she was. Paulette was a social climber at a time and in a country where social advance was all but impossible, especially for women. Those who did make the leap from poverty to wealth, as Paulette had, could often be revealed by their lack of cultivation. Coco Chanel, who began her own rise by making hats, was one of the very few exceptions. Mistinguett was another of these rare birds of paradise. As she recalled in one of her routines, she had begun as a flower girl. Perhaps the rise from poverty is exactly what Wilhelm found appealing in Paulette, and in Mistinguett as well. Even Zita, as Wilhelm the lapsed Catholic would have known, was named for the patron saint of domestic servants.[63]

Wilhelm did kiss Paulette in public. There is no sign that he conferred that particular grace upon anyone else.

Wilhelm's state defender maintained that "he was a puppet in the hands of Mademoiselle Couyba." One of Paulette's lawyers rejoined that if she "had committed a crime, it was a crime of excessive and blind love for a man who treated her as a plaything." Both lawyers were speaking the truth. People who are puppets in each others' hands, who pull the very strings that bind them, are people who are in love.[64]

Paulette did cry through the last half of the trial. It is not easy, even for an adventuress of the highest grade, to shed false tears for an entire afternoon.

And when it was all over, when the verdict was in, she came after him again.

BROWN

◈

Aristocratic Fascism

W HEN THE PRESS attaché of the Austrian legation in Paris
took the telephone call from the Princess of Bourbon-Parma
on 1 April 1936, he was expecting good news. What with the Wilhelm affair and then the rise of the Popular Front to power in
France, there had been precious little of that for the diplomats of
Austria's right-wing regime. So this call was something promising.
The Bourbon-Parmas were a branch of the French royal family, related by marriage to the Habsburgs. Empress Zita, Emperor Karl's
widow, was a Bourbon-Parma. The press attaché, one Dr. Wasserbäck, hoped for an initiative that might improve the parlous state of
Austro-French relations. The feminine voice on the telephone did in-
deed convey an appealing proposition, one that spoke directly to an
Austrian predicament in the difficult Europe of 1936.

Hard hit by the Great Depression, its factories closed and its
fields lying fallow, Austria was desperate for tourism. The Alps appealed to hikers and skiers, the countryside was backward and
beautiful, and the oversized cosmopolitan capital offered more art,
theater, and music than domestic demand could support. Yet Adolf
Hitler had ruined the Austrian tourist industry. To express his dis-
pleasure at the Austrian ban on the Nazi Party, the Führer had required all Germans who wished to travel to Austria to pay a fee of
one thousand marks. Rather than stopping in Austria, German
tourists were now traveling through the Brenner Pass of the Alps to

Italy. To compensate for the loss of German tourism, Austrian diplomats had to redouble their efforts to draw visitors from other European countries. So Wasserbäck was very pleased to hear that the Princess of Bourbon-Parma had a friend, the Countess de Rivat, who wished to undertake a "great propaganda action" for Austria. Would the countess be received by the press attaché at the legation? Of course she would.[1]

The Countess de Rivat made a vivid first impression. From behind a hat and a good deal of makeup, she spoke quickly of her desire to improve the image of Austria in France. She had a great many friends among the Austrian aristocracy, she explained, and wished their country much prosperity. For example, she had known the unfortunate Archduke Wilhelm quite well, and expressed her disappointment that Austrian diplomats had done nothing to aid him during the investigation and trial. As a result of this inaction, she continued, poor Mademoiselle Couyba had been forced to sacrifice herself for her beloved Wilhelm, and was now utterly ruined.

Perhaps sensing that Wasserbäck would be unlikely to endorse that version of events, the countess then rushed forward to make her proposal. She was on good terms, she said, with the French journalist Michel Georges-Michel. The two of them, with official Austrian diplomatic endorsement, would like to travel to Austria. Georges-Michel would then write favorable articles for the press, and a propagandistic book or two, to encourage the French to follow in their footsteps. She proposed to bring Georges-Michel to the legation, and the press attaché agreed. Wasserbäck helped her to the door.

As long as the countess was present, Wasserbäck had some trouble thinking clearly. Now he had occasion to reflect. Ever since Wilhelm's scandal of the previous year—a media disaster for Austria that Wasserbäck had observed in his official capacity—he had regarded Paulette Couyba as a notorious fraud. He was surprised that a lady of society such as the Countess de Rivat would know her, much less defend her.

His suspicions were confirmed at the next meeting. Georges-Michel introduced himself as the author of eighty or ninety books, mentioning that Mussolini had rewarded him for drawing French tourists to Italy. He claimed that his personal connections to the international Wagons-Lits company meant that he never had to pay for train tickets. The countess added that Georges-Michel was so rich that there was no need to speak of financial compensation for his propaganda: a strange way to raise the issue of money, and a strange way to dismiss it, thought Wasserbäck.

Then the subject of Wilhelm arose again, as if irresistibly. The journalist and the countess said that they wished to promote the restoration of the Habsburgs in Austria. They regretted that the Wilhelm affair had done such harm to the worthy monarchist cause. This was a delicate area of policy for the Austrian diplomat to discuss. Austria had indeed made itself far more welcome to Habsburgs in 1935, and a number of them had returned, usually for less colorful reasons than Wilhelm's. That September the Austrian chancellor had met secretly with Otto von Habsburg, the pretender to the throne. Yet there was no official policy of restoration, as Wasserbäck now explained.

The countess tried to strike a light note of compromise. All they wanted from the embassy, she said, was an invitation to Austria. Wasserbäck replied that they would be welcome to visit the country, but that invitations were not standard practice. Something had caught his attention in a most unpleasant way: her wish to associate Austria with a Habsburg restoration, and the restoration with Wilhelm. This reminded him, again, of the Wilhelm affair, when Wilhelm's enemies had tried to prove that the Austrian state was supporting his cause. Because the countess kept mentioning Wilhelm and kept repeating that she wished to accompany Georges-Michel on the trip to Vienna, he intuited that her real object was to see the archduke. Why would that be?

Then, at a certain moment, Wasserbäck understood everything. The woman before him, whom he had now met twice as the Countess de Rivat, was in fact none other than Paulette Couyba herself, in disguise. No doubt it had also been she who had telephoned in the first place, presenting herself as the Princess of Bourbon-Parma. He bade farewell to his two visitors, and then bided his time.

A few days later, a distraught Michel Georges-Michel appeared at the Austrian legation to call on Wasserbäck. He looked terrible. Something was wrong. He had been receiving telephone calls at odd hours from people claiming to represent the Austrian legation. There had been several different voices, and they did not sound like diplomats. Georges-Michel asked Wasserbäck if he knew who the Countess de Rivat really was. When Wasserbäck replied in the affirmative, that the countess was Paulette Couyba in disguise, Georges-Michel wanted to know why Wasserbäck had not warned him. Wasserbäck replied, truly enough, that he had presumed that the two of them had been conspiring together. Georges-Michel defended himself, claiming that he had only recently grasped the truth himself. A detective agency had provided him with evidence, he said, that Couyba had been masquerading as the Countess de Rivat for some time. Couyba had promised him 100,000 francs to petition the legation and travel to Austria. Then he added that Couyba had insisted that the two of them bring along to Austria a certain Vasyl Paneyko, who, she had maintained, had all the connections that they would need in Austria.

The pieces fell together. Paneyko, of course, was the former political advisor of Wilhelm, who quite likely engineered the entire scandal of 1934–1935. Paneyko had spread gossip far and wide about Wilhelm's homosexuality; Wilhelm, forgetting his manners, afterward referred to Paneyko only as "the fruit." It seemed that Paneyko and Couyba now wished to follow Wilhelm to Vienna, in spring 1936, ideally with Austrian money and an Austrian invitation, the better to hurt him and the monarchist cause generally. The Austrian press had published not a word about Wilhelm's Parisian distress. Paneyko and Paulette would have brought the scandal to him, and no doubt to the attention of Austrians as well.[2]

Paulette had added the special touch of presenting herself (on the phone) as a Bourbon-Parma relative of Zita, and then in person as a member of the French aristocracy. Had her scheme worked, she would have taken symbolic revenge on the empress, whom she no doubt saw as Wilhelm's other woman, as well as upon the French journalists who had mocked her class background. How could she be unfashionable, working class, and fat if she could play the glamorous and seductive countess? But her plan did not work, not quite.

Paulette's second set of frauds and deceptions confirms her guilt in the first, and suggests a continuing complicity with Paneyko. What was the role of Michel Georges-Michel, also once a friend of Wilhelm? Could he have been so easily fooled by Paulette's disguise? The journalist knew Wilhelm well, and thus must have known Paulette. He spent much of his life in the dressing rooms of famous women, in the salons of Paris, and on the beaches of the Riviera. He liked pushy females and had made a career of taking their measure. He had quite literally written the book on the love of crazy French women for riches, conspiracy, and thrones.[3]

But then Paulette was something special. Wasserbäck had followed the Wilhelm affair from beginning to end, and had attended the trial. A skeptical and intelligent man, he too knew Paulette. He had watched her in court, and seen her pictures in the newspapers. He nevertheless was taken in by her impersonation of a countess, at least at first. So perhaps Georges-Michel really was an innocent dupe, as he claimed. Perhaps he was not, but decided that he had had enough cooperation with a rather difficult woman. Whatever Georges-Michel's role, he made no trip to Austria. However the story began, it ended with Paulette and Paneyko still in France.

After Wasserbäck warned his superiors, Austrian border guards received an order to permit no one traveling under the names Rivat, Couyba, or Paneyko to cross the border. Wilhelm was sheltered, as much as anyone could be, from the associates he had chosen for himself.

Hearing the news in Vienna, Wilhelm was incensed that Couyba was still free in France, and grateful to the Austrian authorities for their firm action. An encounter with Paneyko or Paulette might have destroyed his standing in Austria, where almost no one knew anything of his doings in France. It might also have shattered him. Paris had been his home; and however painful the circumstances of his parting, he missed what he had lost and could not recover. When Wilhelm fled, he left behind not only Paulette, but also his Arab valet and lover, Maurice Néchadi. More than his woman or his man, though, he seemed to miss his cat. "That cat," he wrote, "was dearer to me than all humanity." He had lost all trust in people. His nerves were "completely destroyed."[4]

From Vienna, Wilhelm tried to protect his good name in Paris. A conservative newspaper, *Le Figaro,* did publish his version of events, editing it in a way that protected him at a moment when he was not at his most reasonable. Wilhelm had written that Paneyko was not to be trusted because he had changed his original nationality—not the best line of argument, perhaps, from someone who had been born a Habsburg, had been educated to be a Pole, had wished to be king of Ukraine, had sought citizenship in France, and was now seeking the right to reside in Austria. Wilhelm, not the most lucid of men in the best of times, was not quite master of his faculties. The editors of *Le Figaro* were tactful enough to excise that passage. It was kind of them to have published his letter at all. After all, Wilhelm's girlfriend Paulette was also the lover of a man whose wife had murdered the newspaper's editor-in-chief. Such, though, was France in the 1920s and 1930s, and perhaps no one could remember such details. Or, just as likely, it was the business of *Le Figaro* to suppress them, just as it had suppressed the details of Wilhelm's scandal while it was taking place, and the indiscretions in Wilhelm's own account of it.[5]

Wilhelm would never return to Paris. The moment he set foot in France he could be arrested and made to serve his five years of prison time. So he was becoming Austrian again, and in this too he had help. His uncle Eugen, his father's brother, had returned to Austria about a year earlier. Eugen was something of a Renaissance man, a supporter of music and the arts, and the onetime commander of Habsburg forces in the Balkans and Italy. As grand master of the Teutonic Knights, he built hospitals and helped to transform the once-feared crusaders into a purely spiritual order with no military mission. One of the vows of Teutonic Knights was "to be as chaste as possible," a formulation that men, of course, could interpret in many ways, but that Eugen took quite seriously, as least as far as women were concerned. When Eugen returned to Austria in September 1934, after a long Swiss exile, his reputed chastity was such that he was allowed to take up residence in a convent.[6]

Though Eugen represented the glory of the old dynasty in the hearts of Austrians, he helped Wilhelm by guiding him through the rigors of the new Austrian regime. A thoughtful man and a returned Habsburg exile, Eugen was able to explain the pertinent laws. Wilhelm appreciated that Eugen "spoke to everyone necessary," and got permission for his nephew to reside in the country. Wilhelm was fortunate in his timing. A few weeks after he had returned to Austria, the Austrian government enacted a new constitution, this time without provisions requiring Habsburgs to renounce their claims to thrones. Laws of a similar character were still on the books, but the change in the constitution was a clear signal. Without ever having to abandon his claim to the Habsburg succession, Wilhelm received Austrian papers. He was now officially Wilhelm Habsburg rather than Vasyl Vyshyvanyi.[7]

In return for an official identity and protection from the scandal, Wilhelm offered the Austrian regime his loyalty, joining its Fatherland Front. When mandatory military service was reinstated in 1936, he trained again as an officer in the Austrian army.[8]

Though Habsburg was once again Wilhelm's legal name, empire was no longer his destiny. The House of Habsburg, led by Zita and Otto, had ways of making him feel excluded. When Wilhelm left Paris, for example, he was still a knight of the Order of the Golden Fleece, the family chivalric society of the Habsburgs. But the Order, now led by Otto, investigated the Couyba affair, using Austrian diplomatic correspondence to which its members had unofficial access. In March 1936, the Order confidentially informed its members that Wilhelm had "voluntarily resigned from the dignity of a Knight of the Order of the Golden Fleece."[9]

More likely he resigned under pressure. Otto's word was more or less law within the Order, and one can easily imagine why he would want Wilhelm sanctioned. The man had embarrassed Otto and his mother Zita, and had compromised the project of restoration at a critical moment. Even so, there was a bit of hypocrisy in the severity of the penalty. Otto's grandfather and namesake Otto Franz, for example, had committed far worse indiscretions without having to leave the Order. Perhaps some of the motivation was political. Otto wanted to create a new reputation for the House of Habsburg, one less tainted by the popular associations of the family with degeneracy, homosexuality, and war. This, over time, he managed to do, by presenting himself always as a respectable gentleman. Zita had raised him well. With Wilhelm disgraced, Otto was the only member of the dynasty with a strong political profile.

As Otto continued to think of a crown, Wilhelm had to return his golden collar, the sign of his knighthood in the Order. It was number eighty-eight of the one hundred or so that were then abroad in the world. He had been deleted from the Habsburgs' legend of themselves, from the line of civilization that ran from Greek myths through modern monarchs. He would be invited to no more secret meetings with fellow archdukes. In all likelihood, the Order had allowed Wilhelm to maintain contact over the years with his brothers Albrecht and Leo. Now he would have to bear the fact that his brothers were still knights, while he was not. Rejected by the Habsburgs, Wilhelm would have to find consolation in another sort of aristocracy.[10]

Wilhelm remained close to one Parisian friend, the Ukrainian aristocrat Tokary. In the years before Wilhelm's departure from France, Tokary had become a source of authority and comfort. In spring 1933, for example, Tokary had consoled Wilhelm upon the death of his father Stefan. Thereafter Tokary, though only ten years older than Wilhelm, began to play the role of the idealized head of the family. Wilhelm could never now reconcile with Stefan, but he could pledge his loyalty and devotion to his friend. As Wilhelm sought the sort of relationship with Tokary that he had not had with his father since the time of the First World War, he put away some of the anger of his youth. Most notably, Wilhelm lost his reflexive hatred for Poland and things Polish. This brought him closer to Tokary, who believed in Polish-Ukrainian cooperation against the Soviet Union; it also removed, if belatedly, the political source of his dispute with his father. In 1935 and 1936, Wilhelm's desire for paternal authority rang out in his letters to his friend. Writing from Vienna to Paris, he pleaded with Tokary not to forget his "child" and begged to be allowed to "confess to you as to a father."[11]

Wilhelm, lonely and disoriented, needed someone upon whom he could rely. The terrible shock of the Paris scandal had taught Wilhelm to distrust. All his life he had been extremely gullible, following the circular logic of Habsburgs and, indeed, many people born to power and wealth. He regarded anyone close to him as part of a charmed inner circle, by definition full of good will and beyond suspicion. He had never reflected on the means that people must have used in the competition to join his entourage. His companions were boon companions, his advisors were wise advisors, his friends were loyal friends, because, after all, they were his. This outlook had brought him much trouble—from his valet Kroll, his secretary Larischenko, his advisor Paneyko, and his lover Paulette. When Wilhelm learned his lesson in 1935, he learned it too well. Suddenly the world could only be understood as a network of conspiracy, and every individual he had ever known was suspect. In such a world, any political activity would have to be secret.

Wilhelm and Tokary had something like their own secret society, the Ukrainian Order of St. George. The Order of St. George, of which at some point he considered himself a formal member, kept up his flagging spirits. Before he left the Order of the Golden Fleece, Wilhelm had considered himself only an ally of the Order of St. George. He may have felt constrained by the rules of the Golden Fleece from joining any other chivalric society. Thus his exit from the Habsburg conspiracy opened the way to a certain kind of closeness with another hierarchy and a renewal of old ties with Ukrainian authorities. Besides Tokary, Metropolitan Andrii Sheptytsky was likely also involved; Wilhelm wrote regularly to Tokary of an unnamed "clergyman." Sheptytsky had been Wilhelm's Ukrainian mentor during the First World War. Though not his first Ukrainian advisor, Sheptytsky had probably been the first man whose influence on Wilhelm was more important than that of Wilhelm's own father. So Wilhelm was trading one kind of family for another. After the trauma of being expelled from the Order of the Golden Fleece by a younger cousin, Wilhelm surely cherished the sense of returning to a world of paternal warmth. Perhaps, too, he liked being the youngest among the elect. He was only forty, a decade younger than Tokary and three decades younger than Sheptytsky—but seventeen years older than the irksomely young and capable Otto.[12]

Wilhelm also needed a reason to believe that his life was not bereft of prospects of power. He could consider the obscurity of the Order not as an escape from politics but as the mystery needed by a group of elite conspirators. The Order was, after all, a secret kept by a few Ukrainians who regarded themselves as the national aristocracy. It offered Wilhelm a form of Ukrainian activity that did not expose him to the unbearable public judgment of other Ukrainians, at a time when he felt very vulnerable. It also provided the opportunity for a kind of hopeful, perhaps desperate, political fantasy. Wilhelm spoke of himself and of Tokary as "knights." The two men corresponded in a mixture of Ukrainian, German, and French, and the French word for "knight"—"chevalier"—suggests a concept that was quite dear to Wilhelm at this time, chivalry. Feeling himself surrounded by plots, he wrote to Tokary that their enemies could never triumph, as they were incapable of doing battle "as knights," "with visors open."[13]

Wilhelm's education, like his existence, was archaic in many ways. Yet even for him, this image of knights jousting in armor, with faceplates raised so that foes could see their eyes, was centuries out of his ken, and indeed quite baseless. Wilhelm was yielding here to a couple of romantic ideas: of medieval history as a time of harmony, and of an inner, spiritual victory that transcends an external, physical defeat on the battlefield. He had known better in 1918, when he compared the medieval founders of the Habsburg dynasty to violent anarchists. Yet it was no longer 1918. Ukraine had been born in an agony that never ceased, from the overwhelming violence of world war, civil war, revolution and pogroms, to the famine and terror of Soviet Ukraine. Wilhelm had seen his star rise and fall, not once but twice, as a Ukrainian Habsburg in 1918 and then as a Habsburg Ukrainian in 1935. He now knew betrayal, and was left to confront desperate failure. In such a situation, the ideas of family, hierarchy, and mystery served a purpose. They gave back to him values that he had often taken for granted, sometimes mocked, but probably always needed.

Wilhelm had been separated from the Habsburg myth, but now he had found a way back to dreams of empire. He had probably laughed as a youth at the representation of medieval history in *The Emperor's Dream* and smirked at the idealization of his Habsburg forebears when he sought his own kingdom in Ukraine; but the eternal glory presented in that play was nevertheless his birthright, as was his tendency to think of himself as a prospective king. The Ukrainian Order, with its own concept of knighthood and its own idea of an ancient aristocracy, helped him to regain something of his pride. Though it amounted to little more than a few Ukrainians writing almost illegibly obscure letters and Wilhelm designing and ordering chivalric insignia in Vienna, the Order nevertheless allowed him to think again that he might ascend to a Ukrainian throne—without the help of the other Habsburgs, and the bothersome Otto.

Wilhelm could now take his bearings. Having reached a delicate point of self-creation, he could reflect again, a year or so after his disgrace, upon how his dream of power might be realized. Having lost the easy confidence of his imperial youth and the naïve faith in the good will of his adult comrades, he began to reconsider Europe in terms of the conspiratorial logic of the included and the excluded, of perfect oppositions and absolute antinomies. Believing that the European left was in league against him after his experience with the Popular Front in France, he decided that the key to power was unity on the right. Since his only politics were, at this point, secretive and elitist, he conceived of this union as an alliance of various chivalric orders, apparently, though the hints are vague, the Papal Order of St. Gregory, the Bavarian Order of St. George, and the Ukrainian Order of St. George. No such unifications were achieved, nor could they have been given the various rules and missions of these organizations. Wilhelm had nonetheless regained his belief in political action.[14]

Even as Wilhelm retreated to a secret world of monarchic nostalgia, the Austrian political system was transforming the public space around him in a way that also seemed to reject modern political ideas such as democracy and individual rights. Wilhelm had stumbled into Austria at precisely the moment when its government was becoming more welcoming of Habsburgs. As he came to see, this change was part of a larger transformation in which the Austrian regime, the Fatherland Front, tried to create a model of politics that drew symbols from the past in order to generate popular support for its new authoritarian order. The Fatherland Front negotiated with Otto and protected Wilhelm, and naturally the Habsburgs welcomed such gestures. Yet the Fatherland Front referred to the past to justify a new kind of regime. Like the Nazis in Germany, it propagated an emblem of state with an unconventional cross; it also, like the Nazis, employed an official greeting that involved a hail with a raised arm.

Austria, in other words, looked like a fascist regime in 1936. From a distance, at least, it seemed to have joined a European movement that rejected democracy and reason in favor of rule by a Leader who presented himself as the voice of the national will. The first fascist regime was Mussolini's in Italy; the next was Hitler's in Germany. Although the two regimes had important differences, they were regarded by many, on the left as well as the right, as representing a powerful kind of mass politics. The left-wing Popular Front in France, from which Wilhelm had just escaped, presented the world as divided between fascists and anti-fascists. Wilhelm, once he took his bearings, was happy to have landed in a country that represented the opposite of the France that he had just been forced to leave. "Here all is well," he wrote to Tokary in November 1935, "and there is fascist law and order and ideologically it's very pleasant."[15]

Rather quickly, Wilhelm began to synthesize the fascism he saw around him with his own private Ukrainian mission. He saw fascism, correctly, as a challenge to the postwar order in Europe. Italian, German, and other fascists rejected the peace treaties, presenting them as unjust and despicable barriers to the realization of the national will. In other words, they aspired to change the map of Europe by force of arms. Fascists were revisionists, believers that the boundaries of European states had to be changed. As Wilhelm knew from his experience of the early 1920s, revisionists could be allies of Ukrainians.

Since Ukraine did not exist, Ukrainian nationalists believed that they needed a European calamity, presumably a war initiated by fascists, to win state independence. For such a scenario to be realized, there would have to be Ukrainian leaders ready and willing to co-operate with European fascists and capable of turning catastrophe to their own ends. This is where Wilhelm and his aristocratic brethren saw their own role. By April 1936, Wilhelm was sure that the only independent Ukraine would be a fascist Ukraine. As he wrote to Tokary that October, their Ukrainian chivalric order would "create the cadres that will be necessary for the reconstruction of a Ukrainian Empire, sovereign and independent, ruled by a single person"—who would, presumably, be Wilhelm himself.[16]

The fascist idea of a Leader had a double significance for Wilhelm in 1936. For the most part, he felt weak and wanted to be led. He wanted to admire Mussolini, and to be instructed by Tokary. Yet he also fantasized about one day becoming a Leader himself. Before he could do that, however, he would have to decide to which nation he belonged. Wilhelm's whole life had exhibited a good deal of ambiguity on this question, an ambiguity that fascism, at first at least, seemed to permit.

The fascism of the 1920s and early 1930s retained something of the fraternity of the patriotic ideas of the nineteenth century. If there was a fascism for each nation, then a person who loved more than one nation could be, if perhaps just barely, a cosmopolitan fascist. Wilhelm and Tokary both met this description. Wilhelm was an Austrian fascist and a Ukrainian fascist and did not experience a contradiction. However, just as Wilhelm was making himself at home in an Austria that he saw as fascist and dreaming of a Ukraine that he hoped would one day be fascist, Nazi Germany was changing the meaning of fascism. Hitler proclaimed that the nation was decided by blood, which meant that Wilhelm's sort of fascism was impossible. According to the Nazi racial logic, Wilhelm was a German, or he was nothing at all.

As Wilhelm began to think politically again in 1936, he had to consider German ideology, because he had to confront German power. In the first few months of Hitler's rule, in spring and summer 1933, he tamed the German state. In March 1935 Germany violated the peace accords by reinstating the military draft and building armaments. A year later German troops marched into the Rhineland, a zone at the French border that was to remain indefinitely demilitarized. Meanwhile, the German economy recovered from the Depression, and German trade policy drew its eastern neighbors into its orbit.

Nazi Germany thus came to rival Mussolini's Italy as the model of European fascism. Tokary, who moved from Paris to Rome, continued to regard Italian fascism as the template for the Ukrainian. As a good Catholic, he saw Nazi Germany as pagan. He also imagined that Italy could somehow help Austria and Ukraine to become independent fascist states. Wilhelm, residing in Austria and hailing from a family of historically German princes, had to react to Hitler's racist understanding of the nation. Unlike Tokary, he himself could be considered a German. His latest homeland, Austria, could be considered a German country, since it was populated by speakers of German. Hitler was himself an Austrian by origin and always regarded his homeland as part of a future, enlarged Germany.

Wilhelm watched as the Fatherland Front, which had welcomed him and which he found to be appealingly fascist, confronted the aggression, racism, and power of Nazi Germany, and its scarcely hidden aspiration to absorb Austria. To survive the rise of Nazi Germany, the Austrian regime needed help from outside. For a few years, Italy had been a loyal ally. In 1934, when Nazis had staged a coup in Vienna, Mussolini dispatched crack infantry units to the Brenner Pass to express support for Austrian independence. Yet by 1936, the year that Wilhelm declared himself for a fascist Europe, the balance of power had changed. Even as Hitler's Germany rose from defeated state to rearming power, Mussolini's Italy alienated possible allies and demonstrated military weakness by botching an invasion of Abyssinia. When Mussolini signed an alliance with Hitler in October 1936, he was abandoning an Austrian ally that he could no longer defend.

As Wilhelm could see, Austria was in no position to defend itself against Germany without Italian help. In July 1936, Austria and

Germany signed a noninterference agreement that, unfortunately for the Austrians, actually legalized a German role in Austrian affairs. A secret clause required the Austrian government to appoint two Nazis to positions of authority, which emboldened Nazis in Austria even as their party remained technically illegal. The Fatherland Front was at a loss as to how to rally the Austrian population in favor of the country's independence. The regime could not call on the left, as the Social Democratic Party had been banned in 1934. It could not call on the Nazi far right, since Austrian Nazis wished for unification with Germany. Some patriotic Austrians began to believe that the country could only be saved by a restoration of the Habsburgs. Austrian towns and villages began to grant Otto honorary citizenship.[17]

Wilhelm found himself confronted, then, not only with evidence of Nazi power, but with signs of Otto's popularity. A restored monarchy under Otto seemed to many Austrians to be the most plausible defense against German aggression. German force provided Wilhelm with a strong reason to accept the German version of fascism, while Wilhelm's jealousy of Otto pushed him away from his tolerant past. As the stakes grew higher and the Austrian confrontation with Nazi power more direct, Wilhelm could no longer be a cosmopolitan fascist. He could either retain some aura of historic Habsburg toleration, with its acceptance of the equality of nations and the presence of Jewish life in Europe, or he could embrace the racism that the Nazis saw as the future. Nazi racism would give Wilhelm a way to express his anger that Otto, as Wilhelm saw matters, had excluded him from the Habsburg restoration.

As 1937 began, Wilhelm made his choice. In January, Wilhelm noted, in a letter to Tokary, that the leader of the restorationist movement in Austria was by birth a Jew. This meant, said Wilhelm, that the movement was morally corrupt and politically doomed. It was an odd thing to say. The man in question was Friedrich von Wiesner, whom Wilhelm had known for more than fifteen years. In 1921, the two of them had collaborated in the Habsburg restorationist politics of Vienna, as well as in the Ukrainian syndicate—the scheme to use Bavarian capital to finance an invasion of Bolshevik

Russia. They remained in touch when Wilhelm was in Madrid in the 1920s. In 1934 Wilhelm had noted with pleasure that Otto had entrusted Wiesner with the leadership of the restorationist movement. Nor were Jewish origins something that had ever troubled Wilhelm. As a young man he had admired Jewish teachers at his military academy and Jewish doctors in the army. In the summer of 1935, he had chosen to reside in a largely Jewish district of Vienna. He knew the city well, and would have understood who his neighbors would be. He even saw something Jewish about the peripatetic course of his own life. Reflecting upon his many journeys in autumn 1935, he referred to himself as "the eternally wandering Jew."[18]

A Habsburg, even a Habsburg fascist, might be tolerant of Jews; anti-Semitism was the mark of a Nazi. Why the sudden and decisive change in the attitudes of a lifetime? Perhaps money was the key. In autumn 1936, Wilhelm experienced a first financial humiliation. That autumn, for three months in a row, his monthly appanage did not arrive from Poland. Poland and Austria did not enjoy good relations, and it was difficult to send Polish currency to Austria. Wilhelm's payments from his brother Albrecht were held in clearing accounts. Since he had no savings and no inclination to work, this reduced him to poverty quite quickly. As he wrote to his brother Albrecht, "I then ask myself what to do in such a situation—and my knowledge comes to an end." He had to write pleading letters to the manager of his family's firm, and pawn his few valuables to pay his rent and gas bill. This humiliated a man who was accustomed to receiving money simply by asking for it and who had never really wanted for anything. Perhaps he somehow associated his sense of powerlessness with the Jews.[19]

Most likely, though, considerations of power and his jealousy of Otto were sufficient to make of Wilhelm a Nazi sympathizer. The Nazis seemed like the only possible ally of Ukraine and the only force that might once again propel Wilhelm toward a throne. He began to consider once more the ways that Germany might bring Ukraine to life. Although he seems never to have joined the Nazi movement in Austria, he began, according to one later report, to speak highly of Hitler.[20]

In February 1937, Wilhelm found a confederate of similar mind and background. Ivan Poltavets-Ostrianytsia, another Ukrainian colonel who admired National Socialism, was a man who had lived a life of uncanny similarities to Wilhelm's own. In 1918, as Wilhelm was fulfilling his special Ukrainian mission in the Habsburg occupation force, Poltavets was working in Kiev as adjutant to Hetman Skoropadsky, the leader of the German-supported government. Poltavets had been in the middle as Wilhelm and Skoropadsky tried to negotiate a common monarchist position in 1920. Poltavets then joined Wilhelm's Ukrainian syndicate. When the Bavarian money dried up in 1922, and the Free Cossacks split into factions, Poltavets had proclaimed himself to be their leader. While at first Poltavets was regarded as Skoropadsky's man, in 1926 he broke with his patron and declared himself hetman of Ukraine.

As Wilhelm whiled away his and his century's twenties and thirties in Spain and France, Poltavets remained in Bavaria. He became friendly with Nazis, who regarded him as one of the first Ukrainian fascists. In the years before the Nazis came to power, Ukraine played an important role in their debates about the future order in Europe. They all regarded the Soviet Union as an enemy to be destroyed, and some believed that nationalism was the key to its destruction. Some Nazis were certainly interested in Ukraine, a large Soviet republic that had suffered enormously under Stalin and that might, therefore, be turned against Russia and, as the Nazis saw matters, the Jewish leadership of the Soviet Union. Alfred Rosenberg, one of Poltavets's backers, believed that Germany should recruit Ukrainians to fight the Soviet Union. In May 1935 Poltavets wrote to Hitler, offering the services of himself and his Free Cossacks.[21]

So Poltavets, like Wilhelm, was a rebellious Ukrainian monarchist and fascist, now looking for a way to return to power and to Ukraine, and seeing the Nazi movement as the most plausible ally. When the two men met again, after fifteen years of separation, enough time had passed since the collapse of the Ukrainian syndicate for the reunion to be a happy one—especially since the backdrop was a skiing vacation. Wilhelm proudly told Poltavets of the Order of St. George and its mission to build a fascist Ukraine.

Wilhelm came away from the encounter of February 1937 with slightly more concrete political ideas for the advancement of the Ukrainian cause in a Europe dominated by Germany. Poltavets had more recent experience with Nazis than did Wilhelm, whose own period of collaboration with the German right had ended in 1922. Most likely Poltavets gave Wilhelm a sense of which Nazis might be sympathetic to the Ukrainian cause and interested in contacts with prominent Ukrainians. Wilhelm wrote to Tokary that their Order would have to penetrate the milieu of Hans Frank, a Nazi who had served as justice minister in Bavaria and was now a minister of government. More grandly, he imagined that he could help the Germans recruit a "Ukrainian Legion."[22]

Using this term in March 1937, Wilhelm was recalling March 1918 when he had been summoned by Emperor Karl to lead a Ukrainian Legion under Austrian command against the Bolsheviks. Likely he imagined that he would one day be summoned by Hitler to do the same in a coming war against the Soviet Union. If so, he was hardly the only Ukrainian to have had this idea. Various Ukrainian political organizations were now banking on some kind of military cooperation with Nazi Germany. Wilhelm and Tokary agreed that no one but their own Order was truly deserving of German support. Tokary wrote to Wilhelm that rival Ukrainian politicians were "idiots," using a German word. Because of his past collaboration with the German right, Wilhelm could imagine that he would have some special access to the Nazis.[23]

The Nazis did not take Wilhelm seriously. Even as Wilhelm was dreaming of a second Ukrainian Legion, in March 1937, the Nazi press was smearing him as a decadent Parisian lowlife. Wilhelm was not much of a reader; if he saw the article, he might have interpreted it, correctly, as part of Hitler's general animus against Austria and the Habsburgs. Wilhelm probably thought that he could explain to Hitler that he himself had turned against Otto and now opposed a Habsburg restoration in Austria. Wilhelm now saw a Habsburg restoration in essentially Nazi terms: as Jewish, illegitimate, and doomed. Any restoration, as he wrote to Tokary in December 1937, would be "by the grace of the Jews and the free masons." The

Habsburg dynasty itself had become a "Jewish enterprise." Wilhelm convinced himself that he had broken with Otto, who was "stubborn and blind," rather than the other way around. If Wilhelm could have no part in a restoration, he wanted no one else to have one either. This was sour grapes, in royal purple—with a bit of Nazi brown around the edges.[24]

As 1938 began, Wilhelm had decided that the Austrian variety of authoritarianism was unsatisfying. Where, after all, was the Austrian nation? A Jew, in Wilhelm's view, at least had some sort of reliable national character, even if that consisted in being "red in the middle" and thus denying the national aspirations of everyone else in the name of communism. An Austrian, Wilhelm now thought, had no character at all, since he had no nation. Wilhelm came to believe that Austrians were simply Germans. Having reinvented himself as an Austrian, he then reconceived Austrian identity as a matter of being racially German. If politics was about nationalism and nationalism was a matter of race, then Austria itself served no purpose. It should be, as Hitler desired, folded into a greater German Reich.[25]

The true significance of his own personal defeat in France, Wilhelm now believed, lay in his participation in a grand war for civilization. To have been attacked by the forces of evil made him a figure of stature among the forces of good. What was more, he now believed that he was on the winning side. Wilhelm saw a Triple Axis (which he anticipated; it had not yet been created) of Berlin, Rome, and Tokyo as "the greatest thing of our era." It would bring about the encirclement and destruction of the Soviet Union. A great victory would follow: "the liquidation of communist ideology and the healing of the entire world!" This total vision of a single and decisive triumph set Wilhelm at odds with Tokary, who still much preferred Italy to Germany and who was more concerned with the "healing of Ukraine." Wilhelm stood by his own ideas of political hygiene. When he had arrived in Austria, he had complained that his nerves were shattered. Now they were "like ropes."[26]

Nationalism was part of his cure. The other parts were snow and sex. Whenever Wilhelm had the money, as he did in those winters of

On the Slopes with a Companion. Wilhelm at left.

1937 and 1938, he traveled to Salzburg and thence to the slopes. The photographs show him dapper and handsome, in the company of beautiful young men.

As Wilhelm calmed his nerves, Austria's leaders grew quite anxious, and with good reason. On 12 February 1938, Hitler gave Chancellor Kurt von Schuschnigg an ultimatum. Austria had three days to conform its policies to Germany's, legalize the Nazi Party, and give a Nazi control over the police. If these conditions were not met, Hitler said, Germany would invade. Schuschnigg accepted the terms.

He did not fulfill them. Though Schuschnigg's Fatherland Front had never created a convincing vision of the Austrian nation, its leaders believed in Austria, and tried, for a moment at least, to defend it. As Hitler proclaimed the coming unification or *Anschluss,*

Schuschnigg summoned Austrians to defend their country to the death. He ordered a referendum on independence, with the question worded (and the votes stacked) to guarantee a victory. He also sought support from foreign powers. None was forthcoming. Italy, the former ally, had abandoned Austria. France's left-wing governments had by early 1938 come to see Austria as a possible barrier to Hitler's expansion, and sought to rally the British to a common position. London declined to support a démarche, regarding Austria's fate as sealed.[27]

The Austrian referendum was prepared but never held. Hitler ordered an invasion, and Schuschnigg instructed Austrian troops not to resist. On 12 March 1938, the German army entered Austria; the next day, Hitler declared that Austria had ceased to exist. Schuschnigg had not, in the end, defended Austria to the death, but he had earned a place in the ranks of Hitler's enemies. After the German invasion, he was arrested and imprisoned. After interrogation, he was dispatched to German concentration camps, first Dachau and then Sachsenhausen.

After the *Anschluss,* Austria's large Jewish population faced restrictions far worse than under the Fatherland Front. Though quotas on Jews in the professions and universities had induced thousands of Austrian Jews to leave the country in the 1930s, Schuschnigg was no Hitler, and the Fatherland Front no Nazi Party. Jews had been allowed to join the Fatherland Front, and indeed many did. German rule was utterly different. Jews lost their jobs, and their property. The *Kristallnacht* pogroms, later in 1938, were incredibly violent in Vienna. Men, women, and children were killed, often after dreadful public humiliations.

Hitler had not only destroyed Austria, he had ended any immediate hope of a Habsburg restoration in Europe. Hitler hated the Habsburgs, so much so that his invasion plan of Austria was called "Operation Otto." Otto had indeed tried to prevent the *Anschluss.* In late 1937 and early 1938, he had said, to anyone who would listen, that a restoration was the only way to keep Hitler from Vienna. On 21 November 1937, Otto's twenty-fifth birthday, Vienna was decorated with the old imperial colors, black and gold. On 17 December the Austrian government restored properties seized from the Habsburgs after the war, making Otto one of the wealthiest men in the country. That month he urged Chancellor Schuschnigg to prepare military resistance to Germany, and suggested that only a legitimate monarch, meaning himself, could lead the people to victory. Right after Hitler's ultimatum, Otto offered his own services as head of government. Schuschnigg politely declined to cede his own position to Otto. Schuschnigg had always repeated, and probably believed, what the Germans had told him: that a restoration would be suicidal since it would bring an instant German attack. In the end, Otto was never asked to return, but the Germans invaded anyway.

Otto, Wilhelm's Habsburg rival, was defeated. Indeed, it seemed as if Nazi power had fulfilled all of Wilhelm's darkest wishes. Germany had swallowed Austria, non-Jewish Austrians had become German citizens, and Jews were fleeing the country. In the aftermath of the *Anschluss,* Germany began to dismember Czechoslovakia: the only European democracy east of France, France's ally, and the state Wilhelm believed had plotted his downfall in Paris. All of his enemies, it might have seemed, had been vanquished. Wilhelm lived in accord with the spirit of the times. His imaginative return to politics, an aristocratic fascism apparently divorced from practical reality, had led him to anticipate exactly what had indeed happened. Next, he believed, the Germans would destroy the Bolsheviks and restore Ukraine.

Of course, an important European country lay between Nazi Germany and the Soviet Union: Poland. Before Hitler could attack Stalin, he would have to destroy Poland, the chosen homeland of Wilhelm's brothers Albrecht and Leo. For Wilhelm's Ukrainian dreams to be fulfilled, his Polish family would have to endure the nightmare of German rule.

BLACK

❧

Against Hitler and Stalin

I N 1939, ALBRECHT WAS still the good son. As Wilhelm drifted from one nation to another, his older brother remained a loyal Polish citizen and a respected Polish businessman. The Polish republic had made peace with the Żywiec branch of the Habsburg family, and Albrecht had returned the favor with an openly patriotic devotion to his chosen homeland. Albrecht and his wife Alice wanted themselves, and their family, to be regarded as Poles. Their children learned English, French, and Polish, but not German.

Their older daughter, Maria Krystyna, lived happily in the family castle in Żywiec. She made her way through its halls by skipping from one white marble tile to another, always avoiding the black. Tutors instructed her in languages, introducing her to the demands of a worldly life she might yet lead. She liked to mock her French tutor, who spoke poor Polish. She was taught to ride by a Polish officer, on a horse so calm that he let the crows nibble at his tail.

For Maria Krystyna, who turned sixteen that year, the summer of 1939 was little different than any other. War with Germany was in the air, but it was a war that her father and other Poles believed that Poland would win. Albrecht had contributed generously to fund drives for Polish anti-aircraft batteries. When units of Poland's elite Border Control Corps were ordered to Żywiec, near the German frontier, Albrecht had them quartered on the grounds of his castle.[1]

The German army invaded Poland on 1 September 1939, unprovoked, without a declaration of war. Unlike Austria and Czechoslovakia, Poland fought; France and Great Britain promised their support and declared war on Germany. As a European war began on the German-Polish frontier, the people of Żywiec fled to the east. Albrecht and Alice had already sent their daughters to Warsaw a few weeks earlier. Their son was on vacation with Alice's family in Sweden.

No doubt urged on by Alice, Albrecht tried to serve Poland in its hour of need. Though released from military service years before for reasons of poor health, Albrecht donned his Polish officer's uniform on 1 September and looked for a unit. The gesture was symbolic, but the struggle was hopeless. Although Polish resistance around Żywiec was fierce and German casualties considerable, he was joining a retreat. The city was taken in three days.[2]

So Albrecht went to Warsaw to fetch his girls, hurrying ahead of the German blitz. In the Polish capital, his daughter Maria Krystyna looked up at the airplanes in the clear blue skies. "Ours," said the people on the streets. They were wrong. The Polish air force had been destroyed on the ground. The planes were German, and they were bombing civilians, right from the beginning of the war.

As German bombs killed tens of thousands of Poles, Albrecht rescued his daughters. He tried to stay ahead of the Germans. Rather than returning to Żywiec, he led the girls southwest toward Alice's estate. It was a journey to another part of Poland, and to another chapter of the Habsburg past. The estate had belonged to Alice's first husband, a Habsburg diplomat; he had inherited it from his father, who was a prime minister under the Habsburgs. It lay in the eastern part of the old Habsburg province of Galicia, in lands where Ukrainians rather than Poles made up the majority of the population.

Albrecht and the girls fled the army of one totalitarian power only to find the army of another. On 17 September, the Red Army invaded Poland from the east, also unprovoked, also without a declaration of war. Nazi Germany and the Soviet Union had signed a nonaggression pact that August, with a secret protocol dividing eastern Europe into spheres of influence. Poland was to be split between them, and Stalin was taking his half.

Albrecht and the girls, confronted with the unexpected Soviet assault, now turned back west toward Żywiec. As a Polish aristocrat and Polish officer, he had good reason to fear the Soviets, who were encouraging Ukrainian peasants to take revenge on Polish landlords. The Soviets would murder more than twenty thousand Polish officers—including the cavalry officer who had taught Maria Krystyna to ride. The German occupation zone was equally frightful. In their absence, Żywiec had already been incorporated into the German Reich. In despair, one of the children's tutors committed suicide.[3]

In that terrible fall of 1939, Polish citizens fled back and forth, east and west, making guesses about personal safety, or trying to rejoin family. The Polish Habsburgs were no exception. On 25 September, having had no word from Albrecht, Alice bravely set out east from Żywiec to find her husband and daughters. She knew that the Soviets had invaded the part of Poland where her estate lay. She was not deterred; indeed, she probably believed that Albrecht and the girls would need her help.

As the invading Soviets urged Ukrainians to make class war in the countryside, there arrived Alice in eastern Galicia: local landowner, Swedish noblewoman, wife of two Polish aristocrats, Habsburg by marriage. Yet once again, as twenty years earlier, the local Ukrainians regarded her as a good neighbor, and did not wish to hurt her. Not finding Albrecht and the girls at her estate, she made her way back to Żywiec. Her husband and daughters had returned to the castle just four days after she had departed. But by the time she reached their home, in the middle of November, he was gone again. All she found was the farewell note, in French. The servants told her the rest.

The gardener had tried to warn Albrecht: "the Germans are coming, they're looking for officers." The German state police, or

Gestapo, knew that Albrecht had funded the Polish military, and that he had reported for duty in its ranks. On 9 November, he had been led from the castle by two policemen, looking, Maria Krystyna thought, "pale as a ghost." He had reasons to fear. His children were without their parents. His wife was somewhere in the east. His army had been annihilated. His own part of Poland, the Żywiec region, had been annexed by the Reich. His property, he must have understood, was at risk of being confiscated. Some of it was already gone, stolen by Hans Frank, the top official of the Generalgouvernement—the German occupation zone made up of Polish lands taken by Germany but not annexed to the Reich. On his way to his assignment, Frank had stopped in Żywiec to steal the Habsburg family silver, originally a wedding gift from Emperor Franz Josef to Stefan and Maria Theresia. He would use it in the former Polish royal castle in Cracow, which he made his headquarters.[4]

As Poland collapsed, Albrecht comported himself with courage. He might have tried to save himself and his possessions by claiming to be German. Instead, in his first Gestapo interrogation on 16 November 1939, he affirmed that he was Polish. Although Albrecht could hardly deny that he was "of German descent," since his forefathers had been Holy Roman Emperors of the German Nation for several hundred years, he repeated that he himself was Polish because he had so decided. He liked Poland, he said. Poland had treated him well. He had raised his children to be Poles.

The Gestapo was annoyed. On 8 December its officers concluded that Albrecht's life "was one long betrayal of Germanness, one that excludes him forever from the community of Germans. His treason can never be redeemed, and he has thus lost any right to his property and any right to live in Germany, even as a foreigner." He was imprisoned indefinitely in Cieszyn, a Polish city that had been, like Żywiec, annexed by the German Reich.[5]

Albrecht's stand was dramatic, but not unrepresentative of the Poles of the region generally. German authorities, in these weeks, were proclaiming that the annexed Żywiec region had always been German, and that its inhabitants were of German origin. Yet even after Żywiec and its surrounding lands had been incorporated by Germany, local Poles decorated the graves of the fallen Polish soldiers who had resisted the German invasion. In December 1939, German authorities conducted a census of the local population. Only 818 people registered themselves as Germans, as against 148,413 Poles.

Whereas Poles were encouraged to register as Germans, but did not, some Jews wished to register as Germans, but could not. Poles might be granted, in certain cases, status as Germans; Polish Habsburgs might be cajoled, interrogated, and tortured. Polish citizens of

Jewish religion or origin were simply registered as Jews, expelled from Żywiec to the Generalgouvernement, and placed in ghettoes.[6]

Albrecht's bravery drew German attention to his family. His Gestapo file listed his siblings, including Wilhelm, residing in Vienna. At some point in late 1939, the Gestapo paid a call on Wilhelm there. Why, they asked him, was Albrecht a Polish citizen? Why had he reported for duty in the Polish army? If Wilhelm had answers to these questions, he did not provide them. There was little he could say that would be intelligible to the policemen of a racial empire. The German police had been taught that family origin was the same thing as nationality. Wilhelm and his brothers came from a family that had abjured national identity for centuries, and then embraced multiple nations at the same time. For the time being, he was one of theirs, a German—or at least that was the impression he gave.

Wilhelm soon donned an officer's uniform himself, a German one. In spring 1940 he was called up for retraining at Wiener-Neustadt. This was the same place where Wilhelm had been a cadet, training for service in the Habsburg armed forces, twenty-five years before. When Wilhelm graduated back in 1915, he could not have been more promising, and could anticipate a secret assignment in Ukraine. In 1940, matters were very different. Although he was only forty-five years old, in the prime of life for an officer, Wilhelm seemed to make little impression. Though his Nazi sympathies were known, he had never, it seems, joined the Nazi Party. He was a Habsburg. He had tuberculosis and a heart condition. Rather than regular duty in the German army, Wilhelm was assigned home defense, generally a task for old men and boys. Wilhelm must have grasped then that the Germans had no plans to ask him to raise a Ukrainian Legion to fight a war of liberation against the Soviet Union. They paid him, it appears, almost no attention at all.[7]

Aware that his grand political plans of the late 1930s had come to naught, Wilhelm turned his attention to family matters. He reported for his home defense duty in Baden, just south of Vienna, where his sister Eleanora lived with her husband Alfons Kloss. Wilhelm and Eleanora, the youngest son and the eldest daughter, had always been close. Eleanora had been the first Habsburg archduchess to follow her heart and marry a commoner for love; Wilhelm had followed his heart, too, in still less conventional directions. Both of them had a weak spot for sailors, of whom Eleanora's husband was one. Eleanora and Kloss were an Austrian family who had become German. They had six sons in the German army. Perhaps, with her sons away on the front, it was a comfort to Eleanora to have her baby brother nearby. Perhaps the consolation was the greater after two of her boys were killed in action. How did the brother and sister discuss the war? Her sons, as part of the German invasion force, had just helped destroy their brother Albrecht's beloved Poland.[8]

Perhaps, though, the family fortune could somehow be saved. If Albrecht was determined to share Poland's fate, Wilhelm and Eleanora could at least try to claim his money. Though the two of them were the rebels of the family, Albrecht had always made sure that they received monthly subsidies. After the arrest of Albrecht and the seizure of his property that followed, their payments had been reduced by the new German administration of the Żywiec brewery and estate. Both Eleanora and Wilhelm hired lawyers and issued protests. Their youthful rejection of Polish identity now worked to their advantage. They were subjects of the Reich, they were racially Germans, and they should not, their lawyers argued, be penalized when the Reich seized a property. Wilhelm wrote directly to Hitler.

Wilhelm and Eleanora sued Albrecht; German courts tried the case as a financial claim against the German administration of the Żywiec estate. The brother and sister most likely knew that Albrecht was in prison. Suing a brother who was being tortured by the Gestapo might be considered an unkind act, but their legal victory did leave a small part of the family wealth in the hands of Habsburgs. Given his extraordinarily thoughtful and generous nature, it seems just possible that Albrecht encouraged them, or would have wanted them, to do just this.

German authorities were certainly sympathetic to Wilhelm and Eleanora's claim. The legal section of the German state paramilitary, the SS, regarded them as "Reichsdeutsch"—Germans by race and culture deserving of full rights. The SS lawyers noted, correctly, that

Eleanora had eight German children. They believed, incorrectly, that Wilhelm had spent all of the 1920s and 1930s in Austria, which by this time was a part of Germany. The nasty articles in Nazi press organs about Wilhelm's scandal in Paris were unread or forgotten. Fortunately for Wilhelm, the Ukrainian and French phases of his life completely eluded their attention. Indeed, it was his good fortune that he had been forced to leave France. Had he remained and become a French citizen, as he had wished, it would have been much harder to leave his scandalous past behind, and press a claim as a German in German courts.

In spring 1941, it appears, Eleanora and Wilhelm were paid off by the German state. Rather than the regular monthly payments to which they were accustomed, they got lump sums: Eleanora 875,000 marks, Wilhelm 300,000—just under $27 million and just over $9 million in today's dollars. They were both set for life.[9]

These generous payments, of course, came from the estate that the Germans had seized from their brother Albrecht in Żywiec. While Wilhelm and Eleanora were free German citizens in Vienna, their oldest brother was in prison in Cieszyn as an enemy of the German nation. While they came into family wealth, he and his wife and children lived from a tiny stipend.

Alice remained an unrepentant Pole. She called the Nazi regime "a robber state"—to the face of her Gestapo interrogator. Him she called a "blackmailer and a criminal." She also promised the Germans the "resurrection of Poland" after the victory of "her friends." When she pronounced these words, in May 1940, Poland was occupied, and the German army was storming through France. Britain was all that stood between Germany and the domination of Europe. So hers was a bold prediction.

Alice was a sufficiently dynastic thinker to have a frame of reference broader than the present time. She thought of Germany as a country that the Habsburgs had ruled for half a millennium. She sensed that Hitler's regime, the so-called "thousand-year Reich," would not last nearly so long. Intimidated by her bravado and beauty, the Gestapo lacked the nerve to arrest Alice. Its officers instead tried to persuade

Polish State Archives, Żywiec

Alice Habsburg

her that, as a perfect female specimen of the Nordic race, she should abandon the Polish nation and join the victorious Germans.[10]

Letters began to arrive at the local Gestapo bureau, forwarded from Berlin, asking for better treatment of Alice and Albrecht. They came from neutral states such as Sweden and Spain, where the couple had royal and aristocratic connections; and from Albrecht's former comrades in arms from the First World War, Germans now in positions of authority in the Reich. The Gestapo had a ready response to such pressure: that Albrecht could not possibly be released given his racial treason, and that Alice was treated very well given her obnoxious performance in interrogations.

In summer 1940 Alice was exiled with the girls to the small town of Wisła, about thirty-five kilometers west of Żywiec. When the family was gone, the family castle was draped with a Nazi banner and put at the disposition of dignitaries of the Reich. Alice was one of some forty thousand Poles to be forcibly resettled from the Żywiec region, making room for some twenty-five thousand Germans who arrived to take their place. Germans were hired, for example, to run the Żywiec brewery in place of fired Polish staff. Production of beer tripled but quality suffered, as the proud European brand became a source of swill for German troops.[11]

After watching the couple throughout 1940, the Gestapo understood "that in the Habsburg family the wife is the active part." They believed, with good reason, that she supported her husband's uncompromising stance. They intercepted a letter from Alice to Albrecht in which she wrote: "don't believe I will lose my courage, just the contrary, that I will never do. Never give up, never bow down—better to be struck to the ground."[12]

Alice never bowed down, nor was she struck to the ground. She worked against the German occupation with the Polish underground from late 1939. Recruited by one of her children's teachers, she was sworn in to the local Secret Independence Organization. This group was one of hundreds that formed in Poland at the time, most of which were later consolidated within the Home Army, the major anti-Nazi resistance organization of continental Europe. Alice listened to the BBC and other illegal radio broadcasts, and helped her comrades get messages to the Polish government in exile.[13]

Alice had foreign connections, and she traveled. In November 1941 she was in the German city of Cologne, the bombing of which she was delighted to watch from the perspective of the target. "It was a beautiful spectacle," she wrote, "like fireworks." As she looked up, her sympathies were entirely with the Royal Air Force, whose deadly cargo might easily have taken her own life. Likely she knew that Polish airmen who had escaped the Germans were flying with the British. She seemed to think of the men in the cockpits, as she thought of men generally, as simple creatures who needed a bit of feminine encouragement. As she watched the German anti-aircraft fire seek its targets, her heart was with the pilots: "I saw the explosions in the air, and the airmen must have felt most uncomfortable, caught there between heaven and earth. The poor boys."[14]

Wilhelm, hopeful about National Socialism in 1939, came to see the war in 1940 and 1941 in much the same way as did his sister-in-law

Alice. The German occupation had been horrible for Albrecht and Alice, as Wilhelm must have guessed after his visit from the Gestapo. Perhaps he heard something from them directly. He had been in touch with his brothers in 1937 and 1938, when Albrecht brought Leo to Vienna to be treated for tuberculosis. Leo, like Albrecht, lived on a portion of the family estate in Żywiec that they had inherited from their father. Although the two brothers were not especially close, in part because Albrecht was a Pole and Leo was raising his children German, they could count on each other in times of need. If Wilhelm got the family news in 1939 and 1940, he would have learned that his favorite Nazi, Hans Frank, had stolen the family silver.[15]

Now, for the first time in his life, Wilhelm was wealthier than his older brother Albrecht. Had he wished to, he could simply have invested the money, and surrounded himself with the pleasures that were so important to him in Paris. Probably he did. According to German police records, he did find himself a girlfriend and complained that she spent all his money. Yet he also chose, from his new position of financial independence, to pass judgment on Hitler and his policies and align himself much more closely with Albrecht's point of view. As he watched German policies toward his family and then toward Ukraine, he came to believe that his brother's choice to resist Hitler had been the correct one. For the first time since the dissolution of the Habsburg monarchy, Albrecht and Wilhelm were on the same side. The First World War, with its promise of independence for Poland and Ukraine, had pushed them apart. The Second, in which Germany oppressed both Poland and Ukraine, drew them together.[16]

War had been Ukrainians' only hope for relief from the horrors of Soviet rule, but Hitler seemed determined to dash that hope. Germany had missed every opportunity to make a gesture toward Ukraine. In 1938, Berlin granted eastern territories taken from Czechoslovakia to Hungary rather than place them under Ukrainian administration. The following year, after Germany invaded Poland, Hitler handed over almost all of Poland's five million Ukrainians to the Soviet Union. When Hitler invaded the USSR on 22 June 1941, he failed to form a Ukrainian puppet state, even though he had done the same for two other nations with a Habsburg history, the Slovaks and the Croats. When Ukrainian nationalists tried that summer to create a nominally independent state that would have been a German ally in the war against the Soviet Union, Hitler had them put in concentration camps. In what had been Soviet Ukraine, Germany established a brutal occupation zone, the Reichskommissariat Ukraine, where Ukrainians were treated as subhumans, and their food as a resource of the Reich.[17]

In his war against the Soviet Union, Hitler did not ally with any Ukrainian entity but, rather, allowed only the collaboration of individual Ukrainians in the crimes of his regime. Some Ukrainian units joined in Hitler's invasion of the Soviet Union, a racial war from the beginning in which Jews were murdered in death pits and Soviet prisoners of war were starved to death. His SS recruited thousands of Ukrainians for police work, which included rounding up Jewish women and children to be shot. The Holocaust—the German policy of murdering every Jewish man, woman, and child in Europe— began with the invasion of the Soviet Union. Wilhelm must have learned of the German killings of Jews, carried out in open fields before death pits. At the end of August, the Germans killed twenty-three thousand Jews at Kamianets Podils'kyi, where Wilhelm had reported for duty to the army of the Ukrainian National Republic in 1919. At the end of September, the Germans shot to death more than thirty thousand Kievan Jews at Babyi Iar. Perhaps these horrors brought Wilhelm, who had protested pogroms in the last world war, to reconsider his newfound anti-Semitism.[18]

Collaboration with the Germans in such a war was a terrible bargain, as Wilhelm seemed to understand. Ukrainians were helping Germans to commit the worst war crimes imaginable, without the promise of any political compensation. Back in 1918, when Wilhelm had visited the German emperor at the end of the First World War, he had warned that exploitative occupation polices could lose Germany the war. Confronted with far blunter German policies now, he seems to have drawn the same conclusion. As the second-largest republic of the USSR, and as its window on Europe, Ukraine was indispensable to Moscow's regime. If Germany had used Ukrainian nationalism against the Soviets, as Wilhelm had in 1918, it would already have won the war—or so Wilhelm believed. Having missed that opportunity, the Germans had already lost Ukraine and thus, as Wilhelm saw matters, the entire war.[19]

By 1942, Wilhelm agreed with his sister-in-law Alice about the outcome of the war. For Alice, of course, the final victory of Poland was an article of faith from the beginning. For Wilhelm, on the other hand, German indifference to him and to Ukraine undermined the previous attractions of fascism. Alice was a woman of unusual grace and will, and it would be easy to contrast her noble loyalty to Poland to Wilhelm's flirtation with Nazi Germany. Yet their different attitudes also flowed from the different interests of their chosen nations. Poland was a beneficiary of the peace settlements after the First World War, and thus a power with an interest in the preservation of the status quo. Ukrainian patriots, by contrast, knew that they needed another war to have a chance at statehood. They were still in the position that Polish patriots had endured before 1918: they needed some sort of cataclysm that would destroy all of the occupying states in order to have a chance to declare their own independence. For Alice, as for Poles generally, it was obvious that German power was a threat. Wilhelm, like many other Ukrainians, could easily see German aggression as an opportunity. When Germany did not support Ukraine, Wilhelm joined Alice in spirited and risky opposition.

Though they chose different nations early in life, Wilhelm and Alice shared an attachment to their people that was highly personal. Alice's love of Poland was also her love for her two Polish husbands and her Polish children. For Wilhelm, the shift towards pro-Ukrainian resistance of the Nazis was motivated by friendship. He began work more important and more dangerous than Alice's when he found men whose company he enjoyed. The most important of them, as it happened, was an unusually handsome Ukrainian student of music.

Roman Novosad, a Ukrainian of Polish citizenship born in the lands of the old Habsburg province of Galicia, was an enterprising young man. Summoned like millions of Polish citizens for forced labor in the German Reich, he had managed to persuade German officials that he

Roman Novosad, second from right, June 1941

should be allowed to enroll at a music academy in Vienna instead. In 1941 he was studying conducting and composition in Vienna and preparing a collection of Ukrainian folk songs for publication. He attracted the attention of Hans Swarowsky, a noted Austrian conductor who was prospering in the Reich.

One evening in February 1942, Roman and a Ukrainian friend decided to attend a concert, and stopped for a bite to eat on the way. They chose the OK restaurant, in the cellar of the Rathaus, the marvelous building on the Ring that houses the office of the mayor of Vienna. It was a cozy place with solid food and Czech waiters, where the Viennese went before crossing the Ringstrasse to go to the opera.

The two friends, looking for a place to sit, saw that German officers occupied most of the tables. They were happy to find one by the window, where a man in civilian clothes was sitting by himself. He smiled kindly and invited them to join him. The two friends spoke to each other in Ukrainian. After a time, they realized that their neighbor was following their conversation. Noticing that he was noticed, he said to them with an engaging smile: "I'm Austrian, but I'm a great friend of the Ukrainians!"

And then, knitting his eyebrows conspiratorially: "I'm Vasyl Vyshyvanyi."

Roman had met a legend, and the legend had time on his hands. Wilhelm, as it happened, was on his way to the same concert, by a Ukrainian cellist. The hall was almost empty, and Wilhelm proposed that they sit together near the front. After the concert, Wilhelm took Roman backstage to meet the performer. It must have been a nice moment for Roman.

Wilhelm and Roman then made for a bar, where they spoke softly to each other in Ukrainian. Wilhelm told Roman about his first love, also a Ukrainian music student. This story was true in its way; twenty years before, Wilhelm and his girlfriend Maria had sat together in Viennese bars, just as Wilhelm and Roman were doing now. Yet Wilhelm had always seemed forlorn in that era; this night, with Roman, he seemed happy.

On this, their very first meeting, Wilhelm delivered himself of an astonishing opinion. As they left the bar for some fresh air, Wilhelm sighed heavily and said: "Somewhere out there in the east there's a deadly war, thousands and thousands of healthy men are dying. And the Germans have already lost this war!" There was some reason to think so. The German army had achieved quick successes in the east, but had not taken Moscow; the decisive victory over the Soviet Union, promised in the press and in propaganda, had not materialized. In December 1941 Japan had brought the United States into the war by bombing Pearl Harbor. A year earlier, Germany faced only Great Britain; now Germany had to contend with Britain, the Soviet Union, and the United States. Still, predicting German defeat to a virtual stranger was a bold thing to do in Vienna in 1942. Vienna was part of the German Reich; such comments, reported to the police, would mean interrogation and much worse. What was Wilhelm doing? No doubt he was expressing a sincerely held belief. Most likely he was also testing Roman.[20]

NAZI EUROPE C. 1942

Axis powers   Vichy France   Occupied territory

Wilhelm was probably, by this time, at work recruiting agents for a western intelligence agency. The agency in question was quite possibly the British Special Operations Executive, which organized cells of resistance in the areas of Europe controlled by Germany. Wilhelm was a lifelong anglophile; he likely knew that the British government was sympathetic to the idea of a restored Austria, perhaps even an enlarged multinational state. Prime Minister Winston Churchill, very much the man of the nineteenth century, was quite nostalgic about the Habsburgs.[21]

Roman was surprised by Wilhelm's declaration, and pleased. He believed that Wilhelm trusted him; and so, in his turn, he trusted Wilhelm. The two men began to meet each week, seeing each other regularly, it seems, throughout 1943. They had dinner at the obscure and cheap restaurants that Wilhelm seemed to favor, and went to concerts together. They became friends.

On 8 February 1944, Wilhelm changed apartments in Vienna, moving from the city's second to its third district. His new place on 49 Fasangasse, which he rented from a retired schoolteacher, was much closer to the districts of Vienna that he had known as a boy. Though the street itself was modest, his building was no more than a half-hour's walk from his father's old residence. It was located in an interesting neighborhood, under the shadow of the Belvedere Palaces, close to the hustle and bustle of the rail station, the Südbahnhof. It made a good shelter for friends who might have good reason to leave the city in haste.

Wilhelm's new apartment soon became a center of anti-Nazi espionage. It was in his rooms on the Fasangasse that he met his handler, a gentleman who called himself Paul Maas. He said that he was a French national working at a German factory and reporting to British intelligence. Wilhelm believed that "Paul Maas" was an alias, as it certainly was. The Maas is the river than runs through Belgium from Liege to Antwerp, and would thus seem to be a name chosen for its plausible anonymity. How much of the rest of Maas's story was true is impossible to say.

Maas wanted Wilhelm to report on German troop movements, and to help establish suitable targets for the allied bombings that began in March 1944. Wilhelm readily agreed. He was eager to help the Royal Air Force target German military sites. Wilhelm spoke to German officers of his acquaintance and reported on these conversations to Maas. One object of interest was the Messerschmitt aircraft factory, located in Wiener-Neustadt, which the allies bombed heavily. Even though Wilhelm had himself studied at Wiener-Neustadt, his sympathies, like Alice's, were with the airmen doing the bombing. This remained true even after the allies destroyed the building next to Wilhelm's on the Fasangasse.[22]

Wilhelm had been right in February 1942 to predict that the war on the eastern front would turn against the Germans. The German surrender at Stalingrad a year later was the symbolic turning point of the war. When the war began, Wilhelm had hoped that a German victory could lead to the creation of a Ukrainian state. As the Germans fell back before the Red Army in 1943, he hoped to prevent a German defeat from becoming a disaster for the Ukrainian nation. In 1944, Ukrainians who had collaborated with the Germans appeared in Vienna, bringing news of German defeats and asking for help. Wilhelm and Roman, who had joined him in the apartment building at Fasangasse, put Ukrainian refugees in touch with local authorities, and served as translators.

Roman, quite the operator, understood that he could have his pick of the desperate Ukrainian women now arriving in Vienna from the east. In September 1944, Novosad chose a young woman he liked, who called herself Lida Tulchyn, to come to his place to cook and clean and, presumably, to perform other duties as well. Roman had more than met his match. Lida had a more complex life than he initially understood. She was in fact Anna Prokopovych, an important Ukrainian nationalist, and a courier for leaders of a faction of the Organization of Ukrainian Nationalists. Once he ascertained her nationalist connections, Roman told an excited Wilhelm of his discovery.[23]

Now, in autumn 1944, Wilhelm had his great chance to rejoin Ukrainian politics, at a time when Ukrainian nationalists needed help. He had lost touch with the Ukrainian national movement after his scandal in 1935, and his main Ukrainian nationalist contact had been assassinated by the Soviets in 1938. Now he could put into motion his larger design: changing the image and enlarging the political possibilities of Ukraine by turning Ukrainians who had been German collaborators into assets of western intelligence. If Ukrainian nationalists were to have any support from abroad after the German defeat, Wilhelm understood, their only hope was to switch sides as soon as possible. They would have to find patrons who were American, British, or French; the Soviets, who claimed Ukraine for themselves, would torture and kill Ukrainian nationalists if they caught them. Wilhelm had the contacts with western intelligence; Lida was just the sort of person he needed to put this plan into motion.

By helping people who had abandoned the Germans make contact with Germany's enemies during wartime, Wilhelm was placing his own life in grave danger. Yet in 1944 he seemed to have regained his youthful calm, and his youthful tact. He asked Roman to acquaint the Ukrainian woman with the Frenchman. "I would like," he said to his friend, "for you to introduce Lida Tulchyn to Paul Maas. But one must think about how this should be done. Perhaps you could invite them, along with your girlfriend Biruta, to a concert? That would be perfectly natural and arouse no suspicion." The arrangement worked very neatly. Biruta, one of Roman's many girlfriends, was a ballerina who spoke French, and so could interpret as necessary. Maas arrived a bit late, and took the empty seat next to Lida. The acquaintance was made. Wilhelm had returned to Ukrainian politics, in style.[24]

Maas gave Lida a difficult assignment. He and his people, he said, were giving shelter to a British airman whose plane had been shot down. Could Lida find some German identification papers for the pilot? She came through, giving Maas the identification papers of a Ukrainian who had left the German armed forces.[25] Quite likely this assignment was a test, which Lida passed. Perhaps there was a downed airman, perhaps not. Lida had proven that she had real contacts with Ukrainians who had borne arms, which was the issue.

Lida no doubt grasped Wilhelm's plans; like thousands of Ukrainian nationalists who had collaborated with the Germans, her only hope now was the West. She put Wilhelm and Maas in touch with Myroslav Prokop, a leader of a faction of the Organization of Ukrainian Nationalists. Wilhelm was back in the thick of Ukrainian politics, helping nationalists in their first awkward conversations with the western powers. Desperate as these encounters must have been, they were in one way relatively promising. Back in 1918, as Wilhelm remembered, Ukrainians had had no contacts with the western powers who won the war. Ukraine was seen then as a phantom of German imperialism, and had little or no support in Paris,

London, or Washington. This time, Wilhelm hoped, the Ukrainians would not have to go down with the Germans.[26]

In Vienna, as Wilhelm risked his life for a vision of a Ukraine in alliance with western powers, he was becoming Ukrainian again. Putting aside the racist ideas that had led him to identify his fate with Germany, he returned to his chosen people and thus to the idea that nationhood was a choice.

In Żywiec, Albrecht and Alice had rejected the idea of race all along. Albrecht remained a Pole, and so sat in prison. Interrogated by the Gestapo in January 1942, Alice spoke of her Polish nationality as a matter of individual political morality. "I regard myself now as before," she said, "as belonging to the community of the Poles, and can only express my admiration of the courageous attitude of the Poles." Her attitude about the Nazi regime was, as ever, categorically negative. "When I am asked about National Socialism, I can only respond that I reject it. The reason for that is the lack of individual freedom."[27]

German policies were based upon a contrary principle: that the nation was race and that race was biological and thus to be determined by science, which in practice meant by the state. In 1940, the Germans had formulated a racial registry of the population, the "Volksliste." Its category one, or "Reichsdeutsch," comprised people believed to be racially, culturally, and politically German. Albrecht and Alice refused to be entered into the Volksliste. Since Poles had no right to property, their rejection of German nationality could be used to justify the nationalization of their property. Heinrich Himmler, chief of both the SS and the Ministry for the Strengthening of Germandom, saw the opportunity. He also wanted the whole family sent to a forced labor camp somewhere deep in Protestant Germany, away from the Catholic Poles of Wisła who, according to police reports, liked Alice and the girls.[28]

Not all of the top Nazis agreed with Himmler. Reinhard Heydrich, Himmler's right-hand man, did not want to see these Habsburgs sent to a camp. In May 1942, however, he was assassinated by members of the Czechoslovak resistance, which removed him from the discussion. Not all of Himmler's subordinates shared his special hostility to the Polish Habsburgs. The local SS refused to interrogate Albrecht further and referred to him respectfully in their internal correspondence as "the archduke." The SS seemed to feel that the Gestapo had handled the matter in a primitive way.[29]

Yet their boss Himmler had his way, or so it seemed. In October 1942, Alice, Albrecht, and their two daughters were sent to a labor camp in Straussberg, Germany. Even there, the Nazi grip was never quite secure. Their foreign protectors protested that Albrecht was too ill and injured by his interrogations to work. He left prison blind in one eye and with only partial use of his limbs. No doubt as a gesture to the Habsburgs' foreign supporters, the Germans allowed the girls to go to Vienna to study. Albrecht, permitted to seek medical attention, joined them there for a time in early 1943. When he returned to the camp that summer, he was still, Alice thought, in "good spirits"; but he seemed in no better health. Only Alice remained at the forced labor camp for the whole year, and she declined to dig potatoes. This was not, she explained, because digging potatoes was undignified—on the contrary. It was rather because she refused to do any work for Hitler's Reich. The girls lost their place at school for exhibiting a similar attitude, and ended up performing forced labor in Vienna. Maria Krystyna was working as a nurse's aid when the American bombs began to fall on the city in March 1944.[30]

Even with the Polish Habsburgs out of the way, the Germans remained unable to establish the legal status of the Żywiec estate. It turned out that there was no single estate. What the Germans wished legally to nationalize was rather two distinct collections of properties owned by Albrecht and Leo that had been managed in the 1930s by a single administration. The Germans were also running the brewery and the timber businesses as a single unit, but to claim them for the state they would have to nationalize property seized not only from Albrecht but from Leo as well. Leo complicated this transaction by being possibly German and certainly dead. He had succumbed to tuberculosis in April 1939.

Since Leo had left no will, all of his property had been inherited by his wife Maja, who naturally objected when her land was seized along with Albrecht's. She had a case. No one doubted that she was German. She also had connections. A brother-in-law hunted with Hermann Göring, head of the German air force and a high official of the Reich. She wrote to Hitler himself, presenting herself as a German widow with five German children, and pleading "deep hardship and unutterable despair."[31]

Hitler and Himmler, frustrated by the complexity of the situation, simply wanted the estate nationalized and the Habsburgs humiliated. In 1941 Himmler declared that Maja, despite all the evidence, was not to be seen as German, since Hitler wanted the property for the German state. This directive was not fulfilled.[32]

The SS instead compiled a careful report on Maja's nationality in 1942. It cited five different German officials on the question, all of whom gave different but entirely reasonable answers. One said that she was German by background and choice; one said that she was German but that he did not wish to answer the question as to whether Habsburgs should own property; one said that she was German but did not have Nazi convictions; one said that she was an aristocrat and therefore of no nationality; and one said that there was nothing in the files that could answer the question. The SS was troubled by her lack of what it took to be normal political commitments: Maja was uninterested in race and anti-Semitism and admitted that she could never raise her children to be Nazis. The SS did conclude that she was, nevertheless, a German of category two, an ethnic German or "Volksdeutsch." This meant that she had the right to property.[33]

In May 1943, Hitler took the matter into his own hands. He ordered that Maja's property be nationalized without compensation along with Albrecht's. Himmler explained the rationale: she was somehow too close to the "traitor" Albrecht. He was misinformed, and in any event, this sort of guilt by association fit poorly with racial ideology and German law (in its application to Germans). Local officials declined again to obey their Führer. They would not nationalize the property of someone who might turn out to be German. Hitler had established a bureaucracy of race that he himself could not always overrule.[34]

By this time, the Germans themselves were realizing, if only by the implications of their own policies, that bureaucracy rather than biology makes race. Beginning in 1942, in accordance with a new racial policy applied to Żywiec and other areas incorporated into the Reich, German officials sought Poles who were tall and beautiful to be sent to Germany for acculturation. The instructions of this policy, known as "Eindeutschung," specified that it made no difference whether these specimens were thought to be of German origin or not. This state policy intended to make Germans from people who would have otherwise become (or remained) members of another nation. The policy was not extended to local Jews, who by this time had been deported to the Generalgouvernement. In 1942 and 1943, they were sent to death camps. At Treblinka, northeast of Warsaw, about eight hundred thousand Polish Jews were killed. At Auschwitz, only forty-five kilometers north of Żywiec, another one million European Jews were gassed.[35]

Since race was a matter for bureaucrats, it was also a matter of interagency dispute. By 1943 the various offices concerned with the Habsburg question were quarreling among themselves. In 1944 the bureaucracies lost their capacity even to argue. That May, the files of the Reich Security Main Office burned after an air raid, as allied airmen, cheered on in those years by Alice and Wilhelm, made an unwitting contribution to the Habsburg cause. Without their paperwork, bureaucrats were unable to recall what had happened to the various Habsburgs in question and where matters stood.[36]

German officials did not give up. Even though files were lost and telephone lines were down, clerks pursued the leads that they had. In May 1944 they searched for a certain Count Romer in the town of Wadowice. He had known Leo before the war and might be able to say something about Leo's nationality, which might then help the Germans decide upon the nationality of Leo's wife and children, and thus perhaps hasten the final disposition of the properties.[37]

It was a curious concern at that point in the war. That summer of 1944, the Americans and their allies landed at Normandy, and the Soviets reached the territories of prewar Poland. Still, that September, the German regional governor insisted that the nationalization of the Żywiec properties was "not a purely formal matter, which during a total war might be deferred, but one that seems quite urgent in light of the goal of administrative simplification." Local authorities called for another personal decision from Hitler. He could not be bothered. Local officials were instructed that the present state of "limbo" would have to be accepted "for the time being." There was no time being. In 1944, the allies were closing in from east, west, and south. In spring 1945, Hitler's Thousand-Year Reich came to an end after just twelve years.[38]

Hitler's dynasty of race proved brittler than the Habsburg dynasty of family. In the confrontation between the two, so apparently unequal, it was the Habsburgs who survived. Hitler committed suicide on April 30, 1945. Albrecht and Alice saw their labor camp in Straussberg liberated by the Americans a few days later. Meanwhile, the Red Army was racing west. Even as the Habsburgs greeted American soldiers, Soviet officers were sleeping in their castle back in Poland. It was the Red Army that liberated Żywiec, and the Soviets had their own ideas about property, politics, and Habsburgs.

Vienna, the family's second home, was also liberated by the Red Army. Vienna and Żywiec, once a Habsburg capital and a Habsburg possession, then cities in Austrian and Polish republics, then added to the German Reich by Hitler, were suddenly both under the power of Stalin.

After the German surrender of 8 May 1945, Stalin succeeded Hitler as the master of eastern and central Europe. He had declared that this war would be like no other in the past, in that the winner would impose its own political system just as far as its army could reach. As the Red Army met the western allies in Germany and Austria, different sorts of occupation zones were established by their respective military police and intelligence services. When Alice and Albrecht hastened from Straussberg to Vienna to find their daughters, they were leaving the American zone and entering the Soviet, and thus taking a certain risk. The Soviet police, and in particular the military counterintelligence service known as SMERSH, had no hesitations whatsoever about arresting civilians thought to be enemies of Soviet power.

Wilhelm remained in Vienna, no doubt keeping a very low profile after the Red Army entered the city in April 1945. He was risking his life in the part of Europe where, at least for the time being, the Soviets made the rules. The Soviet secret police and military intelligence services operated skillfully and energetically behind the lines. They rooted out, with far greater effectiveness than had the Germans, organizations of Polish and Ukrainian opposition. Alice's comrades in the Polish Home Army were overmastered by the Soviets.

In Poland and other countries whose entire territories were liberated by the Red Army, the Soviets proposed a provisional government with a disproportionate role for communists, who then manipulated their way to full control. In Austria, where the Americans and the British liberated the east and the south of the country, the Soviets did the same thing, seeking a non-communist to be the front man for a provisional government. Yet here their maneuver went awry. The Soviets entrusted the responsibility of forming a government to Karl Renner, who appointed a government of the two major parties, now called the Social Democrats and the People's Party, along with the Communist Party of Austria. The Soviets, and then the Americans and the British, recognized the provisional government in spring 1945.

The two major Austrian parties became what they had never been before: unambiguous supporters of democracy in an Austrian republic. The leaders of the Social Democrats and the People's Party understood that their parties had a chance in free and fair democratic elections, while the Soviet-sponsored Communist Party of Austria did not. Never popular in Austria, communism was quickly discredited by the Soviet occupation. Soviet authorities treated all property in their occupation zone as "formerly German," and thus subject to confiscation. Most horribly and unforgettably, Soviet soldiers raped tens of thousands of women, behaving in Vienna as they did in Budapest and Berlin. After the Soviets raised a monument to the unknown soldier on the Schwarzenbergplatz, the Viennese, in a black instance of the city's dark humor, called it the memorial to the unknown father. With fair procedures and a high turnout, the Communist Party of Austria never had a chance in democratic elections.

For the two parties that now supported Austrian democracy, of the center-left and the center-right, a chance in democratic elections was much more than they might have expected from the war. The Social Democrats were happy to return to a political system from which they had been excluded when their party was banned in 1934. The People's Party, effectively a successor of the Fatherland Front, was lucky to take part in politics at all. Elsewhere in Europe the Soviets had presented all right-wing parties as collaborators with the Germans. In Austria they could not quite do this. As everyone knew, the Fatherland Front had tried to defend the country against the Nazis in 1938. The postwar leader of the People's Party, Leopold Figl, had spent most of the war in German concentration camps. What was more, the Americans, the British, and the French clearly wanted a democratic system. Since they also occupied Austria, the Soviets could not so easily determine who took part in elections, and who did not.[39]

Communism followed the Red Army; democracy followed the Americans and the British. Austria fell somewhere in between. Wilhelm, a man of royal birth and aspirations, decided to support the rule of the people. In May 1945, right after the German surrender, Wilhelm threw himself into Austrian democratic politics. He endorsed the Austrian republic after a career as a monarchist, accepted the Austrian nation after a lifetime of believing in empire, and even joined the People's Party after years of bemoaning democracy as a front for Soviet conspiracy. He had some guidance. His handler Paul Maas had left for France, but not before putting Wilhelm in touch with a colleague who called himself Jacques Brier. Brier asked Wilhelm to serve as a mediator between the People's Party and a French party of the center-right, the Mouvement Républicaine Populaire. Wilhelm seems to have introduced French intelligence officers to leaders of the People's Party. In his own special way, Wilhelm did what much of Europe was doing after the German surrender: assembling fragments of a very undemocratic past into a program of democratic action.[40]

The promise of democratic elections in Austria, planned for November 1945, was some distraction from the larger problem— uncertainty about the fate of the entire country. Only one thing was sure: the *Anschluss* was undone, and Austria would be an independent state, distinct from Germany. On that much, the British, Americans, and Soviets had agreed in 1943. In July 1945 the British government of Winston Churchill had fallen, and with it any scarce possibility that Austria might once again be a monarchy, or the center of some sort of central European federation. Otto von Habsburg had spent most of the war in the United States, but had failed to attract meaningful support for his idea of a multinational federation under a Habsburg. Thus the allies generally agreed that Austria would be a republic, although they understood this term rather differently. The Soviets believed that a true republic was one where communists controlled the state in the name of the working class. The other allies believed that a republic would involve the democratic alternation of power by free elections. Everywhere the Soviets agreed upon elections, they expected their local allies to falsify them.

In July 1945 the allies divided Austria into four zones of occupation: Soviet, American, British, and a French zone in the alpine far west. The capital, too, was to be placed under a four-power occupation. British, French, and American authorities moved into Vienna in August. Wilhelm found himself, no doubt to his great pleasure, in the British sector of Vienna. It might have seemed to him that he had taken risks for a good cause, for western intelligence during the war and then for democracy thereafter, and now could reap the rewards. Wilhelm could be proud of his democratic daring in May and June, and relax in the comparative security of British rather than Soviet military police. He could watch as democracy did its own work that autumn, as both the Social Democrats and the People's Party ran effective campaigns. Wilhelm was in a good mood, writing warm letters to his landlady and taking the children of fellow tenants swimming. In November he told his landlady that after a lifetime of wandering he was ready to settle down. He was now a man of fifty. Perhaps it was time.[41]

Just as Wilhelm seemed to be finding a place in the new Austria, his family sought a way out. Once Albrecht and Alice had found their daughters Maria Krystyna and Renata, they had nothing to gain by staying. It is not clear whether Albrecht sought his brother Wilhelm in the city; many years later, Maria Krystyna recalled no such meeting. However that may be, the two brothers had different commitments. Albrecht and his family were Poles rather than Austrians, and they made their way back to Poland. They knew they would find a country occupied by the Red Army and falling under communist control. At a moment when they might easily have fled to a free European country, perhaps to Spain or Sweden where they had family and friends, they chose instead to return to Poland. They watched as communists secured power, forging the results of a referendum in 1946 and then a general election in 1947.

In Austria, Wilhelm's party won the elections of November 1945. The People's Party got almost half the votes, with the Social Democrats close behind. The Communist Party of Austria received only 5.9 percent. The People's Party then formed a government in a capital city liberated by the Soviets. The Soviets were at a loss as to what to do. In Poland, a country where the communists could never have won free elections, the Soviets could and did help them intimidate opponents and falsify results. The Communist Party of Austria did not control the requisite ministries, and the new government was greeted warmly by the British and Americans. The allies were suddenly in disaccord, and the future of the country was uncertain. In March 1946, Winston Churchill, in a speech in the United States, spoke of an "iron curtain" dividing eastern from western Europe. It seemed to run right through Vienna.[42]

Austria, even occupied as it was by the four powers, was in a far more favorable position than Ukraine, which was entirely incorporated by the Soviet Union. The Soviets reconquered their prewar Ukrainian republic and annexed, a second time, the lands granted them by the terms of the 1939 nonaggression pact with Germany. These territorial gains included the eastern half of the old Habsburg province of Galicia. In these Galician or west Ukrainian territories, partisans of the Organization of Ukrainian Nationalists stubbornly resisted Soviet rule. They hoped to defeat the very army that had just defeated the Germans. They desperately needed help.

Wilhelm, who in 1946 might have retired to his businesses and congratulated himself on his Austrian successes, did what he could. Somehow he made contact again with French intelligence. It appears that Wilhelm let his handler Jacques Brier know that he was still available for the mission of acquainting western intelligence agencies with Ukrainian nationalists. In early 1946 Brier introduced Wilhelm to a Frenchman who called himself Jean Pélissier and claimed to be a captain in the French navy. Pélissier had come, he said, on a special mission from the French government. France was interested in cooperating with Ukrainian nationalists. In exchange for intelligence about the Soviet Union, France could promise airdrops of men and propaganda over Soviet territory.

Wilhelm could place his wartime Ukrainian contacts at the disposal of the French. He proposed that Lida Tulchyn, the Ukrainian activist whom he and Roman had befriended during the war, put Pélissier in touch with her colleagues of the Organization of Ukrainian Nationalists. Lida, however, was no longer to be found in Vienna. Fearing the Red Army, she had continued her flight west. Like several thousand other Ukrainian nationalists, she made her way to Bavaria, in the American occupation zone of Germany. Wilhelm, once he learned this, guessed that Roman could be persuaded to go and find her.[43]

So Wilhelm brought his friend Roman Novosad back into intelligence work. Roman, like Wilhelm, had already taken considerable risks during the German occupation. Now, with the Soviets victorious, he was vulnerable in ways that his older friend was not. He was young, without independent means, and carrying a Polish passport—which meant that he could be expelled at any time to a country that was fast becoming communist. Roman was born in the Galician territories that had been incorporated into the Soviet Union, so he might very easily be deported there as well. Roman still had plans and prospects for a future career. He wanted to finish his studies and become a conductor or composer. He had much to lose.

Nevertheless, when Pélissier proposed that Roman travel to Bavaria and find Lida, he immediately agreed. Why? He was patriotic and courageous. Wilhelm had brought him good luck and good company, so far. Perhaps, too, Roman had a soft spot for Lida, the seemingly helpless refugee who turned out to be an impressively resourceful nationalist. Pélissier gave Roman a special pass to the French occupation zone, which lay in western Austria, just south of Bavaria. He wrote that Roman, a Polish citizen, was traveling to Innsbruck to conduct a concert. This phrasing obscured not only his reason for being in the French zone, but also his Ukrainian nationality.[44]

Roman was an able messenger. He reached the French zone without incident and flew onward from Innsbruck to Munich. He found Lida in a displaced persons camp, no mean trick in the chaos of the time, and told her that French authorities wished to meet the leadership of the Organization of Ukrainian Nationalists. She gave him a message concerning Mykola Lebed, a major nationalist. Roman returned to the French zone, left a note as arranged at the desk of a hotel, and went home to Vienna. The note was transmitted to French intelligence, which then prepared for a meeting with Lebed.

On 15 May 1946 Pélissier met Lebed in a small town amidst woods outside Innsbruck. Jacques Brier, Roman Novosad, and Lida Tulchyn were also present, to create an atmosphere of trust. The real discussions, however, were between the French intelligence officer and the Ukrainian nationalist leader. Thanks to Wilhelm, Roman, and Lida, an important Ukrainian activist was in touch with a western intelligence agency. The friends could not know what would happen next, but they saw that they had helped Ukrainian nationalists gain a foothold they might otherwise have missed. Lebed, in the end, went to work for the Americans.[45]

Roman would never know the outcome of his labor, but he did enjoy the work. As his own part in the mission revealed, he liked to take chances, especially when women were involved. Not only did he pursue Lida to Bavaria, he seems then to have followed the female officer sent to watch over him during that mission. Roman had first noticed the attractive Frenchwoman on the plane from Innsbruck to Munich. In Bavaria she had tactfully intervened to help Roman explain to the Americans his business in their occupation zone. A few weeks later he met her again, as if by chance, at the Vienna Philharmonic. They began to attend concerts together, and she invited him to her apartment for dinner.

Wilhelm advised his young friend to be careful. If the woman in question was indeed a French officer, Roman was exposing his private life to observation by an intelligence service. He also risked allowing himself to be recruited for French operations on the traditional but foolhardy basis of sex. Although Wilhelm was willing to take risks with Roman, he also tried to look out for his friend. Or perhaps he was simply jealous.

Wilhelm's attachment to France was neither blind nor sentimental. His own years in Paris had ended in very public humiliation. He had sobered and matured enough during the war to see that France might become an ally of Ukraine. He believed in a certain identity of interests between the western powers, of which France was one, and the Ukrainian movement. He knew that Germany was defeated and that the Soviet Union had no interests in Ukraine beyond restoring its own power and crushing national resistance. He thought that France, Britain, and the United States would be the best possible patrons of Ukraine after the war.[46]

Wilhelm was right that Ukraine had no other possible sponsors, but perhaps too hopeful about what Paris, London, and Washington could do. In the years to come, a few Ukrainian nationalists were supported by western intelligence services. But the Americans, French, and British were overmatched by Soviet counterintelligence. The Soviets usually knew in advance where airdrops of Ukrainians would take place. Ukrainians who crossed the Soviet border with western aid were generally captured, tortured, and shot.

Ukraine's best hope was not much hope at all. From Vienna, where Wilhelm continued to recruit Ukrainian nationalists for French intelligence, he had little idea just how desperate the Ukrainian national struggle had become. The Soviets had returned to western Ukraine determined to crush any resistance. Soviet special forces, under the command of Nikita Khrushchev, were ordered to be more brutal, and thus more feared, than the Ukrainian partisans they

fought. Since the Ukrainian resistance had no qualms about murdering Poles or even Ukrainians thought disloyal to the cause, this
was a high standard. In the end, though, Soviet forces dismembered
enough bodies, burned enough villages, and deported enough family members to defeat their enemies. They had the apparatus of the
state on their side.

In order to make sure that the Ukrainian question could not be
used against them by an outside power, Moscow also imple-
mented ruthless policies to match populations to borders. In two
years of deportations, between 1944 and 1946, about a million
Poles and Ukrainians were deported west and east to communist
Poland and Soviet Ukraine. These actions were meant to drain
support from the Organization of Ukrainian Nationalists. On the
Polish side of the border, the ruling communists took a frankly
racist view of the presence of Ukrainians in their country. One of
the Polish generals proposed, in language redolent of the Holocaust, to "resolve the Ukrainian problem once and for all." He
was one of the commanders of a final operation, in 1947, that resettled Poland's remaining Ukrainians from the south and east to
the north and west. Among the targets were the people of the
Beskidy Mountains around Żywiec, where Wilhelm had heard his
first words of Ukrainian.[47]

The idea of Ukraine was not dead; after all, the Soviets continued
to rule a republic of that name. Extending from the eastern steppe
to the Carpathians, embracing almost all the lands that Ukrainian
patriots had claimed in the First and Second World Wars, Soviet
Ukraine was the second most important republic of the Soviet
Union, after Russia. The struggle of Ukrainian nationalists for true
state independence on these territories, however, was doomed to
failure. Facing overwhelming numbers and the ruthless anti-partisan
tactics of Soviet forces in Soviet Ukraine, they were defeated on that
side of the border by the early 1950s.

In order to crush a Ukrainian national uprising, the Soviets and
their Polish communist allies had removed the traces of national variety in the old Habsburg land of Galicia, now divided between the
Soviet Union and communist Poland. There would be Poles on the

Polish side, and Ukrainians on the Ukrainian side. The Jews had been killed by the Germans in the Holocaust, and the Germans were now expelled to Germany. Multinational Galicia, a creation of the Habsburgs, could not survive Hitler and Stalin.

By 1948, the Habsburg Europe of multiple loyalties and ambiguous nationalities seemed to have reached its end. The Polish Habsburgs went down with the Europe their ancestors had built. The sons and daughters of Stefan had either died or, willingly or unwillingly, abandoned Poland. Of the daughters, Renata had died in 1935; Eleanora was in Austria with her husband, Kloss; and Mechtildis and her husband, Olgierd Czartoryski, had fled to Brazil during the war. The Germans gave her a strange goodbye. While traveling through Germany on her Polish passport, she was stopped by a German policeman. "Habsburg?" he asked, noticing her maiden name. "That sounds Jewish." In her Brazilian exile, Mechtildis spent her time explaining that she was not of German but of Austrian origin, and that she regarded herself as a Pole. Leo had died in 1939; although he and his wife and children were probably more Austrian or German than anything else, he remains forever, because of the grace of that early death, undefined.[48]

In the late 1940s, Alice and Albrecht wished to remain Polish, and to remain in Poland. The Polish communist regime refused to return to them what the Germans had seized—their land and their brewery. Albrecht and Alice had lost their property once because they were loyal to Poland. Now they lost it again to a new regime that claimed to be Polish. In a final insult, Albrecht, who had chosen Poland, who had fought for Poland, who had been tortured for Poland, was told by the new Polish authorities that he was German. Ill and heartsick, he left the country for Sweden, where Alice hoped doctors could restore him to health. His daughters joined him in emigration.

Alice traveled back and forth from Sweden to Poland, still trying vainly to regain the family property. She happened to be in Poland when she learned of her husband's death, in 1951. Then even Alice conceded. Polish for the love of her men, matron of a proud aristocratic home, last of the Habsburgs in Poland, she returned finally to Sweden, the land of her birth.

What would happen to Wilhelm, the Ukrainian Habsburg, in this new Europe of racial clarity and class war? In the Vienna of 1947, he had found a way to reconcile his two identities, Austrian and Ukrainian. He accepted Austrian democracy and supported an Austrian political party. Meanwhile, he hoped that Ukraine, despite the odds, could be liberated from the Soviets. He had made an Austrian home, and kept a Ukrainian dream. Even as the Soviets hunted Ukrainian spies through the streets of Vienna in 1947, he joined his own destiny firmly to that of his Ukrainian friends. If Austria were to regain its sovereignty and the four-power occupation were lifted, he would be safe. If Ukraine were somehow freed from Soviet power, he would be a hero.

As Wilhelm must have known, if the Soviets remained in both countries for long, he would have to disappear from the streets of Vienna, and from the pages of history.

ORANGE

❦

European Revolutions

VIENNA IS THE CITY of music, so long as the music is not too loud. The Viennese have ideas about quiet in the evening, long sanctioned by custom and law, which they are quick to enforce with a call to the police. For generations, foreigners have been surprised by a sharp rap at the door just at the moment when they are losing themselves in a party. The Viennese police are polite, but firm, and sometimes have to take people away. So it was, one evening in spring 1947, when the Ukrainian refugee Vasyl Kachorovsky, an acquaintance of Wilhelm and Roman, was arrested for disturbing the peace. The young man was up late, singing and dancing, celebrating the birthday that would be his last.

Kachorovsky was a spy, a Ukrainian nationalist at work for French military intelligence. His was a typical Ukrainian story. In 1939, without moving an inch, he suddenly found himself in the Soviet Union. By the terms of a secret protocol to the nonaggression pact between Berlin and Moscow of August 1939, the Soviet Union claimed the half of Poland that included the eastern part of old Habsburg Galicia, the city of Lviv, and five million Ukrainians. After these lands were incorporated into the Soviet republic of Ukraine, Ukrainian nationalists fled to the west. Had they remained within Stalin's reach, they would have risked long years of exile in Siberia or Kazakhstan.

Kachorovsky had reached Vienna in 1940, where he found work as a radio operator for German military intelligence. By that time, of course, Austria had already been absorbed by Hitler's Germany, which, having overrun Poland and France, was the dominant power in Europe. Hitler was turning his mind to the east, planning the invasion of the Soviet Union that he believed would seal his final victory in Europe. Kachorovsky's native Ukrainian language skills were put to use when German forces entered Soviet Ukraine in the massive invasion of the Soviet Union in June 1941.

Dashing the hopes of Ukrainian nationalists such as Kachorovsky, Germany neither restored Ukraine nor defeated the Red Army. The Soviet advance of 1943 and 1944 brought another dilemma. As the Soviets defeated the Germans on the eastern front, they reincorporated all of Soviet Ukraine, including the lands Germany once granted them by treaty. Kachorovsky's homeland, eastern Galicia, became once again a western part of Soviet Ukraine. After the German surrender of 8 May 1945, Ukrainians such as Kachorovsky could not go home. From a Soviet perspective they were now even guiltier than before—not only nationalists but German collaborators. They faced interrogation and execution.

As Wilhelm had understood during the war, the only hope for such men and women was to change sides, and find patrons among the western allies. Of course, past collaboration with the Germans aroused little sympathy among the Americans, the French, and the British. Yet as communism spread through eastern Europe in 1946, the western powers realized that they needed to know much more about the Soviet Union; so they recruited, sometimes with Wilhelm's help, Ukrainians such as Kachorovsky. Like Lida before him, Kachorovsky first met Roman, who brought him to Wilhelm, who then helped him make contact with the French.

The French engaged Kachorovsky in August 1946 to observe Soviet military movements in Austria, Hungary, and Romania. In the latter two countries, occupied by the Red Army, communist parties were engaged in a struggle for power that would shortly prove victorious. Though he complained that he did not know the Hungarian and Romanian languages, Kachorovsky did the best he could to create networks of local informants. Provided in December 1946 by the French with Austrian papers, he continued to live in Vienna, making journeys to Budapest and Bucharest as needed.

By the beginning of 1947, Soviet military counterintelligence, the dreaded SMERSH, was hot on Kachorovsky's heels. At least once, Soviet soldiers tried to force Kachorovsky into the back of an automobile on a Vienna street, but he had been strong enough to escape. Now, after the party, the Austrian police gave him to the Soviets, confused, tired, probably drunk. By an accident of fate, the Viennese police took into custody a man urgently sought by the Soviet occupation authorities who exercised real power in their city. The Soviets sometimes told the Austrian police whom they were hunting, and claimed the right to arrest and interrogate anyone they wished. One way or another, they usually got their man, and now, thanks to a loud party and an impatient neighbor, they had Kachorovsky.

He talked. He named names. In his interrogations at Soviet headquarters in Baden, just south of Vienna, Kachorovsky gave the Soviets an astonishing piece of information. He said that Wilhelm von Habsburg, along with his friend Roman Novosad, had put him in touch with French military intelligence. The red prince, enemy of the Soviets in Ukraine in 1918 and Austria in 1921, victim of a scandal that seemed to have destroyed his Ukrainian political career in 1935, was back in action. Wilhelm had been working against the Soviets for over a year without revealing himself. Now the Soviets had their first willing witness. Perhaps Kachorovsky believed that by giving away Wilhelm and Roman he might save his own life. If so, he was mistaken. The Soviets put him to death. Kachorovsky was one of thousands who disappeared from the streets of Vienna during the years of the four-power occupation of the city, never to be seen again. People simply disappeared, falling beyond the limited authority of the Austrian police and state, into the abyss of Soviet power.[1]

Roman was next. On 14 June 1947 Soviet soldiers abducted him from the British sector of Vienna. As the Austrian police recorded, Roman was "taken by unknown civilians into a personal auto with plate number W2038 and driven away." The plate was traced to a Soviet major—which of course ended the Austrian investigation. Austria had free elections and a democratic government, but that government did not enjoy sovereignty over its territory. The Soviet major, a certain Honcharuk, interrogated Roman at Baden. Within three days he had admitted his connection to Wilhelm, and their work for western intelligence agencies. On 19 August Roman defined his relationship with Wilhelm: "We trusted each other as friends."[2]

Without trust their conspiracies would have been impossible. But now that a third man had given them away, the two friends would be reunited in Soviet captivity. The next day, 20 August 1947, the Soviets decided to arrest Wilhelm. He must already have been afraid. Kachorovsky had suddenly disappeared. Then his friend Roman had vanished. He must have been lonely in the apartment on the Fasangasse, and he had every reason to suspect the worst. One day in August, Wilhelm left the office where he did the paperwork for his three small businesses, telling colleagues that he was going out to lunch. Then, it seems, he made for the departure gates of the Südbahnhof, the closest train station. He did not catch a train. The Austrian police again filed a report: "A man who met the description of Wilhelm Habsburg was on 26 August 1947 at 2:00 at the departure gates of the Südbahnhof seized by three Soviet soldiers with red armbands led by a major, and taken to the Soviet command post."[3]

Major Honcharuk interrogated Wilhelm at Baden for the next four months. By Soviet standards, Wilhelm was treated well. While the other prisoners ate from common bowls, he got his own. He even had his own blanket. Still, he looked terrible. He needed regular medical treatment for his tuberculosis and for a heart condition, which he was now denied. Four months after his arrest, when he boarded a plane with Roman and other prisoners on 19 December 1947, they noticed his thinning hair, his fearful eyes, his trembling voice. After the plane took off from the Aspern airfield near Vienna, Wilhelm asked a German prisoner if a Third World War was coming.

This was not at all a strange question, in the time and place. No one could know, in 1947, that the cold war would not grow hot. The United States had offered European states massive aid in the form of the Marshall Plan, which the Soviet Union had ordered its east European clients to reject. President Harry Truman had pronounced that America would use all means necessary to prevent the spread of

COLD WAR EUROPE 1948
Allied occupation zones in Germany and Austria
Communist states

Jonathan Wyss, Topaz Maps

communism to Greece. Stalin feared that the Americans and British would find a way to intervene in the Balkans. Thousands of partisans still fought the imposition of communism in Poland, western Ukraine, and the Baltics. Knowing that they needed help from the outside, many dreamed of a Third World War and an invasion of the Soviet Union by the British and Americans. For the hundred million Europeans who had survived Hitler's empire only to fall under the dominion of Stalin, the thought that the Americans and British would abandon them to totalitarian rule was difficult to accept.[4]

By the time the plane landed in Lviv, Wilhelm had ceased to think of the future, and begun to reflect on the past. That night, in a city now within Soviet Ukraine, Wilhelm dreamt of the First World War, keeping his fellow prisoners awake as his talked in his sleep of his youthful exploits. His journey in Soviet captivity had recapitulated, strangely, the adventures of his youth. The airfield from whence they had departed Vienna, Aspern, was named after the greatest military victory of Wilhelm's most martial ancestor, Archduke Karl. Baden, where he was interrogated by the Soviets from August through December 1947, had been Habsburg army headquarters during the First World War. Perhaps Wilhelm recalled, as his health declined during his interrogations, that Baden was where he took the cure for his illnesses thirty years before. Now they had arrived in Lviv, where soldiers trained by Wilhelm had led a Ukrainian insurrection in 1918. The next day they were to fly to Kiev, the capital of the Ukrainian National Republic that Wilhelm had helped create in 1918, and the seat of his imagined Ukrainian throne during his adventures on the steppe that summer.[5]

On 20 December 1947, Wilhelm shared a blanket with Roman on the flight from Lviv to Kiev, the two men whispering together in Ukrainian. It would be Wilhelm's first visit to the Ukrainian capital; the two men must have known that it would be his last. Their fate was probably sealed at this point; they could only hope not to implicate too many other people. Their interrogations took place at Ministry of State Security headquarters on Volodomyrska Street. This avenue was perhaps the prettiest in Kiev, running across the city's heights. It is just the sort of place to build a palace, or a prison. There was a time, thirty years before, when Bolsheviks and Habsburgs had both dreamed of controlling these heights. In 1918, Wilhelm had made camp on the steppe, waiting for the right moment to advance on Kiev. Now the red prince had reached the city of his dreams, wearing a blindfold instead of a crown, borne to a dungeon rather than a throne. Imprisoned with fellow Ukrainians, men who knew of his adventures in 1918, he made no secret of his youthful dreams of being king. Once he had told the tale of his life a final time, in a second round of interrogations on Volodomyrska Street from January through April 1948, his story seemed to be over.[6]

On 29 May 1948, a Soviet tribunal found Wilhelm guilty of aspiring to be king of Ukraine in 1918; of leading the Free Cossacks in 1921; and of serving British and French intelligence during and after the war. Soviet law was retroactive and extraterritorial, reaching backwards across the decades to a time before the establishment of the Soviet Union, and outwards to territories over which Moscow had never exercised sovereignty. Among other indignities, Wilhelm's espionage work against the Germans during the Second World War was treated as a crime against the Soviet Union. The same had happened to thousands of other east Europeans. Soviet judges regarded noncommunist resistance movements as a form of collaboration with the Germans. Ideologically, this might be justified by the Marxist idea that Nazism was simply the highest form of fascism, and fascism a natural result of capitalism. Thus anyone who struggled for any system other than a communist one was objectively an ally of the Nazis.

The Soviet judicial system had more pragmatic motives. Those who resisted the Germans—people with a sense of national honor and a willingness to take risks, men and women unintimidated by the armbands and the jackboots and the arrogant scowls, mature souls unmoved by the propaganda banners and victory marches— such people might resist the Soviets as well. Not all of them, of course, were as noble as Albrecht or as graceful as Alice; nor, for that matter, were many as charming as Roman or as shameless as Wilhelm. Yet all Europeans who had not been passive under the Germans were a risk to the Soviets. Best to be rid of them. On 12 August 1948 Soviet officers issued instructions to transport Wilhelm to a prison in western Ukraine, where he was to serve a sentence of twenty-five years.[7]

Six days later, on 18 August 1948, after 357 days in Soviet captivity, Wilhelm died of tuberculosis. It was the birthday of Emperor Franz Josef, Wilhelm's first patron, and an even hundred years since Franz Josef had come to power, during the Springtime of Nations, in 1848. Wilhelm's lungs, which had taken their first breaths by the pure Habsburg Adriatic, exhaled for the last time in a Soviet prison hospital in Kiev. The blue eyes that had seen Franz Josef in his glory at the Court Opera in 1908 closed upon a view of rusty bed frames and cracked concrete walls.

It is unclear whether or not the Soviets meant to kill Wilhelm. They could, after all, have sentenced him to death. On the other hand, they could have treated his tuberculosis and his heart ailment during the year of interrogation rather than simply watching him decline. These sorts of deaths were characteristic of the Soviet system; Stalin's police killed by direct order about a million people, whereas untold millions more perished from exhaustion in the labor camps of the Gulag or by maltreatment in prison. Had Wilhelm survived interrogation, he surely would have died quickly in prison.

Soviet policy was murderous, and mendacious. After Wilhelm was dead, the Soviets denied the fact. They let Austrian authorities know of the sentencing, implying that Wilhelm was alive and in a camp. As usually happened in these cases, people returning to Austria from the Soviet Union claimed to have seen Wilhelm alive. Later came reports, equally false, that he had died in captivity in the 1950s. The Austrian state sent inquiries for a few years. In 1952, Austrian authorities decided that Wilhelm was not an Austrian citizen after all. Since he had never renounced his rights to the Habsburg thrones, they reasoned, he should not have received citizenship, as he had in 1936. Austria washed its hands of Wilhelm, four years after his death.

Wilhelm's eternal statelessness, liberating for most of his life, now annihilated him. His restless spirit, a confirmation of the only eternity we know, that of the ambition to be eternal, was long since quiet. His fine body, once admired across the beaches and ski slopes of Europe, was decomposed, anonymous, and forgotten. He had disappeared, body and soul, somewhere between monarchy and modernity, having lived a life so rich and strange as not to require an age of its own.[8]

With Wilhelm seemed to perish a certain Ukrainian dream. Wilhelm was one of tens of thousands of men and women killed by the Soviets in the late 1940s for involvement, real or supposed, with movements for Ukrainian independence. Many if not most of them hailed from the area that had once been Habsburg eastern Galicia. Wilhelm embodied, perhaps more than any of them, the Ukrainian connection to the Habsburg monarchy and to the west, the links to European culture and traditions that distinguished Ukraine, or so many patriots felt, from Russia.

After annexing these western territories in 1945, Moscow quite purposefully severed them from their Habsburg history. Genocide and ethnic cleansing had already changed the population irrevocably. The Germans had killed the vast majority of the Jews between 1941 and 1944; the Soviets then deported the Poles (and the surviving Jews) to Poland. The Soviets did away with an institution that the Habsburgs had created for an earlier age by banning the Greek Catholic Church. The Greek Catholic Church represented not only the Ukrainian nation but also the whole western tradition of the autonomy of the church relative to the state. Back in 1918, Wilhelm had played a small role in the plans of the Greek Catholic metropolitan to convert the Russian Orthodox. Instead, the Russian Orthodox Church, subordinated completely to the Soviet state, absorbed the Greek Catholics of western Ukraine. Their clergy were sent to prison and Siberia. One Greek Catholic clergyman, crossing paths in prison with Roman, gave him an apple.[9]

When Roman was arrested by the Soviets in June 1947, he was close to completing his musical studies, a point to which he returned obsessively in his interrogations. Even after he was transported with Wilhelm to Soviet Ukraine that December, he very much hoped to return to Vienna, complete his education, and become a conductor. Instead, he was sentenced to hard labor at the Soviet labor camp in Norilsk, on the wrong side of the Arctic Circle. In the Gulag, in the worst conditions imaginable, the tireless Roman organized what a fellow prisoner recalled as a "pretty good choir and orchestra."[10]

Roman's former teacher Hans Swarowsky, who had made a good career during the Nazi period, conducted after the war in Vienna, Graz, and Edinburgh, places far more pleasant than the continuous permafrost zone of the Arctic. In his long and successful career, Swarowsky trained a number of conductors of the next generation, some of whom are now well known in the world of classical music. Roman, like countless Ukrainian artists of the twentieth century, left his mark in politics rather than in art. As far as can be ascertained by the writings he left behind, Roman never regretted the risks he took for Wilhelm, and for Ukraine.[11]

Even as Ukraine was absorbed by the Soviet Union and the champions of its national independence killed or sent to the Gulag, Austria was taking on, for the very first time, a nationalism of its own. Just as, in the nineteenth century, the Ukrainian nation emerged as a result of the competition for the lands at borders of the Habsburg and Russian Empires, so the Austrian nation asserted itself during the superpower friction of the early cold war.

The Soviet habit of making people disappear in Vienna was but a very small example of Moscow's policies throughout the regions of Europe it controlled. The same happened, on a far larger scale, in Poland, Hungary, Romania, Bulgaria, and Czechoslovakia, countries that went communist in 1946, 1947, and 1948. In Austria and Germany, the countries the Soviets occupied along with the western powers, the wartime allies found that they could not agree on the terms of their withdrawal. By the late 1940s, Moscow and Washington were clearly engaged in a global competition for power. The cold war had begun in earnest. Absorbed by Germany, Korea, and an atomic arms race, the Americans and Soviets had little time or attention for Austria. Foreign troops did not leave Austria until 1955, a decade after the end of the war. In the state treaty signed that year, Austria regained its sovereignty, agreeing to the strict observance of military and political neutrality.

Subjected to a full decade of the humiliation of the four-power occupation, Austrians supplied themselves with a national myth emphasizing suffering under the Germans in 1938–1945 and then the allies in 1945–1955. The fact that Austria during that first period was rather a part of the German Reich than its victim was obscured. During the Second World War, the allies had agreed to restore Austria as an independent state. In the hopes of rousing some support for the anti-German cause, they had treated Austria as the "first victim" of Hitler. This characterization became dear to Austrians themselves after the war.

Their history would start anew, in 1955, on the premise that Austrians themselves bore little responsibility for their past. Like all of the nations that had challenged the Habsburgs in the nineteenth century, the new Austrian nation embraced a narrative of its history in three parts: a vague golden age in the distant past, a recent middle period of foreign oppression, and a present of national liberation. The popular history of the Habsburg period was reduced to a few images: more or less the same ones that were presented to Franz Josef as dream pictures at his jubilee at the Court Opera in 1908.

Austria's self-presentation, wherever possible, escaped politics to emphasize culture, above all, music. Sometimes, though, the music in Vienna was too soft. Jewish conductors and composers, at the center of Viennese culture since Gustav Mahler took over the Court Opera in 1897, had left the country in the 1930s or been killed in the Holocaust. Roman, a student of music who had set aside his books and his baton to spy against the Germans, had also left unwillingly. He and the Ukrainian cause that had cost him a life of pleasure were forgotten in postwar Austria. Nothing in Austria's present required the recollection of Vienna's past ties with Ukraine.

Ukraine was lost to Austria, not just behind the Iron Curtain that ran just fifty miles east of Vienna, but beyond the intellectual limits of the new national identity that Austrians were creating for themselves. Under the Habsburgs, Austria had never been a nation: it was something above the nations, an identification with monarchy and empire. For Austria to become a nation, it had to shed its position above the others, and descend to modern Europe as one people among many. Neutral Austria sought security, leaning to the West, avoiding risky connections to the East. Its economy performed well in a world where services, finance, and image counted for ever more. Suspended between East and West, occupied by the great powers and then preoccupied with itself, Austria was perhaps the perfect creation of its era. It was rich, successful, democratic, and schizophrenic about its recent past.[12]

Again a republic, Austria defined itself against not only its Nazi but also its Habsburg past. A figure such as Wilhelm, with his

Habsburg name, Ukrainian identity, fascist moment, and provocative anticommunism, was someone who had to be forgotten. And he was, in Austria and throughout the West. When Wilhelm was arrested in August 1947, his Soviet guards removed an Omega watch from his wrist. This was the brand later worn by James Bond on the silver screen. The fictional Bond family even took a Habsburg motto for its own: "The World Is Not Enough." By the time this was revealed by Bond's creator Ian Fleming in 1963, only a very few Europeans would have remembered its Habsburg origins. By the time James Bond wore an Omega Seamaster watch in *GoldenEye* in 1995, it is fair to guess that none of the eighty million or so people who saw the film thought of Wilhelm.

Yet once, not so long before, there had been a real person who wore that watch, a ladies' man of a slightly different sort, whose family used that motto, whose life began with a dream of mastery of the sea and ended with courageous espionage against the Soviet Union. The cold war had become its own culture, absorbing earlier images and ideas, teaching two European generations a history of East-West conflict that left out the Habsburgs, who after all were right at the center of all that had come before.

Yet the cold war did come to an end, and the Habsburgs did not. The two most impressive Habsburg women in Wilhelm's life, his sister-in-law Alice and Empress Zita, lived to see the Soviet Union decline and a new Europe emerge.

By the time Alice died at the age of ninety-six in 1985, a reformer called Mikhail Gorbachev had come to power in the Soviet Union. In 1988, Gorbachev promised that the Soviet Union would no longer interfere in the internal affairs of its east European satellites, thus removing the keystone from the arch of Soviet power in Europe. The communist regimes in eastern Europe all relied on the threat and use of force against their own populations. After crushing the revolution in Hungary in 1956, the Soviets had also intervened in Czechoslovakia in 1968. In 1981 the Soviets had bullied the Polish communist leadership into implementing martial law. Although Poland's self-invasion destroyed the independent labor movement known as Solidarity, it was also a confession that communist leaders had no other resort but force.[13]

Communism collapsed in eastern Europe when Gorbachev sought to reform the Soviet Union. He had wished to revive communism by encouraging open discussions of policy and thus generating authentic political support for change; his policies led to an outcome dramatically different from what he expected. The Polish communist regime, having already tried force in 1981, was the first to follow Gorbachev's new line. In 1989, Polish communists met with the opposition, scheduled elections, and lost them. Leaders of the Solidarity opposition formed a government in August. This was the beginning of the end of communism, though it was the fall of the Berlin Wall that November that provided the durable visible image. In August 1991, Soviet conservatives staged a coup against Gorbachev, protesting an arrangement that would have given the Soviet republics, such as Ukraine, more authority in their dealings with the center. Instead, their coup precipitated the end of the Soviet Union and its disintegration into its constituent republics. By the end of 1991, Ukraine was an independent state.[14]

The short twentieth century was over. One world war had brought the end of traditional empire and an experiment with national self-determination; another had brought the clash of two totalitarian powers and the victory of a new kind of ideological empire, the Soviet Union. The cold war had lasted long enough to seem eternal, its rapid end raising questions about what to do with all the newfound freedom. Moscow's east European satellites, sovereign since 1989, and the former Soviet republics, independent after 1991, had to replace communism with something else. Half the continent embarked on two transformations: from a political system of one-party rule to democracy, and from an economic system of state ownership and planning to some variant of free-market capitalism. The end of communism meant the beginning of mass privatization throughout eastern Europe. Firms that had been nationalized after the communist takeovers of the 1940s were now returned to the private sector, although not usually to their prior owners.

The brewery at Żywiec fell into legal limbo as Poland began to privatize state-owned concerns. It was placed on the Polish stock market in 1991. Enter the Polish Habsburgs, in distress. As the Dutch beer giant Heineken began to buy up shares, the Polish Habsburgs—the two daughters and one son of Alice and Albrecht—made appearances in the Polish media to remind Poles who had owned the Żywiec brewery before the Nazis and the communists. None of the three siblings, though they were all born in interwar Poland, had Polish citizenship. Karl Stefan, the son, was Swedish; Renata, the younger daughter, was Spanish. The older daughter, Maria Krystyna, lived in Switzerland with no citizenship at all. The only member of the family with Polish citizenship, and thus standing in Polish courts, was Alice's son from her first marriage. This gentleman, the son of a Habsburg diplomat and grandson of a prime minister, was born Kazimierz Badeni. He had in the meantime become a Dominican monk, and a rather interesting theologian, known as Father Joachim.

Led by Father Joachim, the four children of Alice, now in their sixties, filed three lawsuits. The first asked that the postwar transfer of the brewery to the Polish state be annulled on the grounds that it violated the law of the day. This was probably a good argument: the brewery had been nationalized on the strength of a law on agriculture. A second claim requested massive damages as compensation for the failure of the Polish state to respect the Habsburgs' legal right to the brewery before privatizing it. This was also not such bad reasoning, but it was unlikely to win the day: the Polish state had no money in reserve to honor such a claim, and indeed the point of privatization was to raise cash. In the third suit, the family asked the courts to forbid the brewery from using the Habsburg crown and coat of arms on the labels of bottles and cans of beer.

The Habsburgs lost the lawsuit about symbols first. In 2003 the Polish supreme court concluded that the Habsburg intellectual patrimony was a public good. Habsburg history was Polish history, so it belonged to everyone. The specific family traditions of Alice, Stefan, Albrecht, and the other Polish Habsburgs belonged to the town of Żywiec. Poland's high court had ruled that Poland had imbibed the Habsburg traditions during the very decades that the Habsburgs themselves had been unable to remain in the country. This was none too pleasing an irony for people who had seen the family property taken by totalitarian powers, and who had spent their adult lives in exile. Alice's children were certainly Poles, at least in some sense, speaking the language as well as the lawyers who represented them and the judges who issued the decisions. They were certainly more Polish than Heineken, the new owners of the brewery.[15]

All that remained was negotiation with Heineken, whose subsidiaries by late 2005 owned some ninety-eight per cent of the shares of the Żywiec brewery. Having dropped their claim of damages for the hasty privatization, the Habsburgs had only one matter to be heard in the courts, on the question of the legality of the initial transfer of the brewery to the Polish state. In December 2005 they agreed to drop this lawsuit in exchange for cash.

The Żywiec brewery is now the undisputed property of Heineken. The Habsburg crown is on every bottle of beer.

Alice's line, the Polish Habsburgs, found themselves reduced to a corporate logo and flattered as national symbols. Zita's successors, heirs to the Habsburg thrones, struggled in these same years to establish the family in the new politics of free Europe.

Zita herself lived until the magical year of 1989, when the peoples of eastern and central Europe, nations of the old Habsburg domains, began again to assert their sovereignty. Poland was followed by Hungary and Czechoslovakia, two countries composed entirely of formerly Habsburg lands. The end of the Soviet Union in 1991 liberated Ukraine, which included part of the old Habsburg crownlands of Galicia and Bukovina. To the south, war broke out in Yugoslavia, the worst fighting taking place in the former Habsburg province of Bosnia. Croatia, a state constituted of former Habsburg possessions, fought Serbia, that eternal Habsburg irritant.

Zita's son Otto, groomed for a Habsburg restoration in the 1930s, was still active in politics sixty years later, as a member of a conservative German party based in Bavaria and as a deputy to the European Parliament. He had much to say about the new Europe.

As Yugoslavia dissolved, Otto pressed European states to recognize newly independent Croatia. A leader of a Serbian paramilitary, Arkan the Tiger, reminded Otto what had happened to Franz Ferdinand when he stuck his nose into Balkan politics. Otto responded to the death threat by visiting Sarajevo in person, coming, he said, "to pray for this circle of tragedies to close." Otto also had visions for other nations whose histories had begun with the Habsburgs, most notably for Ukraine. In 1935, Wilhelm had fallen into scandal in Paris, depriving Otto of a Habsburg ally in Ukraine and embarrassing the whole family. Seven decades after that disappointment, Otto spoke up again about Ukraine. In late 2004, he pronounced that the future of Europe would be decided in Kiev and Lviv.[16]

Otto had a point. Ukraine was the largest and most populous post-Soviet republic in Europe, a country the size of France with fifty million inhabitants. As such, it was the test of whether democracy could extend across post-communist Europe. Most of the formerly communist countries to its west had undergone more or less successful transformations into electoral democracies with market economies. Russia, to its east, failed to establish a recognizable form of either but could rely upon the state infrastructure and state elites of the Soviet Union. Ukraine, a former Soviet republic with little history of independent existence, had to create the entire apparatus of an independent state as well as a democracy and a market. Like all of the European countries that had endured communism from the very beginning, from the foundation of the Soviet Union, Ukraine had certain difficulties with this very fundamental transformation. The idea of the state as something objective, beyond the personal control of its leaders, was something entirely new. As great fortunes were made in an era of very shady privatization, the state came to be seen as the protector of the economic barons known as oligarchs.

In the first years of the twenty-first century, Ukraine was sliding toward oligarchic authoritarianism, as a president with very strong powers ruled with a shifting entourage of very rich men and women who, among other things, controlled the television media. In the most striking of innumerable scandals, a presidential bodyguard revealed in late 2000 what seemed to be audiotapes of the president, Leonid Kuchma, ordering that a journalist be made to disappear. That journalist, Georgii Gongadze, had been the editor of a reliable website called Ukrainian Truth that dodged the corrupt television media and criticized the presidential administration. He had been found decapitated a few months earlier. In the presidential campaign of 2004, the opponent of the president's handpicked successor was poisoned with dioxin. The dose horribly disfigured the face of Viktor Yushchenko, once a handsome man.[17]

Yet Yushchenko fought on, disfigured and in pain, and won the elections, as exit polls revealed. When Kuchma's administration falsified the results in December 2004, his supporters came to Kiev and demanded a recount. They camped on freezing cobblestones near Kiev's Independence Square, in the hundreds of thousands, for weeks. They braved the weather and a very real threat of violence. Unlike Ukrainian patriots at any other point in history, they had powerful allies in the West. With the help of pressure from Europe and the United States and mediation from Poland, they succeeded. The elections were held again, the votes were counted, Yushchenko won, and the principle of democracy was restored.

Meanwhile, in Russia, the United States, and Europe, many people understood the Orange Revolution, as it was known, in ethnic terms. Yushchenko's supporters were portrayed in much of the world media as ethnic Ukrainians, people whose actions were somehow determined by their family origin. Opponents of democracy were, just as dubiously, presented as Russians. While this was the first time that the Ukrainian nation was presented in such a flattering light by major newspapers, journalists had no reason to associate ethnicity and politics in this way. The unthinking haste to classify east European politics as essentially a matter of race was an intellectual victory of the national policies of Hitler and Stalin over the gentler and more ambiguous legacy of the Habsburgs.[18]

Yet the Orange Revolution itself was the political revenge of the Habsburgs. In 1918, Wilhelm had pursued a policy of "Ukrainization," trying to teach peasants who spoke Ukrainian that they belonged to a nation that deserved a state. He did not succeed then, nor did any of the other Ukrainians who fought for independence in those revolutionary years. Yet after 1918, Ukrainian culture could no longer be ignored, even by the Soviets. Despite the terrible political oppressions visited upon Soviet Ukraine, in cultural policy the Soviets generally pursued their own variant of "Ukrainization"—using the same word as Wilhelm—in the hopes of creating a Soviet Ukrainian elite loyal to communism. In 1945 the Soviets did what certain Habsburgs had dreamed of doing in 1918: they assimilated all Ukrainian territory within their own multinational state, thus claiming to resolve the Ukrainian question. When the Soviet Union collapsed in December 1991, Ukraine provided a suitable form for an independent state. The borders of the Soviet republic suddenly defined an independent country.[19]

When Ukraine's government then fell into corruption, the national idea was available again as the principle of rule by the people, or democracy. During the Orange Revolution of 2004, Ukrainian patriots took risks to defend a vision of Ukraine in which citizens would have a voice in governance. In the events of 1991 and 2004, people from the former Habsburg province of Galicia played a disproportionate role. Many Ukrainian patriots were Greek Catholics, members of the church the Habsburgs had protected but the Soviets had banned. Yet they defended the Ukrainian nation not for reasons of ethnicity but rather as a political choice. The courageous journalist who was beheaded was born in the Caucasus, far from Ukraine. The city where the Ukrainian revolution took place, Kiev, speaks Russian.[20]

The nation is more a matter of love than language. In a youthful poem, Wilhelm had written, in a Ukrainian language that he had scarcely then mastered, of marching with his troops towards national freedom over the "cold earth" of Ukraine. In their own more peaceful way, the Orange Revolutionaries also chose the cold earth. They too pitched tents in the hope of realizing a certain idea of national liberty. It was their good fortune to live in a Europe where freedom could be pursued without violence. Some of them spoke Ukrainian, some of them spoke Russian, most of them spoke both. When they warmed the air and the cobblestones by making bilingual love in their orange tents, they were certainly acting in Wilhelm's spirit.[21]

In those orange tents, these revolutionaries sometimes had two flags: that of Ukraine and that of the European Union. Perhaps Otto overstated the case when he said, in 2004, that the future of Europe would be decided in Ukraine. When he returned to Kiev in 2007, he made the point a bit differently: "You are Europeans, we are Europeans." The Orange Revolution was the most important defense of democracy in the Europe of the early twenty-first century.[22]

Europe was an entirely different model for Ukrainians in the early twenty-first century than it had been in the early twentieth. The Europe of the 1910s, 1920s, 1930s, and 1940s had brought the collapse of empire and then of democracy in politics, inflation and then depression in economics, and suspicion and then war in international relations. Fascism and communism were the attractive and modern European models, which some Ukrainians followed. During the cold war, in the 1950s, 1960s, 1970s, and 1980s, free European states took part in a long and peaceful process of economic and political integration. By the 1990s, the European Union included a free trade area, a customs union, a zone of free internal movement, a common external border and currency, and a court of justice. All this progress was enabled by the American military presence and a postwar economic boom. It also required the embrace of democracy, an acceptance of the welfare state, and the endorsement of continental common interests, especially in finance and trade. Thus arose a new vision of Europe, the only one that the Orange Revolutionaries knew.[23]

In a small and circumscribed way, the history of this new and unifying Europe was also a Habsburg history. In 1946 and 1947, Wilhelm risked his life to carry out assignments on behalf of the French political party called the Mouvement Républicaine Populaire. This was the political home of Robert Schuman, who became a founding father of European unity. Schuman designed the European Coal and Steel Community. Established in 1951, it was the first step toward European economic and political integration. Otto put the weight of conservative monarchism, such as it was, behind the project of European integration. He was already sixty-seven years of age in 1979 when he was elected a deputy of the European Parliament. He served there for twenty years, until 1999. Otto advocated the enlargement of the European Union to the east after the revolutions of 1989, and supported democracy in Ukraine in 2004.

Europe was not only a model to be imitated, but an institution to be joined. In the last two decades of the twentieth century, the European Union attracted European states beyond its borders. In 1981, a few years after the establishment of a democratic constitution, Greece joined the European Union. In 1986, Spain too was rewarded with membership after a shift from authoritarianism to democracy. A key role in Spain's political transformation was played by King Juan Carlos—the grandson of King Alfonso and the first cousin twice removed of Wilhelm. In 1995, Austria joined the European Union, abandoning its neutrality, as did Sweden. In 2004, the European Union embraced Poland, along with seven other postcommunist democracies (as well as Cypress and Malta). During the Orange Revolution, the European Union intervened in favor of free elections, in the first consequential example of a European foreign policy. Like the Habsburgs before them, European Union officials intervened, discretely, on the side of the Ukrainian nation.[24]

That collective European action in favor of democracy opened a new chapter in the history of the continent. Wilhelm knew these European societies—German, French, British, Spanish, Austrian, Swedish, Polish, Ukrainian, Greek, and Maltese—in a different guise. In his own peculiar way, Wilhelm took part in the political history of several of these nations in the 1920s and 1930s. Despite all the twists and turns, he was at home in the Europe of the interwar years, dismal and decadent, too passionate in its politics and too political in its passions. But during the 1940s, like millions of other Europeans, Wilhelm followed a certain intellectual shift toward democracy. Democracy could only be realized in politics on the half of the continent not occupied by the Soviet Union, as Wilhelm's abduction by the Soviets and death in the Soviet Union demonstrate.

Wilhelm's death in 1948 coincided with the division of Europe into East and West. His memory fell into the shadow cast by the Iron Curtain, as did much of the history of the Habsburgs themselves. They had been banished from history once already, in 1918, for violating the idea of national self-determination. Their heritage was denounced again, in 1948, in the communist lands that fell into the forgotten half of Europe. Wilhelm has been saved from oblivion by a few devoted Ukrainian historians and monarchists. With the end of communism in the late twentieth century and the enlargement of the European Union in the early twenty-first, the histories of the European nations will perhaps be defined in more cosmopolitan terms, and Wilhelm may find his proper place in each of them. He, and the Habsburgs, will return. Indeed, in the rise of Ukraine, they already have.

Wilhelm's project, bizarre though it seemed at the time, has come to fruition. Seeing that Ukraine had to be made as well as chosen, he devoted himself to the work he called "Ukrainization." Today the population of the country of Ukraine is indeed "Ukrainized," in the sense that most citizens accept a Ukrainian national identity and believe in the future of a Ukrainian state. Almost a century after Wilhelm began to design a Ukrainian destiny for himself, the country is the crucial democratic state of eastern Europe. With Russia lost to electoral autocracy and Poland safely ensconced in the European Union, Ukraine has become the hinge of European politics.

Ukraine is also the test of the viability of that modern European political form, the nation-state. It is an example of the most recent group of European national unifications, after Italy and Germany in the second half of the nineteenth century, and Poland, Czechoslovakia, and Yugoslavia in the first half of the twentieth. What remains to be seen is whether this very success, the unification of a nation within a territorial state, heralds prosperity or ruin. As Wilhelm and his father Stefan understood, history brought the age of national unification, and it, like every age, will pass.

In the nineteenth century, national unifications were brought by monarchs and their ministers, who sought to make from mass politics a new buttress of dynastic rule. Although nationalists presented unification as the choice of the people, no national question was resolved by popular will. Italy and Germany were made by kings at war. Even after Europe's continental empires were destroyed in the First World War, national unifications were more a consequence of diplomacy than of democracy. Czechoslovakia, invented by a few Czechs, was created by the victors of the First World War. Yugoslavia was an enlargement of Serbia the first time it was created, and the creation of communist partisans the second. Even Poland could not have been created without the fortuitous destruction of three empires and the support of powerful allies after the First World War.

Ukraine is an example of a third wave of unified nation-states whose borders arose from Soviet policies, and whose independence was won with the collapse of the Soviet Union. Though Ukrainian patriots are loath to admit it, it was the Soviet Union that brought Ukrainian territory into a single unit. From the 1920s to the 1950s, the Soviet Union added more and more territory to its Ukrainian republic until all but the most stubborn of nationalists had to grant that, at least on that level, the national issue was resolved. So the creation and enlargement of Soviet Ukraine was one more unification from above.

Is the Ukraine of today a glimpse of the future, or of the past? Like the other unified national states of the nineteenth and twentieth centuries, Ukraine is a state named after one nation but is home to a hugely complicated mélange of peoples. Unlike its predecessors in the first and second waves of national unification, Ukraine had a moment, thirteen years after its creation, when democracy and the civic character of the nation were both publicly confirmed. Also unlike most of the other states, Ukraine has been a democracy, albeit a very shaky one, since its establishment as an independent state. Though there is much to complain of in Ukrainian politics, perhaps this unification will prove more solid than the others. Simply by existing for almost two decades within unchanged boundaries, Ukraine has already proven more durable than most of its predecessors.

Other national unifications were brittle indeed. The national movements that so troubled the Habsburgs succeeded in destroying their monarchy, but not in replacing it with a durable national order. Italy, whose partisans rebelled against the Habsburgs in 1859, is the only major national unification to succeed at all durably, although it was briefly divided during the Second World War and lost some of its possessions thereafter. Of course, Italian politics can hardly be landed as an example of successful parliamentarism. In the first half of the century the dominant note in Italian politics was fascism; in the second, European integration.

German unity, the project that began in 1866 with a war against the Habsburgs, proved much less stable. The Germany created in 1871 was much reduced by the defeat of 1918. Hitler's Germany, briefly vast, was shattered in 1945. The postwar Federal Republic of Germany (or West Germany) was less than half the size of Bismarck's unified Germany of 1871, and less than a third the size of Hitler's of late 1938. The Federal Republic was occupied by American troops and was the most important actor, along with France, in European integration. It was thus no longer a sovereign state in conventional terms. By the time West and East Germany unified in 1990, the political commitment to Europe was an axiom among all major political parties in the democratic Federal Republic. United Germany remains the most reliable advocate of the European Union, and so cannot be seen as a traditional national state.[25]

After Italy and Germany, the story of national unification only becomes less impressive. Hungary was unified within the Habsburg domains in 1716 and gained internal sovereignty in 1867. After the First World War, it was reduced to the somewhat pitiable territorial rump of ethnic Hungarians that it remains today. The Polish unification of 1918 lasted only until 1939. In 1939 the country was dismembered by Nazi Germany and the Soviet Union. It was revived in 1945 as a small satellite of the USSR. When it regained sovereignty in 1989, its foreign policy was directed toward joining the European Union. Czechoslovakia was destroyed in 1939 by the Germans, then revived after the Second World War. It was sovereign for less than three years before suffering a communist coup. After four decades as a Soviet satellite, it regained sovereignty in 1989. For a second time in the twentieth century, a free Czechoslovakia lasted for three years. It divided into separate Czech and Slovak republics in 1993. These two states, like Poland, joined the European Union in 2004. Yugoslavia, the other state unified in 1918, was destroyed by the Germans in 1941. It was re-created as a communist federation in the postwar years, only to dissolve in fratricidal warfare in the 1990s. One of its constituent republics, Slovenia, joined the European Union in 2004; another, Croatia, will probably follow in 2009.

The central and east European states that have joined the European Union in the twenty-first century are not the result of the great national unifications that so threatened the Habsburg monarchy. The states created by the great national unifications, all of them now essentially defunct even if their names live on, replayed the multinational history of the Habsburgs, though more rapidly, more brutally, and with a bloodier finale. The states that petitioned to join the European Union are the humbled and ethnically cleansed remnants of the grand national projects of the past. Yugoslavia, Czechoslovakia, and Poland, the national unifications that the Habsburgs rightly feared, either disintegrated or were much reduced in size before they acceded to the European Union. Indeed, the average size of a European country today is comparable to that of a Habsburg province one hundred years ago. The Habsburg crownland of Galicia was larger in size than exactly half the sovereign states of Europe of the early twenty-first century. Although the minor national states today rarely bear the same names as Habsburg provinces, they are in much the same position. Too small to imagine truly sovereign existence, too poor in resources and educated elites to manage in an age of globalization, they seek unification.

Ukraine, the national unification that Wilhelm foresaw, came late and under different auspices. For Ukrainians, and especially Ukrainians hailing from the former Habsburg province of Galicia, the question of the form of a future European unification remains open. Ukraine as a whole, large, ungainly, and poor, is unlikely to join the European Union in the near future. Some Ukrainians in Galicia consider seceding from the independent Ukraine they did so much to form in the hope of joining the European Union. If they did so, they would be joining the Czechs, who left Czechoslovakia, and

THE EUROPEAN UNION

Member states | Candidate countries

Status in 2008. Member states Portugal and Cyprus not shown.

Jonathan Wyss, Topaz Maps

the Slovenes, who left Yugoslavia—former Habsburg peoples who abandoned the grand national projects of the nineteenth century for the European idea of the twenty-first.

Either way, the unification in question would be neither national nor imperial, as in the past, but European, in a sense that no one seems quite able to define. The European Union, unlike the Habsburg monarchy, is an association of sovereign states that have freely chosen to pool their sovereignty. Whereas the Habsburg monarchy was a disorderly accumulation of several kinds of historical entities in various relationships to the crown, the European Union is composed of modern states whose relationship is clearly defined by

European law and administrative practice. European policies are formulated by a collectivity of government ministers from the member states. Thus the comparison between the Habsburg monarchy and the European Union is no more than suggestive.

The resemblances, though, are real enough. The "European" identity of today, like the "Austrian" identity of the late Habsburg period, transcends but does not exclude national feeling. Europeans find what they have in common when they leave Europe, just as Austrian writers created Habsburg nostalgia in exile. In both cases, the non-national identity is best felt and expressed outside the region that gives rise to it. Like Habsburg writers before them, European elites suffer from an inescapable sense of irony, grounded in the horrible muddle of overlapping institutions and multiple languages, confirmed by the dimly remembered truth that the whole system of peace arose from war. The Habsburgs' national compromises arose from the monarchy's inability to win a war; European integration began because Germany lost a war that would have been more horrible still to win. The oppression of irony leaves Europeans unable to boast about their system.

In the early twenty-first century, the European Union is in what might be called the Habsburg position: in control of a massive zone of free trade, at the center of an economic globalization, without far-flung maritime possessions, lacking the ability to project decisive military power, in an age of unpredictable terrorism. In late 2007, an Austrian foreign minister spoke proudly of the removal of border controls between her country and its eastern neighbors. This European Union policy restored the state of affairs of 1914, when Habsburg subjects could travel the length and breadth of these very same territories with no documentation at all. The European Union, like the Habsburg dynasty, is without a national identity, yet fated to address the national question within its constituent parts and along its borders. The Habsburgs were most successful when they addressed national questions with tact, economic pressure, and the promise of bureaucratic jobs. The Europeans, with very limited military forces, have no other choice but precisely this policy. It has worked, in general, rather well.[26]

The Habsburgs believed that they were still a great military power when they were not; the Europeans suffer under no such illusion. Without an army, of course, the European Union was helpless to stop the bloodshed in Yugoslavia in the 1990s, and unable to make its voice heard about the American invasion of Iraq in 2003. When in that year the American wit Robert Kagan compared his own country to warlike Mars and the European Union to loving Venus, he echoed the advice a Hungarian king gave to the Habsburgs more than five hundred years earlier: "Let others fight wars! Thou happy Austria marry. What Mars gives to others, Venus bestows on thee." Unlike the Habsburgs, the European Union cannot actually enlarge its territories by marriage—but it is indeed a political body that attracts many suitors. The Orange Revolutionaries who pitched tents to support democracy the following year were clearly in the camp of Venus, rather than Mars.

The Habsburgs felt themselves constrained to civilize a far-flung empire, spreading regulations and bureaucrats to eastern Europe. The European Union exports the civilizing mission to the candidate countries themselves, requiring them to improve their own regulations and enlighten their own bureaucrats before requesting admission. The Habsburgs found themselves surrounded by nations partly of their own making. The European Union finds itself surrounded by weak states made in its own image.

Wilhelm, a Habsburg and a European, dreamed of America. He came from a realm of national toleration, and was himself evidence of the possibilities it conferred for change and assimilation. As one of his contemporaries, the writer Hugo von Hofmannsthal, said of the Habsburg monarchy during the First World War: "Here, if anywhere, is America." The Latin motto of Emperor Franz Josef, "Viribus unitis," has practically the same meaning as that of the Great Seal of the United States, "E pluribus unum": the first means "with united strength," the second "from many, one." Wilhelm, educated to see lands as personal opportunities, was personally drawn to the land of opportunity. He told a Soviet interrogator that he had wished to fly to America in a Zeppelin, and a fellow Habsburg officer that he wished to emigrate to the United States. This seems perfectly sensible. What better country for a man who chose his nationalities than one that was itself a choice?

How many of the American founding fathers, after all, were born American? Exactly as many as the subjects of this book who were born Ukrainian: none of them. The American founding fathers were born British subjects, of various origins, and became American as they made America. Very much the same is true of the early generations of Ukrainian politicians. Wilhelm was born a Habsburg. Kazimir Huzhkovsky, who introduced him to politics; Andrii Sheptytsky, his most important mentor; and Jan Tokary, his friend of the 1930s, were all Ukrainians who hailed from Polish noble families. His military ally in the steppes of Ukraine was Vsevolod Petriv, who had just joined the Ukrainian cause after a life as a Russian. Wilhelm's constant companion there was François-Xavier Bonne, born a Belgian. His partner during the peace negotiations at Brest was Mykola Vasylko, scion of a family of Romanian nobles. The first president of Ukraine was Mykhailo Hrushevsky, whose mother was Polish. Hrushevsky was one of the two most influential Ukrainian historians of all time. The other, Ivan Rudnytsky, was Jewish by the terms of Jewish religious law.[27]

Such Ukrainians behaved as the American revolutionaries did, resisting an empire while claiming to embody its best principles, struggling to found an independent state and thereby creating for themselves a new political identity. The signal difference resides not in intentions but in outcomes: the Ukrainians did not succeed in building a state on the first try. Their revolutionary wars, in which Wilhelm took part, ended in failure rather than success. They were fought in less propitious circumstances, with weaker allies and against more pitiless enemies, than was the American Revolutionary War. The Ukrainian national idea could not be inscribed in a constitution, as even the monarchist Wilhelm wished. Instead, after the failures of 1918–1922, Ukrainian nationalism was taken up by radicals, some disillusioned, some cynical, some representing foreign powers seeking to dominate and exploit. For much of the twentieth century, the extreme right and the extreme left concentrated upon ethnicity—the right because of a desperate belief in a hidden Ukrainian national will that could liberate the country from communism, the left because it wished to reduce Ukraine to a folk culture requiring Soviet rule. Yet the Ukrainian idea, like the American one, was political in its origins. It was, for Wilhelm as for his friends, a choice.

As states with powerful police forces and extensive bureaucracies came to define and regulate nationality in the twentieth century, such choices became harder to make. Wilhelm's father wanted to be Polish, but had to bribe the Polish state with land and property to get citizenship. Wilhelm's brother Albrecht wished to be Polish, but the Germans tortured him and took his property for not admitting to being German, then the communists seized his lands while claiming that he was in fact German. Wilhelm wished to be Austrian and Ukrainian, but the Austrian state revoked his citizenship after he died in Soviet Ukraine. Wilhelm died in 1948 and Albrecht in 1951, in the dark middle of the twentieth century when the election of nationality became all but impossible. So long as communists remained in power in Poland and Ukraine, their lives could neither be emulated nor recorded.

It would be tempting, of course, to treat their tragedy as belonging to the past. After all, Poland and Ukraine are now free and democratic. Yet even the freest of today's societies would not permit the sorts of choices the Habsburgs made. The state classifies us, as does the market, with tools and precision that were unthinkable in Wilhelm's time. There will never be another life like his. It would be impossible, today, to pose in Europe as a princess of Java, as did Mata Hari, or to keep one spouse on each American coast, as did Anaïs Nin. Perhaps that is not an entirely bad thing. Yet surely the ability to make and remake identity is close to the heart of any idea of freedom, whether it be freedom from oppression by others or freedom to become oneself. In their best days, the Habsburgs had a kind of freedom that we do not, that of imaginative and purposeful self-creation. It would be a mistake to consign it, as was so often done in the twentieth century, to the categories of decadence and degeneracy. Habsburgs benefited from the belief that they were the state rather than its subjects. But in the end, is that not what a free individual wishes to be, a part of a government rather than its instrument?

Even in the minutely controlled public sphere of our own times, outsiders can still join a national polity and influence national politics. Consider the Sephardic Jewish and Hungarian ancestry of Nicolas Sarkozy in France, or the Afro-Hawaiian-Indonesian childhood of Barack Obama in the United States, leading politicians in two of the most nationalist countries in the world. All citizens do have a measure of control, at least in democracies where their votes are counted, of how they belong to their nations. Perhaps they will have more confidence in unconventional choices if they see that each nation's founders were disobedient and unpredictable, men and women of imagination and ambition. The steel of every national monument was once molten.

The nation faces forward. It is made and remade every day. If we believe that the nation resides in the orderly recitations of history given to us by our leaders, then our story is over.

Epilogue

IN ŻYWIEC, AS IN VIENNA, there are certain risks to throwing loud parties. Maria Krystyna Habsburg, resident again in a castle in the middle of the city, has been known to complain. She has also been known to threaten to invite young people in for cake. The castle, no longer her family's, serves the municipality as a museum of art. Some of its holdings were gifts from Maria Krystyna herself.

Maria Krystyna lives alone in a small corner apartment, as a kind of guest of the city. The family brewery belongs to Heineken, which has built its own museum of history, complete with antique equipment, art deco advertising posters, video montages of the Second World War, and perky guides with headsets and microphones. The highlands around the city have also changed. The snowcaps melt faster than they did when Maria Krystyna was a girl, the green rises to the peaks sooner and stays longer every year.

Maria Krystyna, who dresses in black, has blue eyes that regard without making contact. Trying to meet them is like trying to focus on the surface of the sea. She speaks interwar Polish provocatively fast, as if the stories she is telling are not quite meant to be understood. She drops in phrases in English and French, perhaps expressions that a tutor, seventy years ago, told her were colloquial. In the free, democratic Poland of the early twenty-first century, she is a living symbol of the heroic Polish Habsburgs, who chose Poland and suffered for their choice. She never took a citizenship other than Polish, and never married. The mayor's office looks out for her and helps to arrange visits.

One summer Maria Krystyna was visited in Żywiec by a dozen champions of beauty pageants. Like the Heineken deal, this was good press for a tourist town that had seen better days. Beauty queens met a real princess. Presumably this was a meeting of equals. Royals are indulged today, as they were not in her uncle Wilhelm's time, partly because they make no claims to power and partly because scandal itself has become banal. Wilhelm courted very real risks as a certain kind of playboy. Unconcerned with the opinions of others for most of his young life, perfectly insouciant in his own sexual behavior, he was shamed by the popular media in the 1930s as he sought to recommence his political career in Paris. Today, scandal has no power left to tame royalty; royalty is little more than birthright celebrity. When Wilhelm's niece Maria Krystyna met with Miss Playboy, this was no scandal at all. It was nothing more than a bit of celebrity gossip in a regional edition of a newspaper. Poland, unbelievably, has become something very much like a normal European country.

The Habsburg family's other palace, on what is today the Croatian island of Lošinj, is a bit louder. The villa that Stefan completed just after Wilhelm's birth now serves as a sanatorium, specializing in the treatment of allergies. Come summer, Croatian teens, bunking many to a room, blast amplified music from the open windows. The building has been nationalized, in more ways than one. It belongs to the state, and is presented as an achievement of the nation. There is no outward indication that the building was once a Habsburg residence, or associated with figures of Polish and Ukrainian history. The garden is a national park. Stefan's exotic trees and flowers still grow, a century after his departure, though the credit is given to a Croatian scientist.

Time passes; times pass, too. The island began the century as part of the Habsburg monarchy, with its strivings toward eternity and its compromises with those who believed in the progress of nations. Then it was part of fascist Italy, governed by a regime that shared the imperial attachment to symbol, but also believed in a grand Italian modernity that would be hastened by a leader of genius. After the Second World War, the island was incorporated by communist Yugoslavia, a system legitimized by the belief that the forward movement of time brought progress toward a utopia of social justice. Now it is part of independent Croatia, a national state that pallidly revisits the twentieth century's belief that time brings national liberation. Today, however, the mark of national success in Europe is not state independence, but membership in the European Union.

Austrian investors are eager to buy the villa and restore it. An Austrian bank sponsors the park's playground, presumably for the good publicity. Croatian authorities drag their feet. Such a transaction may be difficult to resist once Croatia adapts itself to the legal norms of the European Union. It is easy to imagine the villa restored to its original charm, filled with Austrians drawn by Habsburg nostalgia to a palace built by an archduke—or by Ukrainians or Poles thinking of Wilhelm and Albrecht, or rather, as they are known in Ukrainian and Polish, Vasyl Vyshyvanyi and Karol Olbracht. In the park outside, visitors would tread upon the orange of the fallen pine needles on paths laid down by Stefan. The health they would seek is simple, physical health: the golden fleece of the old nations, or rather the aging peoples, of Europe.

Today, Europe's peoples live longer than ever before, and better. Europeans master time, insofar as they can, by better education, nutrition, and medicine. The typical European has more and better access to all of these than did a Habsburg archduke a century ago. In most of Europe, no one must die, as did Wilhelm, in the prisons of tyrants. And no one must die, as did both Wilhelm and his brother Leo, of tuberculosis. Lives extending into the eighties and even the nineties, such as their sister-in-law Alice's or Empress Zita's, are becoming the European norm. Otto von Habsburg, still quite active at ninety-five, explains his longevity in a way that evokes both modern ideas about physical exercise and the Habsburg cyclical view of time: "Life is like a bicycle. As long as you keep pushing the pedals, you keep going."

The water of the Adriatic Sea around Lošinj is warmer every year. The winds bear the same names as a century ago, the Tramontane, the Scirocco, and the Bora, the sailor's bane from the northeast. As the air continues to warm, the winds too will change, and the navigators will have to make their adjustments. Cartographers, too, will have steady work, adjusting shorelines. The old Habsburg charts will lose their value as the sea level rises. It will be measured on the pretty pier at Rovenska bay, where Archduke Karl Stefan docked his boats. The orange lichen will grow a bit higher on the rocks each year, the orange of iron oxide will discolor a bit more of the hillside.

Such is the gift of the twentieth century to the twenty-first. The sea, a last patch of eternity for the Habsburgs, has become a measure of time. Global warming is all that remains of historical inevitability.

In the Ukrainian city of Lviv, there are no Habsburg palaces. Had Wilhelm succeeded in his ambitions, perhaps he would have left a trace of himself in stone in Lviv, just as his father did in Lošinj and Żywiec. Instead, Wilhelm saw the city ruled from Warsaw, Berlin, and Moscow. Like the island of Lošinj at the other end of the old Habsburg domains, Lviv experienced the twentieth century's ideological empires of the left and right. The suffering was far greater, though, under Nazis and Soviets than it was under Italian fascists and Yugoslav communists.

In the decades after the Second World War, Lviv remained the proudest of Ukrainian cities, even under Soviet rule. It is today the most patriotic city in independent Ukraine, a poor and struggling democracy. There is now a small square, in a quiet part of the city, named after Wilhelm, or rather Vasyl Vyshyvanyi. Its single ornament is a street sign, in black and white. In its center rests a grey plinth, upon which stands no monument. But there are seesaws and swingsets, painted brightly in the primary colors. Vasyl Vyshyvanyi Square is a playground.

Of a summer afternoon, grandmothers sit on a bench, looking after their grandchildren. None of them can say who this Vasyl

Vyshyvanyi was. I tell them Wilhelm's story, and they listen and nod, as though every day someone with a foreign accent comes along to add a Habsburg prince to the national pantheon. My mind is wandering, my eye drawn by the sun in the ladies' lilac hair. They turn their heads, and so I do, too. Their grandchildren are playing on the empty base of the monument, the monument that is not yet.

Since this book ends with them, it ends with a beginning.

ACKNOWLEDGMENTS

The implausibly adventurous wanderings of Wilhelm von Habsburg left written sources in a dozen languages in more than twenty European archives. I would like first of all to thank archivists for their help. Deserving of special mention are Bożena Husar of the Polish State Archives at Żywiec and Leopold Auer of the Haus-, Hof-, und Staatsarchiv in Vienna. I would like to extend my gratitude to Iryna Vushko and Ray Brandon, who supplied me with important Ukrainian and German archival sources. Discussions with each of them also informed my own interpretations of events. I should also signal my great debt to Ivan Bazhynov for his generosity with his time and research in Kiev. More than anyone else, he helped me to see the outline of Wilhelm's early life. My time in Poland was fruitful, thanks in good measure to Andrzej Waśkiewicz, Katarzyna Jesień, and Andrzej Paczkowski.

Because the number of other interpretations of the life of Wilhelm von Habsburg is so limited, I would like to acknowledge the scholars whose published work on the subject preceded my own: Wolfdieter Bihl, Iurii Tereshchenko, Tetiana Ostashko, and Vasyl Rasevych. At Yale University's Sterling Memorial Library, Tatjana Lorković and Susanne Roberts were more helpful and responsive than could reasonably have been expected. While I was finishing the research, lectures at Harvard University, Cornell University, and the Anglo-American Conference in London helped me to formulate arguments. I appreciated the opportunity for discussion afforded by the Russian and East European History Workshop in Washington, DC, the Remarque Institute Seminar in New York, and the Transitions to Modernity Workshop at Yale. While responsibility for this book must remain my own, I am very glad to acknowledge that it only improved with discussion.

Chapters improved after critique by Karen Alter, Holly Case, István Deák, Timothy Garton Ash, Isabel Hull, Jovana Knežević, Hugo Lane, Andrzej Nowak, Dominique Reill, Stuart Rachels, Mary Lou Roberts, Michael Snyder, Piotr Wandycz, and Larry Wolff. Marci Shore and Nancy Wingfield generously read and commented upon full drafts of the manuscript. Ernst Rutkowski, Scott Spector, and Matti Bunzl were kind enough to show me unpublished articles. Conversations with Paul Laverdure and Tirza Latimer alerted me to important sources. Elisabeth Grossegger and Daniel Unowsky answered questions about the commemorations of 1908; Marina Cattaruzza, Alison Frank, and Marion Wullschleger spoke to me of Istria. E. E. Snyder and Christine Snyder introduced me to Malta. Dan Shore answered questions about opera, and Sasha Zeyliger about Russian. Eagle Glassheim sent me Czech materials; Vladyslav Hrynevych located interrogation protocols in Kiev. Oleh Turii gave me rare books about Redemptorists. Galin Tihanov and Adelina Angusheva-Tihanova helped me to think about time and eastern-rite Christianity.

A number of people, places, and institutions facilitated the travel, discussion, and reflection needed to recall the atmosphere of the Habsburg monarchy. Omer Bartov included me in his Borderlands project and thus in his personal encounter with eastern Galicia. Christoph Mick and the Zeit-Stiftung invited me to Lviv at just the right moment. Oxana Shevel taught me how to compare Lviv and Kiev, and much else about the politics of Ukrainian nationality. Ivo Banac taught me what I know about the history of Croatia. Leda Siragusa's Grbica Hotel was an ideal starting point for hiking the island of Lošinj; and her husband Giovanni built me a sailboat. Krzysztof Michalski and his Institute for Human Sciences sheltered me in Vienna. The Department of History and the European Council of the Macmillan Center for International and Area Studies of Yale University supported my research institutionally and financially. Maria Krystyna Habsburg and Georg von Habsburg were gracious enough to answer some of my questions about their family. Steve Wasserman of Kneerim and Williams saw the appeal of the story from the beginning. Lara Heimert of Basic Books was a fitting literary companion for Wilhelm von Habsburg.

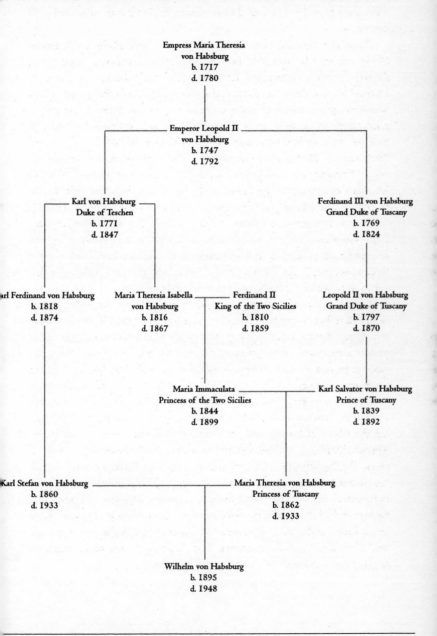

Empress Maria Theresia
von Habsburg
b. 1717
d. 1780

Emperor Leopold II
von Habsburg
b. 1747
d. 1792

Karl von Habsburg
Duke of Teschen
b. 1771
d. 1847

Ferdinand III von Habsburg
Grand Duke of Tuscany
b. 1769
d. 1824

Karl Ferdinand von Habsburg
b. 1818
d. 1874

Maria Theresia Isabella
von Habsburg
b. 1816
d. 1867

Ferdinand II
King of the Two Sicilies
b. 1810
d. 1859

Leopold II von Habsburg
Grand Duke of Tuscany
b. 1797
d. 1870

Maria Immaculata
Princess of the Two Sicilies
b. 1844
d. 1899

Karl Salvator von Habsburg
Prince of Tuscany
b. 1839
d. 1892

Karl Stefan von Habsburg
b. 1860
d. 1933

Maria Theresia von Habsburg
Princess of Tuscany
b. 1862
d. 1933

Wilhelm von Habsburg
b. 1895
d. 1948

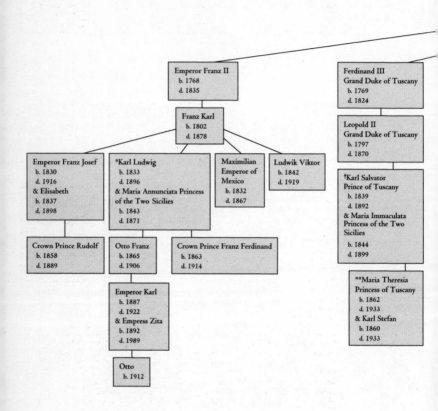

Emperor Franz II
b. 1768
d. 1835

Franz Karl
b. 1802
d. 1878

Emperor Franz Josef
b. 1830
d. 1916
& Elisabeth
b. 1837
d. 1898

°Karl Ludwig
b. 1833
d. 1896
& Maria Annunciata Princess
of the Two Sicilies
b. 1843
d. 1871

**Maximilian
Emperor of
Mexico**
b. 1832
d. 1867

Ludwik Viktor
b. 1842
d. 1919

Crown Prince Rudolf
b. 1858
d. 1889

Otto Franz
b. 1865
d. 1906

Crown Prince Franz Ferdinand
b. 1863
d. 1914

Emperor Karl
b. 1887
d. 1922
& Empress Zita
b. 1892
d. 1989

Otto
b. 1912

**Ferdinand III
Grand Duke of Tuscany**
b. 1769
d. 1824

**Leopold II
Grand Duke of Tuscany**
b. 1797
d. 1870

**†Karl Salvator
Prince of Tuscany**
b. 1839
d. 1892
& Maria Immaculata
Princess of the Two
Sicilies
b. 1844
d. 1899

**°°Maria Theresia
Princess of Tuscany**
b. 1862
d. 1933
& Karl Stefan
b. 1860
d. 1933

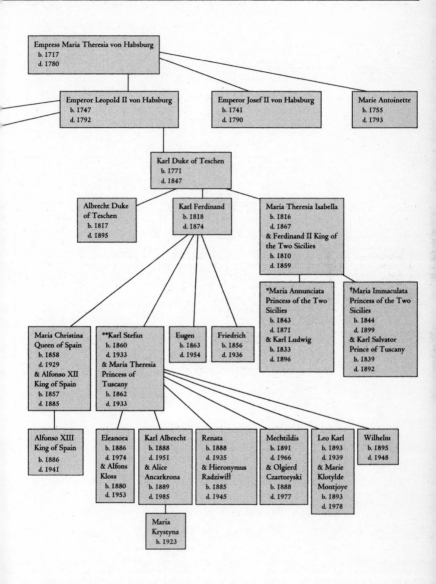

BIOGRAPHICAL SKETCHES

HABSBURG AND ROYAL PROTAGONISTS

Albrecht (1817–1895). Archduke of Austria, etc. Field Marshall of the Habsburg army, victor over the Italians at Custozza in 1866. Adoptive father of Stefan, who inherited his Galician properties.

Albrecht (1888–1951). Archduke of Austria, etc. Eldest son of Stefan and Maria Theresia, husband of Alice Ancarkrona, brother of Wilhelm. Artillery officer in the Habsburg and then the Polish army. Father of Maria Krystyna, Karl Stefan, and Renata. Head of the family after Stefan's death in 1933, main landholder at Żywiec. Wilhelm's financial benefactor. A Pole by nationality, he was imprisoned by the Germans and forced into exile by Polish communists.

Alfonso XIII (1886–1941). King of Spain. Son of Maria Christina, nephew of Stefan, first cousin of Wilhelm. Welcomed Wilhelm and Zita to Madrid in 1922, and sought to preserve Stefan's landholdings in Poland. Left Spain in 1931, bon vivant in Paris in the 1930s. Abdicated shortly before his death in favor of his son. Grandfather of King Juan Carlos.

Eleanora (1886–1974). Archduchess of Austria until the renunciation of her titles necessitated by her marriage to Alfons Kloss. Eldest daughter of Stefan and Maria Theresia, Wilhelm's sister. Broke with Habsburg convention by marrying a sailor, the captain of her father's yacht. An Austrian by nationality before and after the Second World War, during which her sons served in the German army.

Elisabeth (1837–1898). Empress of Austria, etc., wife of Franz Josef, mother of Rudolf. Like Stefan, Maximilian, Rudolf, and a number of other Habsburgs, a warm-water Romantic. Built a palace on Corfu visited by Stefan and the family, identified with Greece.

Eugen (1863–1954). Archduke of Austria, etc. Brother of Stefan, uncle of Wilhelm. Commander of Austrian forces in the Balkans and Italy during the

First World War. Wilhelm's patron after his return to Austria in 1935. Supporter of the arts. The last Habsburg to lead the Teutonic Knights.

Don Fernando (1891–1944). Duke of Durcal. Boon companion of Wilhelm in Paris.

Infante Fernando (1884–1959). Prince of Bavaria, then Infante of Spain. First cousin of Alfonso and Wilhelm, and conspirator with Wilhelm in financial schemes in Madrid in the 1920s.

Franz Ferdinand (1863–1914). Archduke of Austria, etc. Visited Stefan and his first cousin Maria Theresia on the Adriatic in the 1890s. As crown prince was assassinated by Serbian nationalists in Sarajevo. An opponent of war in the Balkans in life, he became the cause of the First World War in death.

Franz Josef (1830–1916). Emperor of Austria, etc. Victor over the national rebellions of 1848, failed absolutist, then sponsor of constitutional reform; pragmatist on national questions. Preserved the monarchy even as national unification changed the geopolitics of Europe. Husband of Elisabeth and father of Rudolf. Apparently encouraged Wilhelm's Ukrainian vocation.

Friedrich (1856–1936). Archduke of Austria, etc. Brother of Stefan, uncle of Wilhelm. Commander in chief of Austrian forces during the First World War through 1916.

Karl (1887–1922). Emperor of Austria, etc. The last Habsburg to rule. Ascended the thrones after the death of Franz Josef in 1916. A proponent of a rapid armistice during the First World War. Tried and failed to negotiate secretly a peace with France. Dispatched Wilhelm to Ukraine in 1918 for special missions. Saw the Habsburg monarchy decline during the war to the status of a German satellite. Resigned from his state responsibilities without formally abdicating at war's end. Died after two failed attempts to restore the monarchy in Hungary. Husband of Zita and father of Otto.

Karl Ludwig (1833–1896). Archduke of Austria, etc. Younger brother of Emperor Franz Josef. Briefly seen as Franz Josef's successor after the death of Rudolf in 1889. Died after drinking the waters of the River Jordan. Father of Franz Ferdinand and Otto Franz.

Karl Stefan (1921–). Prince of Altenburg. Son of Albrecht and Alice. Swedish citizen. Contested the ownership of the Żywiec brewery after 1989. Named for his grandfather, Karl Stefan, who in this book is called Stefan. Wilhelm's nephew.

Leo (1893–1939). Archduke of Austria, etc. Second son of Stefan and Maria Theresia, brother of Wilhelm. Officer in the Habsburg and Polish armies. Landowner of the smaller part of the Żywiec properties after his father's death. Husband of Marie Montjoye.

Ludwig Viktor (1842–1919). Archduke of Austria, etc. Younger brother of Franz Josef. Known for his homosexual adventures and art collection. Banished to a castle near Salzburg by his brother the emperor.

Maria Christina (1858–1929). Archduchess of Austria, etc., then queen and regent of Spain. Sister of Stefan, mother of Alfonso, aunt of Wilhelm. Sheltered Zita and Wilhelm in Spain in the early 1920s.

Maria Krystyna (1923–). Princess of Altenburg. Daughter of Albrecht and Alice, exiled after the Second World War, current resident of the New Castle in Żywiec. Wilhelm's niece.

Maria Theresia (1862–1933). Archduchess of Austria, etc., Princess of Tuscany. Along with her husband, Stefan, the founder of a Polish royal family. Mother of Wilhelm, Leo, Albrecht, Renata, Eleanora, and Mechtildis. Fervent Catholic, lover of the arts. Donated a hospital and served as a nurse during the First World War.

Maximilian (1832–1867). Archduke of Austria, etc., then Emperor of Mexico. Commander and modernizer of the Habsburg navy. Executed by Mexican republicans. Brother of Franz Josef.

Mechtildis (1891–1966). Archduchess of Austria, etc., until the renunciation of her titles necessitated by her marriage to Olgierd Czartoryski. Third daughter of Stefan and Maria Theresia, sister of Wilhelm. A Pole by nationality. Emigrated to Brazil during the Second World War.

Otto (1912–). Archduke of Austria, etc., eldest son of Emperor Karl and Empress Zita, heir to the Habsburg thrones after Karl's death in 1922, head of the House of Habsburg after coming of age in 1932. Statesman and author. Leader of the Austrian restorationist movement of the 1930s, advocate of a Danubian confederation during the Second World War and of European integration thereafter. Member of the Bavarian Christian Social Union, deputy in the European Parliament.

Otto Franz (1865–1906). Archduke of Austria, etc. Remembered for his scandals, perhaps most for appearing in the Hotel Sacher wearing only a sword and the collar of the Order of the Golden Fleece. Seen in the 1890s as the likely heir to the Habsburg thrones after Franz Ferdinand fell ill with tuberculosis. Father of Emperor Karl and grandfather of Otto.

Renata (1888–1935). Archduchess of Austria, etc., until the renunciation of her titles necessitated by her marriage to Hieronymus Radziwiłł. Second daughter of Stefan and Maria Theresia, sister of Wilhelm. A Pole by nationality.

Renata (1931–). Princess of Altenburg. Second daughter of Alice and Albrecht. Spanish citizen. Contested the ownership of the Żywiec brewery after 1989. Wilhelm's niece.

Rudolf (1858–1889). Archduke of Austria, etc., son of Franz Josef and Elisabeth, heir to the Habsburg thrones until his suicide at Mayerling in 1889. A writer, a liberal, and a friend of intellectuals.

Stefan (1860–1933). Archduke of Austria, etc. Naval officer, automotive enthusiast, painter, sailor, aspirant to a nonexistent Polish throne, founder of a Polish royal family, owner of the Żywiec brewery and related properties. Husband of Maria Theresia, father of Albrecht, Eleanora, Mechtildis, Renata, Leo, and Wilhelm.

Vyshyvanyi, Vasyl. *See* Wilhelm.

Wilhelm (1895–1948). Archduke of Austria, etc. Habsburg by birth, child of the Balkans, Polish by upbringing, Ukrainian by choice. Officer in the Habsburg army during the First World War, supporter of a Ukrainian entity under Habsburg rule. Companian of Bavarian imperialists, Spanish royals, and French pleasure-seekers in the 1920s. A Habsburg restorationist and a fascist in the 1930s, then a spy against Nazi Germany and the Soviet Union in the 1940s, and finally a democrat. Lover, orientalist, sportsman. Son of Stefan and Maria Theresia, brother of Albrecht, Leo, Mechtildis, Renata, and Eleanora, cousin of Alfonso, nephew of Maria Christina, Eugen, and Friedrich.

Wilhelm II (1859–1941). Emperor of Germany and king of Prussia, head of the House of Hohenzollern. Met Wilhelm at German headquarters at Spa in August 1918.

Zita (1892–1989). Princess of Bourbon-Parma, then Empress of Austria, etc. Wife of Karl, mother of Otto. The heart and soul of the restorationist politics of the 1930s. Visited by Wilhelm in Belgium.

HABSBURG CONSORTS AND RELATIONS

Ancarkrona, Alice (1889–1985). Created Princess of Altenburg in 1949. Wife of Albrecht, mother of Karl Stefan, Maria Krystyna, Renata, and Joachim Badeni. Patriotic Polish Habsburg of Swedish origin, activist in the Polish underground, author of the memoir *Princess and Partisan.*

Badeni, Joachim (1912–). Polish theologian. Born Kazimierz Badeni, the son of Alice Ancarkrona and her first husband, Count Ludwik Badeni. Raised in eastern Galicia and then, after Alice married Albrecht, in Żywiec with his half-siblings Karl Stefan, Maria Krystyna, and Renata. A soldier in the Polish army during the Second World War before taking orders as a Dominican monk in 1943. Returned to communist Poland to study theology. Author of a memoir that concerns the Polish Habsburgs. After 1989 contested the ownership of the Żywiec brewery.

Chotek, Sophie (1868–1914). Countess of Chotkova and Wognin, then Duchess of Hohenberg. Wife of Franz Ferdinand, murdered at his side at Sarajevo on 28 June 1914 by a Serbian nationalist.

Czartoryski, Olgierd (1888–1977). Prince, Polish aristocrat, husband of Mechtildis, brother-in-law of Wilhelm. Joined his wife in emigration to Brazil during the Second World War.

Kloss, Alfons (1880–1953). Captain of Stefan's yacht in the Adriatic. Married Eleanora in 1913. Austrian by nationality.

Montjoye, Maja (1893–1978). Properly Marie-Klotilde von Thuillieres, Countess of Montjoye et de la Roche. Married Leo in 1922. As his widow, she protested the German attempt to seize the family property during the Second World War.

Radziwiłł, Hieronymus (1885–1945). Prince, Polish aristocrat, husband of Renata, brother-in-law of Wilhelm. In his youth regarded as pro-German and as a candidate for the Polish throne in 1918. Aided the Polish anti-German underground during the Second World War. Died in Soviet captivity as a Polish patriot.

OTHERS

Bauer, Max (1875–1929). German artillery officer, close associate of Ludendorff, advocate of right-wing dictatorship in Germany, sympathizer of monarchy in Austria, and finally military and industrial advisor to Chiang Kai-Shek. Participant in the failed putsch in Berlin in 1920. Comrade of Wilhelm in Vienna in 1921 in the Bavarian plan to invade Bolshevik Russia. Invited to Spain by Alfonso in 1924 at Wilhelm's initiative.

Bonne, François-Xavier (1882–1945). Redemptorist priest of Belgian origin. Took on the eastern (Greek Catholic) rite and Ukrainian nationality. Wilhelm's companion in Ukraine in 1918, envoy of the Ukrainian National Republic to the Vatican in 1920. Died in the United States.

Couyba, Paulette. French adventuress. Wilhelm's lover in Paris.

Dollfuss, Engelbert (1892–1934). Austrian politician, chancellor from 1932 to 1934. Leader of the Christian Social Party, which served as the basis for the Fatherland Front he established in 1933. Dissolved parliament in 1933 and ruled by decree thereafter. After a civil war, he banned the Social Democratic Party in 1934. His clerical authoritarian regime attempted to hold the center of Austrian politics despite the very strong influence of both the left and the Nazi right. Assassinated by Nazis in 1934.

Frank, Hans (1900–1946). Nazi lawyer. Minister of Justice for Bavaria from 1933, chief of the Generalgouvernement (German-occupied Poland) from 1939. Ruled from the former Polish royal palace in Cracow, stole the family silver of the Polish Habsburgs. In 1937 seen by Wilhelm as a possible Nazi partner for Ukraine. Found guilty of war crimes at Nuremberg and executed.

Georges-Michel, Michel (1883–1985). Prolific French journalist, memoirist, and art critic. Friend of Wilhelm in Paris. Recruited by Paulette Couyba for a journey to Vienna in 1936.

Himmler, Heinrich (1900–1945). Nazi leader. Chief of the SS and of the Reich Commission for the Strengthening of Germandom, among other functions. After Hitler, the man most responsible for the Holocaust. A personal enemy of the Habsburgs, he had Albrecht's family sent to a labor camp and repeatedly tried to nationalize the family property. Committed suicide.

Hindenburg, Paul von (1847–1934). German commander and statesman. Regarded, along with his chief of staff Ludendorff, as the victor at Tannenberg over the Russian army in 1914. During the First World War, the two men gained the dominant position in the German Empire, eclipsing Wilhelm II himself. Returned to public life in 1925 to run for president. Reelected in 1932, he appointed Hitler chancellor in 1933.

Horthy, Miklós (1868–1957). Habsburg naval officer and then regent of Hungary. Circumnavigated the globe at the orders of Maximilian, sailed to Spain in the company of Stefan, and served as aide-de-camp to Franz Josef. On Stefan's recommendation was promoted by Karl to admiral and given command of the entire Habsburg fleet. Rose to power in Hungary after a failed communist revolution. As regent opposed his sovereign Karl's two attempts to regain the Hungarian throne.

Huzhkovsky, Kazimir (?–1918). Ukrainian nobleman of Polish origin, officer of the Habsburg army. One of Wilhelm's Ukrainian interlocutors during the First World War.

Ludendorff, Erich (1865–1937). German commander and nationalist. Chief of staff during the First World War to Hindenburg, regarded along with his superior as the victor at Tannenberg in 1914. Participant in the right-wing putsch in Berlin in 1920 and Hitler's Beer Hall Putsch in Munich in 1923. Ally of Wilhelm in Bavarian-backed plots to invade Bolshevik Russia in 1921.

Novosad, Roman (1920?–2004). Ukrainian student of music in Warsaw and then Vienna. Friend and comrade of Wilhelm in wartime and postwar espionage. Soviet political prisoner and author of brief memoirs about Wilhelm.

Hrushevsky, Mykhailo (1866–1934). Ukrainian historian and statesman. Author of the foundational history of Ukraine. Briefly head of state of the Ukrainian National Republic in 1918.

Larischenko, Eduard. Wilhelm's adjutant and secretary. Accompanied Wilhelm in Ukraine and Spain before the two men broke in France.

Lebed, Mykola (1909–1998). Ukrainian nationalist activist, participant in acts of terrorism in interwar Poland. Active in the Bandera faction of the Organization of Ukrainian Nationalists and one of the organizers of the Ukrainian Insurgent Army in 1943. Advocate of ethnic cleansing of Poles. Introduced to French intelligence through Wilhelm's efforts. Postwar operative of American intelligence.

Lincoln, Trebitsch (1879–1943). Hungarian thief, Anglican missionary, British member of parliament, German nationalist, and Buddhist guru. Participant in the White International schemes of the early 1920s to rally revisionist nations against the peace accords and Bolshevik Russia.

Mistinguett (1875–1956). French singer and actress, best known for her song "Mon Homme" and her live performances in Montmartre. Born Jeanne Bourgeois in Enghien-les-Bains, where Wilhelm lived in the late 1920s. The most famous Frenchwoman and the highest-paid performer of her time. A friend of Wilhelm in the early 1930s.

Paneyko, Vasyl. Ukrainian journalist and politician. State secretary for foreign affairs of the West Ukrainian National Republic, representative of the Ukrainian National Republic at the Paris peace negotiations. Known to be pro-Russian, suspected by Ukrainian politicians of collaborating with intelligence services, a naturalized Frenchman. Known to Wilhelm no later than 1918 and his friend and political advisor in Paris in the early 1930s. Possible informer on Wilhelm to Polish intelligence and the likely engineer of the scandal of 1934–1935 that forced Wilhelm to leave Paris.

Piłsudski, Józef (1867–1935). Polish revolutionary and statesman. A socialist who believed in insurrection, he exploited his role in the Habsburgs' Polish Legions to create an armed movement for Polish independence. Head of state and commander in chief of independent Poland from 1918, victor in the wars against the West Ukrainian National Republic and Bolshevik Russia. Came to power in Poland a second time in 1926 in a military coup.

Prokop, Myroslav (1913–2003). Ukrainian nationalist, a leader of the Bandera faction of the Organization of Ukrainian Nationalists. First major nationalist with whom Wilhelm made contact in Vienna during the Second World War.

Prokopovych, Anna. Courier for the Bandera faction of the Organization of Ukrainian Nationalists. As Lida Tulchyn, she made the acquaintance of Roman Novosad and Wilhelm in Vienna in 1944.

Poltavets-Ostrianytsia, Ivan (1890–1957). Ukrainian patriot from the Russian Empire. Active in the Hetmanate government as a close associate of Hetman Pavlo Skoropadsky. Cooperated with Wilhelm in monarchist politics in the early 1920s and made his acquaintance again in 1937. An advocate of a Ukrainian alliance with Nazi Germany.

Schuschnigg, Kurt von (1897–1977). Austrian politician. Chancellor of Austria 1934–1938. Maintained relations with Otto von Habsburg and permitted a certain freedom to the restorationist movement. Sought to find a source of support for the ruling Fatherland Front. Resisted Hitler and the *Anschluss* with fiery rhetoric and a planned referendum on independence in 1938, but ordered Austrian troops not to resist. Held by the Germans in prisons and concentration camps. Emigrated to the United States.

Sheptytsky, Andrii (1865–1944). Ukrainian churchman of Polish origin, Greek Catholic metropolitan of Halych. Transformed the Greek Catholic Church in Austrian Galicia into a Ukrainian national institution and hoped for the conversion of the Orthodox to Greek Catholicism. Mentor of Wilhelm in 1917 and 1918 and perhaps in the 1930s.

Skoropadsky, Pavlo (1873–1945). Ukrainian statesman representing the interests of conservatives and landowners. With German support led a coup d'état against the Ukrainian National Republic in April 1918. Feared the popularity of Wilhelm in the Ukrainian countryside that summer. Rival and occasional ally of Wilhelm in Ukrainian monarchist politics in the early 1920s. An emigrant to Germany, he was killed by an allied air raid.

Tokary. *See* Tokarzewski-Karaszewicz, Jan.

Tokarzewski-Karaszewicz, Jan (1885–1954). Ukrainian diplomat of Polish origin. Official of the Ukrainian National Republic and participant in the Polish-sponsored Promethean movement to weaken the Soviet Union by arousing nationalism. A friend of Wilhelm's in the 1930s and a fellow aristocratic fascist.

Tulchyn, Lida. *See* Prokopovych, Anna.

Vasylko, Mykola (1868–1924). Ukrainian politician of Romanian noble origin. Deputy to the Austrian parliament and proponent, during the First World War, of the creation of a Ukrainian crownland within the Habsburg monarchy. One of Wilhelm's Ukrainian interlocutors during the First World War. Cooperated with Wilhelm in aiding Ukrainian diplomats in January and February

1918 as they negotiated the Bread Peace. A diplomat of the West Ukrainian National Republic and the Ukrainian National Republic.

Wiesner, Friedrich von (1871–1951). Austrian lawyer and diplomat friendly with the House of Habsburg. Assigned by Franz Josef the task of writing a special report on the assassination at Sarajevo. Cooperated with Wilhelm in monarchist and Ukrainian politics in Vienna in 1920 and 1921. Placed in charge of restorationist politics by Otto in 1930. Of Jewish origin, he was the main target of Wilhelm's anti-Semitism in 1937 and 1938.

Wilson, Woodrow (1856–1924). American politician. President of the United States of America, proponent during the First World War of the idea of the self-determination of nations.

CHRONOLOGY OF
HABSBURG HISTORY

1273	Rudolf elected Holy Roman Emperor
1430	Founding of the Order of the Golden Fleece
1522	Separation of Spanish and Austrian lines of Habsburg family
1526	Battle of Mohács, Habsburgs gain Bohemia and Hungary
1618–1648	Thirty Years' War
1683	Ottoman siege of Vienna
1700	Extinction of the Spanish line of the Habsburgs
1740	Accession of Maria Theresia
1740–1763	Wars with Prussia
1772–1795	Partitions of Poland
1792–1814	Wars with France
1793	Execution of Marie Antoinette
1806	End of the Holy Roman Empire
1814–1815	Congress of Vienna
1821–1848	Metternich chancellor
1830	Birth of Franz Josef
1848	Springtime of Nations, accession of Franz Josef
1859	War with France and Piedmont
1860	October Diploma
	Birth of Stefan
1866	War with Prussia and Italy
1867	Compromise with Hungary
	Constitutional laws
	Execution of Maximilian in Mexico
1870–1871	Unification of Germany and Italy
1878	Congress of Berlin, occupation of Bosnia, Serbian independence
1879	Alliance with Germany
	Stefan a naval officer
1886	Wedding of Stefan and Maria Theresia
1888	Birth of Albrecht
1889	Suicide of Crown Prince Rudolf at Mayerling

1895	Birth of Wilhelm
1896	Stefan retires from active duty
1897–1907	Stefan, Willy, and family on Lošinj
1898	Assassination of Empress Elisabeth
1903	Anti-Habsburg dynasty in Serbia
1907	Introduction of general manhood suffrage
1907–1914	Stefan, Willy, and family in Galicia
1908	Annexation of Bosnia and Herzegovina
	Sixtieth jubilee of Emperor Franz Josef
1909–1913	School for Wilhelm, marriage for sisters
1912	First Balkan War
1913	Second Balkan War
1913–1915	Military academy for Wilhelm
1914	Assassination of Franz Ferdinand in Sarajevo
1914–1918	First World War
1915	Wilhelm commands Ukrainian troops
1916	Death of Franz Josef, accession of Karl
	Proclamation of Kingdom of Poland
1917	Bolshevik Revolution, collapse of Russian Empire
1918	Recognition of Ukrainian National Republic
	Austro-German occupation of Ukraine
	Wilhelm in Ukraine
	Austrian, Polish, Czechoslovak, West Ukrainian republics
	Dissolution of the Habsburg monarchy
1919	Destruction of West Ukrainian National Republic
1919–1923	Paris peace settlements
1921	Destruction of Ukrainian National Republic
	Public break between Stefan and Wilhelm
	Stefan becomes Polish citizen, keeps estate
	Wilhelm in White International
1922	Mussolini takes power in Italy
	Alfonso welcomes Habsburgs in Spain
1922–1926	Wilhelm in Spain
1926–1935	Wilhelm in France
1931	Spain a republic, Alfonso departs
1932	Otto comes of age, restorationist politics commences
1932–1933	Famine in Soviet Ukraine
1933	Hitler takes power in Germany
	Death of Stefan and Maria Theresia
	Austrian parliament dissolved, Fatherland Front created
1934	Defeat of Social Democrats in Austria
	Failed Nazi coup in Austria
	Creation of Popular Front in Paris
1935	Trial of Wilhelm and Paulette
1935–1947	Wilhelm in Austria
1936	Germany and Italy ally, Italy abandons Austria
1936–1939	Spanish Civil War
1937–1938	Great Terror in the Soviet Union
1938	*Anschluss*, destruction of Austria
	Kristallnacht pogroms

1939	Nazi-Soviet nonaggression pact
	German and Soviet invasions of Poland
	Arrest of Albrecht by Germans
1939–1940	Germany seizes Habsburg properties
	German expulsions of Poles and Jews
1939–1945	Second World War
1941	German invasion of the Soviet Union
1941–1945	Holocaust of European Jews
1943–1947	Ethnic cleansing of Poles and Ukrainians
1944–1947	Wilhelm at work in espionage
1945	Poland seizes Habsburg properties
1945–1948	Communist takeovers in eastern Europe
1945–1955	Four-power occupation of Austria
1947	Arrest of Wilhelm by Soviets
1948	Death of Wilhelm in Soviet Ukraine
1951	Death of Albrecht in Sweden
	European Coal and Steel Community
1953	Death of Stalin
1957	Treaty of Rome
1979–1999	Otto a deputy to European Parliament
1980–1981	Solidarity movement in Poland
1985–1991	Gorbachev in power in the Soviet Union
1986	Accession of Spain to the European Union
1989	Revolution in eastern Europe
1990–1999	Wars of Yugoslav succession
1991	Dissolution of the Soviet Union
1991	Ukrainian independence
1991–2005	Legal contestation of Żywiec brewery
1995	Accession of Austria to the European Union
2004	Accession of Poland to the European Union
	Orange Revolution in Ukraine

NOTE ON TERMS
AND LANGUAGES

No accurate brief title exists for the empire that is the subject of this book. Until 1804 the Habsburgs had no collective name for their European possessions. Between 1804 and 1867, these lands were known as the "Austrian Empire." Between 1867 and 1918, the state was called "Austria-Hungary." I refer to it as the "Habsburg monarchy." I reserve "Austria" for the small alpine republic formed after each of the world wars, the Austria of today.

The designation "Austria-Hungary" is more confusing than it appears. There was a Hungarian half of the monarchy, but no Austrian half. The official name of the non-Hungarian lands was "the lands and kingdoms represented in the Imperial Council." This book mainly concerns territories within the non-Hungarian part of the empire. The provinces of Istria and Galicia, where much of the action takes place, were both among "the lands and kingdoms represented in the Imperial Council."

Those who study the Habsburg monarchy know the German abbreviations that allowed for administrative precision in the period 1867–1918. Institutions that were imperial or "kaiserlich" were designated as such by the letter "k." Institutions that were Hungarian were royal, and thus "königlich"—also designated by the letter "k." Thus common Austro-Hungarian institutions were known as "K. und. k."—Imperial and Royal. This is why the novelist Robert Musil set *The Man without Qualities* in a land called Kakania. Perhaps this bureaucratic proliferation of the letter "k" also helps explain why Kafka so hated the first letter of his last name. I am avoiding these variants in favor of the adjective "Habsburg."

The institutions that were imperial and royal, K. und k., that appear in this book are the army, the navy, the foreign ministry, and the occupation authority in Bosnia. References to the Habsburg army are to the Imperial and Royal Army, the K. und k. Armee; neither the Austrian nor the Hungarian home guard (the Landwehr and the Honvéd) is much discussed. Both of the latter took part in the 1918 occupation of Ukraine, and it was Honvéd troops who fell victim to a bloody massacre I mention; yet for the purposes of describing the occupation, there is little need to distinguish among these Habsburg armed forces. Institutions that appear in this book that were authoritative in the non-Hungarian half of the empire, imperial but not royal, include the government and the parliament.

Titling Habsburgs is like collecting butterflies, more pleasing in the pursuit than in the pinning down. The full titles of the emperor and of the members of his family run to pages and are almost never printed, even in the most obsequious of heraldic works. Franz Josef and Karl were emperors in Austria and kings in Hungary. Wilhelm and his father and brothers were imperial archdukes in Austria and royal archdukes in Hungary; his mother and sisters were imperial archduchesses in Austria and royal archduchesses in Hungary. I have sometimes translated "Erzherzog" as "prince" rather than the more literal "archduke," to convey the sense of the Austrian usage: that these were princes of the blood, men in line for thrones.

The full name of these Habsburgs was Habsburg-Lothringen. The House of Habsburg-Lothringen arose in 1736 with the marriage of the Duke of Lorraine to Archduchess Maria Theresia von Habsburg. The Pragmatic Sanction allowed Maria Theresia to rule and her children to succeed to the Habsburg thrones. Every modern Habsburg mentioned in this book is a descendant of Maria Theresia and thus a member of the House of Habsburg-Lothringen, or, in English, Habsburg-Lorraine.

There is also no satisfactory way of referring to places once within the Habsburg monarchy. German was the language of administration in the non-Hungarian part of the monarchy, and thus maps before 1918 usually supply German names. The Habsburgs who are the subjects of this book were all born before 1918. Yet they, like their empire, were not German in a national sense. In general I use the English place names. For smaller localities, the English place name is generally the same as the Slavic. This creates a certain amount of anachronism, but it probably causes the least confusion.

Wilhelm used six main languages: German, French, Ukrainian, Polish, Italian, and English. Five of these languages are written in Latin characters. Ukrainian, like Russian, is written in the Cyrillic alphabet. Ukrainian and Russian words are reproduced in a simplified version of the Library of Congress transliteration system. In the main text, Ukrainian and Russian names are given in the simplest possible form, in the notes with more precision. People who know these languages will find this approach legible; others will have no reason to care. With the exceptions of passages from novels cited in the bibliography, any translations from these and other languages are my own—although I shamelessly bothered friends and colleagues for assistance.

All of the men in Wilhelm von Habsburg's immediate family bore the name Karl, after Archduke Karl, Duke of Teschen, his father's grandfather (and his mother's great-grandfather), and more distantly after Emperor Karl, on whose sixteenth-century empire the sun never set. Wilhelm himself was Wilhelm Franz Josef Karl, his father was Karl Stefan, one brother was Karl Albrecht, and the other was Leo Karl. To add to the confusion, the Austrian emperor from 1916 was also Karl. To simplify matters, I have adopted the solution of their contemporaries, referring in the text to Stefan rather than Karl Stefan, Albrecht rather than Karl Albrecht, and Leo rather than Leo Karl. Emperor Karl is thus the only Karl in the story.

Wilhelm was known by different names in different contexts. Family members, friends, lovers, and comrades knew him as Guillaume, Guy, Robert, William, Vasyl, Willy, or Vyshy. I refer to him in boyhood as Willy and then in adulthood as Wilhelm. The use of these German forms does not suggest that he was nationally German, which he was not—most of the time. The German language could once suggest the universal, and the universal inside a man is always ambiguous. After the Nazi period, German has different resonances than it did during much of Wilhelm's lifetime. Before 1933, German culture was the flower of Europe, not only in Germany itself but also in the Habsburg domains. Unlike K., the hero of Kafka's *The Trial,* Wilhelm chose the identity for which he was sentenced and died. Like Ulrich, the hero of Musil's *The Man without Qualities,* he never saw any such choice as final.

NOTES

GOLD: THE EMPEROR'S DREAM

1. The play is *Des Kaisers Traum. Festspiel in einem Aufzuge von Christiane Gräfin Thun-Salm. Musik von Anton Rückauf*, Vienna, 1908. For an introduction to the Ring, see Schorske, *Fin-de-Siecle Vienna*, 24–115. Detail of the day's events from

Vasyl Vyshyvanyi (Wilhelm von Habsburg), "Memuary," TsDAVO 1075/4/18a/2; *Wiener Abendpost*, 3 December 1908, 1–6; *Wiener Bilder*, 9 December 1908, 21; Thun-Salm and Hoffmansthal, *Briefwechsel*, 187, 238. For other discussions of the evening, see Mayer, *Persistence of the Old Regime*, 142–143; and Unowsky, *Pomp and Politics*, 87–89. On other celebrations of 1908, see Grossegger, *Der Kaiser-Huldigungs-Festzug*; and Beller, "Kraus's Firework."

2. The detail about the head of the Princesse de Lamballe, and a good deal of this interpretation, from Blanning, *Pursuit of Glory*, 619–670.

3. On Habsburg symbolism, see Wheatcroft, *Habsburgs*. Unlikely to be surpassed as a study of one Habsburg's universal discourse is Evans, *Rudolf II and His World*. On Rudolf's pamphlet: Hamann, *Kronprinz Rudolf*, 341.

4. On censors and nations, see Zacek, "Metternich's Censors"; and Killem, "Karel Havlicek." For a humorous corrective: Rak, *Byvali Čechové*.

5. I draw these details from Clark, *Iron Kingdom*—except for the melting of gold in 1683, which is mentioned by Stoye, *Siege of Vienna*.

6. Performance detail: Sonnenthal, *Adolf von Sonnenthals Briefwechsel*, 229. See First Corinthians 13:13: "Nun aber bleibt Glaube, Hoffnung, Liebe, diese drei; die größte aber von diesen ist die Liebe." Future in the play: "Das ist das Größte, und ich nenn's: die Liebe."

7. *Wiener Abendpost*, 3 December 1908, 3.

8. "Memuary," TsDAVO 1075/4/18a/1.

9. Austria and Hungary would share an army, a foreign ministry, and a budget, but the Hungarian government would decide upon its own domestic policies. From 1867 forward it would be correct to refer to Franz Josef as "Emperor and King" or "Emperor-King" of Austria (empire) and Hungary (kingdom), his domains as Austria-Hungary, the institutions of his monarchy as Imperial, Royal, or Imperial and Royal, as the case may have been. Please see the Note on Terms and Languages.

10. Consult Cohen, *Politics of Ethnic Survival*; King, *Budweisers into Czechs and Germans*; Kořalka, *Češi v Habsburské říse a v Evropě*.

11. A. J. P. Taylor, in his *Habsburg Monarchy*, wished to make a case that the Habsburg monarchy was doomed, with or without the First World War. This study contests that view. For a barrage of suggestive counter-quotations to Taylor, see Remak, "The Healthy Invalid."

12. Stefan to Franz Ferdinand, 5 or 6 November 1908; Stefan to Franz Ferdinand, 6 or 7 November 1908, APK-OŻ DDŻ 84. Conrad's presence is mentioned in *Wiener Abendpost*, 3 December 1908, 3.

13. *Volksblatt*, 6 December 1908, 3; *Die Neue Zeitung*, 3 December 1908, 1; Wingfield, *Flag Wars and Stone Saints*, 129; Unowsky, *Pomp and Politics*, 181.

BLUE: CHILDHOOD AT SEA

1. *Des Kaisers Traum. Festspiel in einem Aufzuge von Christiane Gräfin Thun-Salm. Musik von Anton Rückauf*, Vienna, 1908, 29; Michel Georges-Michel, "Une histoire d'ancre sympathetique," *Le Jour*, 25 July 1934; "Akt," TsDAHO 26/1/66498-fp/148980/I.

2. Basch-Ritter, *Österreich auf allen Meeren*, 71.

3. *Pola: Seine Vergangenheit, Gegenwart und Zukunft*, 32, 82. The German word for what we call "globalization" was *Welthandel*. I use the term advisedly; the condition of world trade today should be and sometimes is called "the second globalization."

4. Wiggermann, *K.u.k. Kriegsmarine und Politik*, 36.

5. Sondhaus, *Habsburg Empire and the Sea,* 172–212; Perotti, *Das Schloss Mira-mar,* 9–89.

6. Vogelsberger, *Kaiser von Mexico,* 333.

7. Karl was later crushed by Napoleon at Wagram, as the Arc de Triomphe recalls.

8. "Memuary," TsDAVO 1075/4/18a/1; Sondhaus, *Naval Policy,* 61; Hyla, "Habsburgowie żywieccy," 7.

9. HHStA, Fach 1, Karton 189, Folder Vermählung Des Erzherzogs Carl Stephan mit der Erzherzogin Maria Theresia von Toscona zu Wien am 28 February 1886, Grover Cleveland to Franz Josef, 20 May 1886. On the gift of silver, see A. Habsburg, *Princessa och partisan,* 113.

10. On Rudolf's life, see Hamann, *Kronprinz Rudolf,* esp. 330–332, 415–419. The father and son relationship is discussed in Dickinger, *Franz Josef I,* 54–66.

11. Quotations are from Hamann, *Reluctant Empress,* 130, 135.

12. Markus, *Der Fall Redl,* 149–150; Wheatcroft, *Habsburgs,* 283; Gribble, *Life of the Emperor Francis-Joseph,* 281.

13. Ivanova, *Stara bulgarska literatura,* 64.

14. On Rudolf, see Hamann, *Kronprinz Rudolf,* 296–298. For suggestions of mutual influence: "Memuary," TsDAVO 1075/4/18a/1, 2, and 6; and Ryan, *My Years,* 232. On trialism: Dedijer, *Road to Sarajevo,* 93–95, 153, 159. Serbian and Croatian political ideas of the period are discussed in Banac, *National Question,* 70–114. The Yugoslav idea returned after the change of dynasty in 1903. See Jelavich, *South Slav Nationalism,* 19–26.

15. HHStA, Fach 1, Karton 147, Folder Entbindung Erzherzogin Maria Theresia 1895. Wilhelm Franz Josef Karl was his full name. All of these names were dynastic. Karl was his father's grandfather and mother's grandfather; all the boys bore this name, which, in a way, was suitable since it reminded them that they were not only brothers but cousins. Franz Josef was the reigning emperor, and so this name was a gesture in the direction of Vienna. The name Wilhelm was, as well, for the Archduke Wilhelm von Habsburg, the Grand Master of the Teutonic Knights and the former commander of the Austrian army, who had died the previous year. Stefan was thus doubly offering his son to his sovereign, paying his respects directly to Franz Josef and by way of one of the few members of the family whom Franz Jozef had respected. Redlich, *Emperor Francis Joseph,* 200, 476.

16. This brief survey does not do justice to the complexities of Polish history in the nineteenth century. The best guide is Wandycz, *Lands of Partitioned Poland.*

17. Schmidt-Brentano, *Die Österreichische Admirale,* 473.

18. Sondhaus, *Naval Policy,* 136.

19. Ryan, *My Years,* 69.

20. Ryan, *My Years,* 70–73. Ryan says that she wrote her memoir to disprove the notion that all Habsburgs were mad, bad, and unfit to rule, although its contents are a bit ambiguous on this point.

21. Ryan, *My Years,* 83.

22. None of Stefan's artwork seems to have survived. The sketches in his Kopier-Buch, however, are revealing. See APK-OŻ DDŻ 84 and 85.

23. Ryan, *My Years,* 66–67.

24. "Memuary," TsDAVO 1075/4/18a/1; Ryan, *My Years,* 91.

25. The architects and the quotation: Stefan to Cox and King, Naval Architects, London, 1905, APK-OŻ DDŻ 84. The sons' sailing lessons are mentioned in "Memuary," TsDAVO 1075/4/18a/1. The goat episode is recounted in Ryan, *My Years,* 245–246.

26. The trip to St. Petersburg is documented in HHStA, Fach 1, Karton 66, Folder "Erzherzog Karl Stefan," Letter to Seiner Exzellenz Herrn Grafen Gołuchowski, St. Petersburg, 12 August 1900. On contact with Maria Christina: HHStA, Fach 1, Karton 66, Folder "Erzherzog Karl Stefan," Letter, Seiner Exzellenz Herrn Grafen Gołuchowski, San Sebastian, 30 September 1900.

27. The trip to Alfonso's celebration in 1902 is recounted in Ryan, *My Years,* 250.

28. HHStA, Fach 1, Karton 66, Folder "Erzherzog Karl Stefan," An das hohe K. und h. Ministerium des kaiserlichen und königlichen Hauses und des Aeussern, Vienna, 27 January 1905.

29. Contact with sailors: Ryan, *My Years,* 98. Date: Hyla, "Habsburgowie żywieccy," 9. Wilhelm's memory of sailors: "Memuary," TsDAVO 1075/4/18a/1.

30. Stefan to Agenor Gołuchowski, 17 July 1906, HHStA, Fach 1, Karton 66, Folder "Erzherzog Karl Stefan."

31. "Memuary," TsDAVO 1075/4/18a/1.

GREEN: ORIENTAL EUROPE

1. Gribble, *Life of the Emperor Francis-Joseph*, 119; Hamann, *Reluctant Empress*, 288, 301; E. Habsburg, *Das poetische Tagebuch*, 383.

2. For discussions, see Wheatcroft, *Habsburgs;* and especially Tanner, *Last Descendant.*

3. For the trip to Istanbul, see HHStA, Fach 1, Karton 66, Folder "Erzherzog Karl Stefan," Seiner Exzellenz Herrn Grafen Gołuchowski, 3 October 1906 and 23 October 1906. On the trip to Algiers, see ibid., Telegram, Chiffre, Algiers, 2 May 1907.

4. On the visit to Malta, see ibid., Consolato d'Austria-Ungharia, Malta, A sua Eccellenza Il Barone Lexa de Aehrenthal, 22 April 1907. Maltese politics is discussed in Owen, *Maltese Islands,* 63–66.

5. On the 1909 trip, see Stefan in Podjavori to Austrian trade section in Triest, 31 March 1909, APK-OŻ DDŻ 84. On Willy's impressions, see "Memuary," TsDAVO 1075/4/18a/1.

6. Tylza-Janosz, "Dobra czarnieckie i porąbczanskie," 20, 28, 35; Spyra, *Browar Żywiec,* 27–30. On noble capitalism, see Glassheim, *Noble Nationalists;* and Mayer, *Persistence of the Old Regime.*

7. On the family portraits, see Senecki and Piotrowski, "Zbiory malarstwa," 58–60; Kuhnke, "Polscy Habsburgowie"; Mackiewicz, *Dom Radziwiłłów,* 209. The timing of the move is mentioned in "Memuary," TsDAVO 1075/4/18a/1. On national style, see Bożek, *Żywieckie projekty Karola Pietschki.* The chapel is mentioned in Rusniaczek, "Jak powstał," 40–41. Maria Theresia's request to the pope: Maria Theresia to Pope Benedict XV, 1 December 1904; "Sacra Rituum Congregatio . . ." 18 January 1905; [Illegible] to Maria Theresia, 15 May 1912; all in APK-OŻ DDŻ 3.

8. Kuhnke, "Polscy Habsburgowie." The window incident is from Stefan to Entresz, July 1906, APK-OŻ DDŻ 84.

9. Stefan to "Caro Signore Commendatore," 25 September 1909; Stefan to Dr. Weiser & Sohn, Vienna, 8 October 1909; Stefan to Société Lorraine, 2 December 1909; Stefan to Daimler Motor Company, Coventry, 21 March 1910; Stefan to Hieronym Tarnowski, June 1910, all in APK-OŻ DDŻ 85. On automobiles, see Husar, "Żywieccy Habsburgowie," 65.

10. Ryan, *My Years,* 127–134. The yew tree was still there in 2007.

11. HHStA, Fach 1, Karton 200, Folder "Vermählung 74 der Erzherzogin Renata mit dem Prinzen Radziwill," K. und k. Ministerium des kaiserl. und königl. Hauses

und des Äussern, "Eheschliessung Ihrer k.u.k. Hoheit der durchlauchstigsten Frau Erzherzogerin Renata Maria mit dem Prinzen Hieronymus Radziwill"; ibid., Sr. K. und K Apost. Majestät Obersthofmeisteramt, An das löbliche k. und k. Ministerium des k. und k. Hauses und des Aeussern, 18 September 1908. Renata had to accept each of these conditions in notes to the court and repeat her renunciation in a ceremony in November 1908. Even after the partitions of Poland the Radziwiłł family remained wealthy. Hieronymus Radziwiłł had a strong German connection. He hailed from the German Empire, and his father was a deputy in the German parliament.

12. Mackiewicz, *Dom Radziwiłłów*, 210–211.

13. The quotations are from an untitled renunciation document in HHStA, Fach 1, Karton 203, Folder "Vermählung der Erzherzogin Mechtildis mit dem Prinzen Aleksander Olgierd Czartoryski." See also, ibid., the following documents: "Kopie" of "Entwurf," 9 October 1912; K. und k. Ministerium des kaiserl. und königl. Hauses und des Äussern, Vienna, 26 January 1913, 3.518/1, Vertraulich; Vortrag des Ministers des kaiserlichen und königlichen Hauses und des Äussern, 9 October 1912.

14. Hyla, "Habsburgowie Żywieccy,"10. The Czartoryski motto is "Bądź co Bądź."

15. Ryan, *My Years*, 98–99; Hyla, "Habsburgowie Żywieccy," 9; "Memuary," Ts-DAVO 1075/4/18a/1.

16. Stefan's letter: Stefan to Baron Rehmer, Ministerium des Aüssern [December 1912], APK-OŻ DDŻ 85. Reactions are recorded in HHStA, Fach 1, Karton 203, Folder "Vermählung der Erzherzogin Mechtildis mit dem Prinzen Aleksander Olgierd Czartoryski," K. und k. Ministerium des kaiserl. und königl. Hauses und des Äussern, Vienna, 26 January 1913, 3.518/1, Vertraulich. The first wedding "in das Bürgertum" according to Hamann, *Die Habsburger*, 81. Unlike her sisters, Eleanora had to resign from all future access to state funds. HHStA, Fach 1, Karton 203, Folder "Vermählung der Erzherzogin Eleonore mit dem Linienschiffslieutenant von Kloss," Kopie, "Verwurf."

17. The quotation is from Ryan, *My Years*, 99. Example of correspondence: Stefan to L. Bernheimer, 22 December 1912, APK-OŻ DDŻ 85.

18. KA, Personalevidenzen, Qualifikationsliste und Grundbuchblatt des Erzherzogs Wilhelm F. Josef, Klassifikationsliste (15 March 1915).

19. Hull, *Entourage*, 65 and passim; Clark, *Kaiser Wilhelm II*, 73–76; Murat, *La loi du genre*, 265. Proust credited the scandal with making the word "homosexualité" acceptable in French. Lucey, *Never Say I*, 230.

20. Spector, "Countess Merviola," 31–46; ibid., "Homosexual Scandal," 15–24.

21. Deák, *Beyond Nationalism*, 143–145; Palmer, *Twilight*, 318; Ronge, *Kriegs- und Industriespionage*, 79–86; KA, Personalevidenzen, Qualifikationsliste und Grundbuchblatt des Erzherzogs Wilhelm F. Josef, "Hauptgrundbuchblatt."

22. Novosad, "Vasyl' Vyshyvanyi," 24. Or perhaps Willy prepared himself for two kingdoms, as Vasyl' Rasevych maintains in "Vil'hel'm von Habsburg," 212–213. Rasevych argues that Wilhelm first identified with the Jews and only later with the Ukrainians. He seems to be relying on a summary or summaries of a single press article. The original is Henry Hellsen, "Kejser at Ukraine," *Berlinske Tidende*, 31 March 1920, 2. According to Hellsen, Willy drew up a project for a State of Israel and approached the World Zionist Organization in Berlin to offer his services. One can imagine how he might have come to such an idea. Zionism, the idea of the return of the Jews to Palestine and the creation of a Jewish state, was gaining adherents. In 1913 the Third Zionist Congress was held in Vienna, where Willy was living. Willy's move to Vienna, in such a scenario, would have been the crowning moment in his

own discovery of a nation. As it happens, there were no Jews on Lussin, and few if any Jews in Żywiec. There were certainly Jews in Istanbul and North Africa, places Wilhelm loved when saw them during the family sea journeys of 1906, 1907, and 1909. There were Jews in Hranice, where he studied from 1909 to 1912. There was a street called Jewish Street, with a synagogue, a school, and a communal building (see Bartovský, *Hranice*, 225). This is all however very speculative. Wilhelm does not recall this incident himself; the article is the only known source; and Hellsen's chronology is very vague. Some of the details that Hellsen cites about the Jews, for example a conversation Wilhelm had with Kaiser Wilhelm II, are suspiciously similar to actual events that concerned Ukrainians. Hellsen was writing years after the fact, with no particular expertise. Unless further evidence is found, Wilhelm's Jewish episode must be considered possible but unlikely.

23. "Memuary," TsDAVO 1075/4/18a/1–2, quotations at 1 and 2. See also Hirniak, *Polk. Vasyl' Vyshyvanyi*, 7–8.

24. "Memuary," TsDAVO 1075/4/18a/2.

25. Quotation is from "Memuary," TsDAVO 1075/4/18a/2.

26. For greater detail and subtlety, see Markovits and Sysyn, *Nationbuilding*; and Binder, *Galizien in Wien*.

27. A nice summation of the style of east European ethnography can be found in Gellner, *Language and Solitude*, 132ff.

28. On Ukrainian monarchism, see Tereshchenko, "V'iacheslav Lypyns'kyi." On the popular side of the Galician Ukrainian movement, consult the works of John-Paul Himka, for example *Religion and Nationality in Western Ukraine*.

29. Tereshchenko and Ostashko, *Ukrains'kyi patriot*, 8. The advisor was Ievhen Olesnyts'kyi.

30. IPH, 14 April 1948; TsDAHO 26/1/66498-fp/148980/I/132; see also Onats'kyi, *Portrety v profil*, 126. On the officer corps, see Plaschka, Haselsteiner, and Suppan, *Innere Front*, 35.

31. "Memuary," TsDAVO 1075/4/18a/3; Novosad, "Vasyl' Vyshyvanyi," 24.

32. "Memuary," TsDAVO 1075/4/18a/3; Deák, *Beyond Nationalism*, 82.

33. On Ukrainian poverty, see "Memuary," TsDAVO 1075/4/18a/2–3.

34. Stefan to Franz Ferdinand, 5 or 6 November 1908; Stefan to Franz Ferdinand, 6 or 7 November 1908, APK-OŻ DDŻ 84. See also Antonoff, "Almost War."

35. Dedijer, *Road to Sarajevo*, 145. See also Deák, *Beyond Nationalism*, 8.

36. The quotation is from Tunstall, "Austria-Hungary," 124.

37. Wilhelm to Huzhkovs'kyi, 17 November 1916, TsDIAL, 408/1/567/15.

RED: PRINCE AT ARMS

1. MacKenzie, *Apis*. His true name was Dragutin Dimitrijević. Apis the god made his very first appearance in history as a curse of empires. Herodotus, *History*, 192–193.

2. The situation was rather different in Hungary, where Franz Ferdinand's hostility to the Magyars was returned. His plans for a trialist state were intended to reduce the importance of Hungary within the empire.

3. This contrasted with his urging of Germans and Czechs to set aside national quarrels for the duration of the war. No military victory could improve their relative position in the monarchy. Popyk, *Ukraintsi v Avstrii*, 99–100; Judson, *Guardians of the Nation*, 220.

4. On Habsburg perceptions, see Shanafelt, *Secret Enemy*, 45.

5. Deák, *Beyond Nationalism*, 193. For excellent recent treatments of the First World War, see Strachan, *First World War*; Stevenson, *Cataclysm*.

6. More than half of the lieutenants graduated in the class of 1913 were killed or wounded in the war. Deák, *Beyond Nationalism*, 91. The quotation is from KA, Personalevidenzen, Qualifikationsliste und Grundbuchblatt des Erzherzogs Wilhelm F. Josef, Belohnungsantrag (28 March 1915). On the Golden Fleece, see "Liste Nominale des Chevaliers de l'Ordre de la Toison d'Or en vie May 1929," APK-OŻ DDŻ 1.

7. On Albrecht, see KA, Personalevidenzen, Qualifikationslist des Erzherzogs Carl Albrecht. On Wilhelm's graduation, see KA, Personalevidenzen, Qualifikationsliste und Grundbuchblatt des Erzherzogs Wilhelm F. Josef, Belohnungsantrag (21 March 1918), and similar documents.

8. On Wilhelm's designation as the "Red Prince," see "Memuary," TsDAVO 1075/4/18a/4; Onats'kyi, *Portrety v profil*, 126. The regiment was the 13th Uhlans.

9. "Memuary," TsDAVO 1075/4/18a/4–5.

10. On Stefan and Wilhelm during this period, see HHStA, Fach 1, Karton 66, Folder "Erzherzog Stefan," Telegram, Prinz Hohenlohe, Berlin, 7 February 1916. On the rumors and assemblies, see Lubomirska, *Pamiętnik*, 121, 333.

11. Burián, *Austria in Dissolution*, 96–97, 100, 342; Shanafelt, *Secret Enemy*, 71, 80, 90; Zeman, *Breakup*, 100, 104.

12. Wilhelm on his father: Wilhelm to Huzhkovs'kyi, 29 December 1916, TsDIAL, 408/1/567/28–29. On Stefan and Olgierd Czartoryski generally, see Hamann, *Die Habsburger*, 226; Hyla, "Habsburgowie Żywieccy," 14–15; Majchrowski, *Ugrupowania monarchystyczne*, 9–10. For examples of father-son correspondence, see HHStA, Fach 1, Karton 66, Folder "Erzherzog Karl Stefan," Der k. und k. Legationsrath, Warsaw, An das löbliche Politische Expedit des K. und K. Ministeriums des Aeussern, 1 October 1916. For the declaration from the point of view of one of the three members of the Regency Council, see Kakowski, *Z Niewoli*, 333–356. Stefan's public support is discussed in Lubomirska, *Pamiętnik*, 499, 504.

13. Correspondence with Friedrich: Friedrich to Wilhelm, 2 November 1916, TsDIAL, 408/1/567/8. On the audience, see "Memuary," TsDAVO 1075/4/18a/6. On Wilhelm's assignments in 1916, see KA, Personalevidenzen, Qualifikationsliste und Grundbuchblatt des Erzherzogs Wilhelm F. Josef, Vormerkblatt für die Qualifikationsbeschreibung für die Zeit vom 1/IV 1916 bis 30/IX 1917. His promotion is mentioned in KA, Personalevidenzen, Qualifikationsliste und Grundbuchblatt des Erzherzogs Wilhelm F. Josef, Veränderungen. Ethnographic: Huzhkovs'kyi(?) to Olesnyts'kyi, 29 January 1917, TsDIAL 408/1/567/120.

14. Quotations are from Wilhelm to Huzhkovs'kyi, 7 November 1916, TsDIAL 408/1/567/18. In fact, the declaration was a disappointment for Polish advocates of an Austro-Polish solution. This chapter emphasizes Ukrainian perspectives; an excellent treatment of Polish attitudes is Suleja, *Orientacja Austro-Polska*.

15. Correspondence with Stefan is mentioned in Wilhelm to Huzhkovs'kyi, 29 December 1916, TsDIAL 408/1/567/28. On the "Fürstentum Ukraina," see Wilhelm to Huzhkovs'kyi, 29 December 1916, TsDIAL 408/1/567/29.

16. Wilhelm to Huzhkovs'kyi, 8 February 1917, TsDIAL 408/1/567/62–63.

17. Wilhelm's recollections of the doctor are in "Memuary," TsDAVO 1075/4/18a/6. His attendance at Freud's lectures from a newspaper clipping, Michel Georges-Michel, "Ou l'Archiduc Guillaume unit Mlle Mistinguett et l'Archiduc Rodolphe" [summer 1932], HURI, Folder 2. The lectures are published in English as Freud, *Introductory Lectures*, 414–415, 433–435. Peter Gay founded a school of

Freudian interpretation of Viennese life. See for example *Freud, Jews, and Other Germans*.

18. On Wilhelm's 3 April departure see Wilhelm to Huzhkovs'kyi, 22 March 1917, TsDIAL 408/1/567/88. The delivery of alcohol is mentioned in Wilhelm to Huzhkovs'kyi [1917], TsDIAL 408/1/567/124. On the Regency Council, see *Polski Słownik Biograficzny*, vol. 9, 219. The award of the Iron Cross to Wilhelm on 21 May 1917 is mentioned in KA, Personalevidenzen, Qualifikationsliste und Grundbuchblatt des Erzherzogs Wilhelm F. Josef, Veränderungen.

19. Zeman, *Breakup*, 126; Bridge, "Foreign Policy," 28.

20. Wilhelm to Huzhkovs'kyi, 9 June 1917, TsDIAL 408/1/567/100–102.

21. The quotation and details are found in Wilhelm to Vasylko, 1 August 1917, TsDIAL 358/3t/166/34–35. Karl's service in Kolomyja is described in Skrzypek, "Ukraińcy w Austrii," 74.

22. "Vom Tage Metropolit Graf Szeptycki in Lemberg," 11 September 1917, PAAA Wien 342; Deutsches Konsulat, Lemberg, report dated 12 September 1917, PAAA Wien 342; Novosad, "Vasyl' Vyshyvanyi," 22; Rasevych, "Vil'hel'm von Habsburg," 214.

23. The quotation is from Cornwall, *Undermining*, 46. On the peace proposals, see HHStA, Fach 1, Karton 66, Folder "Erzherzog Stefan."

24. Wilhelm to Sheptyts'kyi, 4 December 1917, TsDIAL, 358/3t/166/4; Tereshchenko and Ostashko, *Ukrains'kyi patriot*, 15–16; Grelka, *Die ukrainische Nationalbewegung*, 92; KA, Personalevidenzen, Qualifikationsliste und Grundbuchblatt des Erzherzogs Wilhelm F. Josef, Veränderungen; Wilhelm to Huzhkovs'kyi, 10 January 1918, TsDIAL 358/3t/166/6.

25. On the strikes, see Bihl, *Österreich-Ungarn und die Friedenschlüsse*, 87. On Viennese society under occupation, see Healy, *Vienna*. For Czernin in Vienna on 22 January 1918, see Arz, *Zur Geschichte des Grossen Krieges*, 225. The Habsburg general staff correspondence is in KA, Armeeoberkommando, Op. Abteilung, Op. geh. Akten, Karton 464, K.u.k. AOK zu Op. Geh. Nr. 829, Chef des Generalstabes, "Sitzungsbericht vom 21 Jänner (1918)." On Wilhelm and Vasylko, see Dontsov, *Rik 1918*, 14; Skrzypek, "Ukraińcy w Austrii," 353; Hirniak, *Polk. Vasyl' Vyshyvanyi*, 13; Bihl, *Österreich-Ungarn und die Friedenschlüsse*, 98; Zalizniak, "Moia uchast," 80–81; Popyk, *Ukraintsi v Avstrii*, 134–143.

26. Wilhelm to Sheptyts'kyi, 14 February 1918, TsDIAL 358/3t/166/7–8.

GREY: SHADOW KINGS

1. Lersner to Auswärtiges Amt, 18 March 1918, PAAA R14363; Arz, *Zur Geschichte des Grossen Krieges*, 240.

2. Quotation from the army chief of staff in KA, Armeeberkommando, Quartiermeisterabsteilung, 2626, Folder "Ukraine. Geheimakten," Chef des Generalstabes, Arz, K. u. k. Armeeoberkommando, Ukrainische Abteiling, to Austrian General Staff in Baden, "Klärung von Fragen in der Ukraine," 4 October 1918. Quotation from the envoy in Forgách to Burián, 10 August 1918. n Hornykiewicz, *Ereignisse*, vol. 3, 322. Quotation from the Habsburg military intelligence officer in KA, Armeeoberkommando, Quartiermeisterabteiling, Karton 2634, "Referat über die ukr. Legion," Hptm. Kvaternik, K. u. k. AOK (Opabt.), 25 February 1918. The enterprising military intelligence officer, Kvaternik, had in mind not the original Ukrainian Legion, the Sich Marksmen formed in 1914, but rather a new unit composed of prisoners of war. It was soon dissolved by the Germans.

3. On German priorities see Mumm, cited in Eudin, "German Occupation," 93. See also Mędrzecki, "Bayerische Truppenteile," 458. On the oil fields, see Baumgart, *Deutsche Ostpolitik*, 123. A debate over imperial German war aims and practices was initiated by Fischer with his *Griff nach der Weltmacht*. A useful document collection is Feldman, *German Imperialism*.

4. Officially it was known as the Ukrainian State. I will refer to the state created from the territories of the Russian Empire as the Ukrainian National Republic throughout, in order to avoid confusion.

5. The summons is found in Wilhelm to Sheptyts'kyi, 19 February 1918, TsDIAL, 358/3t/166/15–16; and Rutkowski, "Ukrainische Legion," 3. The men's conversation is described in Wilhelm to Vasylko, 18 March 1918, TsDIAL, 358/3t/166/17–18 (emphasis in original). The throne: IPH, 23 September 1947, TsDAHO 26/1/66498-fp/148980/I/47. On the formation of the Legion, see Vasyl' Vyshyvanyi, "U.S.S. z vesny 1918 r. do perevorotu v Avstrii," 25 October 1920, HURI, Folder 2. For its history before 1918, see Popyk, *Ukraintsi v Avstrii*, 40–62.

6. For Wilhelm's impressions, see Vasyl' Vyshyvanyi, "U.S.S. z vesny 1918 r. do perevorotu v Avstrii," 25 October 1920, HURI, Folder 2.

7. The quotation from Wilhelm is in Vasyl' Vyshyvanyi, "U.S.S. z vesny 1918 r. do perevorotu v Avstrii," 25 October 1920, HURI, Folder 2. On the Cossacks, see "Memuary," TsDAVO 1075/4/18a/8.

8. Wilhelm's statement on Ukrainization is in Wilhelm to Vasylko, 24 May 1918, TsDIAL 358/3t/166/21–22. His policies are discussed in Hirniak, *Polk. Vasyl' Vyshyvanyi*, 15. The information on the stable performances comes from Vasyl' Vyshyvanyi, "U.S.S. z vesny 1918 r. do perevorotu v Avstrii," 25 October 1920, HURI, Folder 2.

9. Sheptyts'kyi to Wilhelm, 13 June 1918, *Documents ruthéno-ukrainiens*, 13; Petriv, *Spomyny*, 550. See also: Onats'kyi, *Portrety v profil*; Podvyzhnyky Chynu Naisviatishoho Izbavitelia v Ukraini; and Skrzypek, "Ukraińcy w Austrii," 381. fn. 47. On the Redemptorists in Ukraine, see Houthaeve, *De Gekruisigde Kerk*, 323–324; Laverdure, "Achille Delaere," 85–90; Turii, "Istorychnyi shlakh," 49–51; and Bubnii, *Redemptorysty*, 24–33. In the early twentieth century, Belgian Redemptorists volunteered for service in western Canada, where Ukrainian Greek Catholic immigrants lacked religious services in their language and rite. These Redemptorists began to learn Ukrainian and exchange the Greek Catholic for the Roman Catholic rite. Sheptyts'kyi, visiting Canada in 1910, met Redemptorists who had become Greek Catholics to minister to Ukrainians in the Canadian prairies. Sheptyts'kyi, impressed, arranged that Redemptorists be sent to eastern Galicia as well. Bonne was one of the first Redemptorists to settle in Galicia, in 1913. Bonne, like other Redemptorists, began to identify with the Ukrainian nation. Bonne, like Wilhelm, was in Lviv to greet Sheptytsky in 1917.

10. "Memuary," TsDAVO 1075/4/18a/8; Tereshchenko and Ostashko, *Ukrains'kyi patriot*, 27.

11. Quotations from this paragraph are from, respectively, Forgách to Burián, 22 June 1918, HHStA, Politisches Archiv X/Russland, Liasse Russland XI d/8, Karton 154, p. 149; K. u. k. Ministerium des Äußern, Referat I, "Tagesbericht," 27 August 1918, in Hornykiewicz, *Ereignisse*, vol. 3, 352; KA, Oberkommando, Quartiermeisterabteilung, 2626, Folder "Ukraine. Geheimakten," Nachrichtenabteilung an Ukr. Abt. des AOK, "Bericht über die ukr. Verhältnisse," 16 June 1918; K. u. k. Armeeoberkommando, Operations-Abteilung, Streng vertraulich, nicht für Deutsche, 30 June 1918, in Hornykiewicz, *Ereignisse*, vol. 3, 139.

12. Malynovs'kyi, "Arkhykniaz Vil'hel'm fon Habsburh," 30; Petriv, *Spomyny*, 537. The Corpus was composed of one cavalry and one infantry regiment.

13. Quotations are from Petriv, *Spomyny*, 546.

14. Hirniak, *Polk. Vasyl' Vyshyvanyi*, 27. See also Wilhelm to Vasylko, 24 May 1918, TsDIAL 358/3t/166/21–22.

15. Bolbochan's proposal is found in Petriv, *Spomyny*, 547. On Wilhelm and Karl's discussion, see HHStA, Politisches Archiv I 523, Liasse XL VII/12/d, 517, "Entwurf eines Allerhöchsten Telegramms an Seine k.u.k Hoheit Erzherzog Wilhelm," May 1918. See also IPH, 23 September 1947, TsDAHO 26/1/66498-fp/148980/I/45; "Memuary," TsDAVO 1075/4/18a/9; and Bihl, "Beitrage zur Ukraine-Politik," 55.

16. On Habsburg soldiers as plunderers, see KA, Oberkommando, Quartiermeisterabteilung, 2626, Folder "Ukraine. Geheimakten," Nachrichtenabteilung an AOK Ukraine, "Bericht über Ukraine,"15 June 1918. On food payments, see Krauss, "Die Besetzung," 360. The peasantry's attitude is discussed in KA, Oberkommando, Quartiermeisterabteilung, 2626, Folder "Ukraine. Geheimakten," Nachrichtenabteilung an Ukr. Abt. des AOK, 6 October 1918. On the protocol, see Borowsky, *Deutsche Ukrainepolitik*, 139.

17. On the hanging, see KA, Armeeoberkommando, Operationsabteilung, Op. Akten, Karton 723, Evidenzgruppe "R," Telegram, 1 June 1918. For the railway official tied to the tracks, see KA, Armeeoberkommando, Operationsabteilung, Op. Akten, Karton 724, Evidenzgruppe "R," Telegram, 5 July 1918. The incident of the artillery bombardment is mentioned in KA, Armeeoberkommando, Operationsabteilung, Op. Akten, Karton 724, Evidenzgruppe "R," Telegram, "Bericht fuer s. m.," 20 July 1918. The quotation from military intelligence is in KA, Oberkommando, Quartiermeisterabteilung, 2626, Folder "Ukraine. Geheimakten," Chef des Generalstabes, "Lage in der Ukraine," 7 August 1918.

18. KA, Armeeoberkommando, Op. Abteiling, Op. Akten, Karton 723. Report from Odessa, "Bericht über die Niedermetzlung der Honvedhusaren bei Wladimirowka am 31/5[1918]," 21 June 1918. The anarchist to whom I refer is Makhno.

19. Habsburg officers' views on Ukraine are found in KA, Oberkommando, Quartiermeisterabteilung, 2626, Folder "Ukraine. Geheimakten," Nachrichtenabteilung an Ukr. Abt. des AOK, "Bericht über die ukrainischen Verhältnisse," 26 June 1918; and KA, Armeeoberkommando, Operationsabteilung, Op. Akten, Karton 724, Evidenzgruppe "R," Telegram, 5 July 1918. See also KA, Armeeoberkommando, Operationsabteilung, Op. Akten, Evidenzgruppe "R," Karton 792, Telegram, 21 May 1918. On Makhno, see Dontsov, *Rik 1918*, 14. On the commander's question to Wilhelm see Forgách to Burián, 16 June 1918, in Hornykiewicz, *Ereignisse*, vol. 3, 339. The plea to the emperor is in Forgách to Burián, 24 June 1918, HHStA, Politisches Archiv X/Russland, Liasse Russland XI d/8, Karton 154, p. 141.

20. For the intelligence report on this plot, see "Monarchistische Bewegung in der Ukraine,"18 February 1918, PAAA R13461. The quotation on Habsburg goals comes from Lersner to Auswärtiges Amt, 20 March 1918, PAAA R14363. The 13 May quotation comes from Stoltzenberg to Oberost, 13 May 1918, PAAA R14365. The German report on Wilhelm as successor to the hetman is in Mumm to Chancellor Hertling, 13 May 1918, PAAA R14365.

21. The telegram from Stalin is in KA, Armeeoberkommando, Operationsabteilung, Op. Akten, Evidenzgruppe "R," 22 May 1918, Karton 793.

22. The view of Wilhelm as fantasist is in General Gröner to Mumm, 20 May 1918, PAAA 14374. For espionage reports, see respectively, "Protokol pro dii USS na terytorii Annins'koi volosti," Hetmanate, 26 June–9 July 1918, in Malynovs'kyi, "Arkhykniaz Vil'hel'm fon Habsburh," 37–38; Mumm to Hertling, 2 June 1918,

PAAA Wien 342; and (last three quotations), "L'Archiduc Wilhelm," Informer's Report, 1918, PAAA 14379.

23. The quotations are from Mumm to Chancellor Hertling, 7 July 1918, PAAA 14376. See also Pelenski, "Hetman Pavlo Skoropadsky," 75. Skoropadsky recalls his suspicions in Skoropads'kyi, *Spohady*, 208; see also Pressebericht der Press-Warte, 28 July 1918, PAAA 14366.

24. "Memuary," TsDAVO 1075/4/18a/9.

25. "Memuary," TsDAVO 1075/4/18a/9.

26. Information on Wilhelm's entourage in Legionsrat to Auswärtiges Amt, 8 August 1918, PAAA 14379. On the meetings, see Niemann, *Kaiser und Revolution*, 36; Hussche to Auswärtiges Amt, 13 August 1918, PAAA 14379. The emperor conveyed his impressions of Wilhelm in Wilhelm II to Karl, 8 August 1918, PAAA 14379. The comparison of Wilhelm to the dynasty is in Plessen to Gräfin Brockdorff, 8 August 1918, in Afflerbach, *Kaiser Wilhelm II als Oberster Kriegsherr*, 926.

27. Niemann, *Kaiser und Revolution*, 35–36; Burián, *Austria in Dissolution*, 352–355; Ludendorff, *General Staff*, 595; Strachan, *First World War*, 317–318; Rumpler, *Max Hussarek*, 50–55.

28. The Germans claimed that Wilhelm spoke of his royal ambitions while at Spa. German diplomats claimed to possess a letter in which Wilhelm described himself as a fitting ruler of Ukraine. For examples of German claims to have evidence of Wilhelm's ambitions, see Bussche to Berkheim, 14 August 1918, PAAA 14379; Forgách to Burián, 18 August 1918, in Hornykiewicz, *Ereignisse*, vol. 3, 347, citing Mumm.

29. Forgách to Burián, 11 August 1918, in Hornykiewicz, *Ereignisse*, vol. 3, 345. For Wilhelm's return in September, see Wilhelm to Sheptyts'kyi (September 1918), TsDIAL, 358/3t/166/19–20. For reactions to Wilhelm's proposal to go to Kiev, see Mumm to Auswärtiges Amt, 27 August 1918, PAAA R14380; Mumm to Auswärtiges Amt, 28 August 1918, PAAA R14380; Mumm to Auswärtiges Amt, 4 September 1918, PAAA R14382.

30. On the annexations and ethnic cleansing, see Geiss, *Der Polnische Grenzstreifen*, 125–146. Stefan's position: Paul von Hintze, Auswärtiges Amt, Telegram, 28 August 1918, PAAA Wien 342.

31. The promise to Skoropadsky is in Borowsky, *Deutsche Ukrainepolitik*, 264–265. On the concerns for Wilhelm's safety, see Trautmansdorff to Burián, 23 September 1918, in Hornykiewicz, *Ereignisse*, vol. 3, 358. The Austrian commander was Alfred Krauss.

32. Bolshevik Ukraine: Wilhelm to Tokary, 12 October 1918, HURI, Folder 1. Wilhelm was removed from formerly Russian lands occupied by Austria to an Austrian province. Yet, as Ukrainians saw matters, he was still in Ukraine. The Ukrainian crownland in Austria was to have included both eastern Galicia and Bukovina. Chernivtsi was not far (164 miles by rail) from Lviv. Wilhelm's orders were to defend the city against Romania, which claimed Bukovina on ethnic grounds. Chernivtsi had become a large, modern city under the Habsburgs, and Habsburg modernity meant variety. The city of some seventy thousand boasted churches of the Roman, Greek, and Armenian Catholic rites, as well as synagogues. It was a center not only of the Ukrainian and Romanian but also of the Yiddishist movement, and perhaps best known for its excellent German-language university.

33. Wilhelm to Vasylko, 18 October 1918, TsDIAL 358/3t/166/23–24; Wilhelm to Sheptyts'kyi, 18 October 1918, TsDIAL 358/3t/166/23.

34. On the replacement of Wilhelm by someone else, see Klimecki, *Polsko-ukraińska wojna*, 47, 55. Karl's decree applied to the Austrian portion of Austria-Hungary; the Hungarian government was immovable on the question of autonomy.

35. Plaschka, Haselsteiner, and Suppan, *Innere Front*, vol. 2, 304, 316. The Polish Ministry of Foreign Affairs acquired copies of the orders: AAN MSZ 5350/254–257. See also Ezherzog Wilhelm, 1 November 1918, "Dringend," *Documents ruthéno-ukrainiens*, 32; Vasyl' Vyshyvanyi, "U.S.S. z vesny 1918 r. do perevorotu v Avstrii," 25 October 1920, HURI, Folder 2; Klimecki, *Polsko-ukraińska wojna*, 68, 73, 91.

36. The Serbs were able to regroup because Entente forces knocked the Habsburg ally Bulgaria out of the war.

37. Wilhelm's journey is recounted in "Memuary," TsDAVO 1075/4/18a/9.

38. "Memuary," TsDAVO 1075/4/18a/11.

WHITE: AGENT OF IMPERIALISM

1. Wilhelm's locale: "Memuary," TsDAVO 1075/4/18a/11.

2. See Żurawski vel Grajewski, *Sprawa ukraińska*; Pavliuk, *Borot'ba Ukrainy*.

3. Personified: *Documents ruthéno-ukrainiens*, 21. Polish arguments: Tereshchenko and Ostashko, *Ukrains'kyi patriot*, 37. See also Milow, *Die ukrainische Frage*, 312–313, 324.

4. Health: Rasevych, "Vil'hel'm von Habsburg," 217. Capture: "Memuary," TsDAVO 1075/4/18a/11; IPH, 4 September 1947; TsDAHO 26/1/66498-fp/148980/I/20. Romanian demands: HHStA, Archiv der Republik, F1, Karton 68, Rumänische Liquidierungskommission to Staatsamt für Äüsseres, 10 June 1919. Austria was actually called Deutschösterreich at this early point. The story was somewhat more complex. Romania had reentered the war just before its end and claimed vast territories from the Habsburg monarchy at the Paris peace talks. Like Poland, Romania was a purported ally of the victorious powers. Though the Romanian army had done little or nothing to win the war, Romania would benefit as the victors carved up the territories of the Habsburg monarchy. Having captured a member of the former ruling dynasty, Romanian authorities used the arrest to embarrass Wilhelm and cause trouble for the new Austrian republic. With Wilhelm in custody, the Romanians claimed that he owed them money and that Austria should repay them. In the chaos of November 1918, Wilhelm, cut off from his family and from the court, had in fact borrowed some money from what was then the Habsburg provincial government at Chernivtsi. Romania had taken Chernivtsi with the rest of Bukovina, and it now sought the return of the money Wilhelm had borrowed. Even as Romanian soldiers were keeping watch over Wilhelm, Romanian officials wrote to Vienna seeking information about his whereabouts. This was either disingenuous or incompetent, but it was hardly endearing. The Entente's allies, on an appropriately smaller scale, thus replicated the humiliations dealt out by the great powers in Paris.

5. Hirniak, *Polk. Vasyl' Vyshyvanyi*, 31.

6. I am simplifying a complex event. See Bruski, *Petlurowcy*; Ullman, *Anglo-Soviet Relations*; Wandycz, *Soviet-Polish Relations*; Reshetar, *Ukrainian Revolution*; Abramson, *Prayer for the Government*.

7. Tereshchenko and Ostashko, *Ukrains'kyi patriot*, 38–39

8. Wasserstein, *Secret Lives*, 1–127. On the Galician oil fields, see Frank, *Oil Empire*.

9. Hull, *Entourage*, 269; Cavallie, *Ludendorff och Kapp*, 327; Evans, *Coming of the Third Reich*, 61, 177.

10. Hitler's quotation is from Kellogg, *Russian Roots of Nazism*, 105. See Evans, *Coming of the Third Reich*, 67–68, 97; Cavallie, *Ludendorff och Kapp*, 329.

11. Wasserstein, *Secret Lives*, 163.

12. Henry Hellsen, "Kejser at Ukraine," *Berlinske Tidende*, 31 March 1920, 2. The quotation is from Onats'kyi, *Portrety v profil*, 135.

13. The details of the scheme are elaborated by V. V. Biskupskii, in Williams, *Culture in Exile*, 100. See also Rape, *Die österreichischen Heimwehren*, 246–248; Thoss, *Der Ludendorff-Kreis*, 444; Naczelne Dowództwo W.P., Oddział II, "Skoropadski i arcyksiążę Wilhelm," 1921, CAW I.303.4.2718/99.

14. His brothers' service: CAW, Teczka personalna, Leon Karl Habsburg: "Wniosek na odznaczenie 'Krzyże Walecznych' w myśl rozporządzenia ROP z dnia 11 sierpnia 1920 r.," Leon Habsburg, 3 September 1920; "Główna karta ewidencyjna," [1929]; CAW, Teczka personalna: Karol Habsburg, "Wniosek na odznaczenie 'Krzyże Walecznych' w myśl rozporządzenia ROP z dnia 11 sierpnia 1920 r.," Leon Habsburg, 11 April 1922; "Karta ewidencyjna," 1927. Wilhelm's services: "Notiz," Vienna, 17 August 1920, PAAA Wien 342; Auswärtiges Amt, Report on meeting with Larischenko, 26 August 1920, PAAA R84244. Lincoln: Wasserstein, *Secret Lives*, 175.

15. Badeni, *Autobiografia*, 11; Chłopczyk, "Alicja Habsburg," 29–31.

16. Stefan to "Kochany Hrabio" (Potocki?), 10 August 1920, APK-OŻ DDŻ 85.

17. Wilhelm, "Das Ukrainische Problem," *Neues Wiener Journal*, 9 January 1921.

18. Stefan, "Nadesłane," Żywiec, 31 January 1921, APK-OŻ DDŻ 754; Polizeidirektion Wien to Bundesministerium für Äusseres, 7 February 1921, in Hornykiewicz, *Ereignisse*, vol. 4, 284.

19. Contestation of property: HHStA, Fach 1, Karton 66, Folder "Erzherzog Karl Stefan," "Rozporządzenie Ministra Rolnictwa i Dóbr Państwowych w przedmiocie ustanowienia zarządu państwowego nad dobrami arcyksięcia Karola Stefana Habsburga z Żywca, położonemi na terytorjum b. zaboru austrjackiego," 28 February 1919, in *Monitor Polski*, 6 March 1919, Number 53. Worry: Stefan to [Potocki?], 10 August 1920, APK-OŻ DDŻ 85. Stefan: Stefan to Polish Council of Ministers, February 1922, APK-OŻ DDŻ 754. Propaganda: K. O. Habsburg, *Na marginesie sprawy Żywieckiej*, 18.

20. Arrangement: Kancelarja Cywilna Naczelnika Państwa to Stefan, 26 August 1921, APK-OŻ DDŻ 757; "Informacja w sprawie dóbr Żywieckich," 1923, APK-OŻ DDŻ 754; "Rozporządzenie," 24 August 1924, APK-OŻ DDŻ 755. Italy: C. Canciani to Kloss, 6 July 1919, APK-OŻ DDŻ 757; "Akt darowizny," draft, September 1920, APK-OŻ DDŻ 757. "Dear Papa": Kloss in Rome to Stefan, 22 November 1921, APK-OŻ DDŻ 757.

21. Quotation is from Wilhelm, "Das Ukrainische Problem," *Neues Wiener Journal*, 9 January 1921. Tereshchenko and Ostashko, *Ukrains'kyi patriot*, 46; Bruski, *Petlurowcy*, 332–333.

22. Disguise: Williams, *Culture in Exile*, 148. Deal: Dashkevych, "Vil'hel'm Habsburg i istoriia," 65.

23. Germans: Naczelne Dowództwo W.P., Oddział II, "Skoropadski i arcyksiążę Wilhelm," 1921, CAW I.303.4.2718/102–104.

24. Democracy: Tereshchenko, "V'iacheslav Lypyns'kyi." Rumors: MSZ, "Projekt Referatu 'Ukraina,'" November 1921, AAN MSZ 5354/671–681; Kellogg, *Russian Roots of Nazism*, 181. Maria: Onats'kyi, *Portrety v profil*, 144. Leading role: Polizeidirektion Wien to Bundesministerium für Äusseres, 7 February 1921, in Hornykiewicz, *Ereignisse*, vol. 4, 284. Emigration: Wilhelm to Tokary, 23 January

1921, HURI, Folder 1; Julius Lustig-Prean von Preansfeld, "Lebensskizzen der von 1870 bis 1918 ausgemusterten 'Neustädter,'" KA, Gruppe 1, Band 2, 536.

25. Predictions and popularity: Polizeidirektion Wien to Bundesministerium für Äusseres, 7 February 1921, in Hornykiewicz, *Ereignisse*, vol. 4, 284. On the Varangian episode, see Dashkevych, "Vil'hel'm Habsburg i istoriia," 67; Tereshchenko, "V'iacheslav Lypyns'kyi." Ievhen Chykalenko's article was published in *Volia*, 23 April 1921.

26. Calamity: Vivian, *Life of Emperor Charles*, 224. See also Vasari, *Otto Habsburg*, 32–34; and Cartledge, *Will to Survive*, 351–352.

27. Rape, *Die österreichischen Heimwehren*, 260–263.

28. July: Nußer, *Konservative Wehrverbände*, 225; Rape, *Die österreichischen Heimwehren*, 263. August: Vogt, *Oberst Max Bauer*, 340, 383. Modern monarch: Spectator, "Monarkhiia i respublika," *Soborna Ukraina*, 1 November 1921, 2. On political activities, see Polizeidirektion Wien to Bundesministerium für Äusseres, 14 November 1921, in Hornykiewicz, *Ereignisse*, vol. 4, 307–308; IPH, 2 March 1948; TsDAHO 26/1/66498-fp/148980/I/118; Onats'kyi, *Portrety v profil*, 149. Though funded by Germans, Wilhelm's newspaper took a pro-English line. Wilhelm was a sailor, who saw Ukraine as a future maritime power, and an anglophile who spoke English and knew the royal family (at this moment, he himself was about 358th in the British succession).

29. Aufbau's founding document is "Die Grundlage für die Statuten einer Gesellschaft m.b.H. des Wiederaufbaus der vom Weltkriege geschädigten Staaten," November 1920, BK 22/74, fiche 1, 18–20. See also Fiutak, "Vasilij von Biskupskij," 32–33; Kursell, "Erinnerungen an Dr. Max v. Scheubner-Richter," 19; and Baur, *Die russische Kolonie*, 258, 267. On Wilhelm and the Ukrainian syndicate, see Vogt, *Oberst Max Bauer*, 383. On the syndicate's operations, see Nußer, *Konservative Wehrverbände*, 226; and Thoss, *Der Ludendorff-Kreis*, 446–447.

30. Onats'kyi, *Portrety v profil*, 150.

31. Ludendorff: Georg Fuchs, "Zur Vorgeschichte der Nationalsozialistischen Erhebung," BA NS26, 38, 130. Arms: "Nr. 282/21 von 11.IX.1921," BHStA, Kriegsarchiv, Bayern und Reich Bund 36. Green International: UNR Mission in Hungary, to UNR Minister of Foreign Affairs, 12 December 1921, TsDAVO 3696/2/466/86; Wilhelm, "Das Ukrainische Problem," *Neues Wiener Journal*, 9 January 1921. Training: Kellogg, *Russian Roots of Nazism*, 181. Fatherland: "Abschrift eines Briefes vom Führer der deutschen Kolonisten Dr. Jakob Flemmer an Obersten Wasyl Wyschywanij, Kischineff, 30 August 1921," BHStA, Kriegsarchiv, Bayern und Reich Bund 36.

32. Viennese press: *Wiener Mittag*, 2 September 1921. The French: "Abschrift des Originalberichts der französischer Spionagestelle in Wien," 30 August 1921, BHStA, Kriegsarchiv, Bayern und Reich Bund 36. The Russians: Zolotarev, *Russkaia voennaia emigratsiia*, 446. The Czechs: "Ruští monarchisté v Praze" [1921], AKPR, ič 276/k. 17. Poles: Embassy in Copenhagen, "Informacje rosyjskie z Berlina," 24 September 1921, AAN MSZ 5351 234.

33. Ukrainians: Directory Chief of Staff to UNR Ministry of Foreign Affairs, 17 September 1921, TsDAVO 3696/2/466/84; UNR MFA to Ambassador in Berlin, 16 November 1921, TsDAVO 3696/3/19/119; Bruski, *Petlurowcy*, 335–336.

34. Rape, *Die österreichischen Heimwehren*, 273; Tereshchenko and Ostashko, *Ukrains'kyi patriot*, 57.

35. Dowództwo Okręgu Korpusnego Nr. II w Lublinie, "Raport Ukraiński," Lublin, 19 April 1922, CAW I.303.4.6906. Support: Vertraulich Abschrift, 11 February 1922, BHStA, Kriegsarchiv, Bayern und Reich Bund 36. Perfidy: Bauer in Vienna

to Ludendorff, 3 February 1922, BK 22/77, fiche 1, 18. See also Sendtner, *Rupprecht von Wittelsbach*, 462–463.

36. Ludendorff and Scheubner-Richter, who was killed.

37. Bauer to Pittinger, 12 March 1922, BHStA, Kriegsarchiv, Bayern und Reich Bund 36.

LILAC: GAY PARIS

1. Armie, *Maria Cristina de Habsburgo*, 200, 205; Brook-Shepherd, *The Last Empress*, 219.

2. Here met the traditional and the modern ideas of dictatorship: a transitional period within which to restore an established political order, and a permanent state of one-man rule.

3. C. Fuchs to Luise Engeler, 20 October 1931, BK 22/70, fiche 2, 62–63; Vogt, *Oberst Max Bauer*, 406–408; Wilhelm's letters to Piegl in BK 22/71, fiche 2.

4. Piegl to Wilhelm, 14 March 1929, BK 22/71, fiche 4, 138; Vogt, *Oberst Max Bauer*, 422, 432; Wasserstein, *Secret Lives*, 214ff.

5. J. Piegl to Wilhelm, 23 June 1927, BK 22/71, fiche 2, 42; Piegl to Wilhelm, 17 January 1928, ibid., 60, 102–103; Piegl to Wilhelm, 21 June 1928, BK 22/71, fiche 3, 102–103; Piegl to Pallin, 8 February 1929, BK 22/71, fiche 4, 131–132; Wilhelm to Piegl, 16 February 1929, ibid., 133. On Alfonso, see Gortazar, *Alfonso XIII*.

6. Wilhelm to Piegl, 25 May 1928, BK 22/71, fiche 2, 69.

7. Loan: "A.S. de l'archiduc Guillaume de Habsbourg," 2 August 1935, APP, B A/1680; Carl Schuloff, Vienna, 12 January 1934, copy of letter, APK-OŻ DDŻ 753. Brothers: information from István Déak, who cites József Kardos, *Legitimizmus: legitimista politikusok Magyarországon a két világháború között*, Budapest: Korona, 1998, 280, 303, 571.

8. A. Bonnefoy-Sibour, Le Préfet de Seine-et-Oise to Ministre de l'Intérieur, 24 April 1929, AC, Fonds de Moscou, Direction de la Sûreté Générale, 19949484/154/9722.

9. Contact: Wilhelm to Sheptyts'kyi, 14 February 1927, TsDIAL, 358/3t/166/26. Police: "A.S. de l'archiduc Guillaume de Habsbourg," 2 August 1935, APP, B A/1680. Travel: Wilhelm to Piegl, 2 June 1928, Wilhelm to Piegl, 9 June 1928, Piegl to Wilhelm, 13 June 1928, all in BK 22/71, fiche 3, 85–92.

10. Kroll: "L'archiduc Guillaume de Habsbourg condamné par défaut à cinq années de prison," *Le Populaire*, 28 July 1935, 1, 2; Ostashko, "Pol's'ka viiskova spetssluzhba." See the records of transfers in APK-OŻ DDŻ 753, 894.

11. Romanov, *Twilight of Royalty*, 27; on polo, see Georges-Michel, *Autres personnalités*, 122.

12. Georges-Michel, *Autres personnalités*, 130–131. Sometimes a cigar is just a cigar.

13. Michel Georges-Michel, "Une histoire d'ancre sympathetique," *Le Jour*, 25 July 1934.

14. "A.S. de Couyba Paule et Guillaume de Habsburg," 23 January 1935, APP, B A/1680. Compare Brassaï, *Secret Paris*.

15. "A.S. de l'archiduc Guillaume de Habsbourg," 2 August 1935, APP, B A/1680.

16. Newspaper clipping, Raymonde Latour, "En regardant poser S.A.I. l'archiduc Guillaume de Lorraine-Habsbourg," 28 October 1931, HURI, Folder 2. On the proximity of agape and philia in slumming, see Koven, *Sexual and Social Politics*, 276–277 and passim.

17. "A.S. de Couyba Paule et Guillaume de Habsburg," 23 January 1935, APP, B A/1680.

18. Madame Caillaux: Berenson, *Trial of Madame Caillaux*. Paulette and Caillaux: [Legionsrat] Wasserbäck, Osterreichische Gesandschaft, Pressedienst, Paris, to Eduard Ludwig, Vorstand des Bundespressediensts, Vienna, 22 December 1934, AR, Neue Politisches Archiv, AA/ADR, Karton 416, Folder: Liasse Personalia Geh. A-H. Monzie: "A.S. de Couyba Paule et Guillaume de Habsburg," 23 January 1935, APP, B A/1680; "Bericht in der Sache gegen Erzherzog Wilhelm und Paule Couyba" [August 1935], AR, Neue Politisches Archiv, AA/ADR, Karton 416, Folder: Liasse Personalia Geh. A-H.

19. Rothschild: "A.S. de Couyba Paule et Guillaume de Habsburg," 23 January 1935, APP, B A/1680; Germaine Decaris, "L'archiduc de Habsbourg-Lorraine est condamné par défaut à cinq ans de prison," *L'Oeuvre*, 28 July 1935, 1, 5; Georges Oubert, "La 'fiancée' de l'Archiduc Guillaume de Habsbourg est en prison depuis d'un mois," *Le Populaire*, 15 December 1934.

20. Préfecture de Police, Cabinet du Préfet, 7 July 1932, APP, B A/1680. All the documents concerning the three naturalization attempts are in this file.

21. It was not unusual in the Paris of the early twentieth century for men of Wilhelm's tastes to have friendships with actresses and other celebrities. Compare Vicinus, "Fin-de-Siècle Theatrics," 171–173.

22. Kings: Mistinguett, *Queen of the Paris Night*, 60–63. Friedrich Wilhelm: "Friedrich Leopold, Kin of Kaiser, Dies," *New York Times*, 15 September 1931; "Potsdam Sale Fails to Draw High Bids," *New York Times*, 21 February 1931.

23. "Michael Winburn Dies; Paris Soap Firm Head," *New York Times*, 14 November 1930.

24. Quotations, respectively, are from Michel Georges-Michel, "Ou l'Archiduc Guillaume unit Mlle Mistinguett et l'Archiduc Rodolphe" [summer 1932], HURI, Folder 2; and Mistinguett, *Queen of the Paris Night*, 1.

25. Brook-Shepherd, *The Last Empress*, 215ff.

26. Andics, *Der Fall Otto Habsburg*, 67, 74; Vasari, *Otto Habsburg*, 150–151; Interview, *Die Presse*, 10 November 2007, 2.

27. Vasari, *Otto Habsburg*, 125–126.

28. Habsburg future: Binder, "Christian Corporatist State," 80. Towns: Vasari, *Otto Habsburg*, 109. Schuschnigg's predicaments are discussed in Goldinger and Binder, *Geschichte der Republik Österreich*.

29. Leo later claimed to have been expelled from the family. SS Rechtsabteilung, "Volkstumszugehörigkeit der Familie des verstorbenen Erzherzogs Leo Habsburg in Bestwin," Kattowitz, 19 April 1941, BA R49/37.

30. Freiherr von Biegeleben, Kanzlei des Ordens vom Goldenen Vlies, Vienna, 1 June 1934, 22 May 1934, 10 December 1934, APK-OŻ DDŻ 1. The dangling: Brook-Shepherd, *The Last Empress*, 243–244.

31. The cook: Chłopczyk, "Ostatni właściciele," 23.

32. Stefan Habsburg, "Mein Testament," 12 June 1924, APK-OŻ DDŻ 85; "Układ spadkowy," 4 May 1934, APK-OŻ DDŻ 753.

33. "Wykaz wypłaconych i przekazanych apanaży dotacji i spłaty na rach. Kasy Dworskiej," 15 May 1934, APK-OŻ DDŻ 894.

34. Charity: A.S. de l'archiduc Guillaume de Habsbourg, 2 August 1935, APP, B A/1680; Andrii Sheptyts'kyi to Ilarion Svientsits'kyi, 5 April 1933, in Diakiv, *Lysty Mytropolyta Andreia Sheptyts'koho*, 50. OUN: "Znany Wasyl Wyszywanyj," 1 July 1934, RGVA, 308k/7/322/4; Wilhelm to Oksana de Tokary, 20 November 1933,

HURI, Folder 1. See also IPH, 26 September 1947, TsDAHO 26/1/66498-fp/ 148980/I/54; Tereshchenko and Ostashko, *Ukrains'kyi patriot*, 58. Hitler: Winter, *Die Sowjet union*, 146.

35. Polish Ministry of Internal Affairs, Wydział Narodowościowy, Komunikat Informacyjny, 7 June 1933, AAN MSW 1041/68; "Znany Wasyl Wyszywanyj," 1 July 1934, RGVA, 308k/7/322/4. On Paneyko's other contacts, see the scattered mentions in *Zhyttia i smert' Polkovnyka Konovaltsia*.

36. Zeppelin and Otto: "Pobyt Otty Habsburka v Berlíne," 6 February 1933, AUTGM, fond TGM, R-Monarchie, k. 1; IPH, 5 September 1947, TsDAHO 26/1/66498-fp/148980/I/27. Hitler: Wilhelm to Tokary, 8 August 1934, HURI, Folder 1. Wiesner: Wilhelm to Tokary in Paris, 21 December [1934?], HURI, Folder 1; Vasari, *Otto Habsburg*, 114.

37. Brook-Shepherd, *Uncrowned Emperor*, 83, 85.

38. Hendrix, *Sir Henri Deterding*; IPH, 14 April 1948, TsDAHO 26/1/66498-fp/148980/I/82.

39. The rescue of the *Eros*: Schmidt-Brentano, *Die Österreichische Admirale*, 474. Rothschild: Ferguson, *World's Banker*, 971, 992.

40. The account of the dinner draws from: "Bericht in der Sache gegen Erzherzog Wilhelm und Paule Couyba" [August 1935], AR, Neue Politisches Archiv, AA/ADR, Karton 416, Folder: Liasse Personalia Geh. A-H; "A.S. de Couyba Paule et Guillaume de Habsburg," 23 January 1935, APP, B A/1680; Germaine Decaris, "L'archiduc de Habsbourg-Lorraine est condamné par défaut à cinq ans de prison," *L'Oeuvre*, 28 July 1935, 1, 5.

41. Osterreichische Gesandschaft, Paris, to [Generalsekretär] Franz Peter, Bundeskanzleramt, Vienna, 5 December 1934, AR, Neue Politisches Archiv, AA/ADR, Karton 416, Folder: Liasse Personalia Geh. A-H.

42. "Une escroquerie au rétablissement des Habsbourg," *Matin*, 15 December 1934. Fraud: [Legionsrat] Wasserbäck, Osterreichische Gesandschaft, Pressedienst, Paris, to Eduard Ludwig, Vorstand des Bundespressediensts, Vienna, 22 December 1934. Nobles: Österreichische Gesandschaft, Paris, to Generalsekretär Franz Peter, Vienna, 28 December 1934. Legation: Maurice Bourgain, Paris, to Légation d'Autriche, 26 June 1935. All three letters in AR, Neue Politisches Archiv, AA/ADR, Karton 416, Folder: Liasse Personalia Geh. A-H.

43. Burrin, *Fascisme, nazisme, autoritarisme*, 202, 209.

44. Georges Oubert, "La 'fiancée' de l'Archiduc Guillaume de Habsbourg est en prison depuis d'un mois," *Le Populaire*, 15 December 1934.

45. Ibid.

46. Eugen: Bundeskanzleramt, Auswärtige Angelegenheiten, "Erzherzog Wilhelm," 15 July 1935; Colloredo: Österreichische Gesandschaft, Paris, to Generalsekretär Franz Peter, Vienna, 28 December 1934; both in AR, Neue Politisches Archiv, AA/ADR, Karton 416, Folder: Liasse Personalia Geh. A-H. Veterans: Union des Anciens Combattants de l'Armée de la Republique Ukrainniene en France to Georges Normand (Juge d'Instruction), 20 May 1935, HURI, Folder 1. Friends: Tokary to Le Baron de Villanye, Hungarian Ambassador in Rome, 6 April 1935, ibid.

47. He was in Vienna no later than 19 June. Wilhelm to Tokary, 19 June 1935, HURI, Folder 1.

48. The trial began with a song. The Palais de Justice is on an island, neither on the left bank nor the right bank of the Seine. It is a landmark on the walk from the left bank, say the Senate, to the right bank, say Montmartre, perhaps a guilty one in the evening, or a cheery one in the morning. It was fitting, then, that the first person

defended in this trial was the recently deceased Senator Charles Couyba, alias bar singer Maurice Boukay, a man who had made that walk many times. The presiding judge allowed a lawyer representing his family to make a special opening statement. The senatorial Couyba family wanted the record clear that the defendant Paulette was in no way their relation. Their lawyer recited some lines of Couyba/Boukay's greatest hit, "Manon," and closed by asking that the song's "immaculate glory" not be tarnished. Germaine Decaris, "L'archiduc de Habsbourg-Lorraine est condamné par défaut à cinq ans de prison," *L'Oeuvre*, 28 July 1935, 1, 5.

49. "Bericht in der Sache gegen Erzherzog Wilhelm und Paule Couyba" [August 1935], AR, Neue Politisches Archiv, AA/ADR, Karton 416, Folder: Liasse Personalia Geh. A-H; Geo. London, "Il fallait d'abord faire manger le prince," *Le Journal*, 28 July 1935.

50. AP, D1U6 3068, case 299814, Seizième Chambre du Tribunal de Premier Instance de Département de la Seine séant au Palais de Justice à Paris, "Pour le Procureur de la République et Pour Paneyko Basile et Evrard Charles contre Couyba Paule et De Habsbourg-Lorraine Archiduc d'Autriche Guillaume François Joseph Charles"; "Bericht in der Sache gegen Erzherzog Wilhelm und Paule Couyba" (August 1935), AR, Neue Politisches Archiv, AA/ADR, Karton 416, Folder: Liasse Personalia Geh. A-H.

51. Her man: Germaine Decaris, "L'archiduc de Habsbourg-Lorraine est condamné par défaut à cinq ans de prison," *L'Oeuvre*, 28 July 1935, 5.

52. Quotations are from "Bericht in der Sache gegen Erzherzog Wilhelm und Paule Couyba" [August 1935], AR, Neue Politisches Archiv, AA/ADR, Karton 416, Folder: Liasse Personalia Geh. A-H.

53. AP, D1U6 3068, case 299814, Seizième Chambre du Tribunal de Premier Instance de Département de la Seine séant au Palais de Justice à Paris, "Pour le Procureur de la République et Pour Paneyko Basile et Evrard Charles contre Couyba Paule et De Habsbourg-Lorraine Archiduc d'Autriche Guillaume François Joseph Charles."

54. Berenson, *Trial of Madame Caillaux*, 1–42.

55. Paneyko to L. Beberovich, 30 April 1935, HURI, Folder 1; [Österreichische Gesandschaft, Paris], July 1935, AR, Neue Politisches Archiv, AA/ADR, Karton 416, Folder: Liasse Personalia Geh. A-H. This was a typical French stereotype of Germans: Murat, *La loi du genre*, 294–295.

56. "L'archiduc Guillaume de Habsbourg est condamné par défaut à cinq années de prison," *Le Populaire*, 28 July 1935, 1, 2; *L'Oeuvre*, 28 July 1935, 1.

57. Geo. London, "Il fallait d'abord faire manger le prince," *Le Journal*, 28 July 1935.

58. Wilhelm to Tokary, 22 June 1935, HURI, Folder 1.

59. Czechoslovaks: Wilhelm to Tokary, 18 August 1935, HURI, Folder 1. Belgian press article produced by Eugen. In July 1935: "Une Machination Bolchevique," AR, Neue Politisches Archiv, AA/ADR, Karton 416, Folder: Liasse Personalia Geh. A-H. For a confession to the Konovalets murder, see Sudoplatov and Sudoplatov, *Special Tasks*, 7–29.

60. "Les Habsbourgs vont-ils rentrer en Autriche?" *Le Figaro*, 4 July 1935, 1.

61. "A.S. de Couyba Paule et Guillaume de Habsburg," 23 January 1935, APP, B A/1680.

62. Century: Germaine Decaris, "L'archiduc de Habsbourg-Lorraine est condamné par défaut à cinq ans de prison," *L'Oeuvre*, 28 July 1935, 1, 5. Hat: Georges Claretie, "La fiancée d'un prétendant du trône d'Ukraine," *Le Figaro*, 28 July 1935, 1, 3.

63. Social advance: Weber, *Hollow Years*.

64. Both quotations are from Germaine Decaris, "L'archiduc de Habsbourg-Lorraine est condamné par défaut à cinq ans de prison," *L'Oeuvre*, 28 July 1935, 1, 5.

BROWN: ARISTOCRATIC FASCISM

1. This incident is recounted on the basis of Österreichische Gesandschaft, Paris, to Bundeskanzleramt, Auswärtige Angelegenheiten, Vienna, "Betrügerische Maneuver der im Prozess gegen Erzherzog Wilhelm verurteilten Mlle. Couyba," 19 May 1936, AR, Neue Politisches Archiv, AA/ADR, Karton 416, Folder: Liasse Personalia Geh. A-H.

2. Wilhelm to Tokary, 19 June 1935 and 27 November 1935, HURI, Folder 1.

3. *Folles de Luxes et Dames de Qualité*, Paris: Editions Baudinière, 1931.

4. Cat: Wilhelm to Tokary, 27 August 1935, HURI, Folder 1. Nerves: Wilhelm to Tokary, 19 June 1935, HURI, Folder 1.

5. Compare [Wilhelm], Declaration to French Press, 1935, HURI, Folder 1 to "Une lettre de l'archiduc Guillaume Habsburg-Lorraine d'Autriche," *Le Figaro*, 13 August 1935, 3.

6. Chastity gossip: Gribble, *Life of the Emperor Francis-Joseph*, 279. On Eugen's return: "Viennese Hail Archduke," *New York Times*, 11 September 1934. Generally: Hamann, *Die Habsburger*, 101.

7. Everyone necessary: Wilhelm to Tokary, 27 November 1935, HURI, Folder 1. Name: Bundes Ministerium für Inneres, Abteilung 2, "Wilhelm Franz Josef Habsburg-Lothringen," 29 November 1952, AR GA, 69.002/1955.

8. Training: Gauleitung Wien, Personalamt, to NSDAP, Gauleitung, 8 May 1940, AR GA, 170.606.

9. Freiherr von Biegeleben, Ordenskanzler, Kanzlei des Ordens vom Goldenen Vlies, Vienna, 26 March 1936, APK-OŻ DDŻ 1.

10. "Es existieren laut Inventar 89 Collanen des Ordend vom goldenen Vlies," Vienna, 26 May 1930, APK-OŻ DDŻ 1.

11. Wilhelm to Tokary, 27 August 1935, HURI, Folder 1; Wilhelm to Tokary, 18 October 1935, HURI, Folder 1.

12. Wilhelm to Tokary, 18 October 1935, HURI, Folder 1.

13. Wilhelm to Tokary, 7 October 1936, HURI, Folder 1.

14. Wilhelm to Tokary, 24 October 1936, HURI, Folder 1.

15. Wilhelm to Tokary, 27 November 1935, HURI, Folder 1. On aristocratic adaptations to national socialism, see generally Burrin, *Fascisme, nazisme, autoritarisme*.

16. April: Wilhelm to Tokary, 22 April 1936, HURI, Folder 2. The quotation is from Wilhelm to Tokary, 7 October 1936, HURI, Folder 2.

17. Goldinger and Binder, *Geschichte der Republik Österreich*, 246. It could not even count on the loyalty of the right-wing self-defense militias, whose representatives had just been excluded from the government.

18. Doomed: Wilhelm to Tokary, 27 January 1937, HURI, Folder 2. 1934: Wilhelm to Tokary, 21 December 1934, HURI, Folder 1. Wandering: Wilhelm to Tokary, 18 October 1935, HURI, Folder 1.

19. Wilhelm to Albrecht, 15 July 1936, APK-OŻ DDŻ 894; Wilhelm to Negriusz, 31 October and 1 December 1936, APK-OŻ DDŻ 894.

20. Gauleitung Wien, Personalamt, to NSDAP, Gauleitung, 8 May 1940, AR GA, 170.606.

21. The summary of Poltavets's career draws from: Kentii, *Narysy*, 30; Bolianovs'kyi, *Ukrains'ki viiskovi formuvannia*, 177; Torzecki, *Kwestia ukraińska*, 119,

125; Lacquer, *Russia and Germany*, 156; and Ostashko, "Pol's'ka viiskova spetss-luzhba." The letter: Poltavets-Ostrianytsia to Hitler, 23 May 1935, BA R43I/155.

22. Wilhelm to Tokary, 25 February 1937, 19 March 1937, HURI, Folder 2.

23. Tokary to Wilhelm, 23 November 1937, HURI, Folder 2, "Trottel."

24. Article: "Habsburger Kriminalgeschichte," *Völkischer Beobachter*, 11 March 1937. Enterprise: Wilhelm to Tokary, 19 December 1937, HURI, Folder 2. Grace, Stubborn: Wilhelm to Tokary, 19 March 1937, HURI, Folder 2.

25. Quotation and context from Wilhelm to Tokary, 27 January 1937, HURI, Folder 2.

26. Era: Wilhelm to Tokary, 19 December 1937, HURI, Folder 2. Liquidation: Wilhelm to Tokary, 19 December 1937, HURI, Folder 2. Healing: Tokary to Wilhelm, 2 March 1938, HURI, Folder 2. Ropes: Wilhelm to Tokary, 25 February 1937, HURI, Folder 2. Germany, Italy, and Japan signed a military agreement on 18 January 1942.

27. See for example Hills, *Britain and the Occupation of Austria*, 18.

BLACK: AGAINST HITLER AND STALIN

1. Chałupska, "Księżna wraca"; Marcin Czyżewski, "Arcyksiężna przypilnuje dzieci," *Gazeta Wyborcza* (Katowice), 21 September 2001; Krzyżanowski, "Księżna arcypolskości"; Badeni, *Autobiografia*, 75.

2. A. Habsburg, *Princessa och partisan*, 83.

3. On Soviet practices, the classic work is Gross, *Revolution from Abroad*. On the murder of Polish officers, see Cienciala et al., *Katyń*. On the first weeks of German occupation, see Rossino, *Hitler Strikes Poland*. Maria Krystyna is the source on the fate of these two teachers; see endnote 4. The German annexation of Żywiec took place on 6 September.

4. Quotations and events as recalled by Maria Krystyna Habsburg, cited in Bar, "Z Życia koła." Silver: "Vermerk," 19 May 1943, BA R49/38.

5. Descent: Sicherheitspolizei, Einsatzkommando z. b. V. Kattowitz, "Niederschrift," 16 November 1939, BA R49/38. Treason: Gestapo, Teschen, to Gestapo, Kattowitz, 8 December 1939, BA R49/38.

6. Dobosz, *Wojna na ziemi Żywieckiej*, 41–48.

7. IPH, 14 April 1948, TsDAHO 26/1/66498-fp/148980/I/143, 145; Gauleitung Wien, Personalamt, to NSDAP, Gauleitung, 8 May 1940, AR GA, 170.606.

8. Hirniak, *Polk. Vasyl' Vyshyvanyi*, 35; Wien Stadt und Landesarchiv, Meldezettel, "Habsburg-Lothringen," 1944, AR GA, 170.606.

9. "Entwurf," Saybusch, 22 October 1940, APK-OŻ DDŻ 1161; Finanzamt Kattowitz-Stadt, "Prufungsbericht," 23 June 1941, APK-OŻ DDŻ 1160. Dollars and marks were convertible as late as 1941. The projection from 1941 dollars is by consumer price index. One can make these projections in various ways, none of them perfect. The point here is that they got a lot of money.

10. Friends: Reichssicherheitsamt to Stab Reichsführer SS (Wolff), 25 May 1940, BA NS19/662 PK D 0279. Nordic race: A. Habsburg, *Princessa och partisan*, 113–114.

11. Letters: Botschafter v. Mackensen, 13 February 1940; Hermann Neumacher to Himmler, 19 June 1940, both at BA NS19/662 PK D 0279. Resettlements and brewery: Dobosz, *Wojna na ziemi Żywieckiej*, 69–74; Spyra, *Browar Żywiec*, 61.

12. Active part: "Schlußbericht," Kattowitz, 30 January 1941, BA R49/38. Letter: Alice to Albrecht, 15 November 1941, BA R49/38.

13. See A. Habsburg, *Princessa och partisan*, 122–123; Dobosz, *Wojna na ziemi Żywieckiej*, 102.

14. Alice to Albrecht, 15 November 1941, Gestapo translation, BA R49/38.

15. Leo: Wilhelm to Tokary, 10 December 1937, HURI, Folder 2.

16. Girlfriend: Bundesministerium für Inneres, Abteiling 2, "Bericht: Wilhelm Franz Josef Habsburg-Lothr," 18 September 1947, AR GA, 69.002/1955.

17. See Berkhoff, *Harvest of Despair*.

18. On the Holocaust in Ukraine, see Brandon and Lower, *Shoah in Ukraine*.

19. Hirniak, *Polk. Vasyl' Vyshyvanyi*; IPN, 19 August 1947, TsDAHO 263/1/66498-fp/148980/II/19. There were different views among the Nazi leadership about how to treat Ukraine; Rosenberg's attempts to exploit the Ukrainian question failed in the face of the actual policies of Eric Koch in the Reichskommissariat Ukraine and the conceit of Hitler.

20. Novosad's past: IPN, 3 July 1947, TsDAHO 263/1/66498-fp/148980/I/224, 185, 236. Quotations are from Novosad, "Vasyl' Vyshyvanyi," 22–23; see also Protokol Doprosa (of their joint interrogation), 12 May 1948, TsDAHO 263/1/66498-fp/148980/II/195–211.

21. Novosad, "Vasyl' Vyshyvanyi," 23; Hills, *Britain and the Occupation of Austria*, 100–111; Beer, "Die Besatzungsmacht Großbritannien," 54.

22. Move: WSL, Meldezettel, "Habsburg-Lothringen," 1944, AR GA, 170.606. Maas: IPH, 26 September 1947, TsDAHO 26/1/66498-fp/148980/I/58–59; IPH, 14 April 1948, TsDAHO 26/1/66498-fp/148980/I/150–154; Balfour and Mair, *Four-Power Control*, 318. My efforts to locate files under this and succeeding names at French and British archives came to nothing, but there might be any number of reasons for that. I am hopeful that others will have better luck; there is much more to be known about Wilhelm's contacts with the British and the French in the 1940s and indeed in the 1930s. His frequent travels to London in the 1930s, and his particular sensitivity to having been expelled from France in 1935, suggest that certain relationships might have existed even then.

23. Lida: IPN, 19 August 1947, TsDAHO 263/1/66498-fp/148980/II/21.

24. Novosad, "Vasyl' Vyshyvanyi," 25.

25. The Waffen-SS Galizien, IPN, 19 August 1947, TsDAHO 263/1/66498-fp/148980/II/23–26.

26. Rasevych, "Vil'hel'm von Habsburg," 220.

27. Gestapo, Kattowitz, Interrogation of Alice von Habsburg, Vistula, 27 January 1942, BA R49/38. See also Badeni, *Autobiografia*, 141.

28. Stab Reichsführer SS to Greifelt, Reichskommissar für die Festigung deutschen Volkstums, 1 December 1942, BA NS19/662 PK D 0279.

29. Chef der Sicherheitspolizei to Stabshauptamt des Reichskommissars für die Festigung deutschen Volkstums, 20 July 1942, BA R49/38.

30. A. Habsburg, *Princessa och partisan*, 169. Heydrich was also Reichsprotektor of Bohemia-Moravia, which is why he was chosen as a target.

31. Marie Klotilde Habsburg to Hitler, 29 May 1940, BA, R43II/1361.

32. Greifelt to Heydrich, 23 September 1941, BA R49/39; "Aktenvermerk," 26 June 1941, BA R49/39.

33. SS Rechtsabteilung, "Volkstumszugehörigkeit der Familie des verstorbenen Erzherzogs Leo Habsburg in Bestwin," Kattowitz, 19 April 1941, BA R49/37.

34. Maja: Der Amtskomissar und k. Ortsgruppenleiter to the SS-SD Abschnitt Kattowitz, 2 August 1940, BA R49/37. Category: Bezirkstelle der Deutschen Volksliste

to Zentralstelle der Deutschen Volksliste in Kattowitz, 19 November 1941, BA R49/37. Traitor: "Vermerk zu einem Vortrag des SS-Gruppenführer Greifelt beim Reichsführer SS am 12 Mai 1943," BA NS19/662 PK D 0279; "Besitzregelung der Herrschaft Saybusch," 18 May 1943, BA R49/38.

35. Der Hauptbeauftrage "Eindeutschung von Polen," 13 August 1942, APK-OŻ DDŻ 1150.

36. "Aktenvermerk," 18 May 1944, BA NS19/662 PK D 0279.

37. "Angelegenheit Saybusch-Bestwin," 19 May 1944, BA NS19/662 PK D 0279.

38. The first quotation in this paragraph is from Gauleiter von Oberschlesien to SS Gruppenführer Greifelt, September 1944, BA NS19/662 PK D 0279. Local authorities: Beauftragte für den Vierjahresplan to Reichskommissar für die Festigung deutschen Volkstums, 26 November 1943, BA R49/38; "Vermerk für SS Standartenführer Dr. Brandt," 18 November 1944, BA NS19/662 PK D 0279. The second quotation is from "Vermerk für SS Standartenführer Dr. Brandt," 18 November 1944, BA NS19/662 PK D 0279.

39. Dachau and Mauthausen. In countries such as Poland, this would not have prevented the Soviets from presenting him as a German collaborator; in Austria, where the Americans and British were also present, they had to take a bit more care.

40. IPH, 26 September 1947, TsDAHO 26/1/66498-fp/148980/I/59; IPH, 14 April 1948, TsDAHO 26/1/66498-fp/148980/I/28; IPN, 19 June 1947, TsDAHO 263/1/66498-fp/148980/I/216; IPH, 5 September 1947, TsDAHO 26/1/66498-fp/148980/I/39–40. Consult generally Müller, *Die Sowjetische Besatzung*, 39–89; Buchanon and Conway, *Political Catholicism in Europe;* Boyer, "Political Catholicism," 6–36.

41. Hirniak, *Polk. Vasyl' Vyshyvanyi*, 38–39.

42. Rauchensteiner, *Der Sonderfall*, 131.

43. As students of the subject will know, the OUN in question was the Bandera faction, which itself at this time was riven by internal dispute. Wilhelm's contacts were with the Supreme Ukrainian Liberation Council, a Banderite attempt to create a general political and military organization under the auspices of which nationalists could prepare themselves for the end of the war. In this work I have avoided discussions of Ukrainian internecine strife; on that issue see my *Reconstruction of Nations* and the pertinent Ukrainian, Polish, and other works cited therein.

44. IPH, 11 November 1947, TsDAHO 26/1/66498-fp/148980/I/72–74.

45. Otto: Brook-Shepherd, *Uncrowned Emperor*, 176. The chain of events of 1946: IPN, 27 August 1947, TsDAHO 263/1/66498-fp/148980/II/30–38; IPN, 19 June 1947, TsDAHO 263/1/66498-fp/148980/I/204–206; IPN, 23 April 1948, TsDAHO 263/1/66498-fp/148980/II/146–147; Novosad, "Vasyl' Vyshyvanyi," 25. On Lebed's American career, see Burds, "Early Cold War."

46. IPN, 24 July 1947, TsDAHO 263/1/66498-fp/148980/II/1–5.

47. See Snyder, "To Resolve"; Snyder, "The Causes"; for these quotations, on this point, and for the succeeding paragraphs.

48. Mackiewicz, *Dom Radziwiłłów*, 211; Hamann, *Die Habsburger*, 401. Mechtildis's husband, Hieronymus Radziwiłł, a German speaker who in his younger days was seen as pro-German, had assisted the Polish anti-German resistance during the war. At war's end he was arrested by the Soviets and died in Siberian exile.

ORANGE: EUROPEAN REVOLUTIONS

1. Novosad, "Vasyl' Vyshyvanyi," 25; Vasyl Kachorovs'kyi, interrogation protocol, TsDAHO 263/1/66498-fp/148980/II/160–164; Rasevych, "Vil'hel'm von Habs-

burg," 220. For numbers, see "Stalins letzte Opfer" and succeeding articles at www.profil.at. Kachorovs'kyi gave the name of his French contact as Boudier.

2. Bundes-Polizedirektion Wien to Bundesministerium für Inneres, "Habsburg-Lothringen Wilhelm Franz Josef; Information," 2 March 1952, AR GA, 69.002/1955. The Novosad quotation is from IPN, 19 August 1947, TsDAHO 263/1/66498-fp/148980/II/20.

3. Lunch: Hirniak, *Polk. Vasyl' Vyshyvanyi*, 38. The police quotation is from Bundes-Polizeidirektion Wien to Bundesministerium für Inneres, "Habsburg-Lothringen Wilhelm Franz Josef; Information," 2 March 1952, AR GA, 69.002/1955. Wilhelm on Kachorov'skyi: IPH, 11 November 1947, TsDAHO 26/1/66498-fp/148980/I/80.

4. The debate on the origins of the cold war is too massive to be considered here. On the Greco-Yugoslav-Soviet crisis, see Banac, *With Stalin against Tito*, 117–142. On American perceptions, see Gaddis, *United States*. A general guide to Soviet policy in these months is Mastny, *Cold War*, 30–46.

5. Kryvuts'kyi, *De sribnolentyi Sian plyve*, 321–322; Novosad, "Iak zahynul," 57.

6. Fellow prisoner Orest Matsiukevych, in his interrogation protocol, TsDAHO 26/1/66498-fp/148980/2/178.

7. See Lymarchenko, "Postanovlenie," 29 May 1948, and Tkach, "Akt," in TsDAHO 26/1/66498-fp/148980.

8. Austria: Bundes Ministerium für Inneres, Abteilung 2, "Wilhelm Franz Josef Habsburg-Lothringen," 29 November 1952, AR GA, 69.002/1955.

9. It was Klymyntii Sheptyts'kyi, the brother of Wilhelm's patron Andrii Sheptyts'kyi and a fascinating figure in his own right. The postwar history of western Ukraine cannot be summarized here. Consult Magocsi, *History of Ukraine*; Hrytsak, *Narys*; Yekelchyk, *Ukraine*. Good introductions to the Soviet camp system are Applebaum, *Gulag*, and Khlevniuk, *History of the Gulag*. On the Holocaust in eastern Galicia, see Pohl, *Nationalsozialistische Judenverfolgung*. On the disappearance of historic Galicia, consult Snyder, *Reconstruction of Nations*; Pollack, *Nach Galizien*.

10. Norilsk: Kryvuts'kyi, *Za poliarnym kolom*, 39 for quotation, also 59–61, 204.

11. Swarowsky: see *Die Musik in Geschichte und Gegenwart* or Baker's *Biographical Music Dictionary of Musicians*.

12. A separate study would be needed to explore the peculiarities of Austrian national identity. The classic work on Austrian high politics through 1955 is Stourzh, *Um Einheit und Freiheit*. On neutrality: Gehler, "From Non-Alignment to Neutrality." On culture: Menasse, *Erklär mir Österreich*; and Wagnleitner, *Coca-colonization and the Cold War*.

13. Wilhelm's sister Renata had died in 1935, his brother Leo in 1939, and his brother Albrecht in 1951. His sister Mechtildis lived until 1966 in Rio, his sister Eleanora until 1974 in Vienna.

14. On Solidarity, see Garton Ash, *Polish Revolution*. Definitive on the relationship between 1989 and 1991 is Kramer, "Collapse of East European Communism."

15. See Badeni, *Autobiografia*. The history of the lawsuits is drawn from press reports in *Gazeta Wyborcza* and *Rzeczpospolita*, as well as Spyra, *Browar Żywiec*, 73–75.

16. Croatia: Brook-Shepherd, *Uncrowned Emperor*, 193–194. Sarajevo: *New York Times*, 7 April 1997, 6. Ukraine: Dashkevych, "Vil'hel'm Habsburg i istoriia," 68. See also the interview in *Korespondent*, 15 June 2007.

17. Those looking for Habsburg parallels can find them: Yushchenko was treated at the same private hospital in Vienna as was Leo von Habsburg in 1937; and the attack itself, like Wilhelm's scandal in 1935, destroyed the image of an attractive

Ukrainian leader. The Orange Revolutionary who most resembled Wilhelm was probably Julia Tymoshenko. Wilhelm was the red prince, an archduke who identified with the peasants; she was the gas princess, an energy oligarch who learned to love the common people. And while they both cut a fine figure in traditional embroidered Ukrainian shirts, she wore dresses with greater public success. For a longer account, see Garton Ash and Snyder, "Ukraine: The Orange Revolution." See also two books by Andrew Wilson: *Ukraine's Orange Revolution* and *Virtual Politics*.

18. In 1991, Ukrainian patriots had little support from either Europe or the United States. In the hope of keeping the Soviet Union together, President George Bush made his famous "Chicken Kiev" speech. In the late 1940s and early 1950s, a few Ukrainian nationalists were employed by Western intelligence services, but that was a marginal effort in a hopeless cause. The closest thing to an exception to the rule would be Wilhelm's occupation policy in 1918. Also worthy of mention is Henryk Józewski's tolerant policy toward Ukrainians in interwar Polish Volhynia. See Snyder, *Sketches from a Secret War*. On Ukraine as a political choice, consult Rudnytsky, *Essays*; Szporluk, *Russia*; and Shevel, "Nationality in Ukraine."

19. On this complex history, see Martin, *Affirmative Action Empire*; and Yekelchyk, *Stalin's Empire of Memory*.

20. Richard Pipes, in a later edition of *Formation of the Soviet Union*, notes the Habsburg influence on Ukrainian nation-building as an issue he had overlooked. For discussion of the dilemmas inherent in the Soviet incorporation of western Ukraine, see Szporluk, *Russia*, 259–276. The best definition I have seen of national identity is in Golczewski, "Die ukrainische und die russische Emigration," 77: "Die Zugehörigkeit sagte weniger etwas über Ethnos, Sprache, Konfession, als über das Bekenntnis zu einer historisch-politischen Ordnungsmöglichkeit aus."

21. Another view of the historic role of Vienna and Galicia can be found in Szporluk, "The Making of Modern Ukraine."

22. The quotation from Otto is in *Korespondent*, 15 June 2007.

23. The best introduction to the period is now Judt, *Postwar*. Extremely valuable are also Mazower, *Dark Continent*; and James, *Europe Reborn*.

24. I write anachronistically of the "European Union" before 1992 since that seems less confusing than shifting back and forth between "European Union" and "European Community" to name the same institution.

25. The unified Germany of the late twentieth and early twenty-first centuries is still less than half the size of the Germany of 1938. For a more critical view of Europe as an articulation of West German interests, see Garton Ash, *In Europe's Name*.

26. On borders: Ursula Plassnik's lunchtime remarks at the Kanzleramt, Vienna, 10 November 2007.

27. Wilhelm's desires: IPH, 5 September 1947, TsDAHO 26/1/66498-fp/148980/I/27; Julius Lustig-Prean von Preansfeld, "Lebensskizzen der von 1870 bis 1918 ausgemusterten 'Neustädter,'" KA, Gruppe 1, Band 2, p. 536. By Jewish law I mean the Halakha. Rudnyts'kyi's mother was Milena Rudnyts'ka, one of the Ukrainian "Group of Five" and an impressive parliamentarian, feminist, and writer. Her mother was Olga Spiegel.

BIBLIOGRAPHY

Printed Primary Sources

Epigraph

Nietszche, Friedrich. "Nachgelassene Fragmente Frühjahr 1881 bis Sommer 1882." *Nietzsche Werke. Kritische Gesamtausgabe.* Berlin: Walter de Gruyter, 1973, Fünfte Abteilung, Zweiter Band, 411.

Libretto

Des Kaisers Traum. Festspiel in einem Aufzuge von Christiane Gräfin Thun-Salm. Musik von Anton Rückauf. Vienna, 1908.

Novels

Musil, Robert. *The Confusions of Young Törless,* trans. Shaun Whiteside. New York: Penguin, 2001.

Musil, Robert. *The Man without Qualities,* trans. Burton Pike and Sophie Wilkins. New York: Vintage, 1995.

Newspapers

Berlinske Tidende, 31 March 1920; *Die Neue Zeitung,* 3 December 1908; *Die Presse,* 10 November 2007; *Gazeta Wyborcza,* 1991–2005; *Korespondent,* 15 June 2007; *Le Figaro,* 4 July, 28 July, 13 August 1935; *Le Jour,* 25 July 1934; *Le Journal,* 28 July 1935; *Le Populaire,* 15 December 1934, 28 July 1935; *L'Oeuvre,* 28 July 1935; *Matin,* 15 December 1934; *Neues Wiener Journal,* 9 January 1921; *New York Times,* 14 November 1930, 21 February 1931, 15 September 1931, 11 September 1934, 17 December 1937, 7 April 1997; *Rzeczpospolita,* 1991–2005; *Soborna Ukraina,* 1 November 1921; *Völkischer Beobachter,* 11 March 1937; *Volksblatt,* 6 December 1908; *Wiener Abendpost,* 3 December 1908; *Wiener Bilder,* 9 December 1908; *Wiener Mittag,* 2 September 1921.

Printed Secondary Sources

Abramson, Henry. *A Prayer for the Government: Ukrainians and Jews in Revolutionary Times, 1917–1920.* Cambridge, MA: Harvard University Press, 1999.

Afflerbach, Holger, ed. *Kaiser Wilhelm II als Oberster Kriegsherr im Ersten Weltkrieg.* Munich, Germany: R. Oldenbourg, 2005.

Andics, Hellmut. *Der Fall Otto Habsburg: Ein Bericht.* Vienna: Verlag Fritz Molden, 1965.

Antonoff, Anne Louise. "Almost War: Britain, Germany, and the Balkan Crisis, 1908–1909." PhD diss., Yale University, 2006.

Applebaum, Anne. *Gulag: A History.* New York: Doubleday, 2003.

Armie. *Maria Cristina de Habsburgo Reina de España.* Barcelona, Spain: Ediciones Maria Rosa Urraca Pastor, 1935.

Arz, Artur. *Zur Geschichte des Grossen Krieges 1914–1918.* Vienna: Rikola Verlag, 1924.

Badeni, Joachim. *Autobiografia.* Cracow, Poland: Wydawnictwo Literackie, 2004.

Balfour, Michael, and John Mair. *Four-Power Control in Germany and Austria.* London: Oxford University Press, 1956.

Banac, Ivo. *The National Question in Yugoslavia: Origins, History, Politics.* Ithaca, NY: Cornell University Press, 1984.

———. *With Stalin against Tito: Cominformist Splits in Yugoslav Communism.* Ithaca, NY: Cornell University Press, 1988.

Bar, Jacek. "Z Życia koła." Unpublished manuscript, available at http://www.przewodnicy.net/kpt/zycie04/04_10_20.html. 20 October 2004.

Bartovský, Vojtěch. *Hranice: Statisticko-Topografický a kulturný obraz.* Hranice: Nakladem Vojt. Bartovského, 1906.

Basch-Ritter, Renate. *Österreich auf allen Meeren: Geschichte der k. (u.) k. Marine 1382 bis 1918.* Graz, Austria: Verlag Styria, 2000.

Baumgart, Winfried. *Deutsche Ostpolitik 1918.* Vienna: R. Oldenbourg Verlag, 1966.

Baur, Johannes. *Die russische Kolonie in München 1900–1945.* Wiesbaden, Germany: Harrassowitz Verlag, 1998.

Bayer v. Bayersburg, Heinrich. *Österreichs Admirale.* Vienna: Bergland Verlag, 1962.

Beer, Siegfried. "Die Besatzungsmacht Großbritannien in Österreich 1945–1949." In *Österreich unter Alliierter Besatzung 1945–1955,* ed. Alfred Ableitinger, Siegfried Beer, and Eduard G. Staudinger, 41–70. Vienna: Böhlau Verlag, 1998.

Beller, Steven. "Kraus's Firework: State Consciousness Raising in the 1908 Jubilee Parade in Vienna and the Problem of Austrian Identity." In *Staging the Past: The Politics of Commemoration in Habsburg Central Europe, 1848 to the Present,* ed. Maria Bucur and Nancy Wingfield, 46–71. West Lafayette, IN: Purdue University Press, 2001.

Berenson, Edward. *The Trial of Madame Caillaux.* Berkeley: University of California Press, 2002.

Berkhoff, Karel C. *Harvest of Despair: Life and Death in Ukraine under Nazi Rule.* Cambridge, MA: Harvard University Press, 2004.

Bihl, Wolfdieter. "Beitrage zur Ukraine-Politik Österreich-Ungarns 1918." *Jahrbücher für Geschichte Osteuropas* 14 (1966): 51–62.

———. *Österreich-Ungarn und die Friedenschlüsse von Brest-Litowsk.* Vienna: Böhlau Verlag, 1970.

———. "Zur Tätigkeit des ukrainophilen Erzherzogs Wilhelm nach dem Ersten Weltkrieg." Sonderdruck aus *Jahrbücher für Geschichte Osteuropas.* Munich: Osteuropa-Institut, 1971.

Binder, Dieter A. "The Christian Corporatist State: Austria from 1934 to 1938." In *Austria in the Twentieth Century*, ed. Rolf Steininger, Günter Bischof, and Michael Gehler, 72–84. New Brunswick, NJ: Transaction Publishers, 2002.

Binder, Harald. *Galizien in Wien: Parteien, Wahlen, Fraktionen und Abgeordnete im Übergang zur Massenpolitik*. Vienna: Verlag der Österreichischen Akademie der Wissenschaften, 2005.

Blanning, Tim. *The Pursuit of Glory: Europe 1648–1815*. New York: Penguin, 2007.

Bolianovs'kyi, Andrii. *Ukrains'ki viiskovi formuvannia v zbroinykh sylakh Nimechchyny (1939–1945)*. Lviv, Ukraine: CIUS, 2003.

Borowsky, Peter. *Deutsche Ukrainepolitik 1918*. Lübeck, Germany: Matthiesen Verlag, 1970.

Boyer, John W. "Political Catholicism in Austria, 1880–1960." *Contemporary Austrian Studies* 13 (2004): 6–36.

Bożek, Gabriela, ed. (Bożena Husar and Dorota Firlej, authors) *Żywieckie projekty Karola Pietschki*. Katowice, Poland: Śląskie Centrum Kultorowego, 2004.

Brandon, Ray, and Wendy Lower, eds. *The Shoah in Ukraine: History, Testimony, and Memorialization*. Bloomington: Indiana University Press, 2008.

Brassaï, *The Secret Paris of the 1930s*. New York: Pantheon Books, 1976.

Bridge, F. R., "The Foreign Policy of the Monarchy 1908–1918." In *The Last Years of Austria-Hungary: Essays in Political and Military History 1908–1918*, ed. Mark Cornwall. Exeter, UK: University of Exeter Press, 1990.

Brook-Shepherd, Gordon. *The Last Empress: The Life and Times of Zita of Austria-Hungary, 1892–1989*. New York: HarperCollins, 1991.

———. *Uncrowned Emperor: The Life and Times of Otto von Habsburg*. London: Hambledon and London, 2003.

Bruski, Jan Jacek. *Petlurowcy: Centrum Państwowe Ukraińskiej Republiki Ludowej na wychodŸstwie (1919–1924)*. Cracow, Poland: Arcana, 2004.

Bubnii, Mykhailo. *Redemptorysty*. Lviv, Ukraine: Monastyr Sv. Alfonsa, 2003.

Buchanon, Tom, and Martin Conway, eds. *Political Catholicism in Europe*. New York: Oxford University Press, 1996.

Burds, Jeffrey. "The Early Cold War in Soviet West Ukraine." Carl Beck Papers, Pittsburgh, no. 1505, 2001.

Burián, Stephen. *Austria in Dissolution*. London: Ernst Benn, 1925.

Burrin, Philippe. *Fascisme, nazisme, autoritarisme*. Paris: Éditions du Seuil, 2000.

Cartledge, Bryan. *The Will to Survive: A History of Hungary*. London: Timewell Press, 2006.

Cavallie, James. *Ludendorff och Kapp i Sverige*. Stockholm: Almqvist & Wiksell International, 1993.

Chałupska, Anna. "Księżna wraca do Żywca." *Nad Sołą i Koszarową* 4, no. 11 (June 2001).

Chłopczyk, Helena. "Alicja Habsburg–Księżna–Partyzant." *Karta groni* 26 (1991): 28–36.

———. "Ostatni właściciele dóbr Żywieckich." Unpublished paper. Żywiec, 1986.

Cienciala, Anna, Natalia Lebedeva, and Wojciech Materski, eds. *Katyń: A Crime without a Punishment*. New Haven, CT: Yale University Press, 2007.

Clark, Christopher. *Iron Kingdom: The Rise and Downfall of Prussia, 1600–1947*. Cambridge, MA: Harvard University Press, 2006.

———. *Kaiser Wilhelm II*. London: Longman, 2000.

Cohen, Gary. *The Politics of Ethnic Survival: Germans in Prague, 1861–1914*. West Lafayette, IN: Purdue University Press, 2006.

Cornwall, Mark. *The Undermining of Austria-Hungary: The Battle for Hearts and Minds*. New York: St. Martin's, 2000.

Dashkevych, Iaroslav. "Vil'hel'm Habsburg i istoriia." *Rozbudova derzhavy* 1, no. 4 (2005): 57–69.

Deák, István. *Beyond Nationalism: A Social and Political History of the Habsburg Officer Corps 1848–1918*. New York: Oxford University Press, 1990.

Dedijer, Vladimir. *The Road to Sarajevo*. New York: Simon and Schuster, 1966.

Diakiv, Solomiia, ed. *Lysty Mytropolyta Andreia Sheptyts'koho do Ilariona Svientsits'koho*. Lviv, Ukraine: Ukrainski tekhnolohii, 2005.

Dickinger, Christiane. *Franz Josef I: Die Entmythisierung*. Vienna: Ueberreuter, 2002.

Dobosz, Stanisław. *Wojna na ziemi Żywieckiej*. Żywiec, Poland: Gazeta Żywiecka, 2004.

Documents ruthéno-ukrainiens. Paris: Bureau Polonais de Publications Politiques, 1919.

Dontsov, Dmytro. *Rik 1918*. Toronto: Homin Ukrainy, 1954.

Eudin, Xenia Joukoff. "The German Occupation of the Ukraine in 1918." *Russian Review* 1, no. 1 (1941), 90–105.

Evans, R. J. W. *Rudolf II and His World*. London: Thames and Hudson, 1997.

Evans, Richard J. *The Coming of the Third Reich*. New York: Penguin, 2003.

Feldman, Gerald. *German Imperialism 1914–1918: The Development of a Historical Debate*. New York: John Wiley & Sons, 1972.

Ferguson, Niall. *The World's Banker: The History of the House of Rothschild*. London: Weidenfeld and Nicolson, 1998.

Fischer, Fritz. *Griff nach der Weltmacht*. Düsseldorf, Germany: Droste, 1961.

Fiutak, Martin. "Vasilij von Biskupskij und die russische politische Emigration in München." Master's thesis, Ludwig-Maximilians-Universität, 2004.

Frank, Alison Fleig. *Oil Empire: Visions of Prosperity in Austrian Galicia*. Cambridge, MA: Harvard University Press, 2005.

Freud, Sigmund. *Introductory Lectures on Psychoanalysis*. New York: Norton, 1966.

Gaddis, John Lewis. *The United States and the Origins of the Cold War*. New York: Columbia University Press, 2000.

Garton Ash, Timothy. *In Europe's Name: Germany and the United Continent*. London: Jonathan Cape, 1993.

_____. *The Polish Revolution: Solidarity*. New Haven, CT: Yale University Press, 2002.

Garton Ash, Timothy, and Timothy Snyder. "Ukraine: The Orange Revolution." *New York Review of Books*, 28 April 2005, 28–32.

Gay, Peter. *Freud, Jews, and Other Germans*. New York: Oxford University Press, 1978.

Gehler, Michael. "From Non-Alignment to Neutrality? Austria's Transformation during the First East-West Détente, 1953–1958." *Journal of Cold War Studies* 7, no. 4 (2005): 104–136.

Geiss, Imanuel. *Der Polnische Grenzstreifen 1914–1918*. Lübeck, Germany: Matthiesen, 1960.

Gellner, Ernest. *Language and Solitude: Wittgenstein, Malinowski, and the Habsburg Dilemma*. Cambridge: Cambridge University Press, 1998.

Georges-Michel, Michel. *Autres personnalités que j'ai connues, 1900–1943*. New York: Brentano, 1943.

_____. *Folles de Luxes et Dames de Qualité*. Paris: Editions Baudinière, 1931.

_____. *Gens de Théatre que j'ai connus*. New York: Brentano's, 1942.

Glassheim, Eagle. *Noble Nationalists: The Transformation of the Bohemian Aristocracy*. Cambridge, MA: Harvard University Press, 2005.

Golczewski, Frank. "Die ukrainische und die russische Emigration in Deutschland." In *Russische Emigration in Deutschland 1918 bis 1941*, ed. Karl Schlögel. Berlin: Akademie Verlag, 1995, 77–84.

Goldinger, Walter, and Dieter A. Binder. *Geschichte der Republik Österreich 1918–1938*. Oldenbourg, Germany: Verlag für Geschichte und Politik, 1992.

Gortazar, Guillermo. *Alfonso XIII, hombre de negocios*. Madrid: Alianza Editorial, 1986.

Grelka, Frank. *Die ukrainische Nationalbewegung unter deutscher Besatzungsherrschaft 1918 und 1941/1942*. Wiesbaden, Germany: Harrassowitz Verlag, 2005.

Gribble, Francis. *The Life of the Emperor Francis-Joseph*. New York: Putnam's Sons, 1914.

Gross, Jan. *Revolution from Abroad: The Soviet Conquest of Poland's Western Ukraine and Western Belorussia*. Princeton, NJ: Princeton University Press, 2002.

Grossegger, Elisabeth. *Der Kaiser-Huldigungs-Festzug, Wien 1908*. Vienna: Verlag der Österreichischen Akademie der Wissenschaften, 1992.

Gumbrecht, Hans Ulrich. *In 1926: Living at the Edge of Time*. Cambridge, MA: Harvard University Press, 1997.

Habsburg, Alice. *Princessa och partisan*. Stockholm: P. A. Norstedt & Söners Förlag, 1973.

Habsburg, Elisabeth. *Das poetische Tagebuch*. Vienna: Verlag der Österreichischen Akademie der Wissenschaften, 1984.

Habsburg, Karol Olbracht. *Na marginesie sprawy Żywieckiej*. Lviv: privately printed, 1924.

Halpern, Paul G. "The Cattaro Mutiny, 1918." In *Naval Mutinies of the Twentieth Century*, ed. Christopher M. Bell and Bruce A. Ellman. London: Frank Cass, 2003, 54–79.

Hamann, Brigitte. *Kronprinz Rudolf: Ein Leben*. Vienna: Amalthea, 2005.

_____. *The Reluctant Empress: A Biography of Empress Elisabeth of Austria*. Berlin: Ellstein, 1996.

Hamann, Brigitte, ed. *Die Habsburger*. Munich, Germany: Piper, 1988.

Healy, Maureen. *Vienna and the Fall of the Habsburg Empire*. New York: Cambridge University Press, 2004.

Hendrix, Paul. *Sir Henri Deterding and Royal Dutch Shell: Changing Control of World Oil 1900–1940*. Bristol, UK: Bristol Academic Press, 2002.

Herodotus. *The History*, trans. Henry Clay. Buffalo, NY: Prometheus Books, 1992.

Hills, Alice. *Britain and the Occupation of Austria, 1943–1945*. New York: St. Martin's Press, 2000.

Himka, John-Paul. *Religion and Nationality in Western Ukraine: The Greek Catholic Church and the Ruthenian National Movement in Galicia, 1867–1900*. Montreal, QC: McGill University Press, 1999.

Hirniak, Nykyfor. *Polk. Vasyl' Vyshyvanyi*. Winnipeg, MB: Mykytiuk, 1956.

Hornykiewicz, Teofil, ed. *Ereignisse in der Ukraine 1914–1923*. Vols. 3–4. Philadelphia, PA: Lypynsky East European Research Institute, 1968–1969.

Houthaeve, Robert. *De Gekruisigde Kerk van de Oekraïne en het offer van Vlaamse missionarissen*. Moorslede, Belgium: R. Houthaeve, 1990.

Hrytsak, Iaroslav. *Narys istorii Ukrainy*. Kiev, Ukraine: Heneza, 1996.

Hull, Isabel. *Absolute Destruction: Military Culture and the Practices of War in Imperial Germany*. Ithaca, NY: Cornell University Press, 2004.

_____. *The Entourage of Kaiser Wilhelm II, 1888–1918.* Cambridge: Cambridge University Press, 1982.

Husar, Bożena. "Żywieccy Habsburgowie." In *Kalendarz Żywiecki 1994,* 65. Żywiec, Poland: Gazeta Żywiecka 1993.

Hyla, Bogumiła. "Habsburgowie Żywieccy w latach 1895–1947." In *Karta groni,* (1991): 7–27.

Ivanova, Klimentina, ed. *Stara bulgarska literatura.* Vol. 4. Sofia, Bulgaria: Bulgarski pisatel, 1986.

James, Harold. *Europe Reborn: A History, 1914–2000.* Harlow, UK: Pearson, 2003.

Jászi, Oskar. *The Dissolution of the Habsburg Monarchy.* Chicago: University of Chicago Press, 1929.

Jelavich, Charles. *South Slav Nationalism: Textbooks and Yugoslav Union before 1914.* Columbus: Ohio State University Press, 1990.

Judson, Pieter M. *Guardians of the Nation: Activists on the Language Frontiers of Imperial Austria.* Cambridge, MA: Harvard University Press, 2006.

Judt, Tony. *Postwar: A History of Europe since 1945.* New York: Penguin, 2005.

Kakowski, Aleksander. *Z Niewoli do Niepodległości.* Cracow, Poland: Platan, 2000.

Kellogg, Michael. *The Russian Roots of Nazism: White Émigrés and the Making of National Socialism, 1917–1945.* Cambridge: Cambridge University Press, 2005.

Kentii, A. V. *Narysy istorii Orhanizatsii Ukrains'kykh Natsionalistiv.* Kiev, Ukraine: NAN Ukrainy, 1998.

Khlevniuk, Oleg V. *The History of the Gulag: From Collectivization to the Great Terror.* New Haven, CT: Yale University Press, 2004.

Killem, Barbara. "Karel Havlíček and the Czech Press before 1848." In *The Czech Renascence of the Nineteenth Century,* ed. Peter Brock and H. Gordon Skilling, 113–130. Toronto, ON: University of Toronto Press, 1970.

King, Jeremy. *Budweisers into Czechs and Germans: A Local History of Bohemia, 1848–1914.* Princeton, NJ: Princeton University Press, 2002.

Klimecki, Michał. *Polsko-ukraińska wojna o Lwów.* Warsaw: Wojskowy Instytut Historyczny, 1997.

Knežević, Jovana. "The Austro-Hungarian Occupation of Belgrade during the First World War." PhD diss., Yale University, 2004.

Kořalka, Jiři. *Češi v Habsburské říse a v Evropě.* Prague, Czech Republic: Argo 1996.

Koselleck, Reinhart. *Futures Past: On the Semantics of Historical Time.* Cambridge, MA: MIT Press, 1985.

Koven, Seth. *Sexual and Social Politics in Victorian London.* Princeton, NJ: Princeton University Press, 2004.

Kramer, Mark. "The Collapse of East European Communism and the Repercussions within the Soviet Union." *Journal of Cold War Studies* 5, no. 1 (2003), 3–16; 5, no. 4 (2003), 3–42; 6, no. 4 (2004), 3–64; 7, no. 1 (2005), 3–96.

Krauss, Alfred. "Die Besetzung der Ukraine 1918." In *Die Militärverwaltung in den von den Österreichischen-Ungarischen Truppen Besetzen Gebieten,* ed. Hugo Kerchnawe, Rudolf Mitzka, Felix Sobotka, Hermann Leidl, and Alfred Krauss. New Haven, CT: Yale University Press, 1928.

Kryvuts'kyi, Ivan. *De sribnolentyi Sian plyve . . .* Kiev, Ukraine: Brama, 1999.

_____. *Za poliarnym kolom: Spohady viaznia Hulah Zh–545.* Lviv, Ukraine: Poltava, 2001.

Krzyżanowski, Piotr. "Księżna arcypolskości." *Wprost,* 11 January 2004.

Kuhnke, Monika. "Polscy Habsburgowie i polska sztuka." *Cenne, bezcenne/utracone*, March–April 1999.

Kursell, Otto v. "Erinnerungen an Dr. Max v. Scheubner-Richter." Unpublished manuscript, BA. Munich, Germany, 1966.

Lacquer, Walter. *Russia and Germany*. Boston: Little, Brown, 1965.

Laverdure, Paul. "Achille Delaere and the Origins of the Ukrainian Catholic Church in Western Canada." *Australasian Canadian Studies* 24, no. 1 (2006): 83–104.

Liulevicius, Vejas. *War Land on the Eastern Front: Culture, National Identity, and Occupation in World War I*. Cambridge: Cambridge University Press, 2000.

Lubomirska, Maria. *Pamiętnik*. Poznań, Poland: Wydawnictwo Poznańskie, 1997.

Lucey, Michael. *Never Say I: Sexuality and the First Person in Colette, Gide, and Proust*. Durham, NC: Duke University Press, 2006.

Ludendorff, Erich. *The General Staff and Its Problems*. Vol. 2. London: Hutchinson & Co., n.d.

MacKenzie, David. *Apis: The Congenial Conspirator*. Boulder, CO: East European Monographs, 1985.

Mackiewicz, Stanisław. *Dom Radziwiłłów*. Warsaw: Czytelnik, 1990.

Magocsi, Paul Robert. *A History of Ukraine*. Toronto: University of Toronto Press, 1996.

Majchrowski, Jacek M. *Ugrupowania monarchystyczne w latach Drugiej Rzeczypospolitej*. Wrocław, Poland: Ossolineum, 1988.

Malynovs'kyi, B. V. "Arkhykniaz Vil'hel'm fon Habsburh, Sichovi Stril'tsi ta 'Zaporozhtsi' u 1918 r." *Arkhivy Ukrainy* 1–6 (1997).

Markovits, Andrei, and Frank Sysyn, eds. *Nationbuilding and the Politics of Nationalism*. Cambridge, MA: Harvard University Press, 1982.

Markus, Georg. *Der Fall Redl*. Vienna: Amalthea, 1984.

Martin, Terry. *The Affirmative Action Empire: Nations and Nationalism in the Soviet Union, 1923–1939*. Ithaca, NY: Cornell University Press, 2001.

Mastny, Vojtech. *Cold War and Soviet Insecurity: The Stalin Years*. New York: Oxford University Press, 1996.

Mayer, Arno J. *The Persistence of the Old Regime: Europe to the Great War*. New York: Pantheon Books, 1981.

Mazower, Mark. *Dark Continent: Europe's Twentieth Century*. New York: Knopf, 1999.

Mędrzecki, Włodzimierz. "Bayerische Truppenteile in der Ukraine im Jahr 1918." In *Bayern und Osteuropa*, ed. Hermann Bayer-Thoma, 442–458. Wiesbaden, Germany: Harrassowitz Verlag, 2000.

Menasse, Robert. *Erklär mir Österreich*. Vienna: Suhrkamp, 2000.

Michalski, Krzysztof. *Płomień wieczności: Eseje o myślach Frydyryka Nietzschego*. Cracow, Poland: Znak, 2007.

Miller, Aleksei. *Imperiia Romanovykh i natsionalizm*. Moscow: Novoe Literaturnoe Obozrenie, 2006.

Milow, Caroline. *Die ukrainische Frage 1917–1923 im Spannungsfeld der europäischen Diplomatie*. Wiesbaden, Germany: Harrassowitz Verlag, 2002.

Mistinguett. *Mistinguett: Queen of the Paris Night*. London: Elek Books, 1954.

Monitor Polski, 6 March 1919, Number 53.

Mosse, George. *The Fascist Revolution: Towards a General Theory of Fascism*. New York: Howard Fertig, 1999.

Müller, Wolfgang. *Die Sowjetische Besatzung in Österreich 1945–1955 und ihre politische Mission.* Vienna: Böhlau Verlag, 2005.

Murat, Laure. *La loi du genre: Une histoire culturelle du "troisième sexe."* Paris: Fayard, 2006.

Niemann, Alfred. *Kaiser und Revolution.* Berlin: August Scherl, 1922.

Novosad, Roman. "Iak zahynul Habsburh-Vyshyvanyi." *Zona* 10 (1995): 56–58.

———. "Vasyl' Vyshyvanyi, Iakyi ne stav korolom Ukrainy." *Ukraina* 26 (1992): 22–25.

Nußer, Horst G. W. *Konservative Wehrverbände in Bayern, Preußen und Österreich 1918–1933.* Munich, Germany: Nußer Verlag, 1973.

Onats'kyi, Ievhen. *Portrety v profil.* Chicago: Ukrainian-American, 1965.

Ostashko, Tetiana. "Pol's'ka viiskova spetssluzhba pro ukrains'kyi monarkhichnyi rukh." *Ucrainika Polonika* 1 (2004): 240–256.

Owen, Charles. *The Maltese Islands.* New York: Praeger, 1969.

Palmer, Alan. *Twilight of the Habsburgs: The Life and Times of Emperor Francis Joseph.* New York: Atlantic Monthly Press, 1994.

Pavliuk, Oleksandr. *Borot'ba Ukrainy za nezalezhnist' i polityka SShA, 1917–1923.* Kiev, Ukraine: KM Akademia, 1996.

Pelenski, Jaroslaw. "Hetman Pavlo Skoropadsky and Germany (1917–1918) as Reflected in His Memoirs." In *German-Ukrainian Relations in Historical Perspective,* ed. Hans-Joachim Torke and John-Paul Himka. Edmonton, AB: CIUS, 1994.

Perotti, Eliana. *Das Schloss Miramar in Triest (1856–1870).* Vienna: Böhlau Verlag, 2002.

Petriv, Vsevolod. *Viis'kovo-istorychni pratsi. Spomyny.* Kiev, Ukraine: Polihrafknyha, 2002.

Pipes, Richard. *The Formation of the Soviet Union.* Cambridge, MA: Harvard University Press, 1997.

Plaschka, Richard Georg, Horst Haselsteiner, and Arnold Suppan. *Innere Front: Militärassistenz, Widerstand und Umsturz in der Donaumonarchie 1918.* Munich, Germany: R. Oldenbourg Verlag, 1974.

Podvyzhnyky Chynu Naisviatishoho Izbavitelia v Ukraini. Ternopil, Ukraine: Monastyr, Uspennia Presviatoi Bohorodytsi, 2004.

Pohl, Dieter. *Nationalsozialistische Judenverfolgung in Ostgalizien 1941–1944: Organisation und Durchführung eines staatlichen Massenverbrechens.* Munich, Germany: R. Oldenbourg Verlag, 1996.

Pola: Seine Vergangenheit, Gegenwart und Zukunft. Vienna: Carol Gerold's Sohn, 1887.

Pollack, Martin. *Nach Galizien: Von Chassiden, Huzulen, Polen und Ruthenen: Eine imaginaire Reise durch die verschwundene Welt Ostgaliziens und der Bukowina.* Vienna: C. Brandstätter, 1984.

Polski Słownik Biograficzny. Vol. 9. Wrocław, Poland: Polska Akademia Nauk, 1960–1961.

Popyk, Serhii. *Ukraintsi v Avstrii 1914–1918.* Kiev, Ukraine: Zoloti Lytavry, 1999.

Rak, Jiří. *Byvali Čechové: České historické mýty a stereotypy.* Prague, Czech Republic: H & H, 1994.

Rape, Ludger. *Die Österreichischen Heimwehren und die bayerische Recht 1920–1923.* Vienna: Europaverlag, 1977.

Rasevych, Vasyl'. "Vil'hel'm von Habsburh-Sproba staty ukrains'kym korolom." In *Podorozh do Evropy,* ed. Oksana Havryliv and Timofii Havryliv, 210–221. Lviv, Ukraine: VNTL-Klasyka, 2005.

Rauchensteiner, Manfried. *Der Sonderfall: Die Besatzungszeit in Österreich 1945 bis 1955.* Vienna: Verlag Styria, 1979.

Redlich, Joseph. *Emperor Francis Joseph of Austria.* New York: Macmillan, 1929.

Remak, Joachim. "The Healthy Invalid: How Doomed the Habsburg Empire?" *Journal of Modern History* 41, no. 2 (1969): 127–143.

Reshetar, John. *The Ukrainian Revolution.* Princeton, NJ: Princeton University Press, 1952.

Roberts, Mary Louise. *Civilization without Sexes: Reconstructing Gender in Postwar France, 1917–1927.* Chicago: University of Chicago Press, 1994.

Romanov, Alexander. *Twilight of Royalty.* New York: Ray Long and Richard R. Smith, 1932.

Ronge, Max. *Kriegs- und Industriespionage.* Zurich: Amalthea, 1930.

Rossino, Alexander. *Hitler Strikes Poland: Blitzkrieg, Ideology, and Atrocity.* Lawrence: University of Kansas Press, 2003.

Rudnytsky, Ivan. *Essays in Modern Ukrainian History.* Edmonton, AB: CIUS, 1987.

Rumpler, Helmut. *Max Hussarek: Nationalitäten und Nationalitätenpolitik im Sommer des Jahres 1918.* Graz, Austria: Verlag Böhlau, 1965.

Rusniaczek, Jerzy. "Jak powstał zamek w Żywcu." *Karta groni* (1991): 37–51.

Rutkowski, Ernst. "Ukrainische Legion." Unpublished manuscript, in the author's possession. Vienna, 2005.

Ryan, Nellie. *My Years at the Austrian Court.* London: Bodley Head, 1916.

Schmidt-Brentano, Antonio. *Die Österreichische Admirale.* Osnabrück, Germany: Biblio Verlag, 1997.

Schorske, Carl E. *Fin-de-Siecle Vienna: Politics and Culture.* New York: Vintage, 1981.

Sendtner, Kurt. *Rupprecht von Wittelsbach: Kronprinz von Bayern.* Munich, Germany: Richard Pflaum, 1954.

Senecki, Ireneusz, and Dariusz Piotrowski. "Zbiory malarstwa w pałacu Habsburgów w Żywcu." *Gronie* 1, no. 25 (2006): 58–60.

Shanafelt, Gary W. *The Secret Enemy: Austria-Hungary and the German Alliance.* Boulder, CO: East European Monographs, 1985.

Shevel, Oxana. "Nationality in Ukraine: Some Rules of Engagement." *East European Politics and Societies* 16, no. 2 (2002): 386–413.

Skoropads'kyi, Pavlo. *Spohady.* Kiev, Ukraine: Knyha, 1995.

Skrzypek, Józef. "Ukraińcy w Austrii podczas wojny i geneza zamachu na Lwów." *Niepodległość* 19 (1939): 27–92, 187–224, 349–387.

Snyder, Timothy. "The Causes of Ukrainian-Polish Ethnic Cleansing, 1943." *Past and Present* 179 (2003): 197–234.

_____. *The Reconstruction of Nations: Poland, Ukraine, Lithuania, Belarus, 1569–1999.* New Haven, CT: Yale University Press, 2003.

_____. *Sketches from a Secret War: A Polish Artist's Mission to Liberate Soviet Ukraine.* New Haven, CT: Yale University Press, 2005.

_____. "'To Resolve the Ukrainian Problem Once and for All': The Ethnic Cleansing of Ukrainians in Poland, 1943–1947." *Journal of Cold War Studies* 1, no. 2 (1999): 86–120.

Sondhaus, Lawrence. *The Habsburg Empire and the Sea: Austrian Naval Policy, 1797–1866.* West Lafayette, IN: Purdue University Press, 1989.

_____. *The Naval Policy of Austria-Hungary, 1867–1914: Navalism, Industrial Development, and the Politics of Dualism.* West Lafayette, IN: Purdue University Press, 1994.

Sonnenthal, Hermine von, ed. *Adolf von Sonnenthals Briefwechsel*. Stuttgart, Germany: Deutsche Verlags-Anstalt, 1912.

Spector, Scott. "Where Personal Fate Turns to Public Affair: Homosexual Scandal and Social Order in Vienna 1900–1910." *Austria History Yearbook* 38 (2007): 15–24.

———. "The Wrath of the 'Countess Merviola': Tabloid Exposé and the Emergence of Homosexual Subjects in Vienna in 1907." *Contemporary Austrian Studies* 15 (2006): 31–46.

Spyra, Adam. *Browar Żywiec 1856–1996*. Żywiec, Poland: Unigraf, 1997.

Stevenson, David. *Cataclysm: The First World War as Political Tragedy*. New York: Basic Books, 2004.

Stourzh, Gerald. *Um Einheit und Freiheit: Staatsvertrag, Neutralität, und das Ende der Ost-West-Besatzung Österreichs 1945–1955*. Vienna: Böhlau, 1998.

Stoye, John. *The Siege of Vienna*. London: Collins St. James's Place, 1964.

Strachan, Hew. *The First World War*. New York: Penguin, 2005.

Sudoplatov, Pavel, and Anatoli Sudoplatov. *Special Tasks: The Memoirs of an Unwanted Witness, a Soviet Spymaster*. Boston: Little, Brown, 1994.

Suleja, Włodzimierz. *Orientacja Austro-Polska w latach I Wojny Światowej*. Wrocław, Poland: Wydawnictwo Uniwersytet Wrocławskiego, 1992.

Szporluk, Roman. "The Making of Modern Ukraine: The Western Dimension." *Harvard Ukrainian Studies* 25, nos. 1–2 (2001): 57–91.

———. *Russia, Ukraine, and the Breakup of the Soviet Union*. Stanford, CA: Hoover Institution, 2000.

Tanner, Marie. *The Last Descendant of Aeneas: The Hapsburgs and the Mythic Image of the Emperor*. New Haven, CT: Yale University Press, 1993.

Taylor, A. J. P. *The Habsburg Monarchy, 1809–1918: A History of the Austrian Empire and Austria-Hungary*. London: Macmillan, 1941.

Tereshchenko, Iu. I., and T. S. Ostashko. *Ukrains'kyi patriot z dynastii Habsburhiv*. Kiev, Ukraine: NAN Ukrainy, 1999.

Tereshchenko, Iurii. "V'iacheslav Lypyns'kyi i Vil'hel'm Habsburg na politychnykh perekhrestiakh." *Moloda Natsiia* 4 (2002), 91–126.

Thoss, Bruno. *Der Ludendorff-Kreis 1919–1923: München als Zentrum der mitteleuropäischen Gegenrevolution Zwischen Revolution und Hitler-Putsch*. Munich, Germany: Kommissionsbuchhandlung R. Wölfle, 1977.

Thun-Salm, Christiane, and Hugo von Hoffmansthal. *Briefwechsel*, ed. Renate Moering. Frankfurt, Germany: S. Fischer, 1999.

Torzecki, Ryszard. *Kwestia ukraińska w polityce Trzeciej Rzeszy*. Warsaw: Książka i Wiedza, 1972.

Tunstall, Graydon A., Jr. "Austria-Hungary." In *The Origins of World War I*, ed. Richard F. Hamilton and Holger H. Hertwig, 112–149. Cambridge: Cambridge University Press, 2003.

Turii, Oleh. "Istorychnyi shlakh redemptoristiv skhidnoi vitky na ukrainskoi zemli." In *Redemptorysty: 90 lit v Ukraini*, ed. Iaroslav Pryriz. Lviv, Ukraine: Misia Khrysta, 2003.

Tylza-Janosz, Marta. "Dobra czarnieckie i porąbczanskie Habsburgów Żywieckich w XIX i XX wieku." Master's thesis, Akademia Pedagogiczna, Cracow, Poland, 2003.

Ullman, Richard. *Anglo-Soviet Relations 1917–1920*. 3 vols. Princeton, NJ: Princeton University Press, 1961–1973.

Unowsky, Daniel. *The Pomp and Politics of Patriotism*. West Lafayette, IN: Purdue University Press, 2005.

Vasari, Emilio. *Dr. Otto Habsburg oder die Leidenschaft für Politik.* Vienna: Verlag Herold, 1972.

Vicinus, Martha. "Fin-de-Siecle Theatrics: Male Impersonation and Lesbian Desire." In *Borderlines: Genders and Identities in War and Peace, 1870–1930,* ed. Billie Melman, 163–192. New York: Routledge, 1998.

Vivian, Herbert. *The Life of the Emperor Charles of Austria.* London: Grayson & Grayson, 1932.

Vogelsberger, Hartwig A. *Kaiser von Mexico.* Vienna: Amalthea, 1992.

Vogt, Adolf. *Oberst Max Bauer: Generalstaboffizier in Zwielicht 1869–1929.* Osnabrück, Germany: Biblio Verlag, 1974.

Vushko, Iryna. "Enlightened Absolutism, Imperial Bureaucracy and Provincial Society: The Austrian Project to Transform Galicia, 1772–1815." PhD diss., Yale University, 2008.

Vyshyvanyi, Vasyl. "U.S.S. z vesny 1918 r. do perevorotu v Avstrii," 1920. Typescript at HURI.

Wagnleitner, Reinhold. *Coca-colonization and the Cold War: The Cultural Mission of the United States in Austria after the Second World War.* Chapel Hill: University of North Carolina Press, 1994.

Wandycz, Piotr. *The Lands of Partitioned Poland.* Seattle: University of Washington Press, 1979.

_____. *Soviet-Polish Relations, 1919–1921.* Cambridge, MA: Harvard University Press, 1969.

Wasserstein, Bernard. *The Secret Lives of Trebitsch Lincoln.* New Haven, CT: Yale University Press, 1988.

Weber, Eugen. *The Hollow Years: France in the 1930s.* New York: Norton, 1996.

Wheatcroft, Andrew. *The Habsburgs: Embodying Empire.* London: Penguin, 1996.

Wiggermann, Frank. *K.u.k. Kriegsmarine und Politik: Ein Beitrag zur Geschichte der italianischer Nationalbewegung in Istrien.* Vienna: Österreichische Akademie der Wissenschaften, 2004.

Williams, Robert C. *Culture in Exile: Russian Émigrés in Germany, 1881–1941.* Ithaca, NY: Cornell University Press, 1972.

Wilson, Andrew. *Ukraine's Orange Revolution.* New Haven, CT: Yale University Press, 2005.

_____. *Virtual Politics: Faking Democracy in the Post-Soviet World.* New Haven, CT: Yale University Press, 2005.

Wingfield, Nancy. *Flag Wars and Stone Saints: How the Bohemian Lands Became Czech.* Cambridge, MA: Harvard University Press, 2007.

Winter, Eduard. *Die Sowjetunion und der Vatikan, Teil 3: Russland und das Papsttum.* Berlin: Akademie-Verlag, 1972.

Yekelchyk, Serhy. *Stalin's Empire of Memory: Russian-Ukrainian Relations in Soviet Historical Memory.* Toronto, ON: University of Toronto Press, 2004.

_____. *Ukraine: The Birth of a Modern Nation.* Oxford: Oxford University Press, 2007.

Zacek, Joseph. "Metternich's Censors: The Case of Palacky." In *The Czech Renascence of the Nineteenth Century,* ed. Peter Brock and H. Gordon Skilling, 95–112. Toronto, ON: University of Toronto Press, 1970.

Zalizniak, Mykola. "Moia uchast u myrovykh perehovorakh v Berestiu Litovs'komu." In *Beresteis'kyi Myr: Spomyny ta Materiialy,* ed. Ivan Kedryn, 51–81. Lviv-Kiev: Kooperatyvna Nakladna Chervona Kalyna, 1928.

Zeman, Z. A. B. *The Breakup of the Habsburg Empire: A Study in National and Social Revolutions.* London: Oxford University Press, 1961.

Zhyttia i smert' Polkovnyka Konovaltsia. Lviv, Ukraine: Chervona kalyna, 1993.

Zolotarev, V. A., et al., eds. *Russkaia voennaia emigratsiia: Dokumenty i materialy.* Moscow: Geiia, 1998.

Żurawski vel Grajewski, Przemysław Piotr. *Sprawa ukraińska na konferencji pokojowej w Paryżu w roku 1919.* Warsaw: Semper, 1995.

INDEX